I0817192

NANTUCKET

NANTUCKET

Classic American style 30 miles out to sea

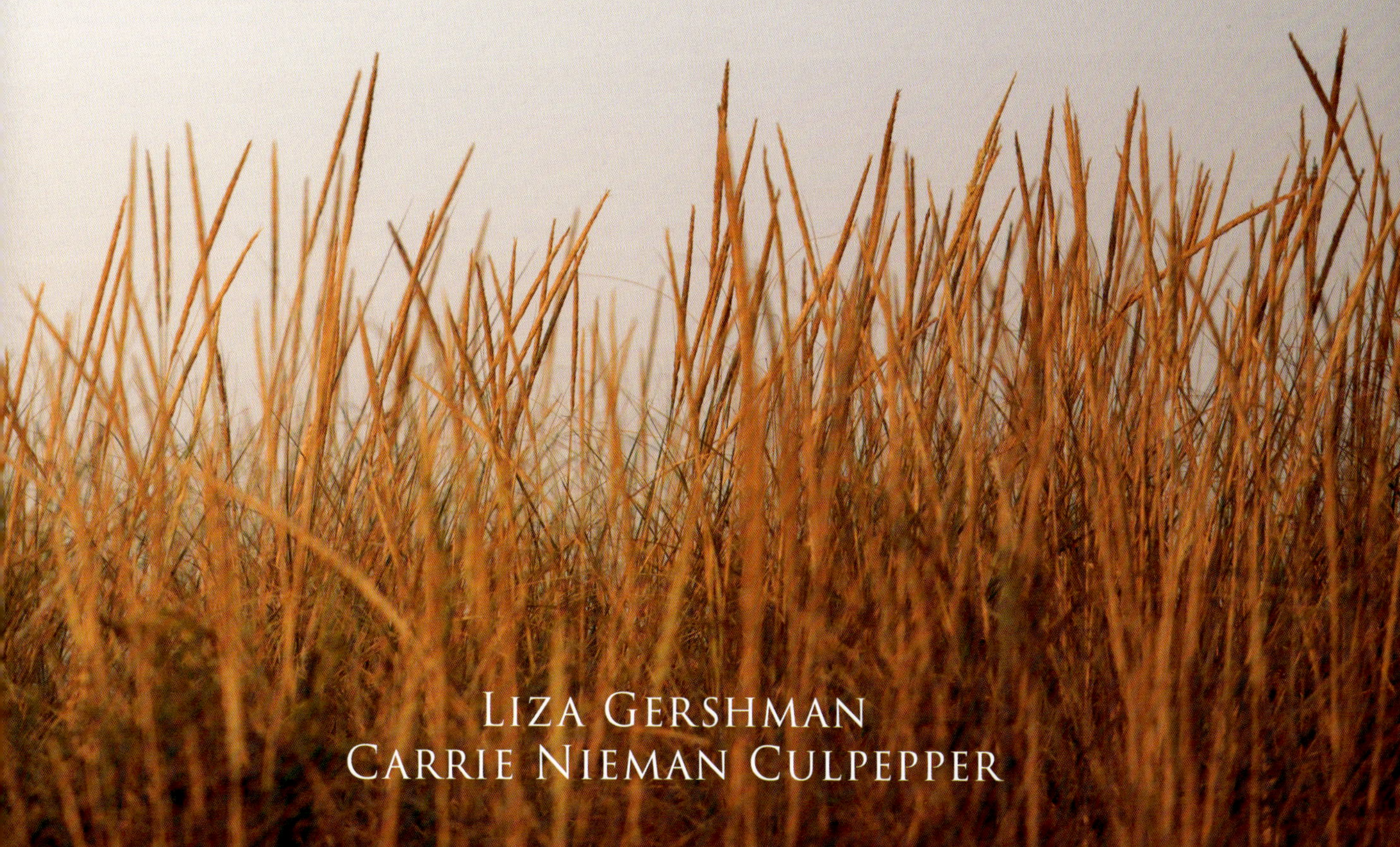

LIZA GERSHMAN
CARRIE NIEMAN CULPEPPER

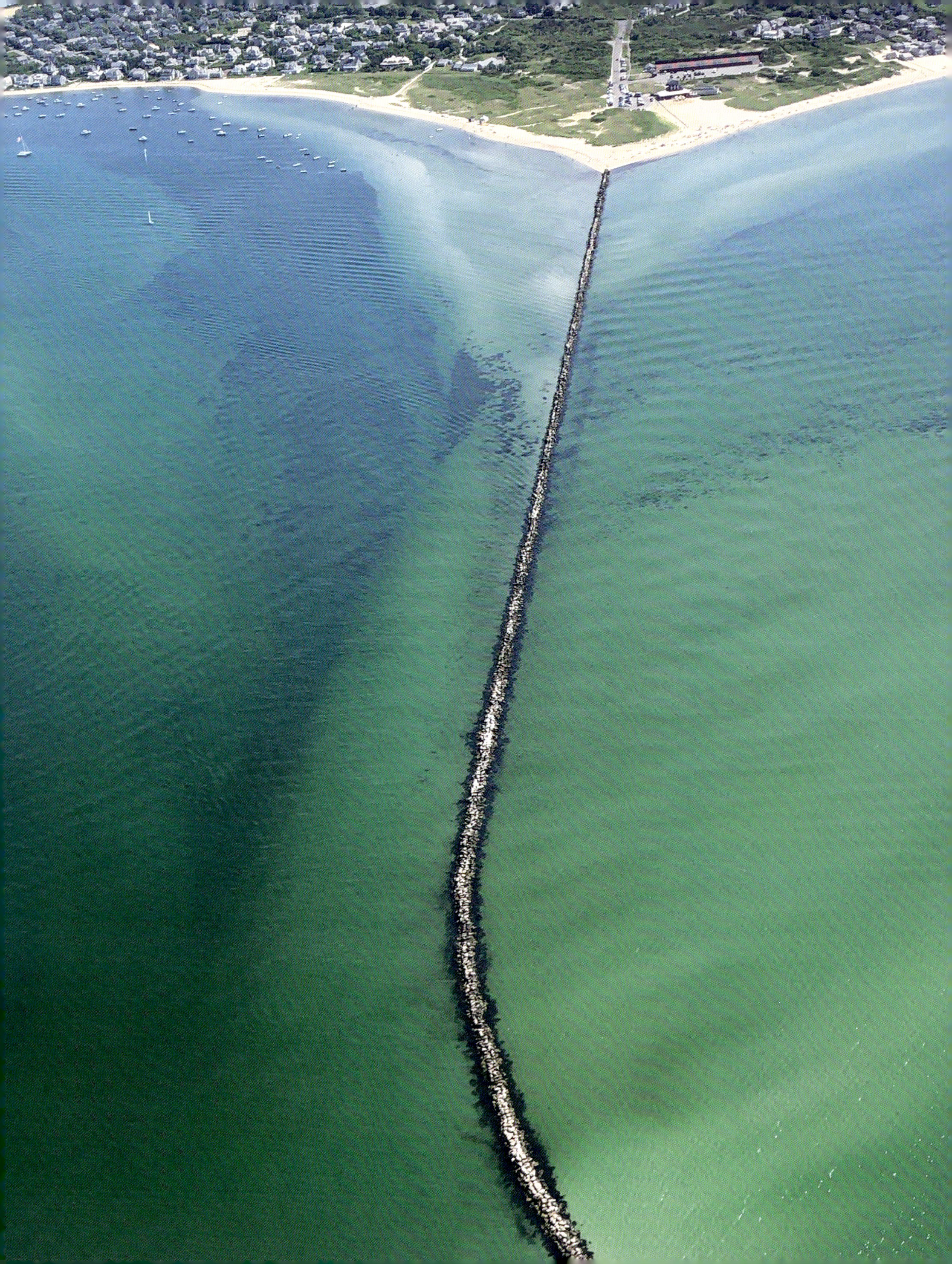

"What wonder, then, that these Nantucketers, born on a beach, should take to the sea for a livelihood! They first caught crabs and quohogs in the sand; grown bolder, they waded out with nets for mackerel; more experienced, they pushed off in boats and captured cod; and at last, launching a navy of great ships on the sea, explored this watery world; put an incessant belt of circumnavigations round it ... And thus have these naked Nantucketers, these sea hermits, issuing from their ant-hill in the sea, overrun and conquered the watery world like so many Alexanders."

—**From Herman Melville's** *Moby-Dick* **(1851)**

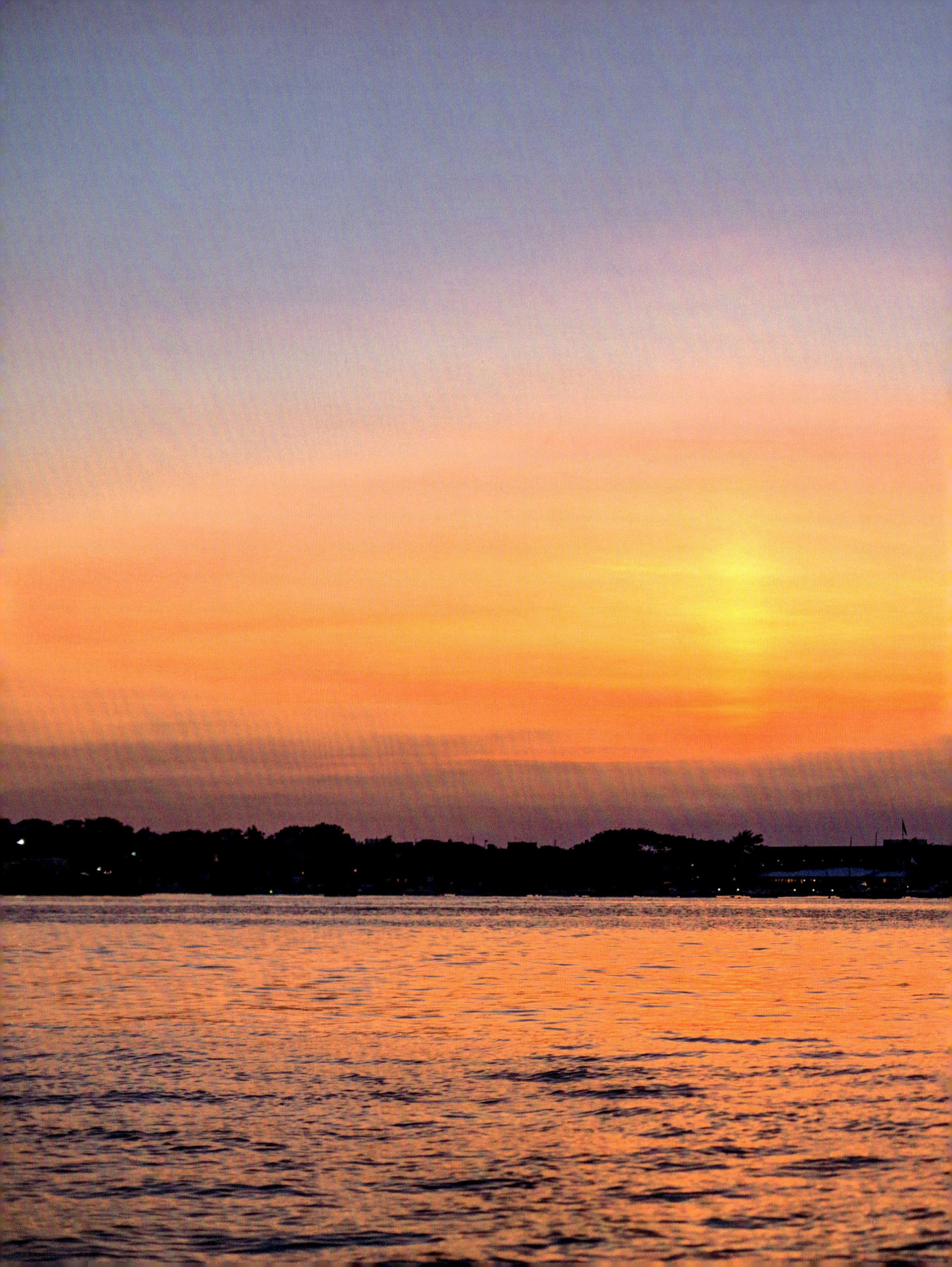

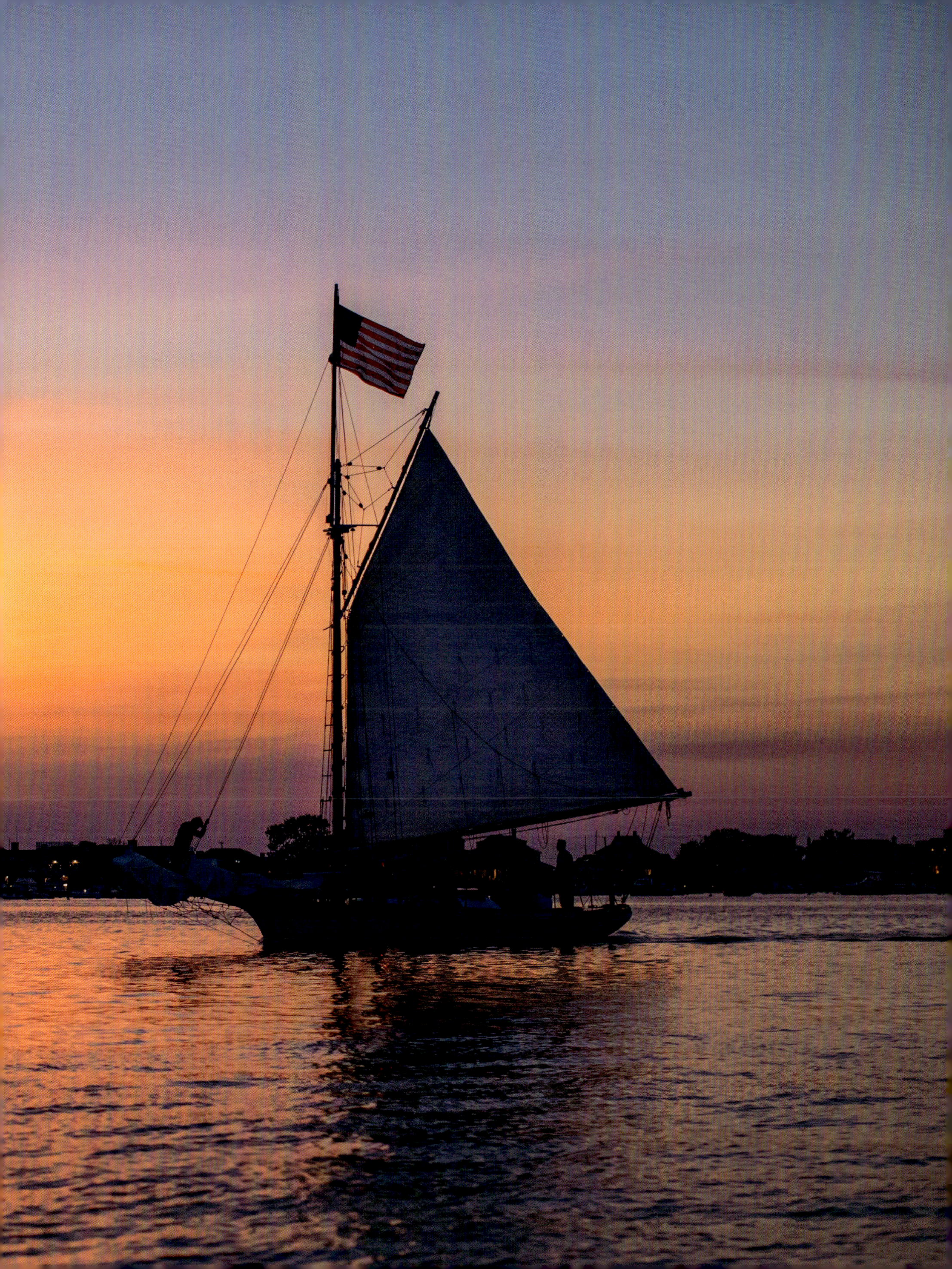

"It was always a journey, a real journey. You left the sight of land. Then you could see it on the horizon. 'Oh, there it is!' And it would take all day, you probably had a flat tire. It was never easy."

—**Patricia Anathan, lifelong summer resident whose parents first arrived in the 1930s**

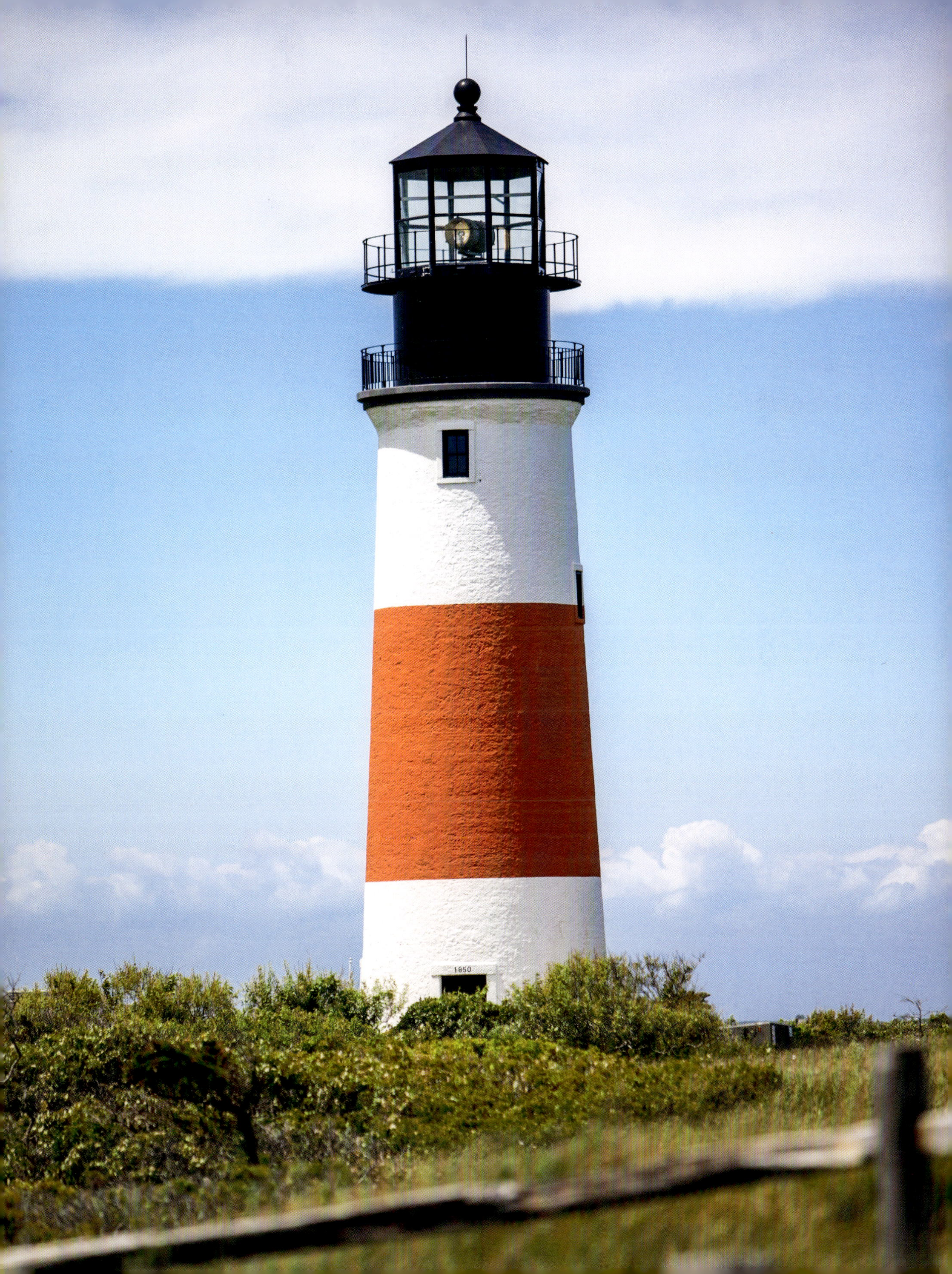
1850

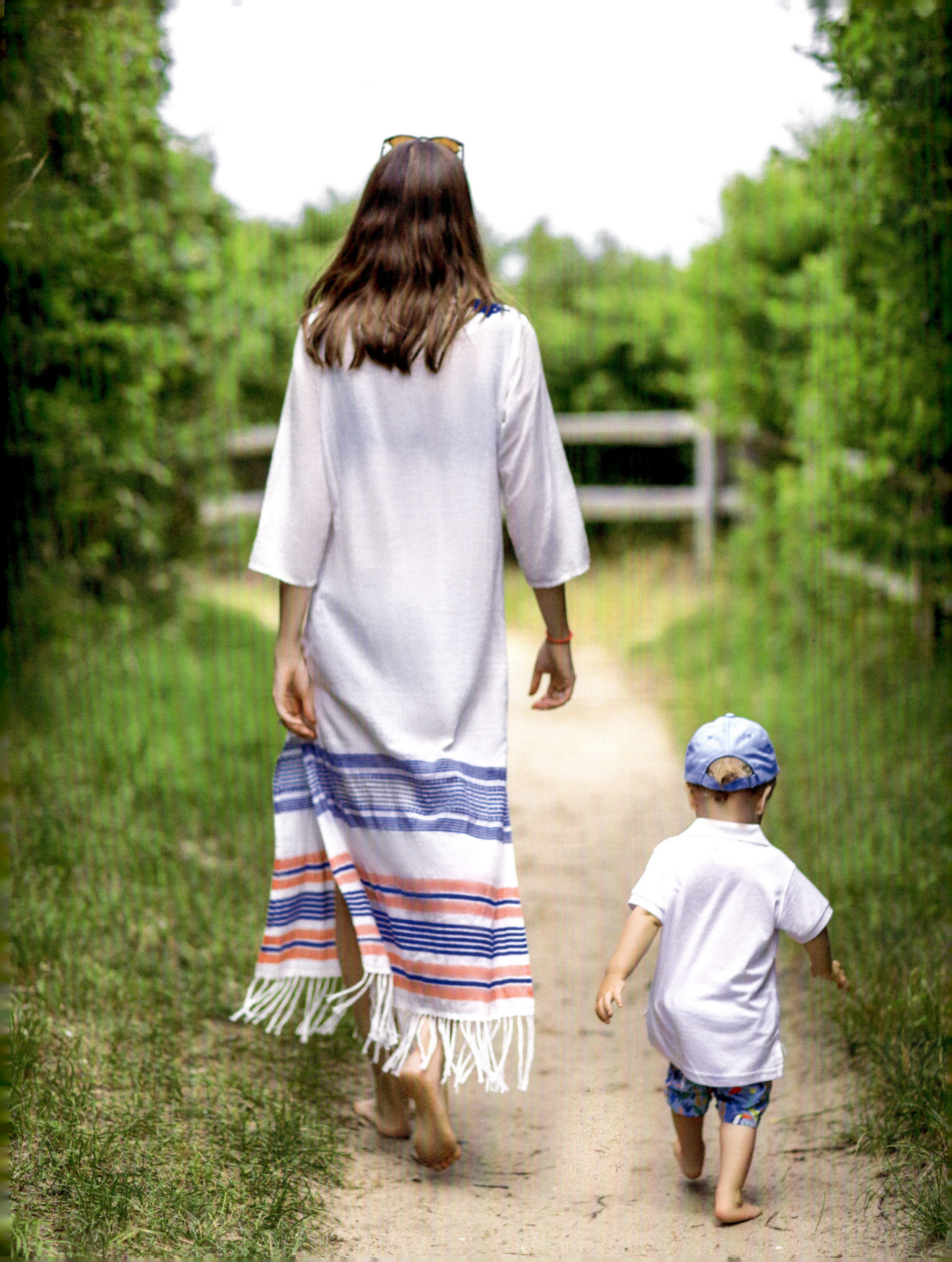

CONTENTS

22 The Island's Allure

70 Rebellious Stock: Whalers, Quakers, Artisans, Entrepreneurs

89 History of Independent Women

102 Finding Inspiration: Actors, Artists, Authors, Creatives

114 Classic American Style

143 Summer Love

166 The Club Life

202 Philanthropy

208 Conservation and Historic Preservation

219 Island Traditions

225 Nantucket Travel Guide

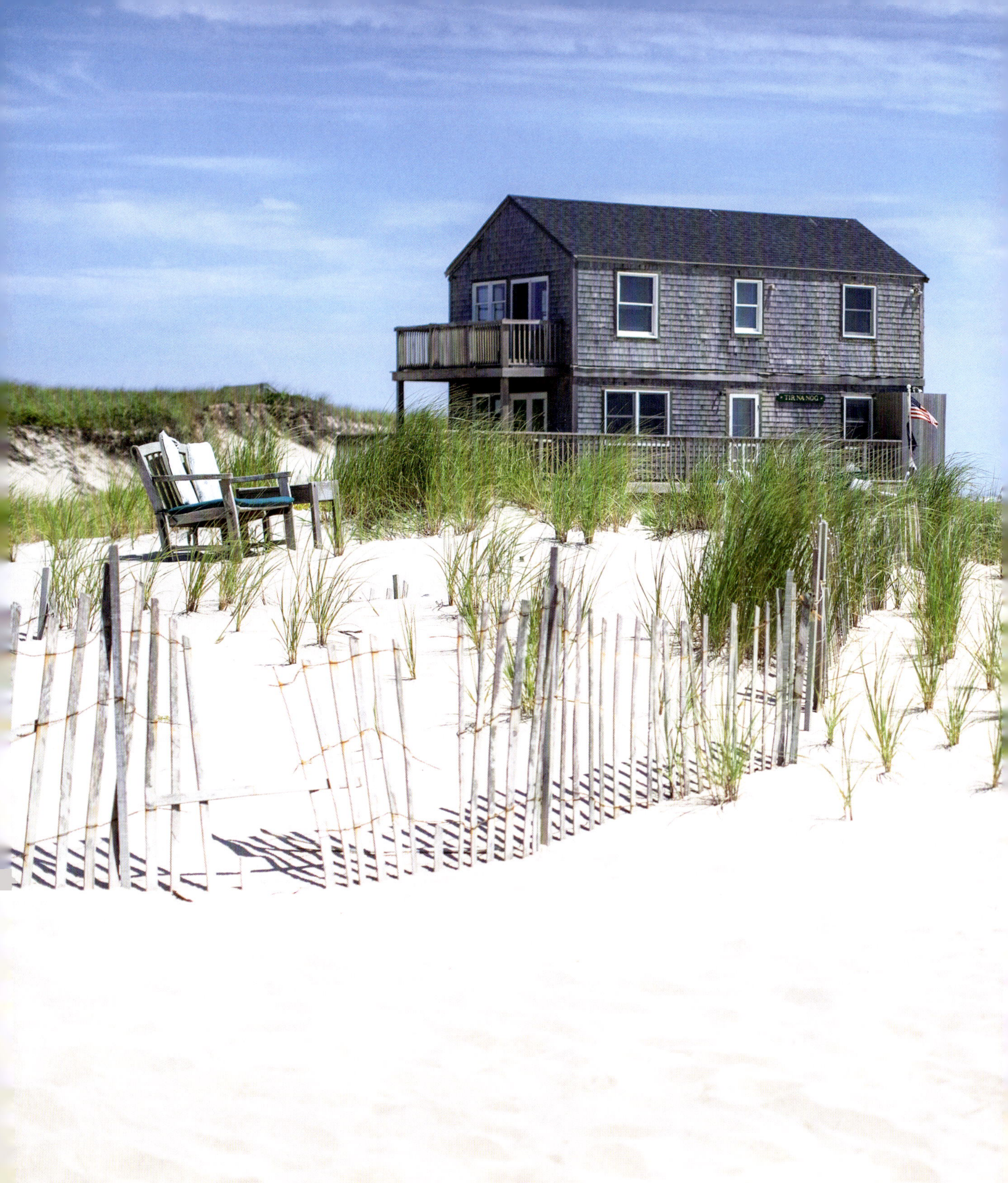
TIR NA NOG

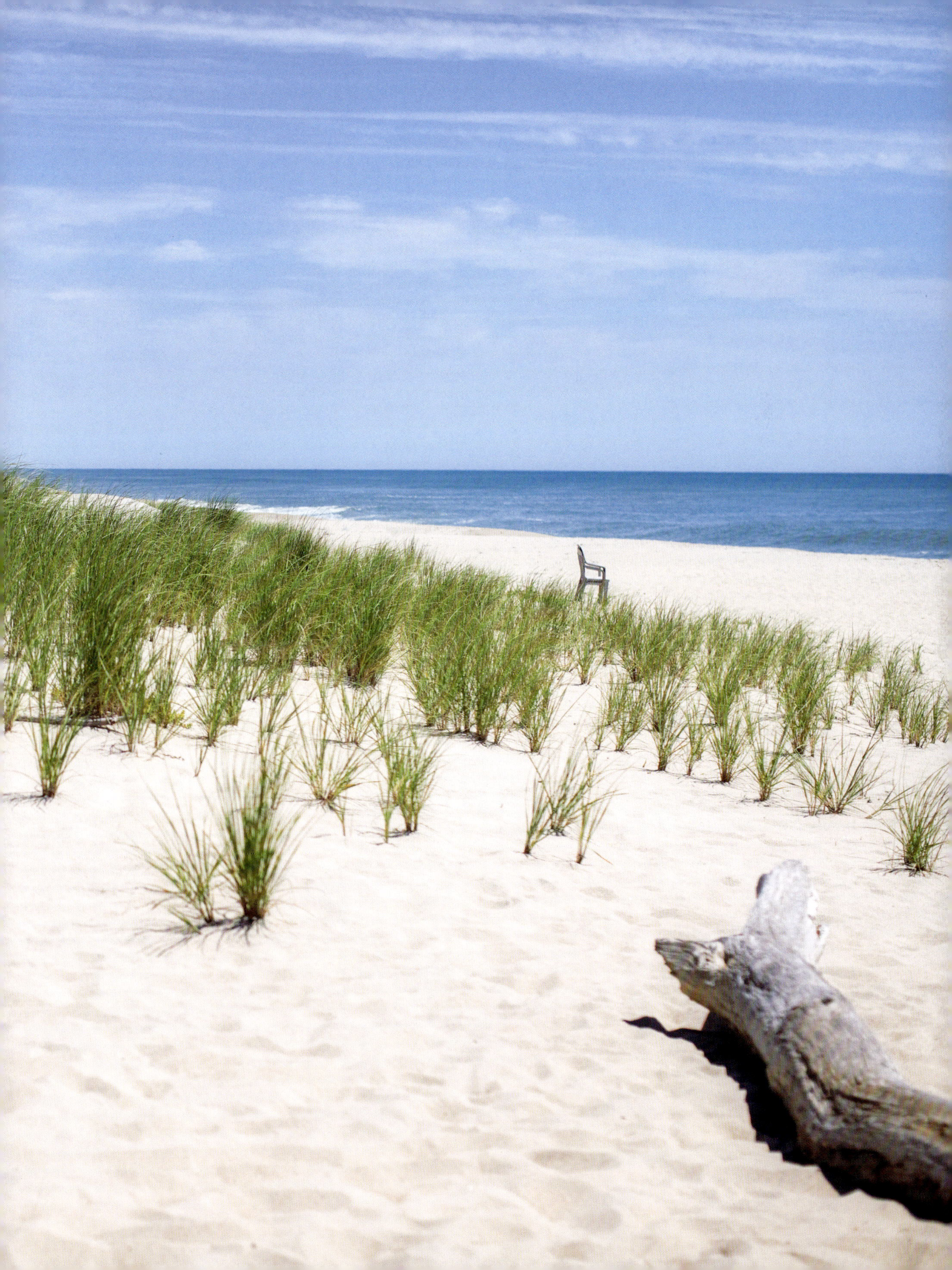

"There is something about Nantucket that inspires people to embrace old traditions while trying new things. There isn't a summer where I haven't tried something new and felt like a kid all over again. Your relationships with everything—from your family and friends, to nature and yourself—feel deeper and more meaningful. These days **my** Nantucket happens to revolve around reconnecting with nature and its beauty, sporty competition, and simple wholesome pleasures with my kids and family, like sprinklers, strawberry picking, and ice-cream cones."

—Jocelyn M. Gailliot, founder and CEO of Tuckernuck retailer

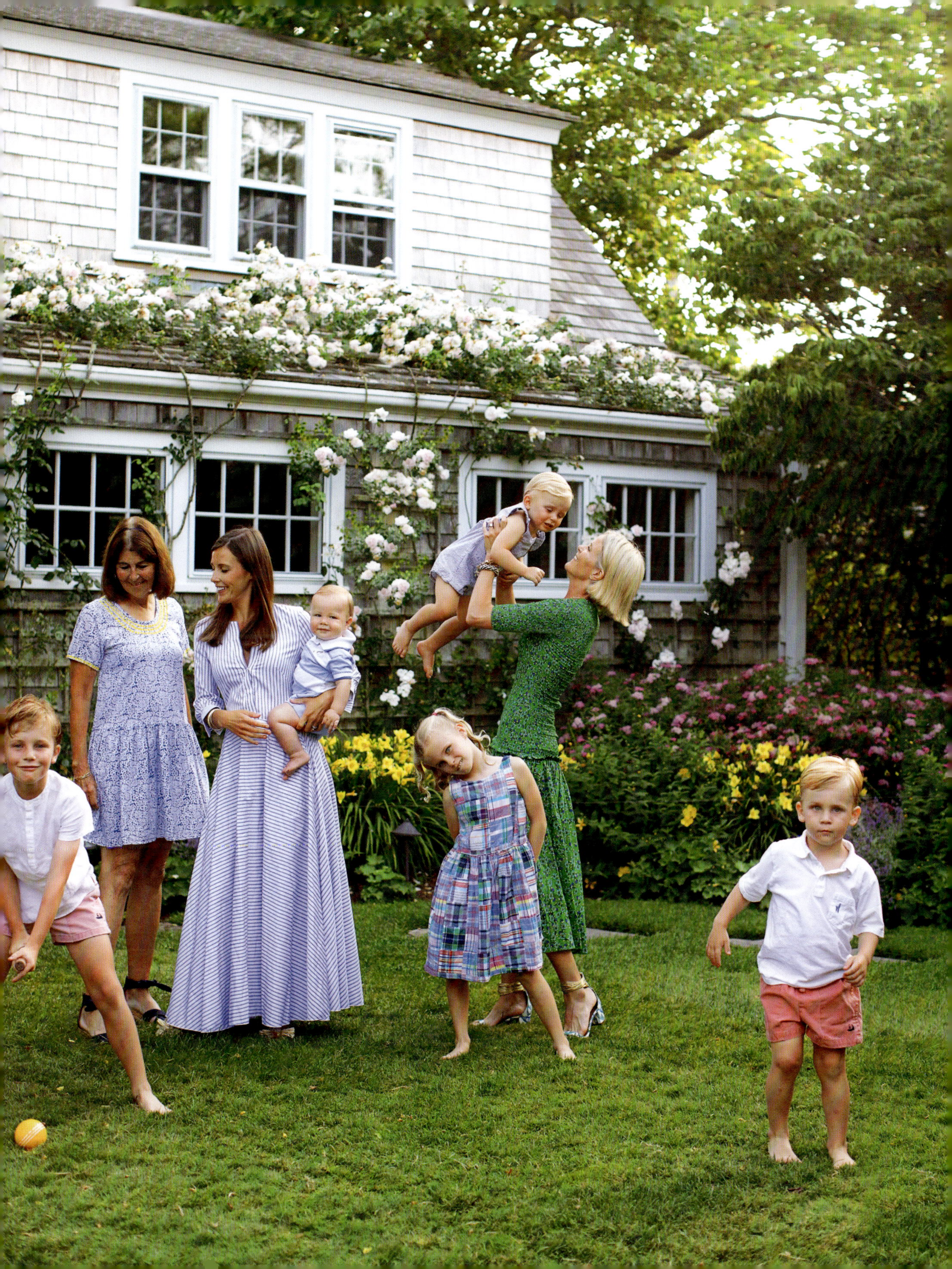

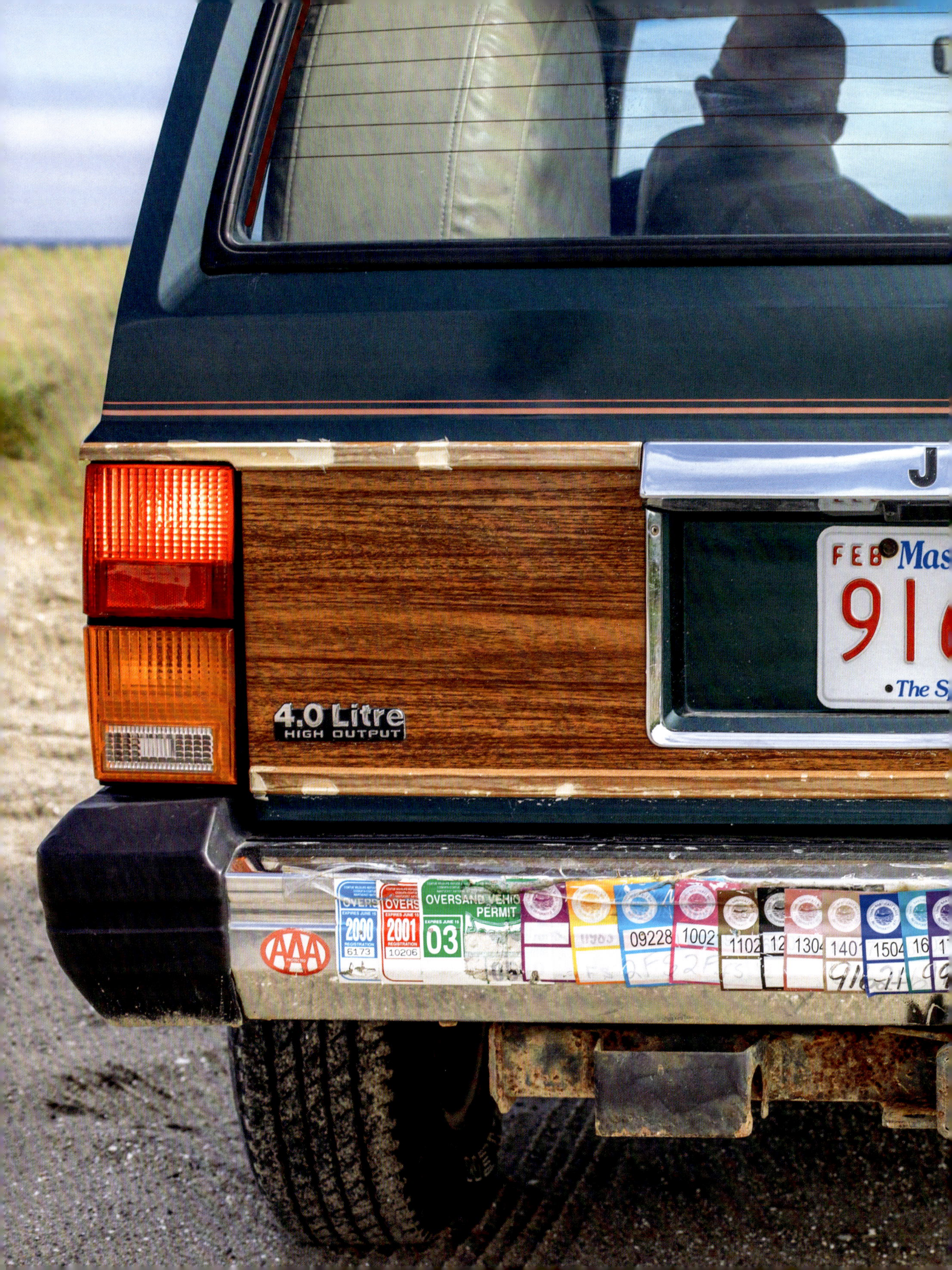
4.0 Litre
HIGH OUTPUT
FEB
AAA
2000
2001
03
PERMIT
09228

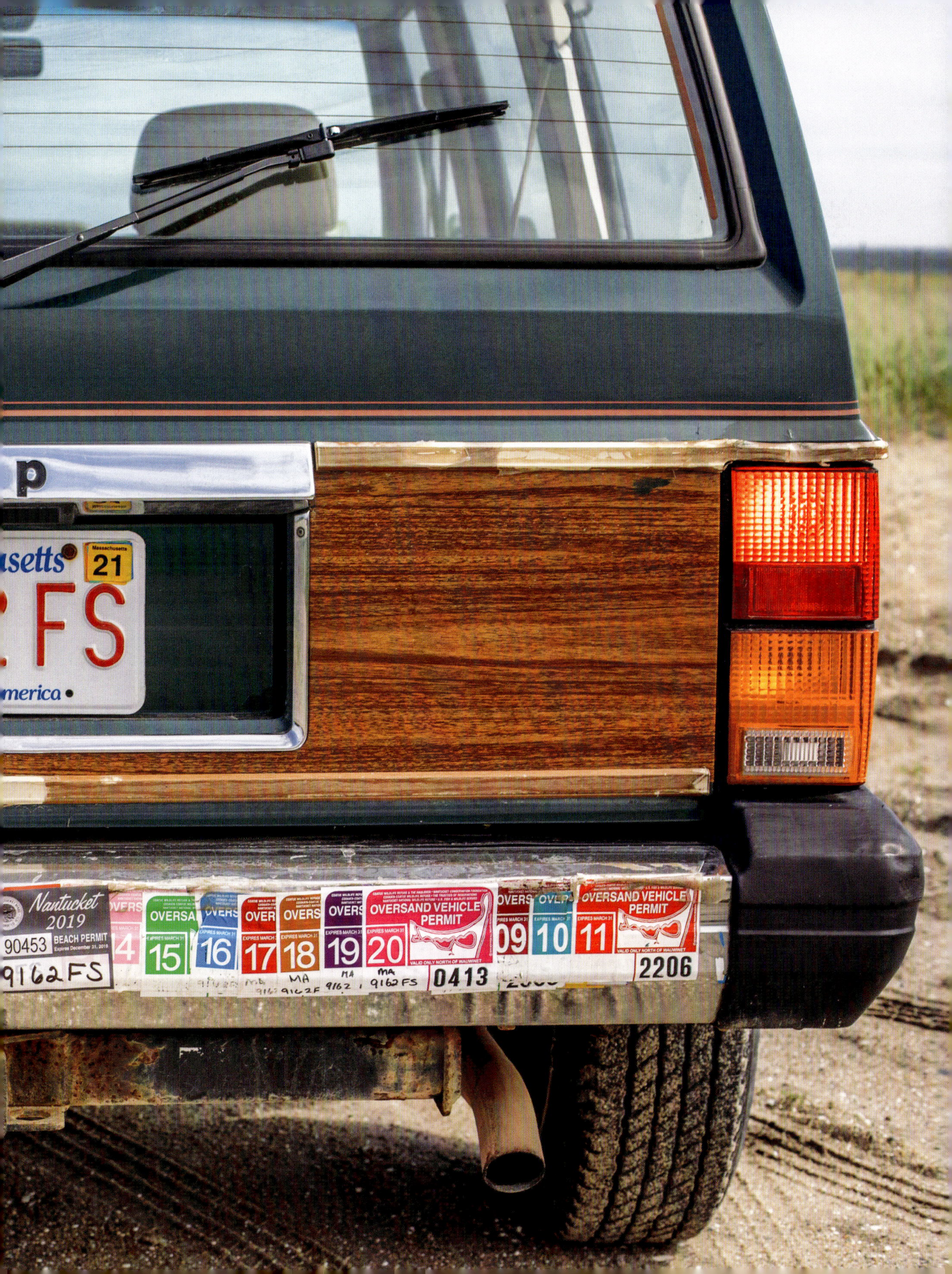

usetts
21
FS
merica
Nantucket
2019
90453
BEACH PERMIT
9162FS
15
16
17
18
19
20
OVERSAND VEHICLE
PERMIT
0413
09
10
11
OVERSAND VEHICLE
PERMIT
2206

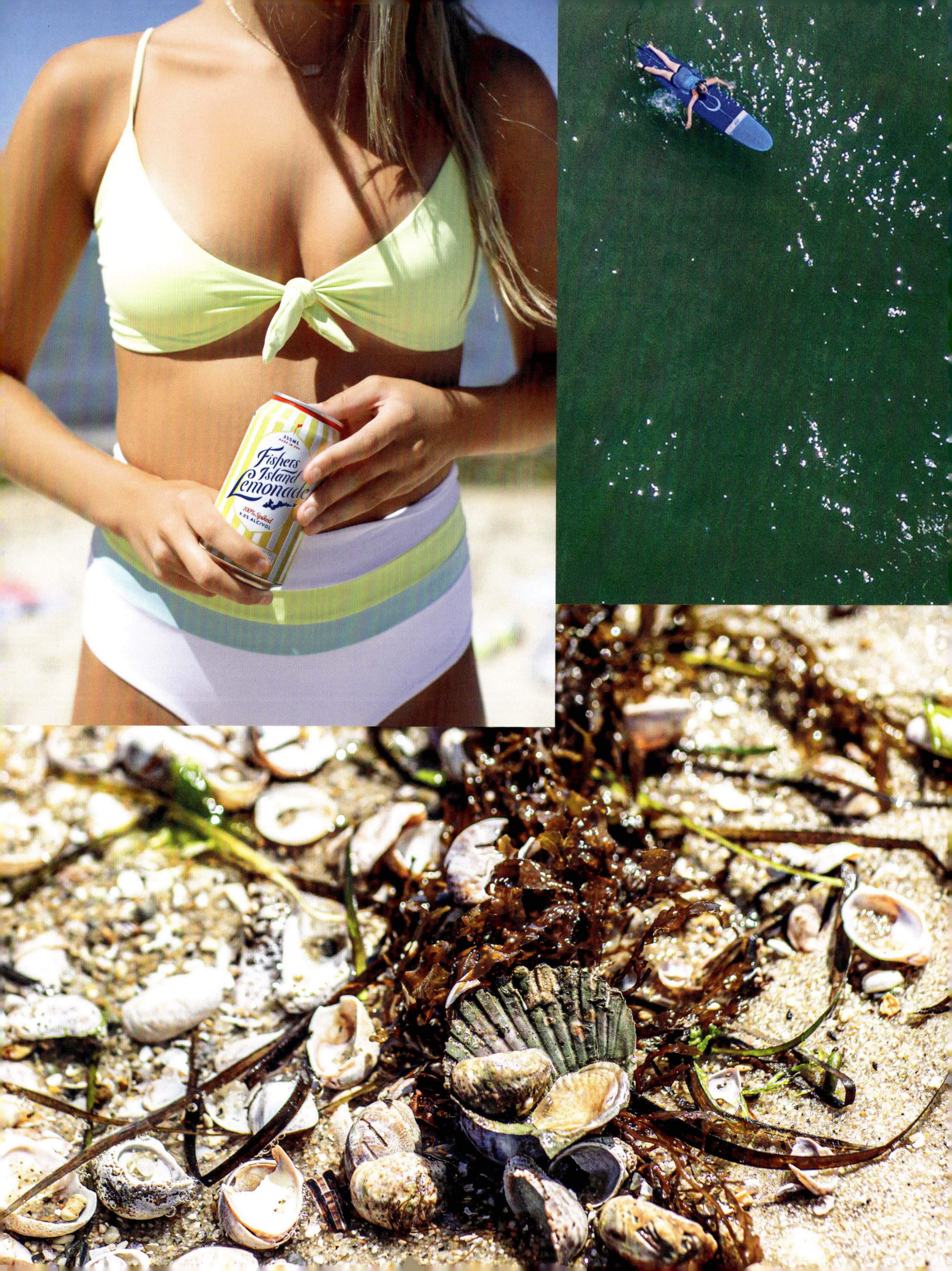
355ML
MADE IN USA
Fishers Island Lemonade
100% Spiked
9.0% ALC/VOL

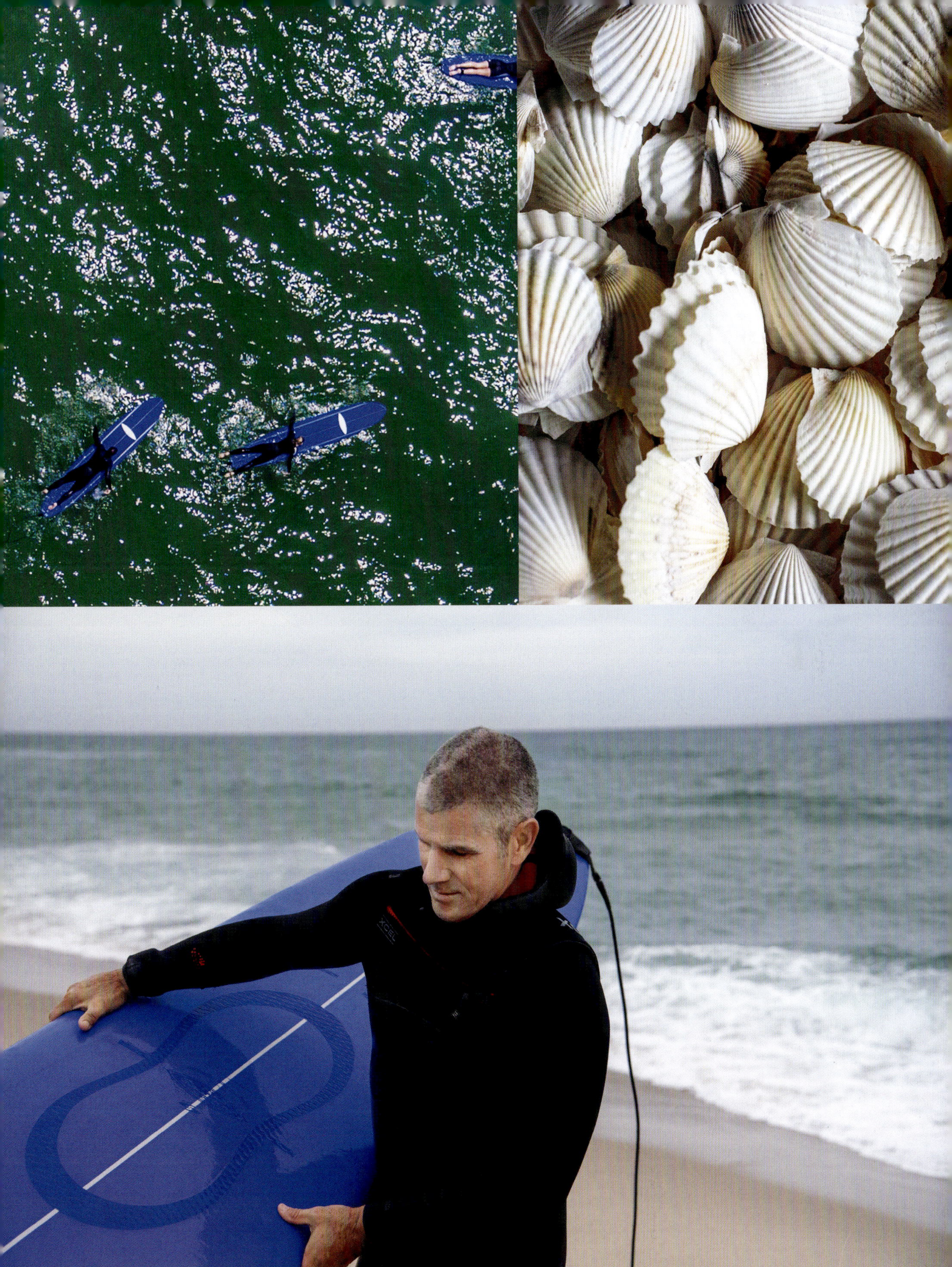

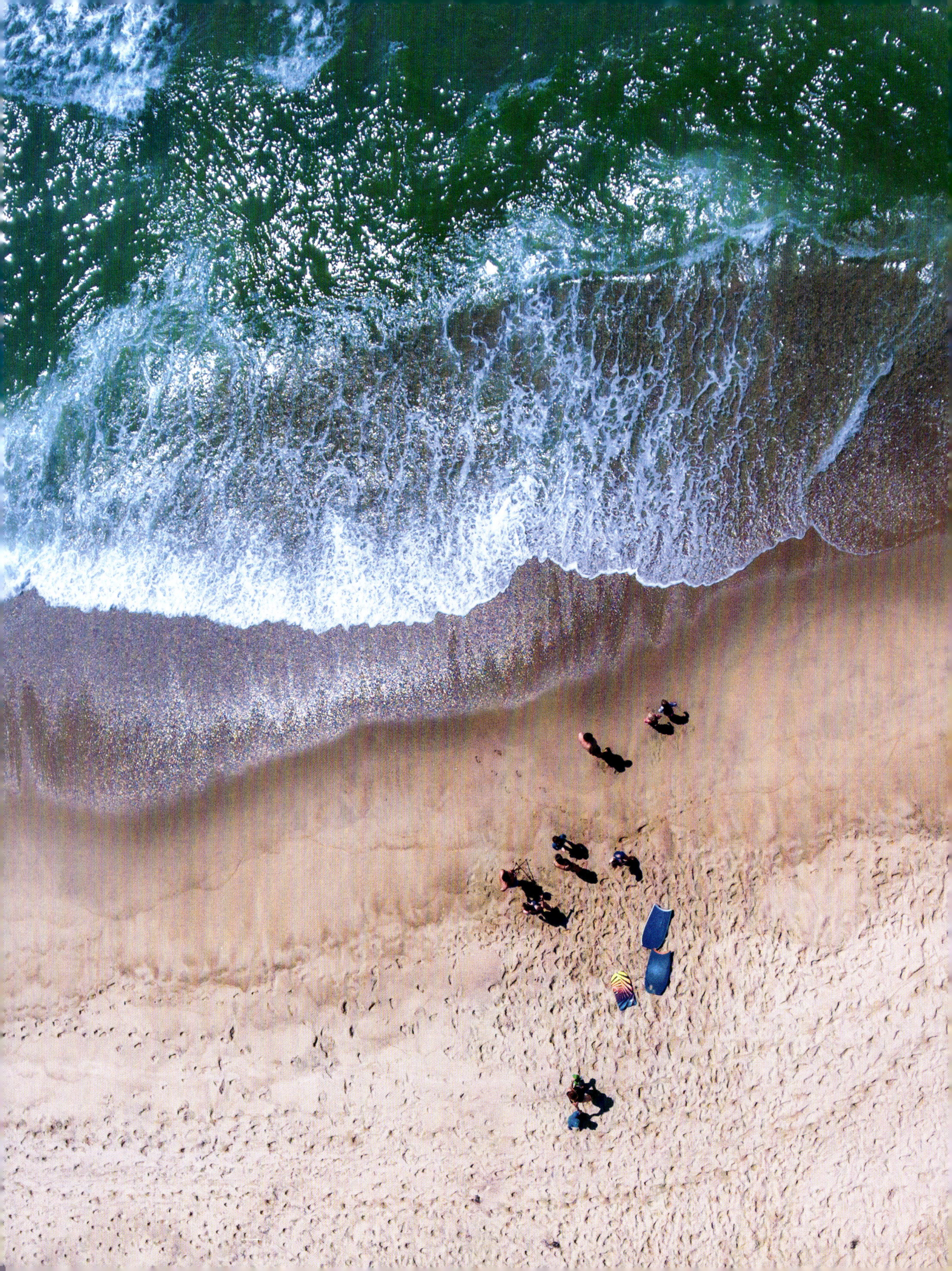

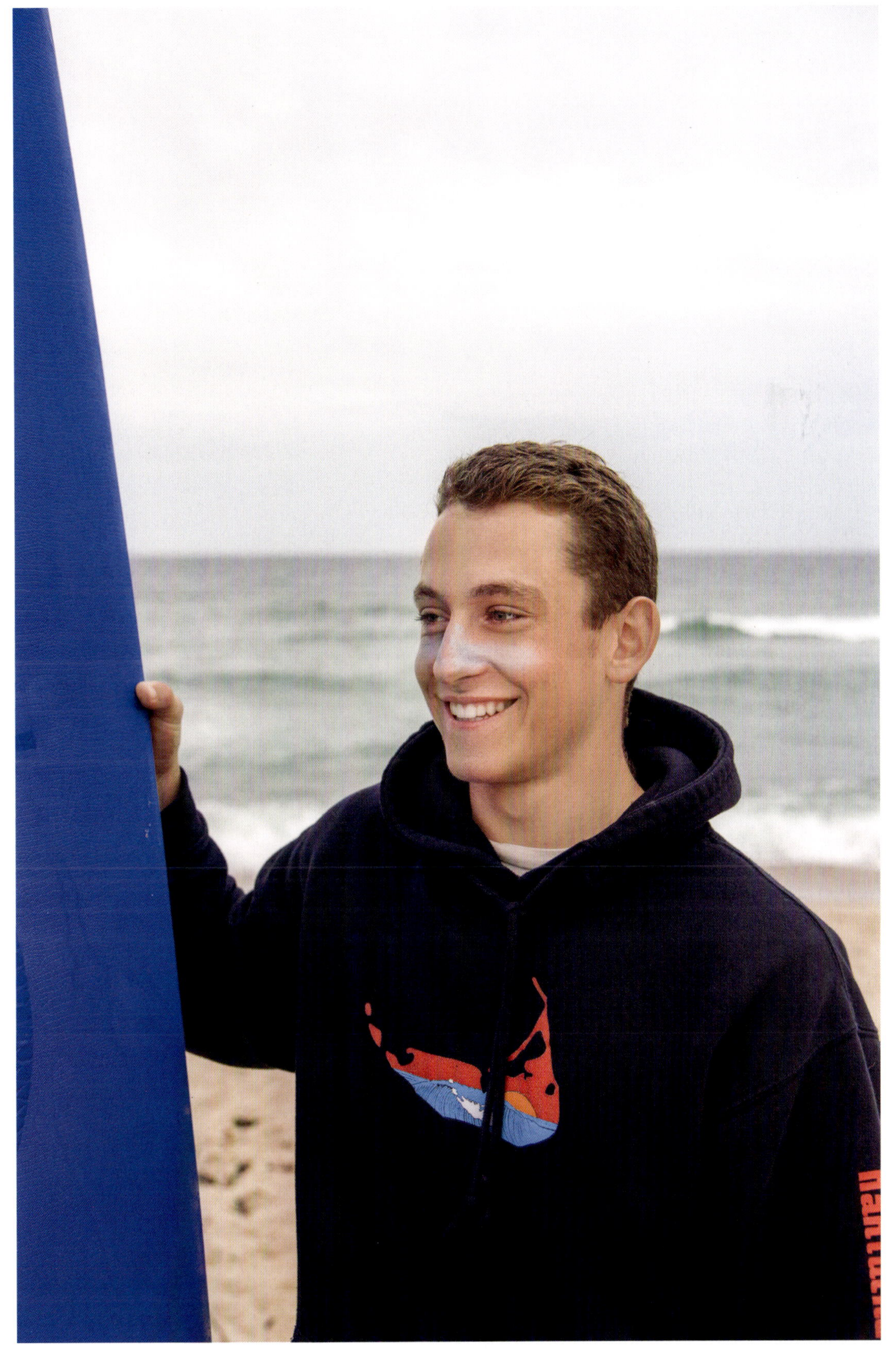

THE ISLAND'S ALLURE

This book is a glimpse in time of a place we cherish. It touches on an island that's so full of history and character, shaped by interesting people and scenery, that once you meet Nantucket it's nearly impossible not to fall madly in love.

Nantucket was once called the island of love. "People would either fall in love with each other or with the island," says eighth-generation resident Wendy McCrae, descendant of the founding Swain, Starbuck, and Coffin families. "And for sure they fall in love with nature. Once you live here, there is really no other place. It's in your blood: you know it, feel it, and love it."

If you are lucky enough to live here for the season or year-round, your connection to Nantucket deepens with each day. It's a gift to be on Nantucket, and there is a sense that most everyone shares this view. Even if you are away for seven or eight months of the year, when you return, you return home. The remoteness and difficult journey to get there means everyone who is on Nantucket wants to be there, and that's a dynamic not found in many places.

Nantucket is its native islanders, washashores, and summer residents. Its many annual festivals, and its ghosts. Throwing a penny off the boat as you round the Brant Point bend and standing in line at the Juice Bar for a tasty scoop of ice cream. Everyone has their own experience, but most agree: the moment when you first fall in love with the island is the one you want to freeze in time. "The island has always been very good to me," says "whale woman" Jean Rioux, known for her work as a conservationist and educator. "In 1957 I washed up on the shore and in the span of a morning I got a job, bike, and housing. If you are meant to be here the island will give you what you need."

Our connection to the island runs deep, if not as long as many featured in this book. We both experienced a spiritual connection that made our discovery of the island feel written in the stars. The island also brought us together, and made this project possible, through the generosity and openness of so many wonderful island characters, of whom we are forever grateful, and now forever connected. That's just what Nantucket does.

"Once you live here, there is really no other place. It's in your blood: you know it, feel it, and love it."

—**Wendy McCrae, descendant of founding Swain, Starbuck, and Coffin families**

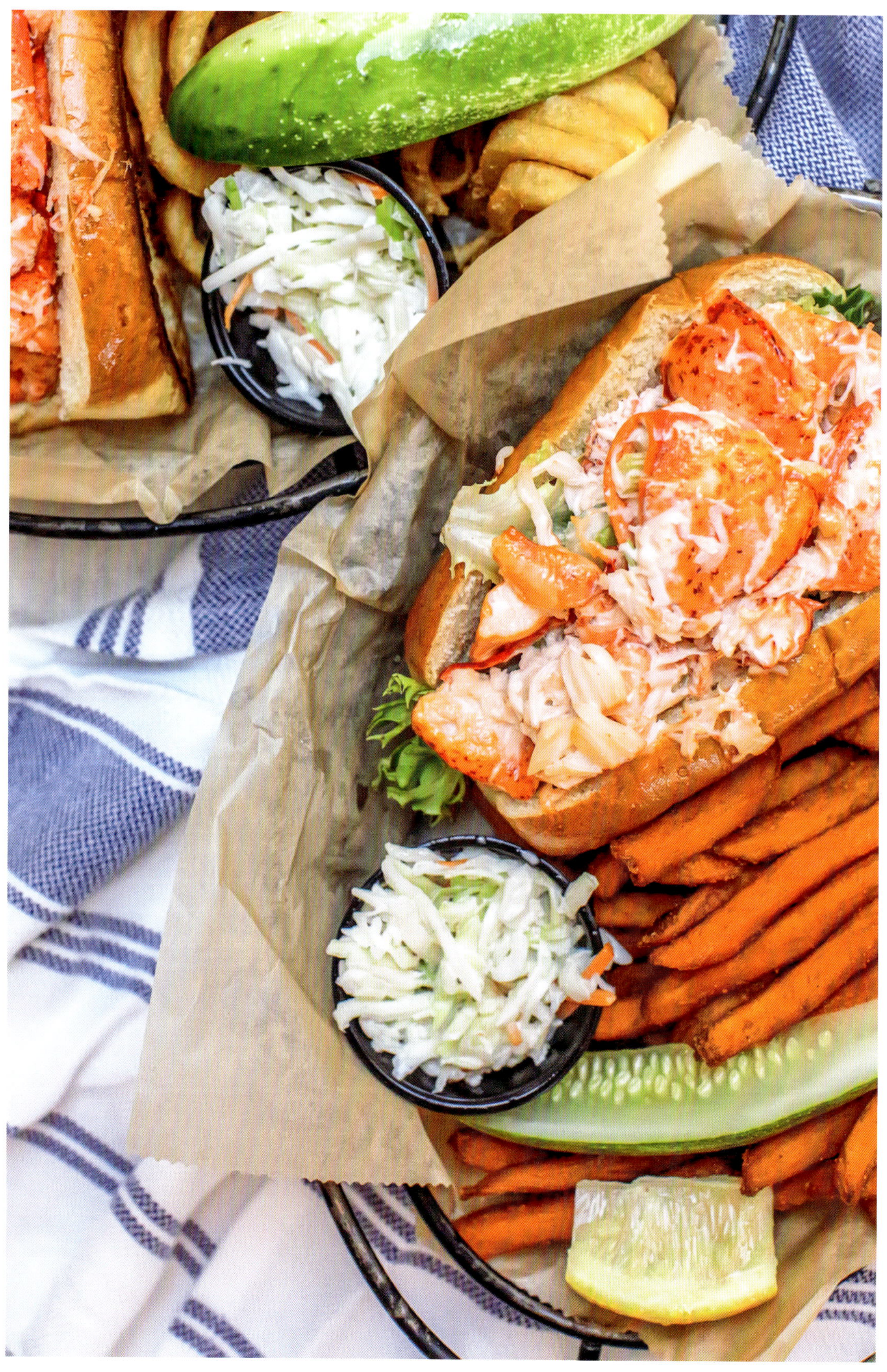

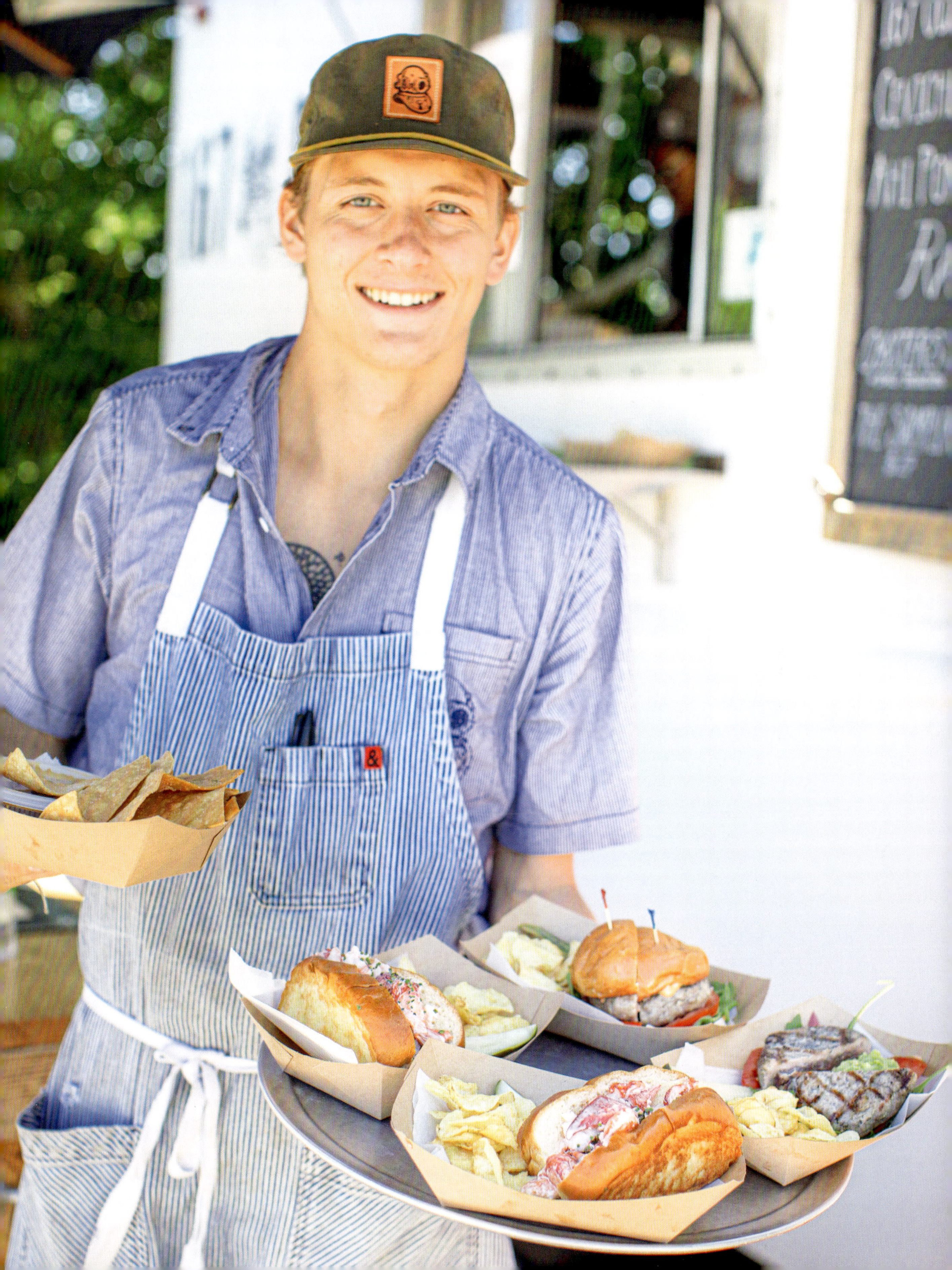

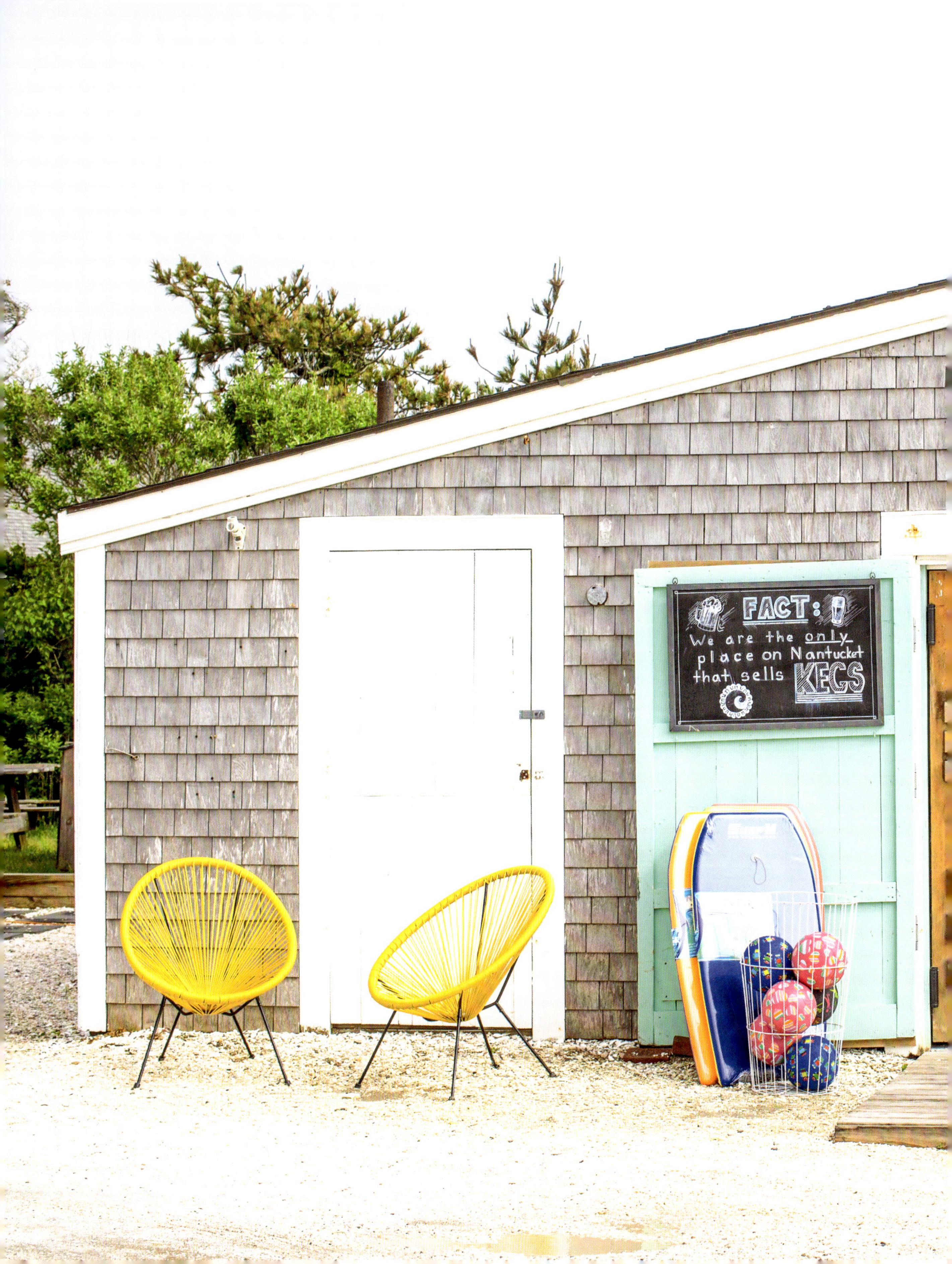
FACT:
We are the only
place on Nantucket
that sells KEGS

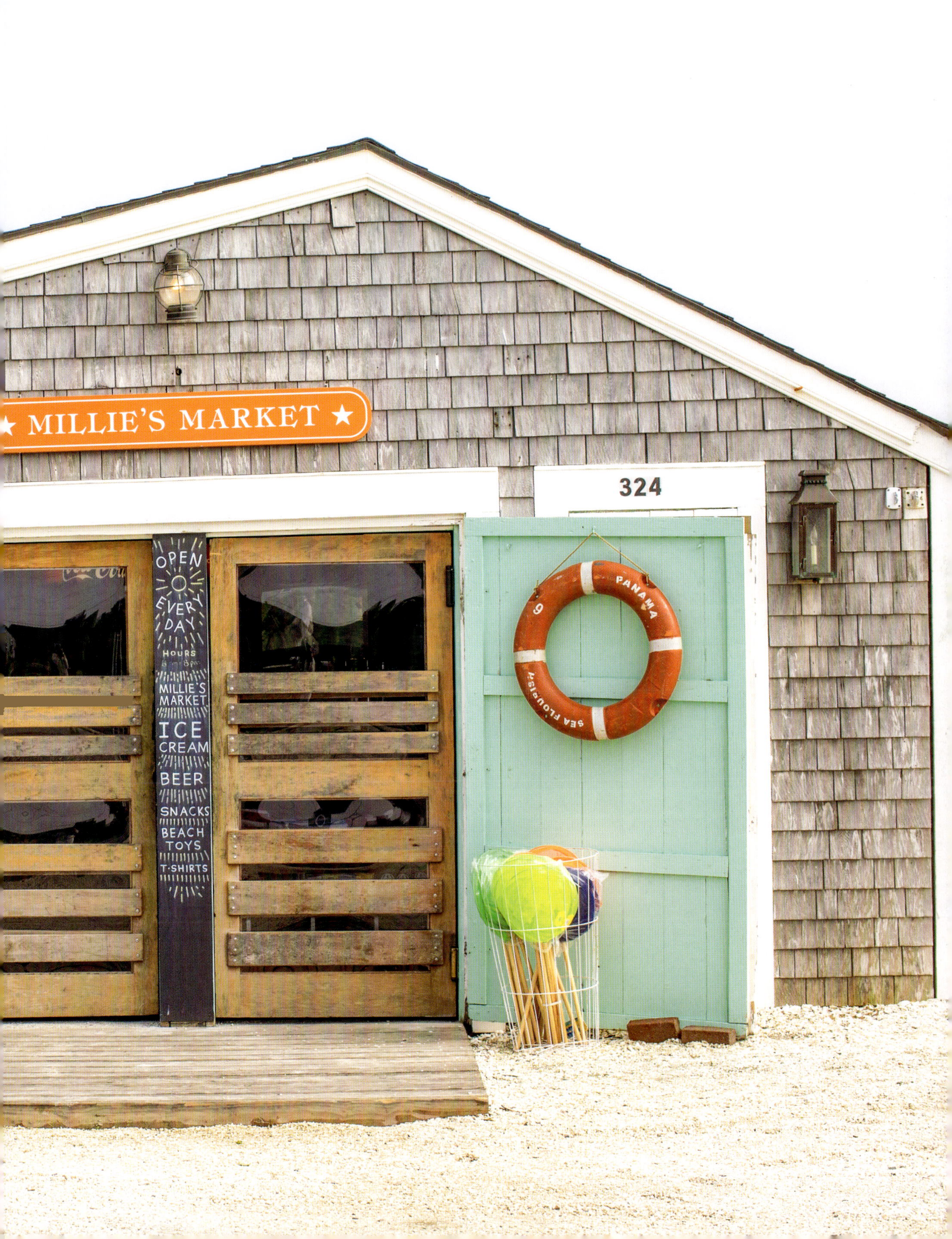
★ MILLIE'S MARKET ★
324
OPEN
EVERY
DAY
HOURS
MILLIE'S
MARKET
ICE
CREAM
BEER
SNACKS
BEACH
TOYS
T-SHIRTS
PANAMA

"We like to take chairs out to the west end for sunset cocktails on the beach as boats roll by. It's stunning. Your whole week has been made because you spent two hours at the beach. It's too easy to enjoy your life when you take a moment like that."

—Marty McGowan, owner of 'Sconset Gardener and Pumpkin Pond Farm

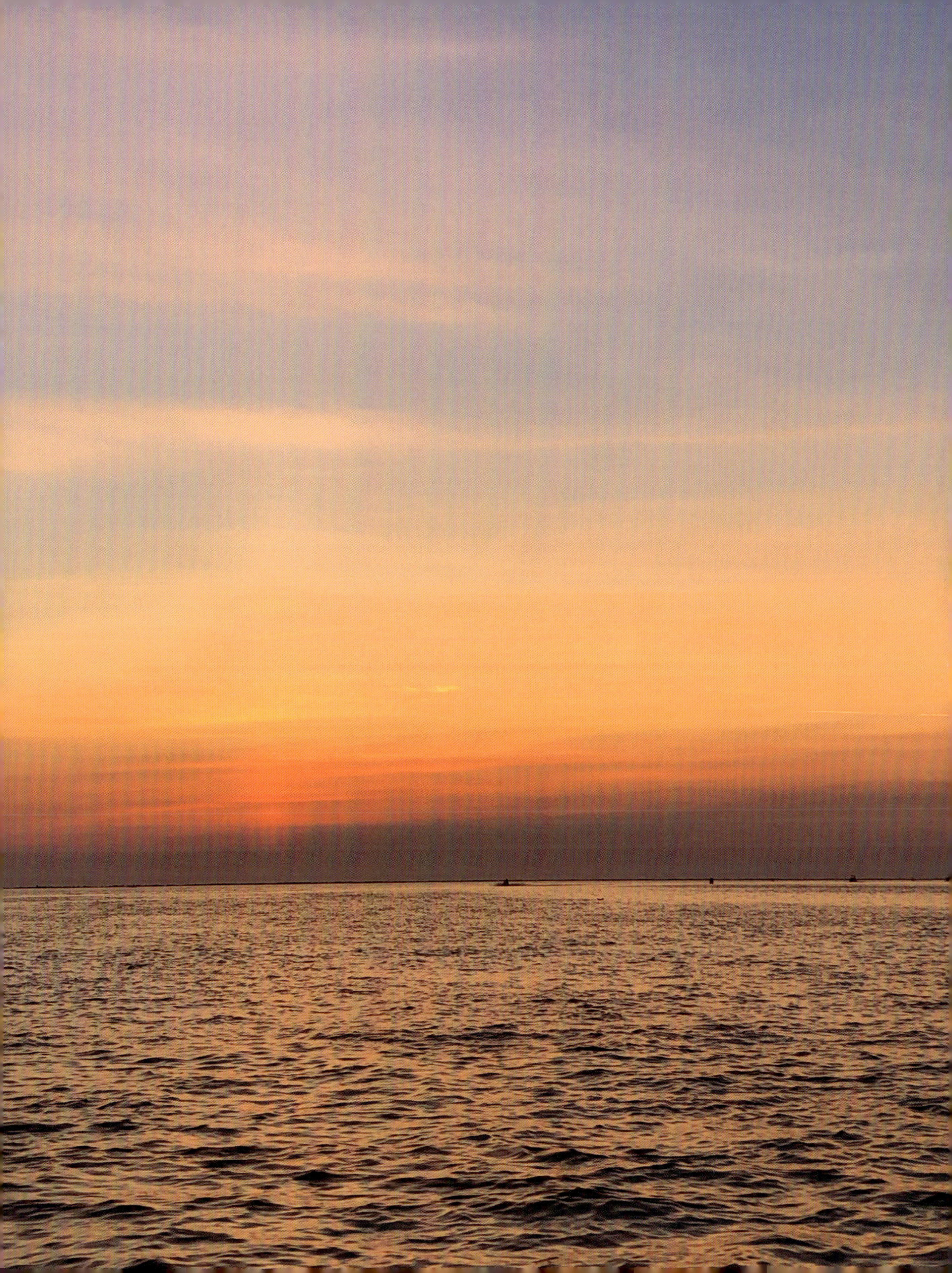

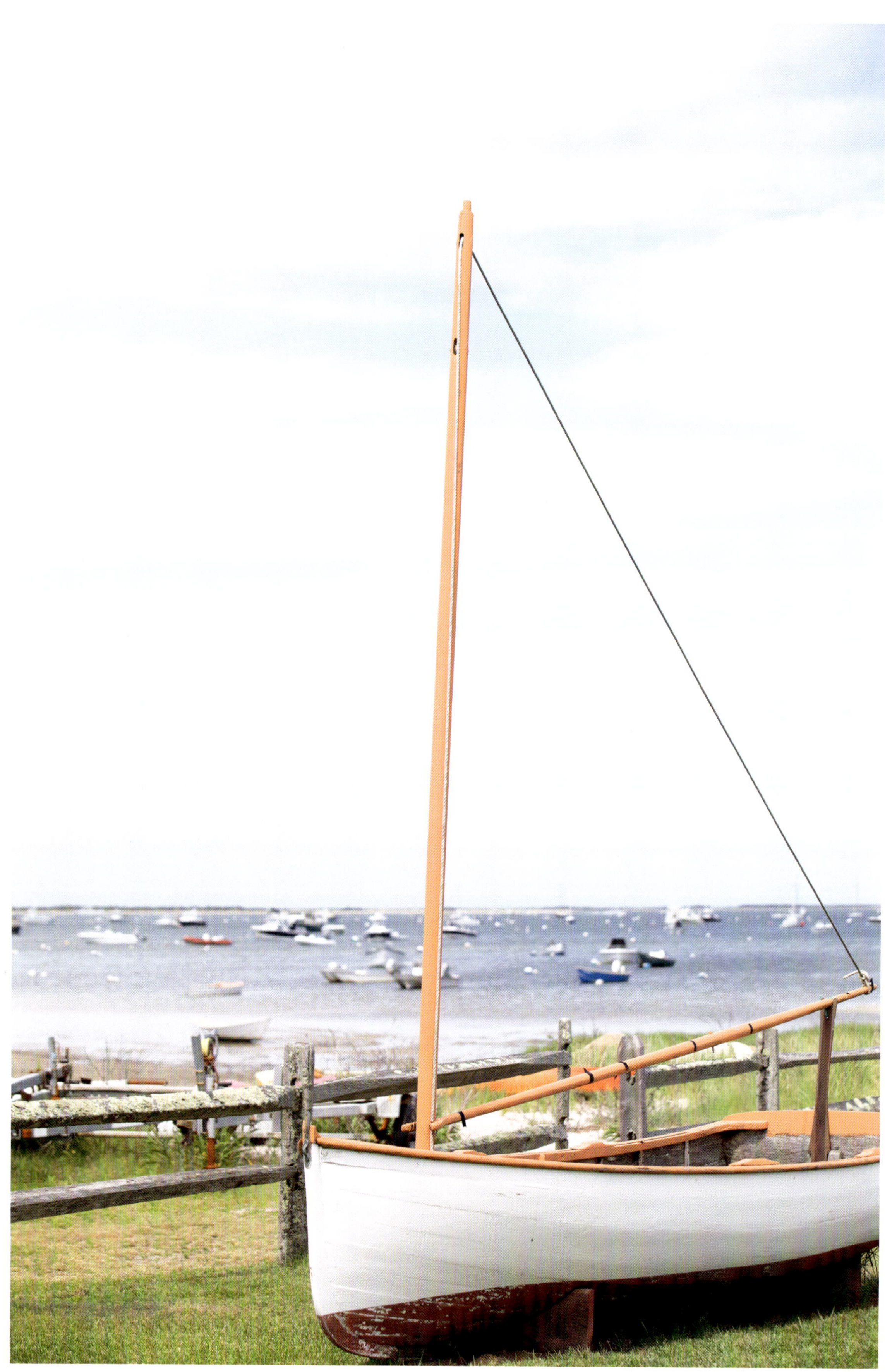

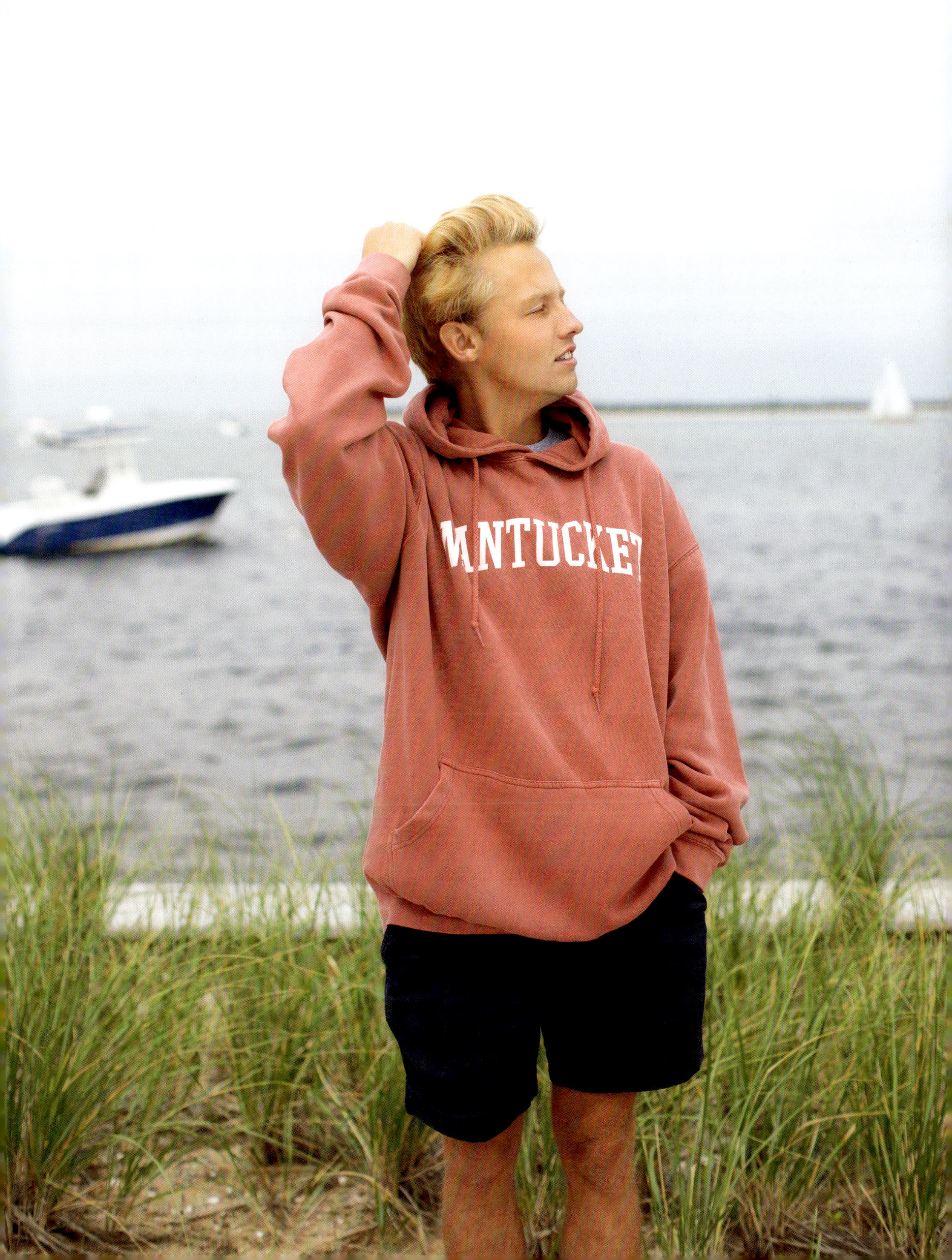

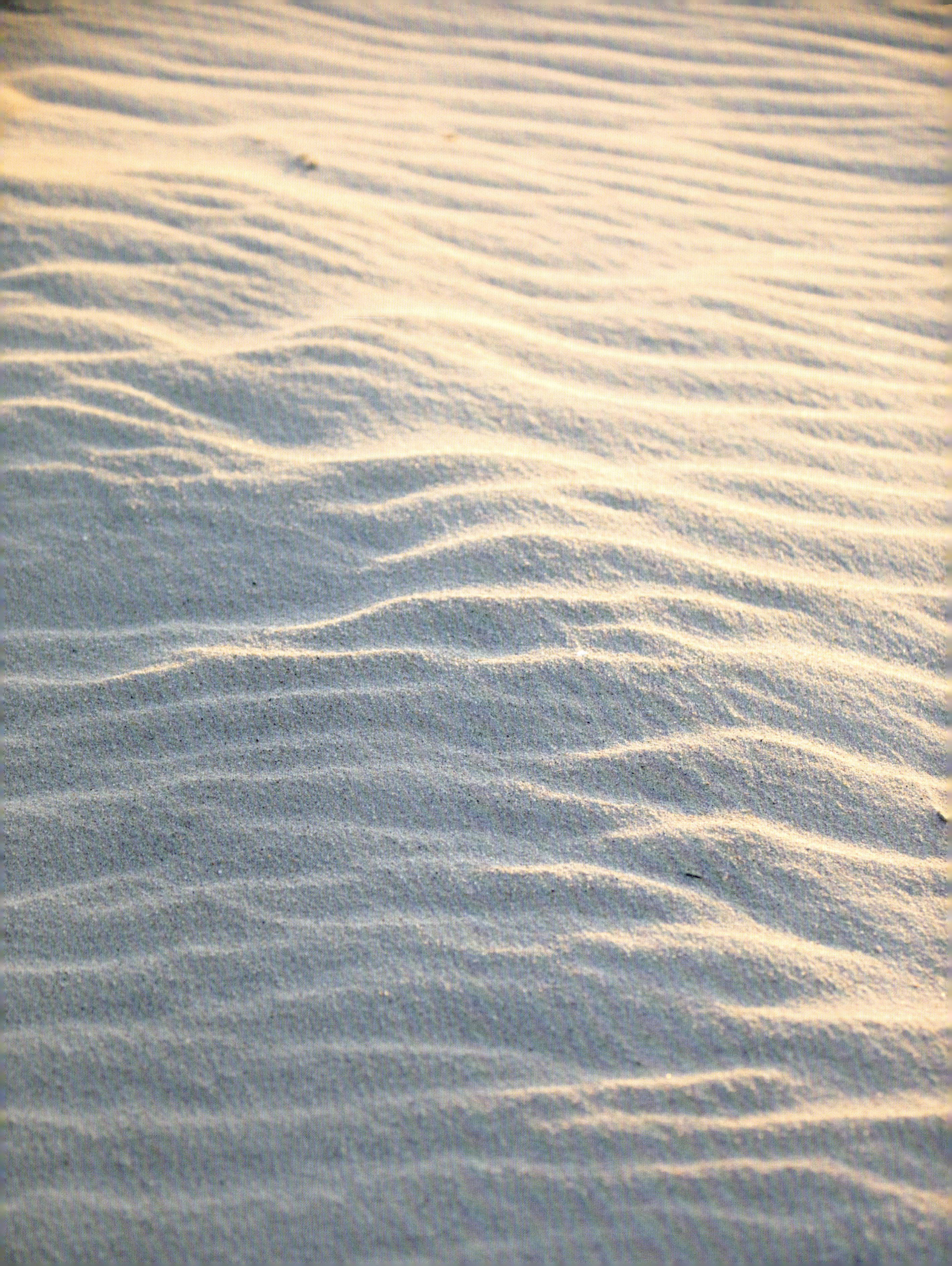

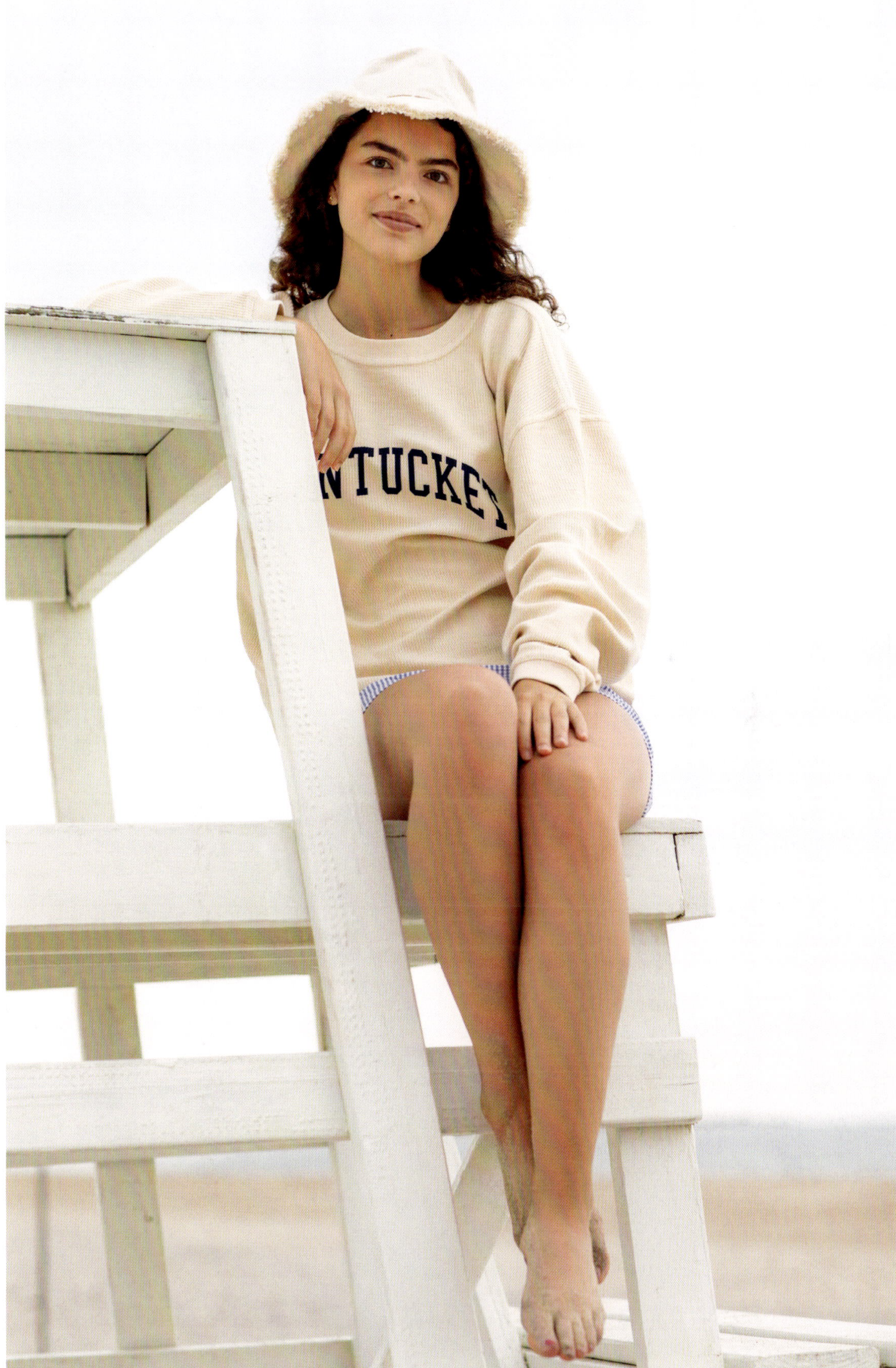
NTUCKET

Nobody accidentally happens upon Nantucket

Nantucket means "faraway island" in the language of the Wampanoag tribe who first inhabited the land. Throughout its last 400 years, the boomerang-shaped island has always required a healthy dose of determination, perseverance, and means, either financial or cunning, to step onto its shores. Even today it's undeniably an effort to arrive, requiring boat or plane, and often a long-haul journey in the car before that. To come to Nantucket is a purposeful choice and arriving feels earned, worth celebrating. The fastest ferry is still an hour from mainland Massachusetts, and flights from Hyannis (when they aren't grounded by fog) are a bumpy twenty-minute ride. But it is worth the effort to get here and settle into the scene: plentiful beaches, hundreds of species of birds, the sunsets of paintings, and a community of smart, charismatic, creative people all contribute to the magic. And that aura of intention and love for the island shows. This tight-knit community of achievers, dreamers, and rebels has created an enviable lifestyle and aesthetic that's an amalgamation of the people, historic grey-shingle homes, and the 14-mile-long island itself, its wind, sea, and wild landscape.

Nantucket has shaped its people and they've developed a unique life 30 miles out to sea. The look, feel, and culture that define what's classic about American style in many ways began here, and Nantucket continues to push cultural boundaries because of influences drawn from around the world, innovative thinking, hard work, and a shared love for the beautiful lifestyle one can have here.

As Nantucket has always been a notoriously difficult place to get to, this has helped it develop and maintain a character all its own. Now more than 11,000 year-round residents inhabit the island, and summer families, no matter where they arrive from—Boston, Chicago, Washington D.C., Greenwich, or San Francisco—all subscribe to its unwritten rules. Many residents slip on colorful sundresses, break out their boat shoes, sun-bleached L.L.Bean bags, and proudly add another beach permit to their vintage Land Rover each season. This is not a self-conscious style capital, absorbed in labels and trends, quite the opposite. Instead, style here is shaped by wind, cobblestones, cliffs, beaches, sailboats, surfboards, and for a long time, the blue-blood idea that showiness is less tasteful than something practical that's tattered and aged by the sun. The island's inaccessibility has preserved the look, which is equal parts blue blazer, decade-old Sperry Top-Siders, and salty Mount Gay cap earned at a regatta. In just the last few years the barrier to get to Nantucket has lifted some. Flights into ACK (the famed airport code) have brought more visitors from New York and other East Coast cities, and many more people live year-round than ever before. Yet the island's steadfast ethos and aesthetics prevail.

"I always say about Nantucket that after a day you can throw away your watch and after a week your calendar. It's murderous trying to get here, but once you arrive you never want to leave."

—**Walter Beinecke, Jr. told** Life **magazine in 1968**

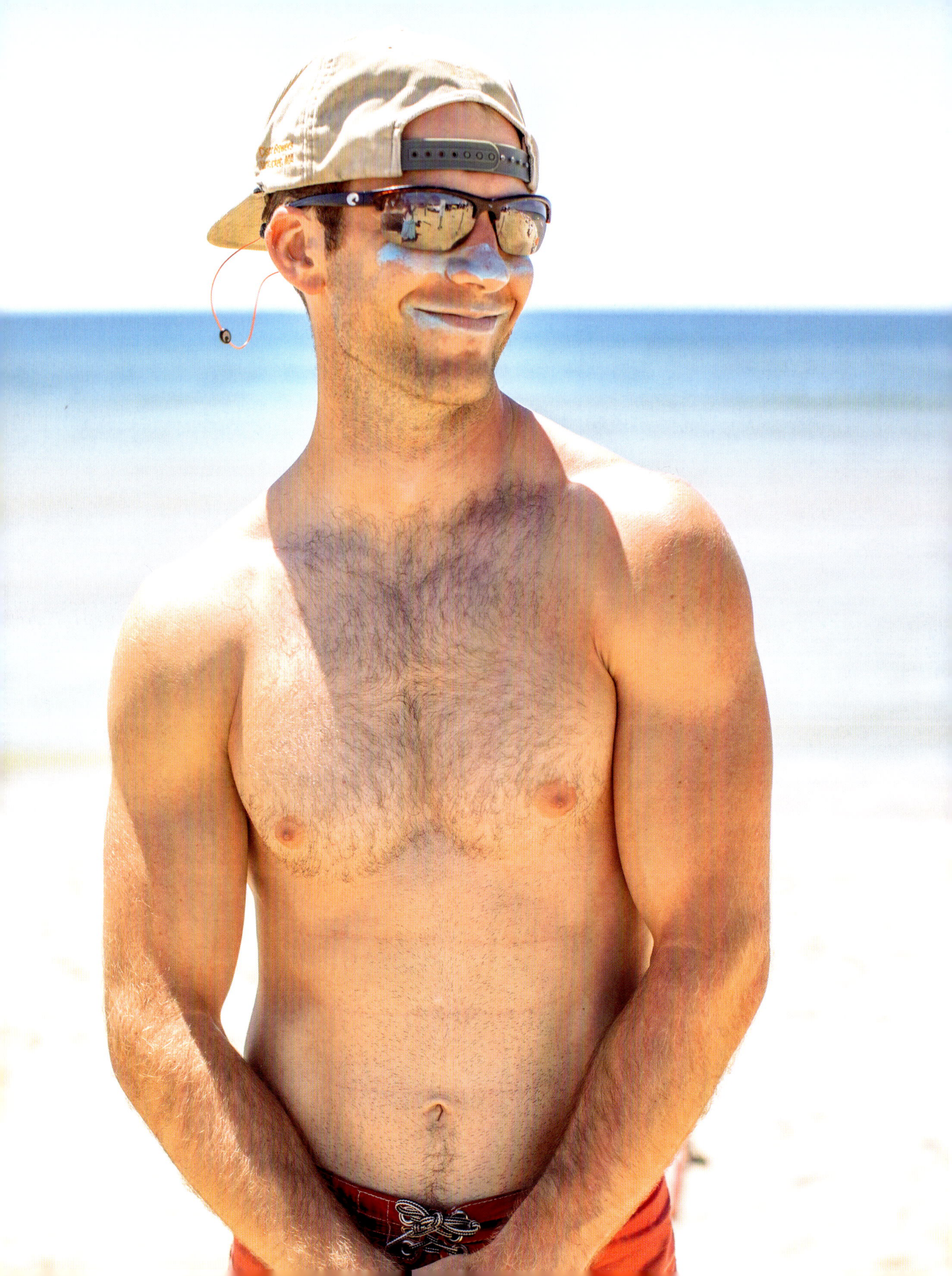

ow Tide: 1:22 p.m.
Alexis +
Water Tem
STAY AWAY FROMTHE SEAL!!!

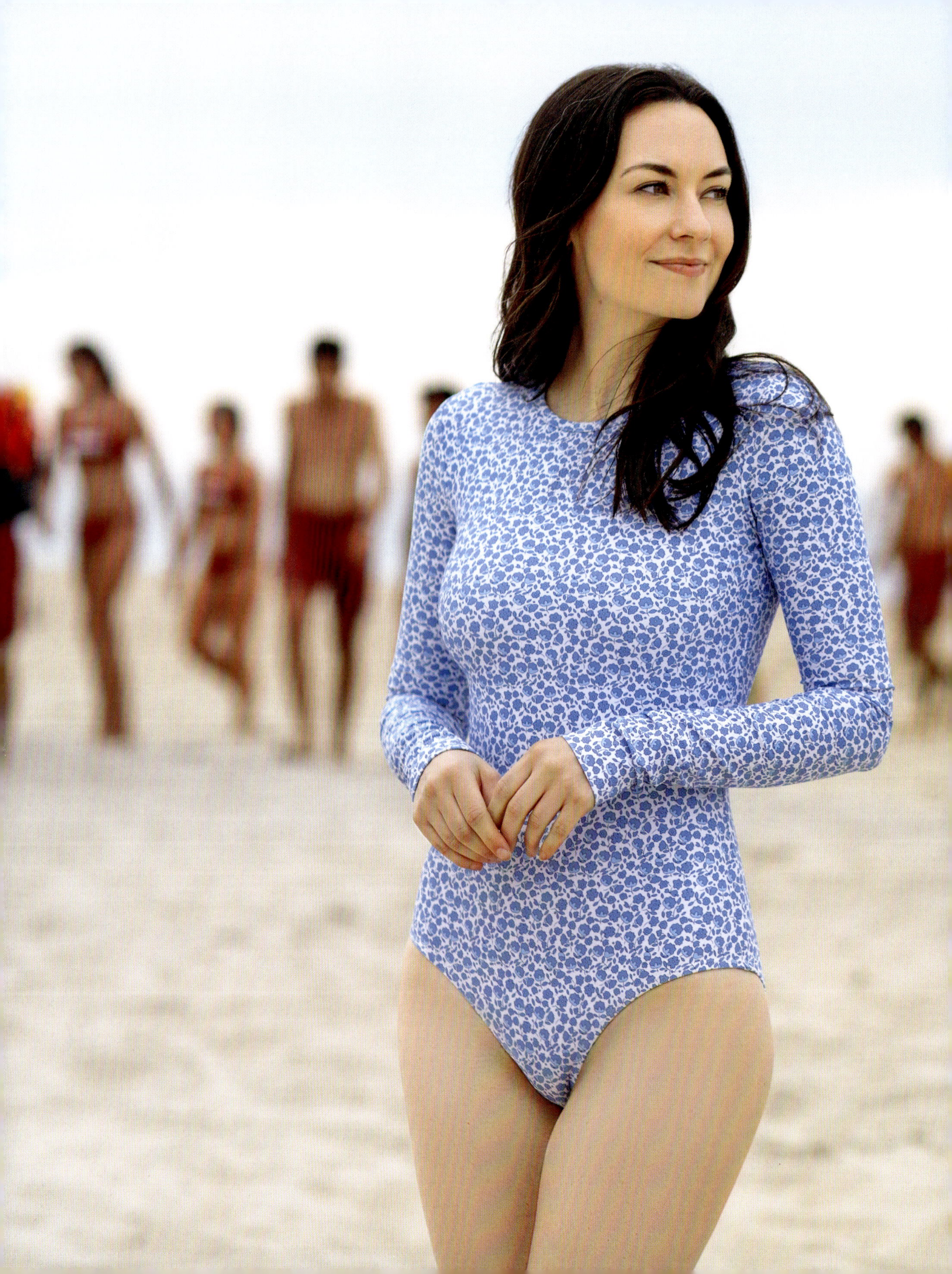

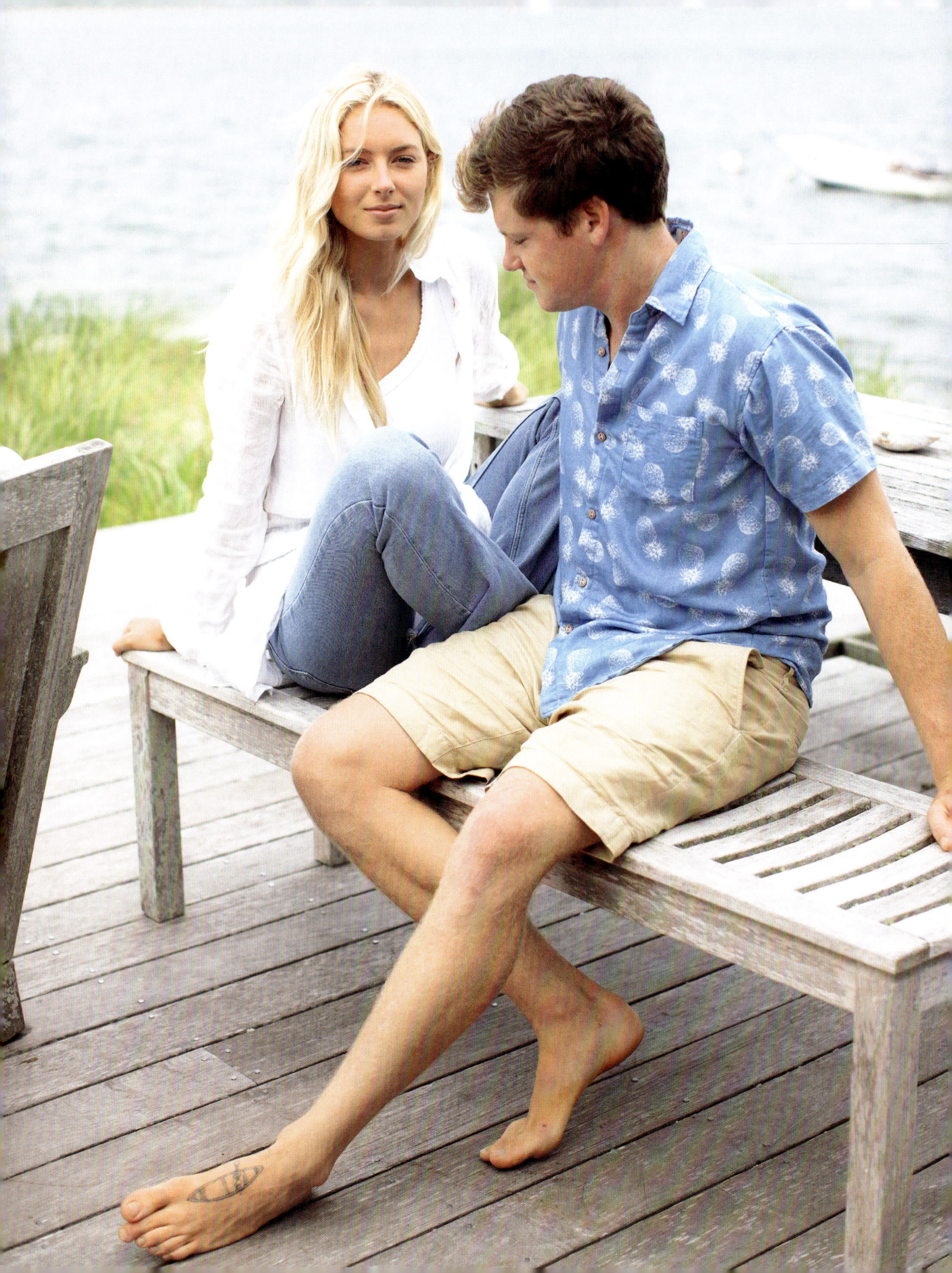

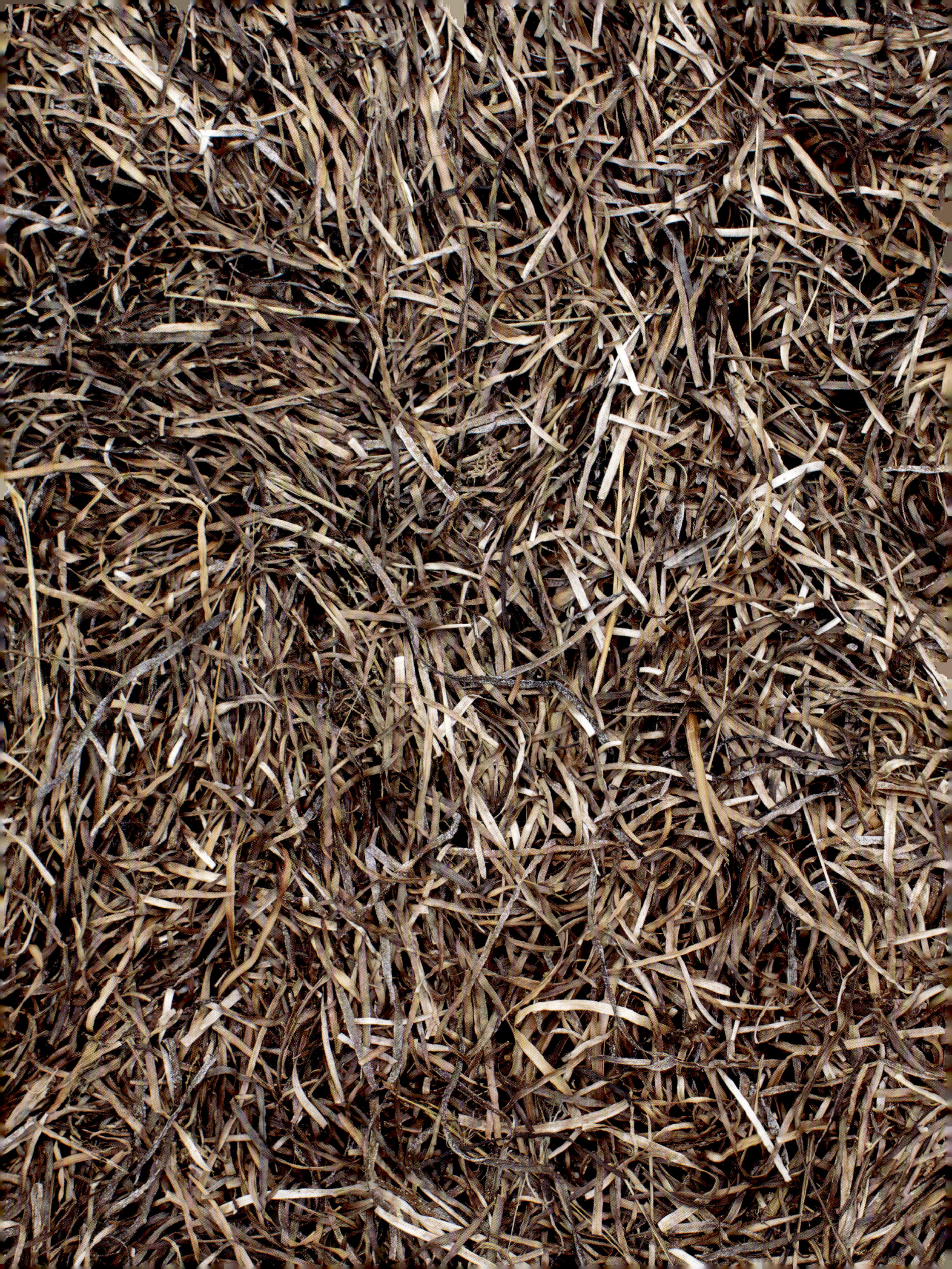

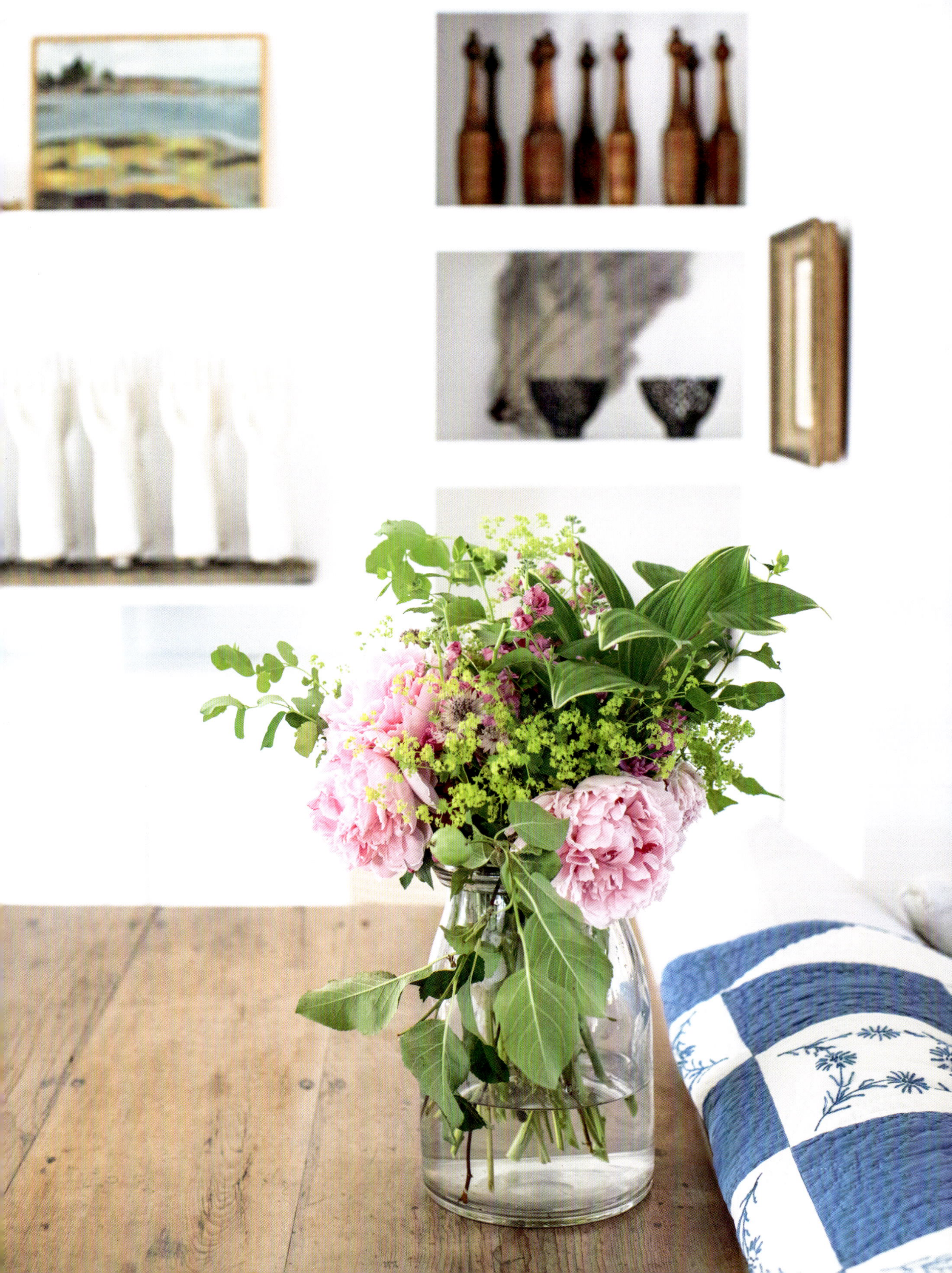

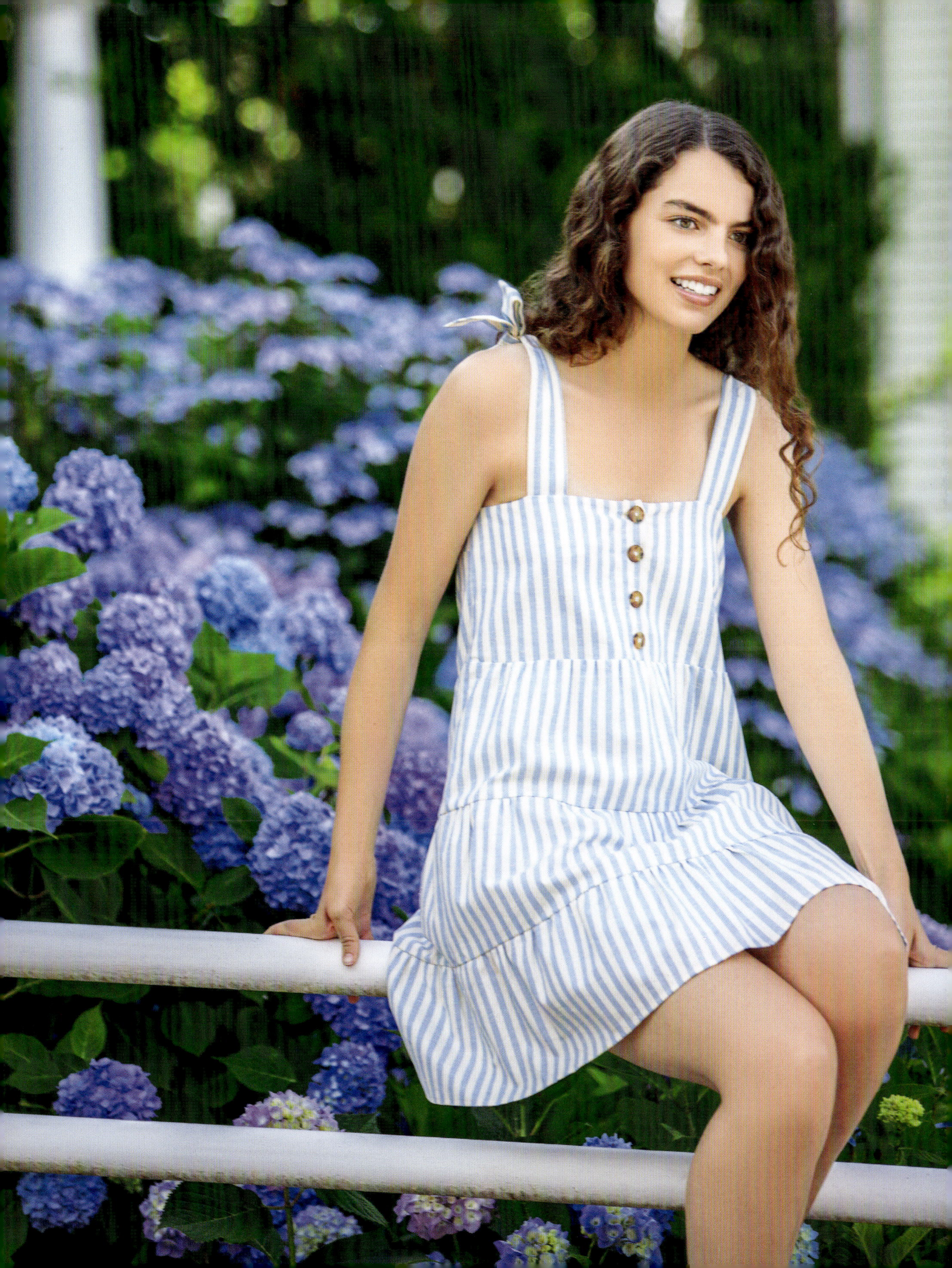

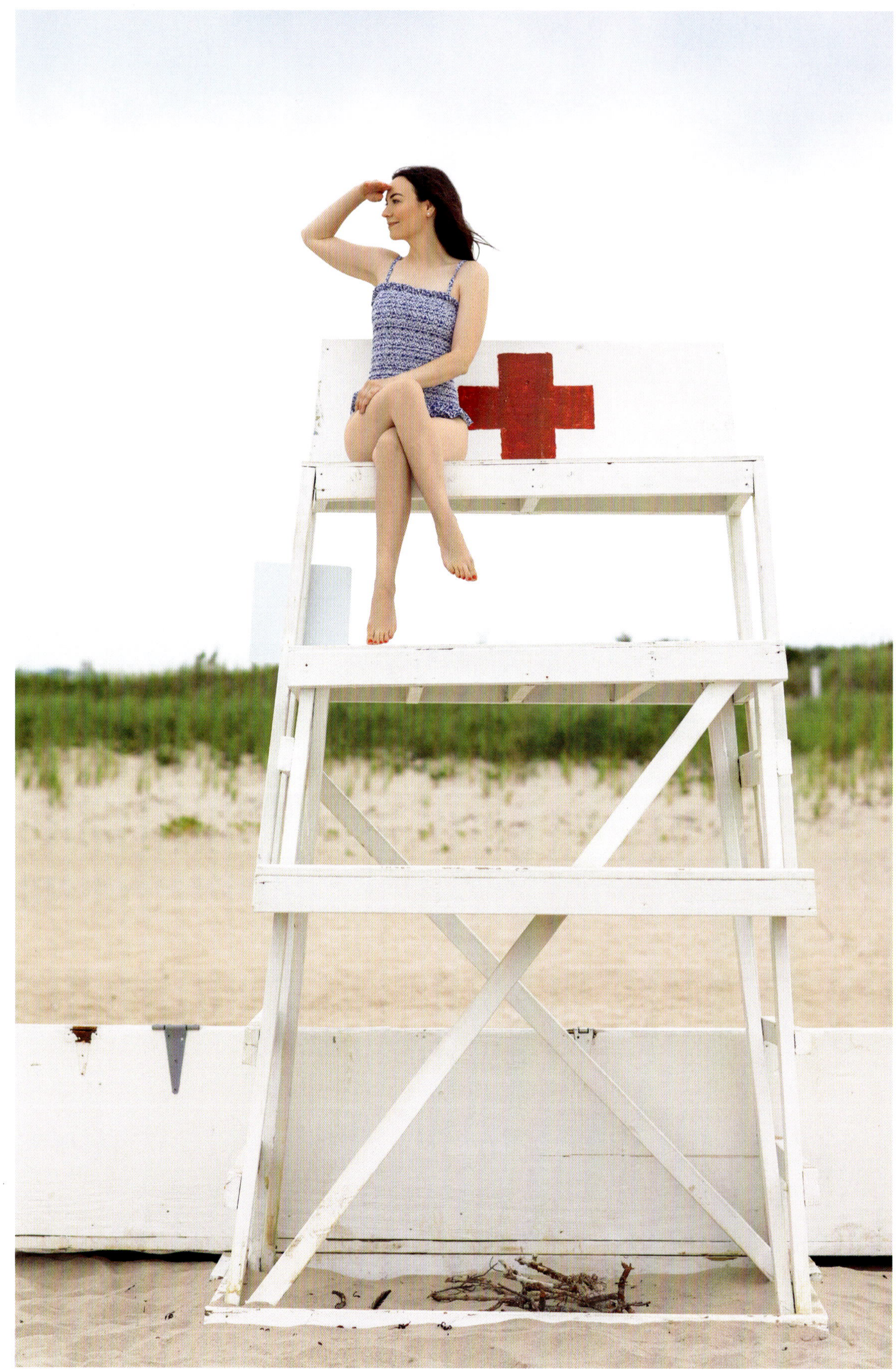

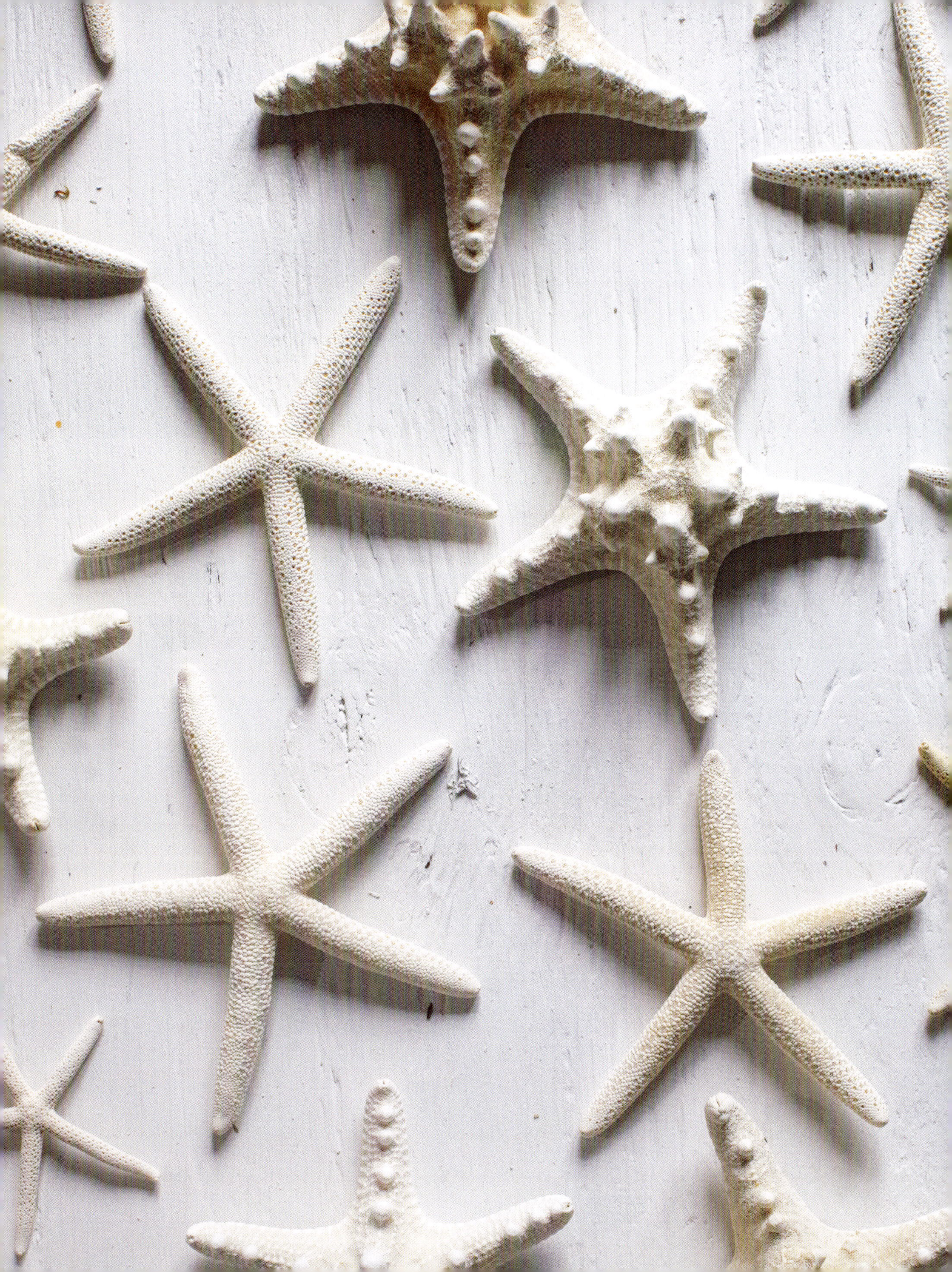

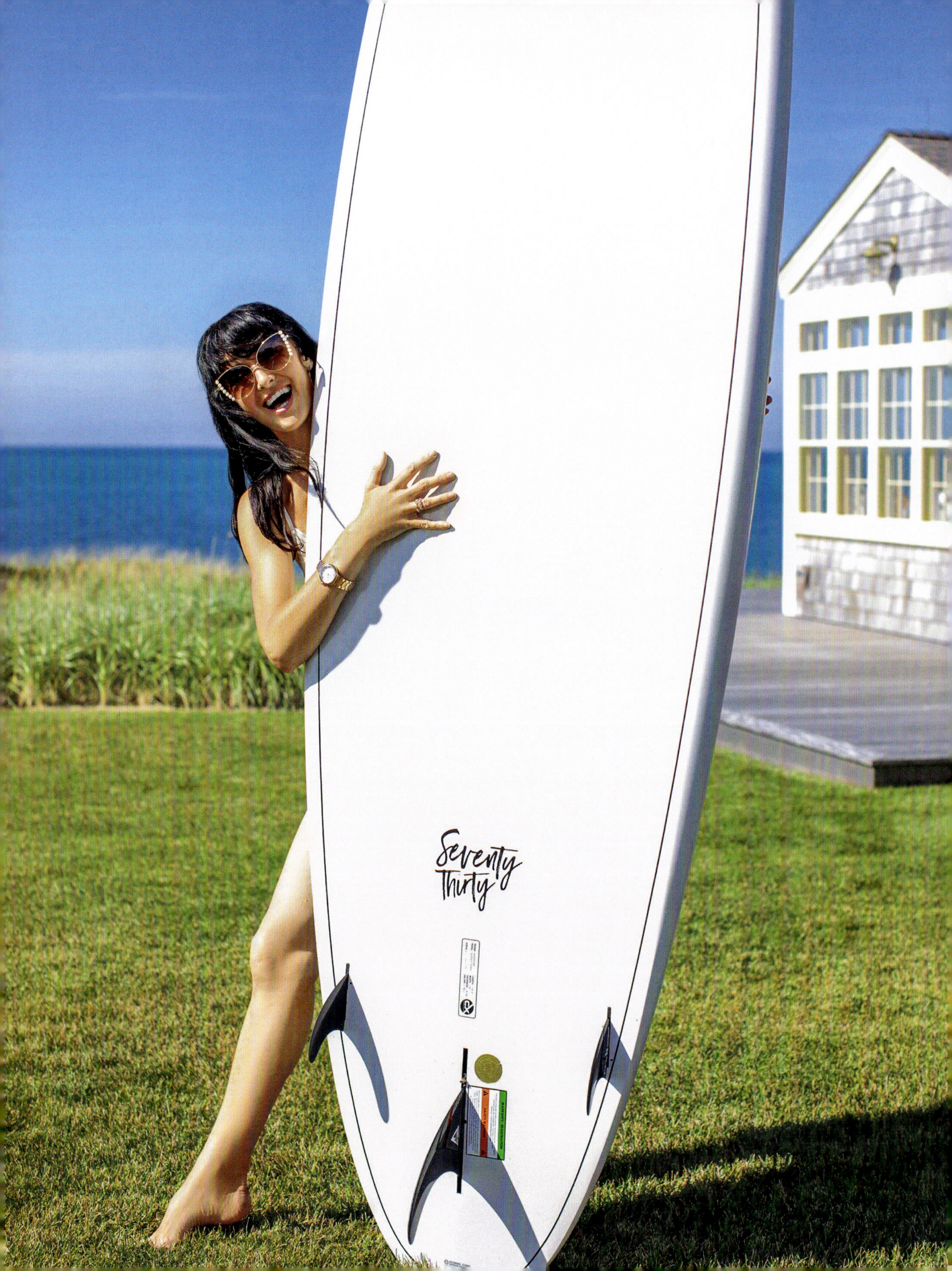
Seventy
Thirty

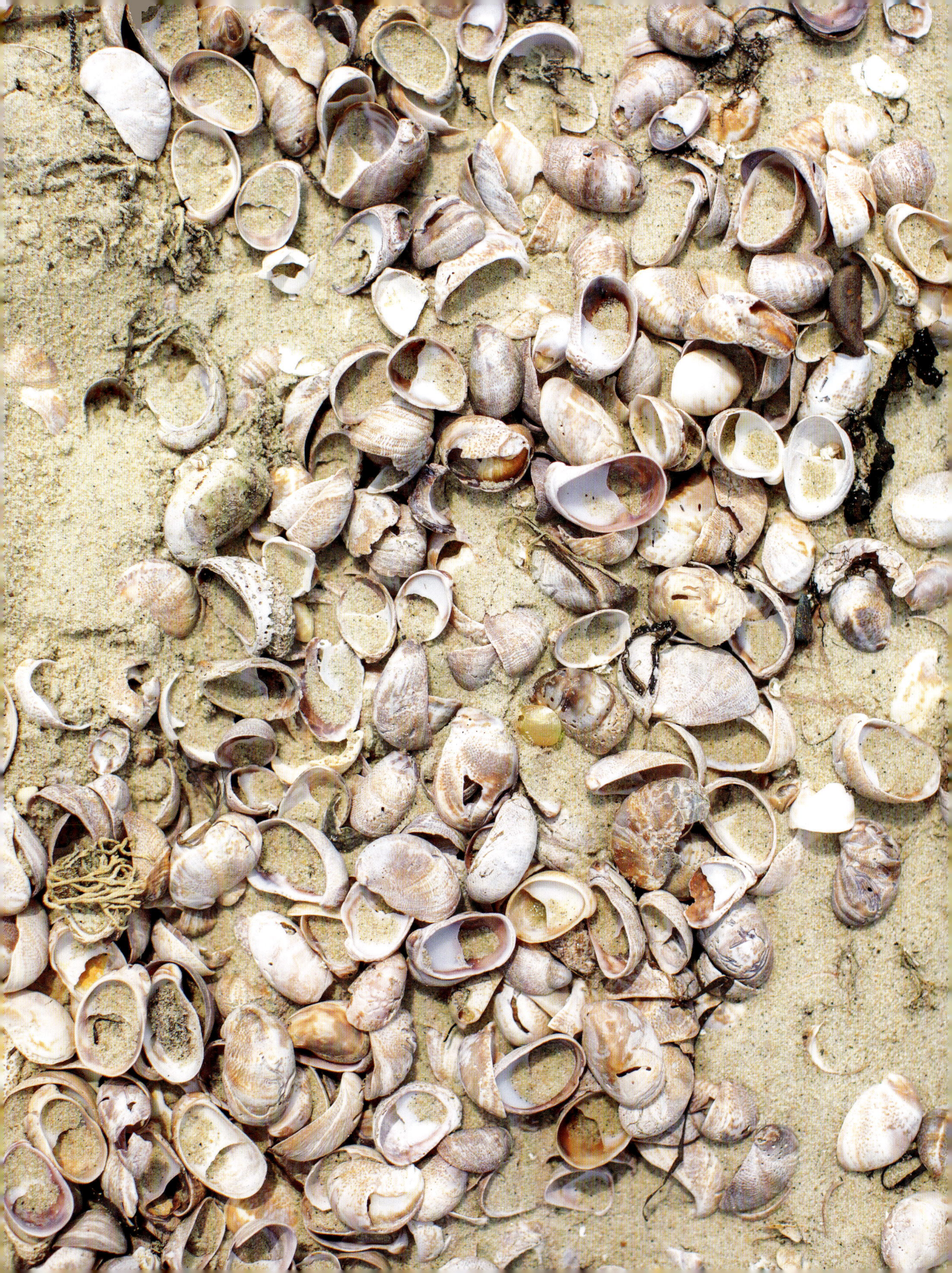

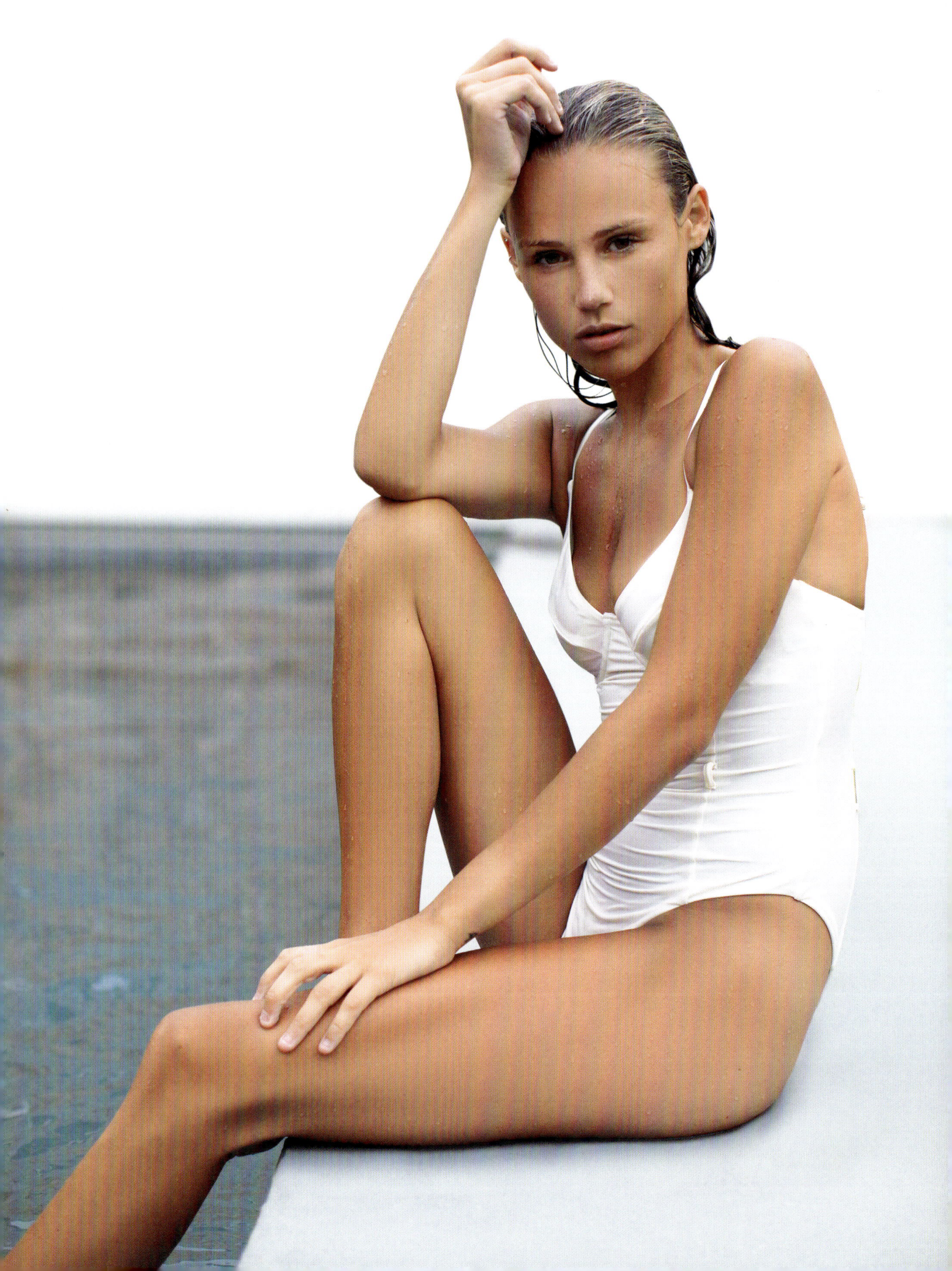

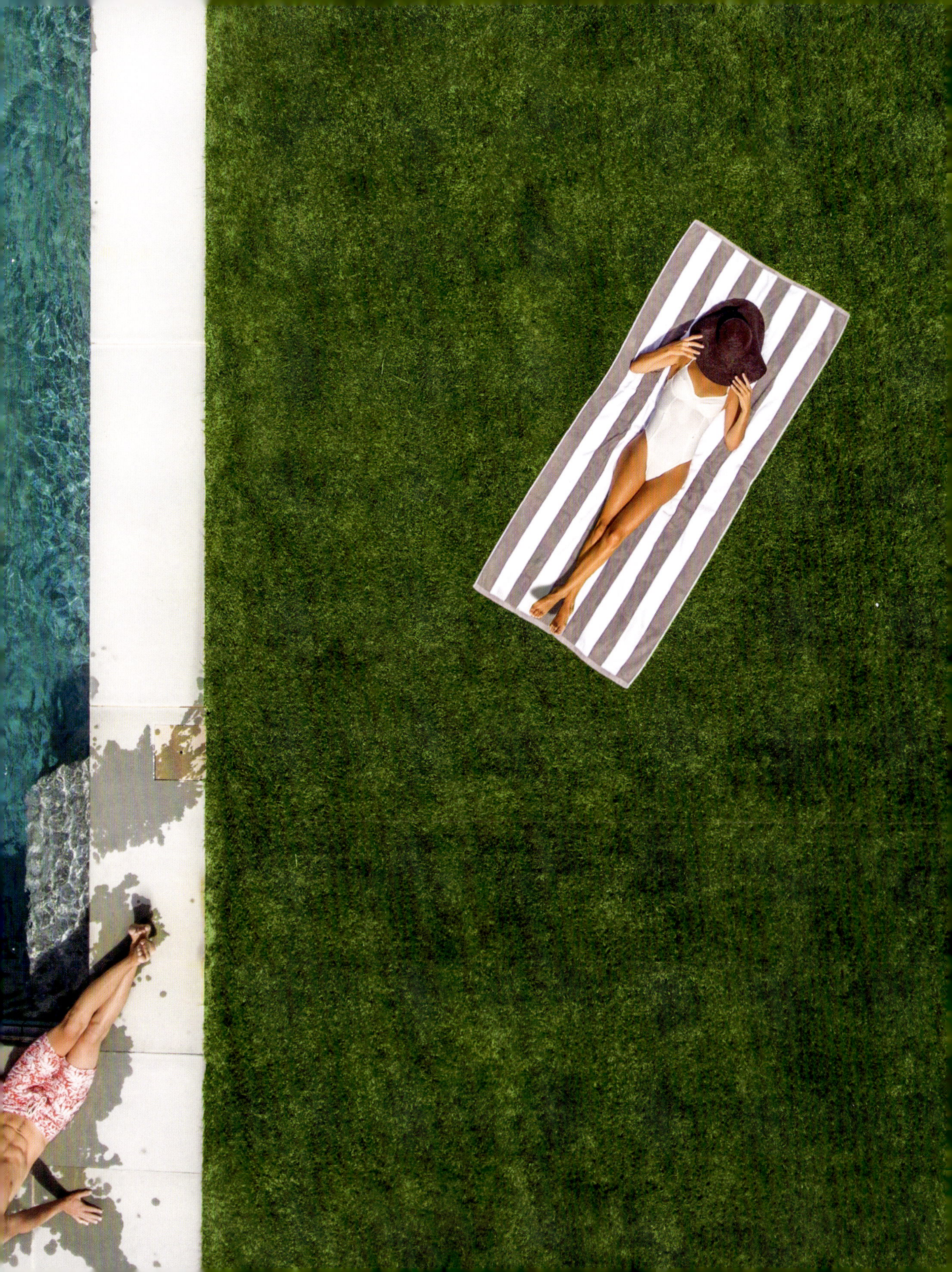

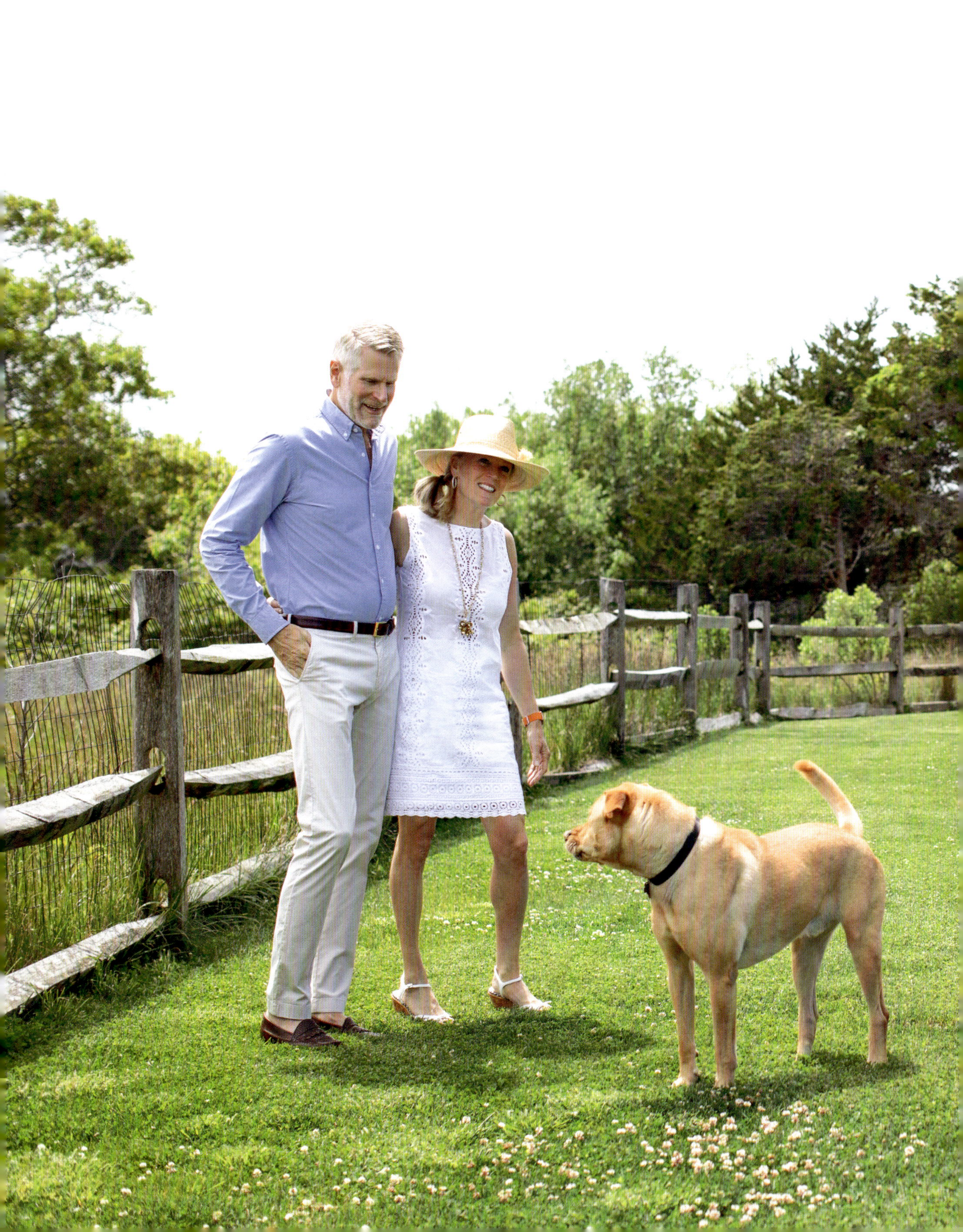

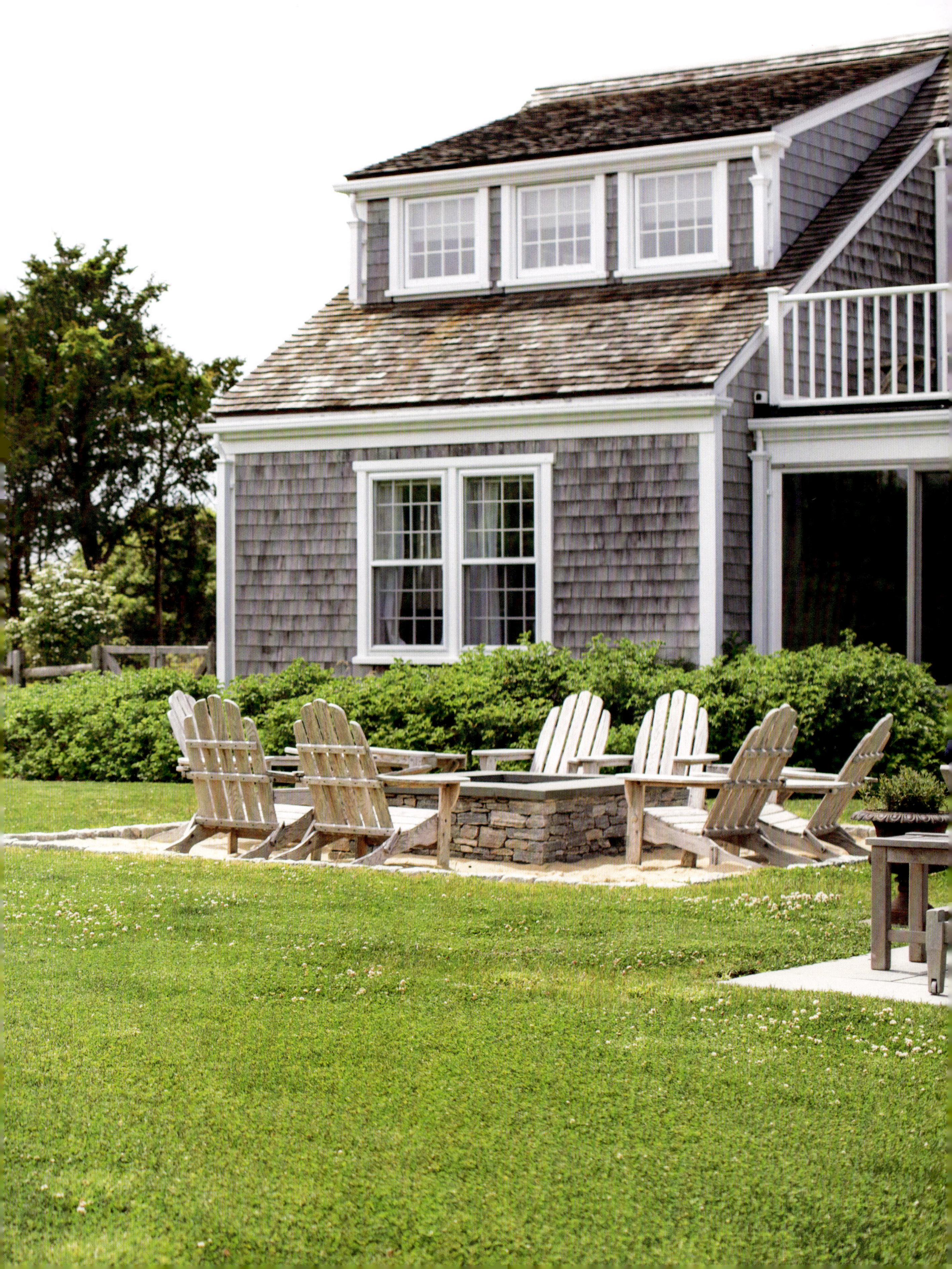

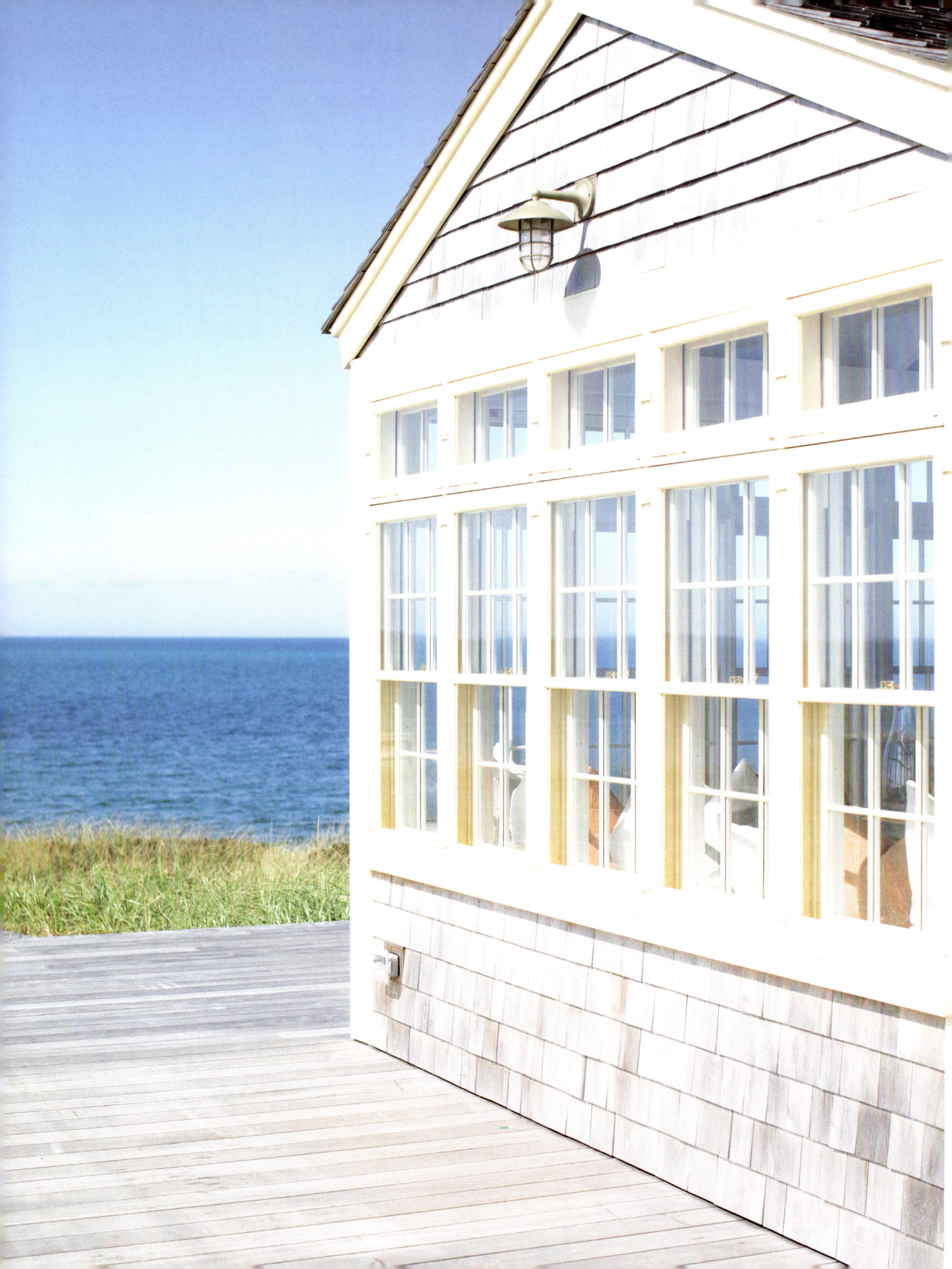

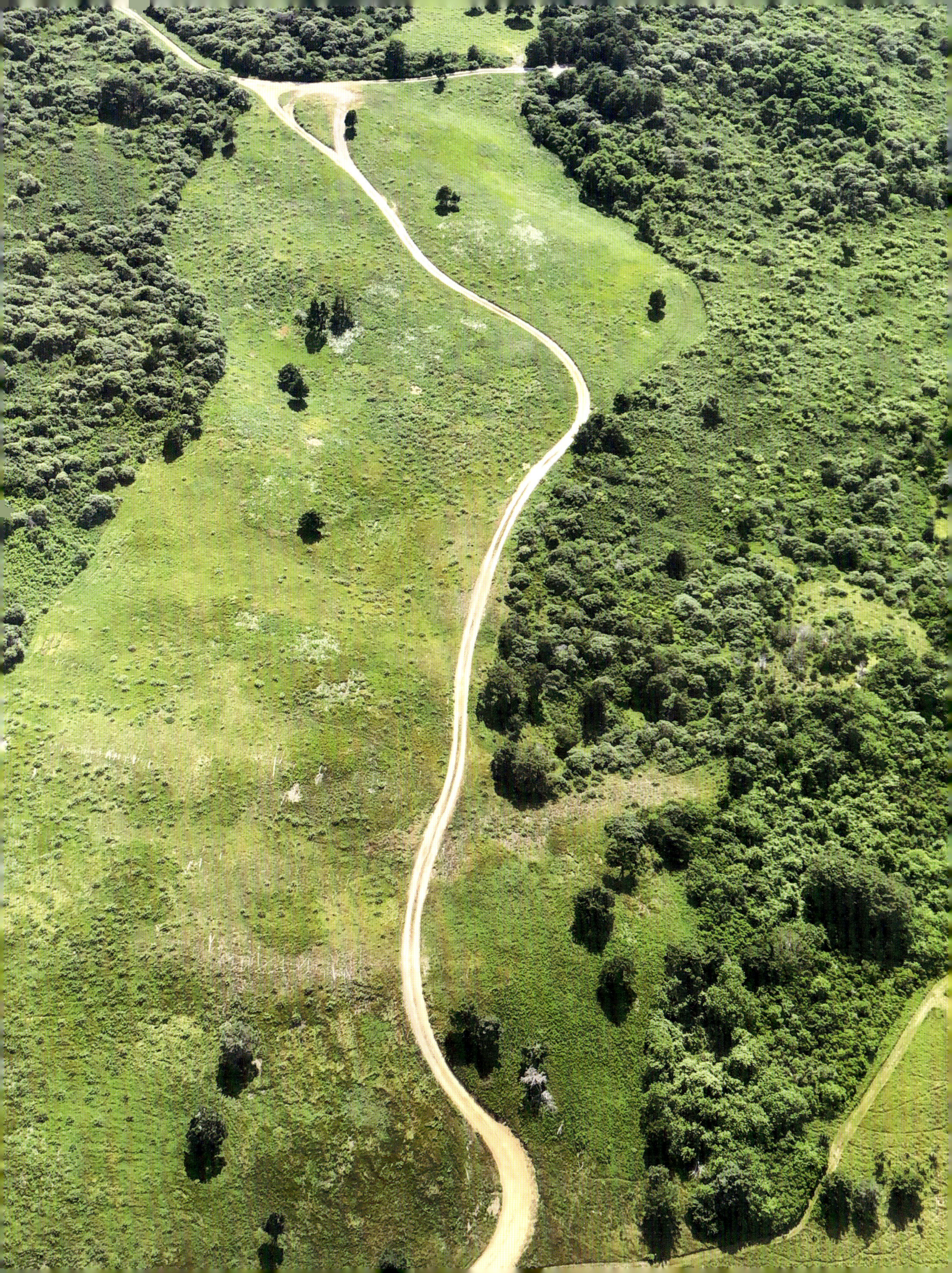

Individualism still reigns

For its first 200 years of European settlement, Nantucket sea captains went out exploring the world. For the last 200, the world has come to Nantucket, and this sentiment is echoed at the Nantucket Historical Association's Whaling Museum.

From Nantucket's start as a settlement of liberal entrepreneurs who escaped their Plymouth Colony brethren's narrow mindedness, later embracing Quaker egalitarianism, Nantucket's individualism and self-reliance can still be seen today in its year-round artists and makers carving a life on the windy, foggy faraway island. For a tiny island, Nantucket holds a powerful role in shaping American culture and style.

One of the United States' most significant ports during the eighteenth and nineteenth centuries, Nantucket's sea captains journeyed to the Orient, Africa, Europe, and the far corners of the world to trade whale oil. They returned with wealth, stories, and souvenirs. Today, Nantucket is often only thought of as an idyllic natural playground for the American elite, but its inhabitants are varied and the island is home to many international residents, including those from the Dominican Republic, Costa Rica, Jamaica, Nepal, Sri Lanka, Russia, and elsewhere.

"The first person from my hometown to come to Nantucket was a woman named Victoria. Because of her, more than 200 people from Cabrera, Dominican Republic, are here now raising families and living year-round," says Diony Gil, a successful builder. "A friend who was building the post office told me to come help for the summer and one summer turned into thirteen years." Diony's story is not uncommon. Many come to Nantucket for the summer and stay for a lifetime. "The island is so quiet, I feel safe here," he says, describing leaving the house unlocked and keys in the car. "I never had that experience anywhere else." Diony, like many, loves the tranquility, and the community. "Everyone knows each other here and it's like a big family," he smiles. Of course, the people make the place.

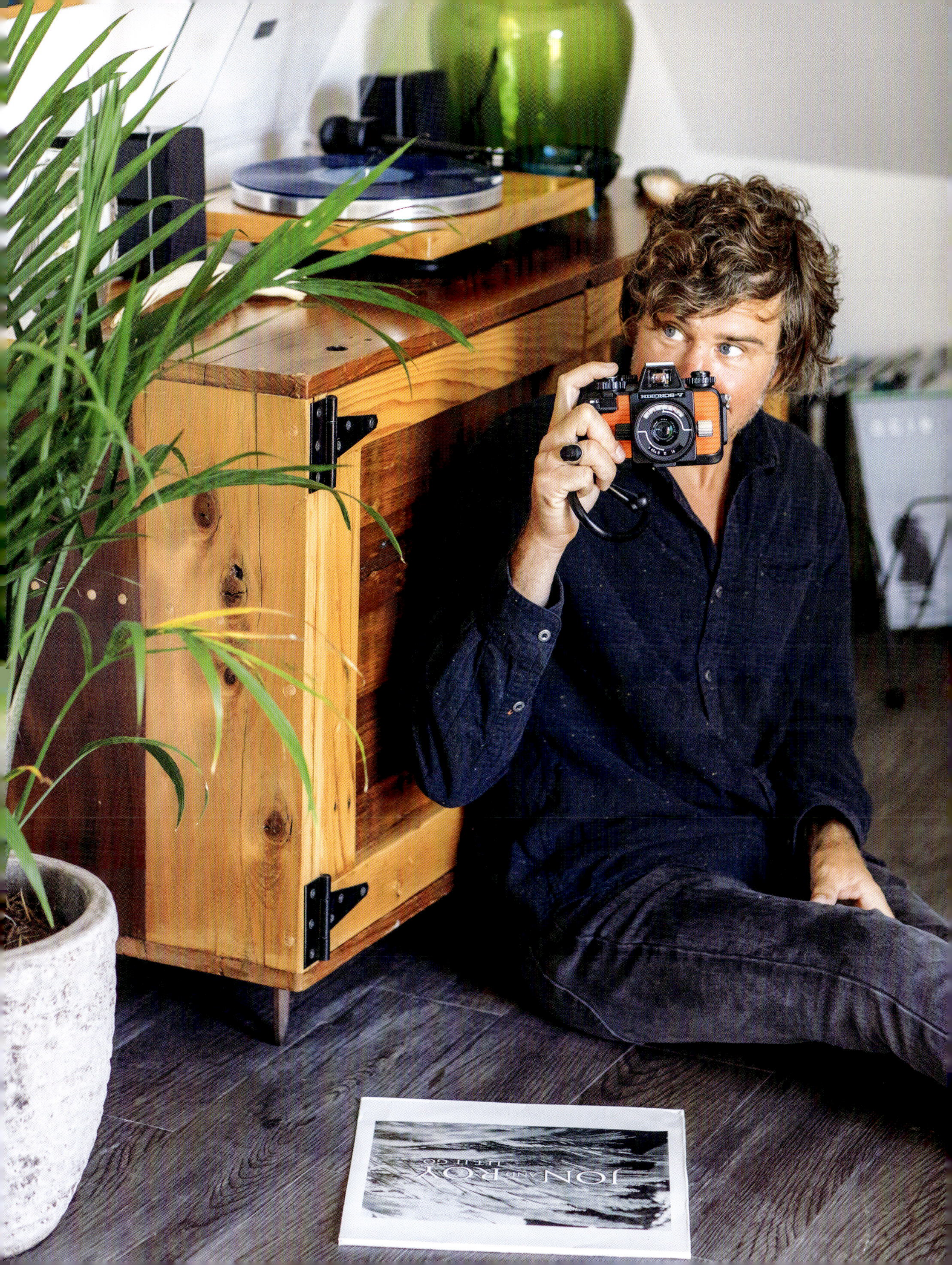

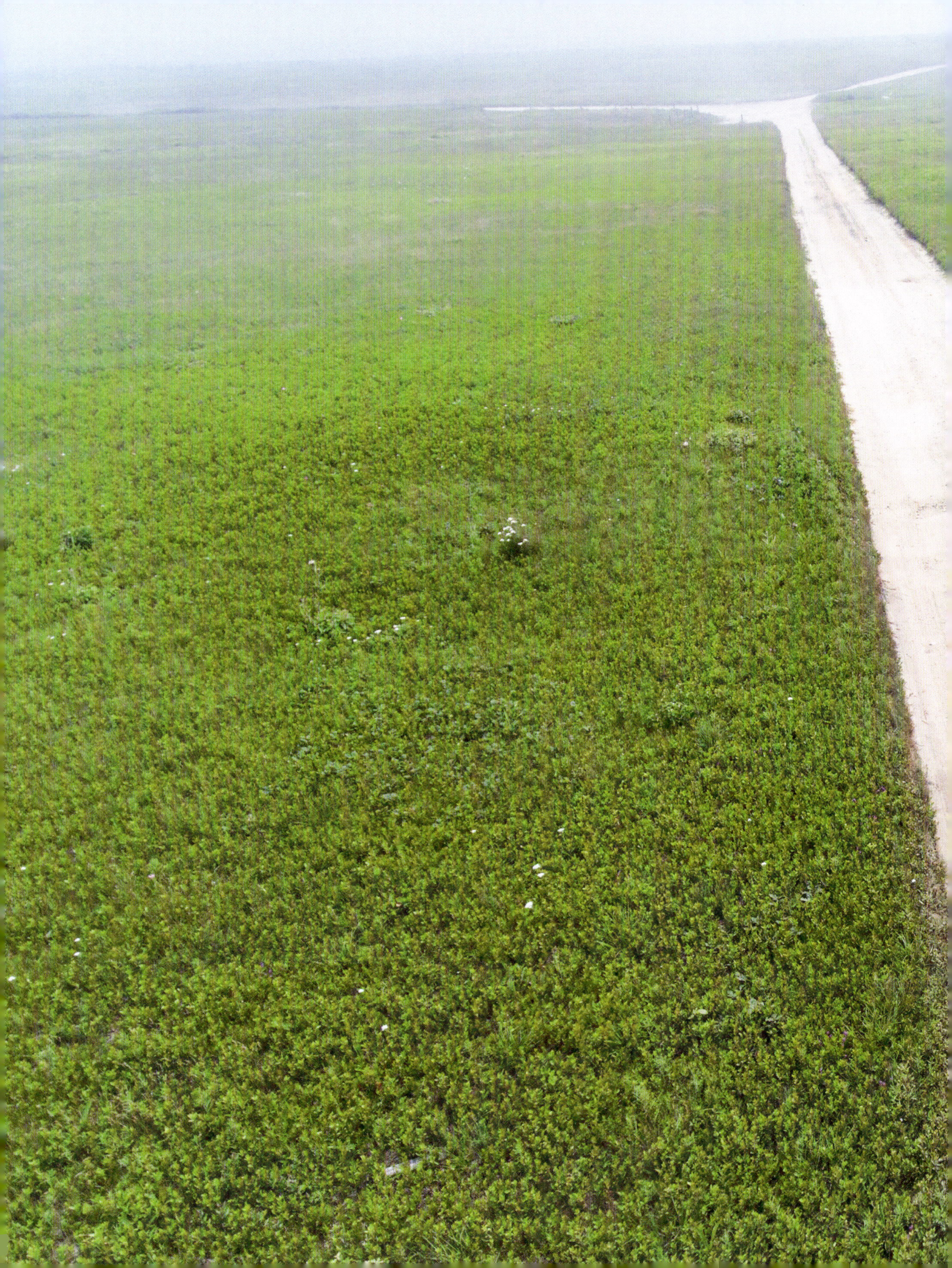

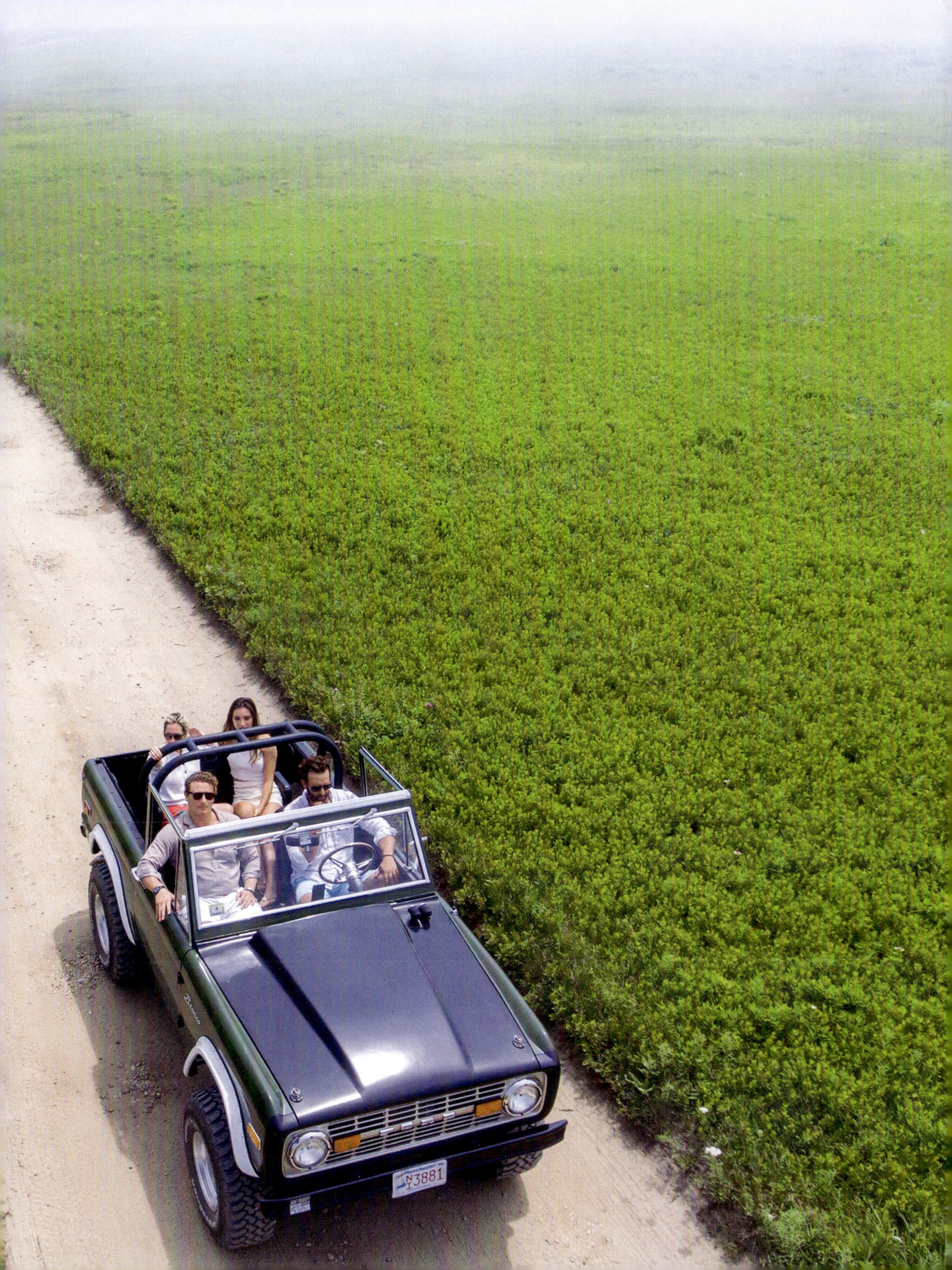
N I 3881

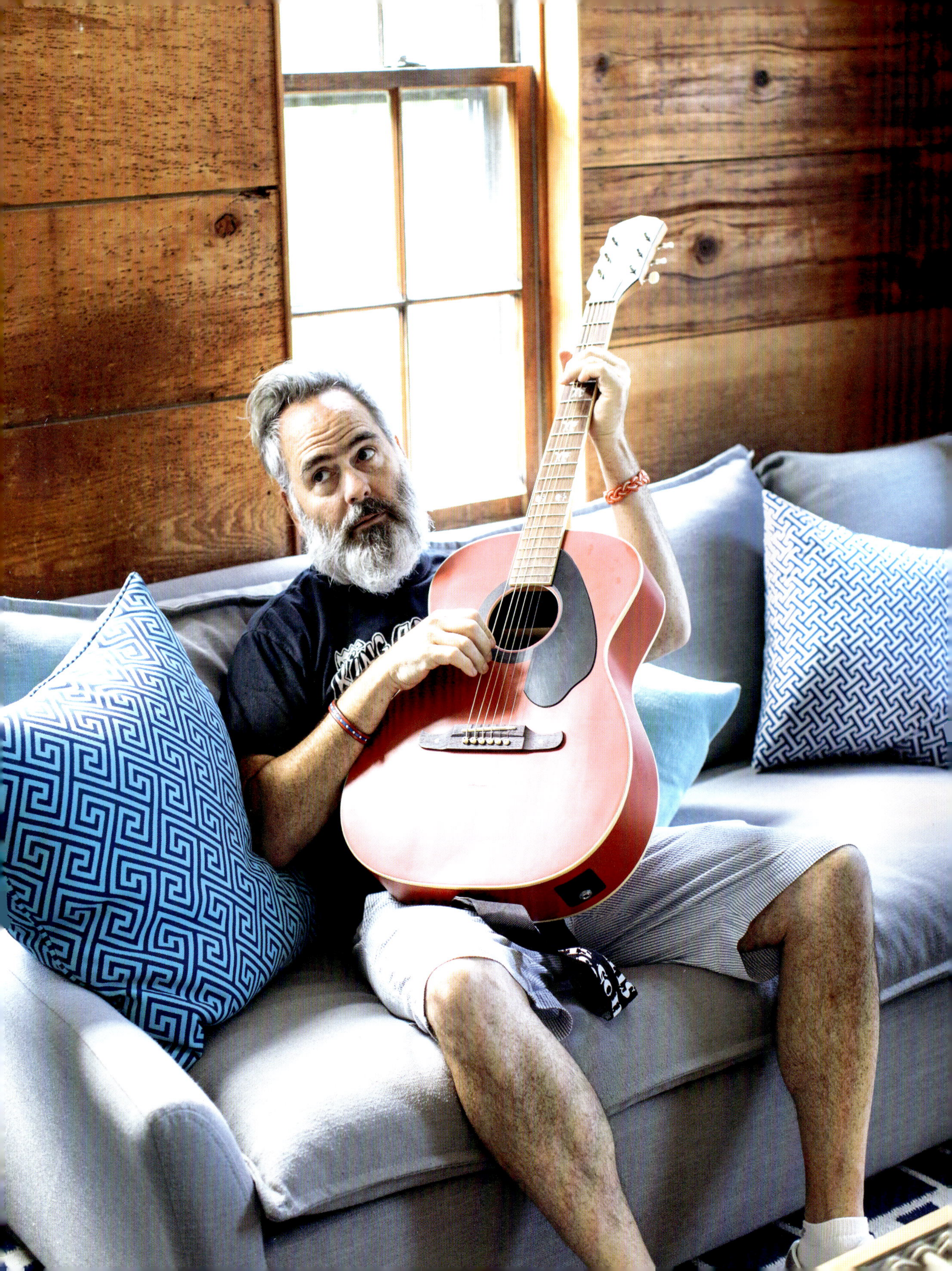

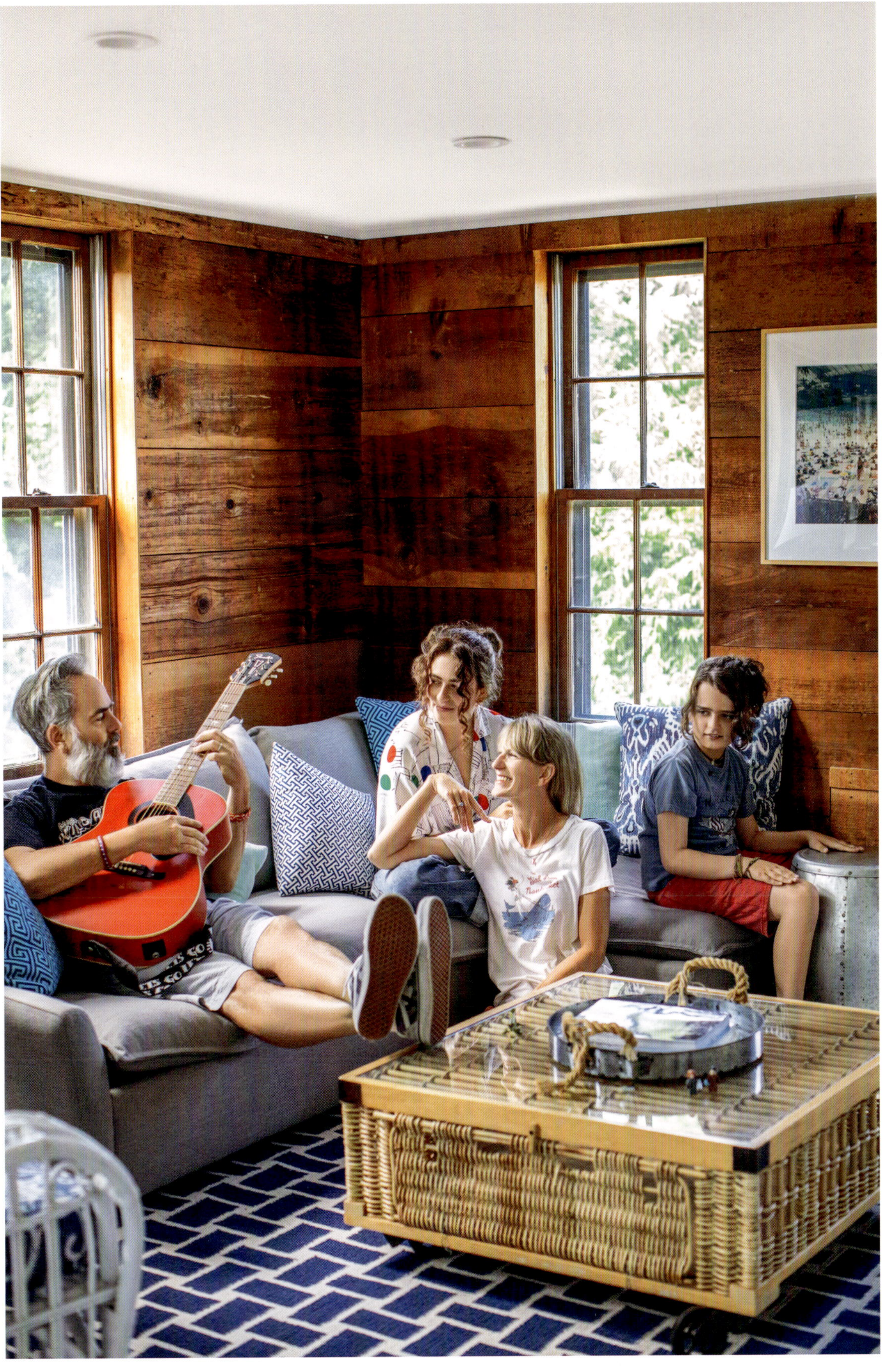

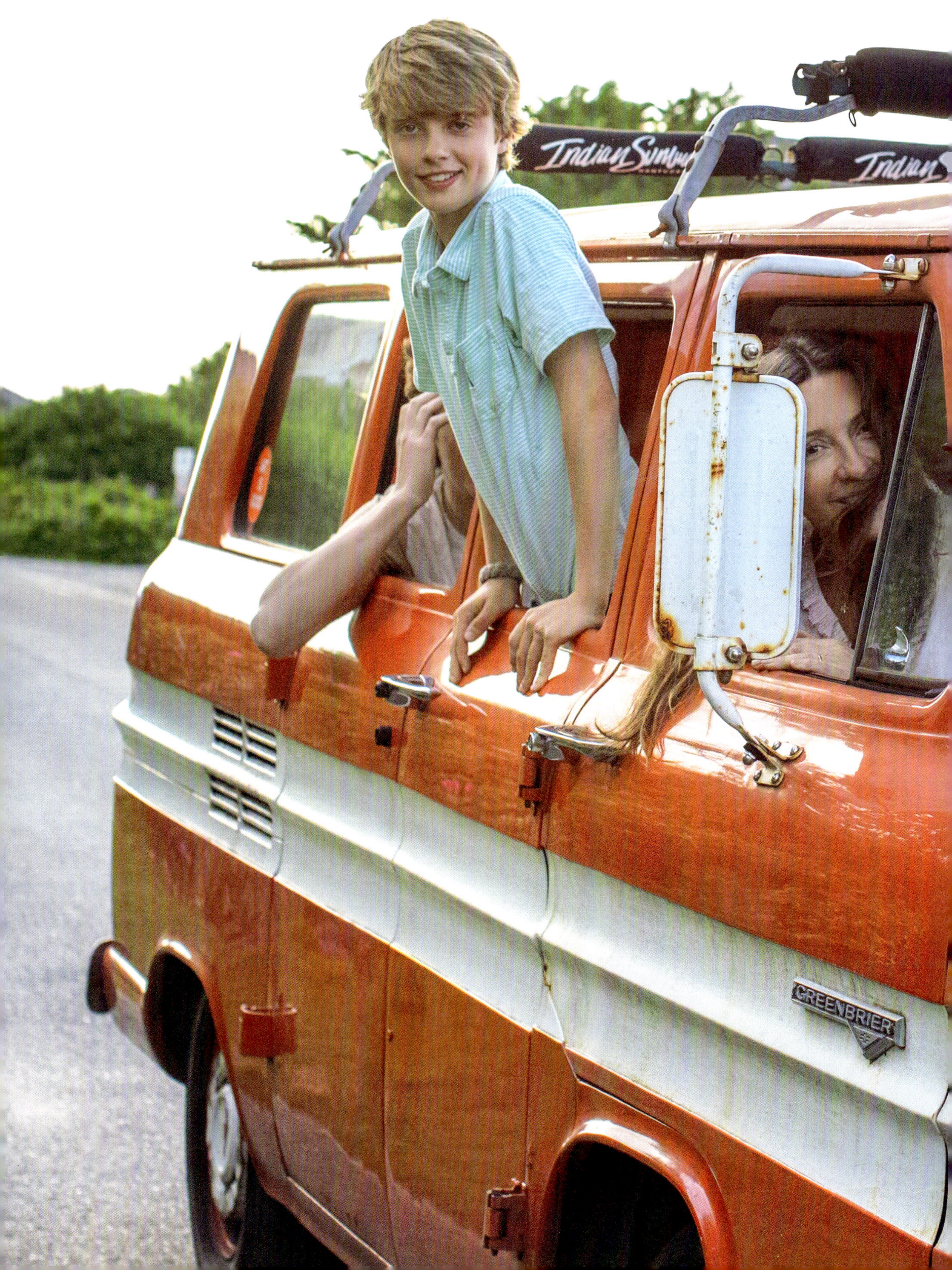
GREENBRIER

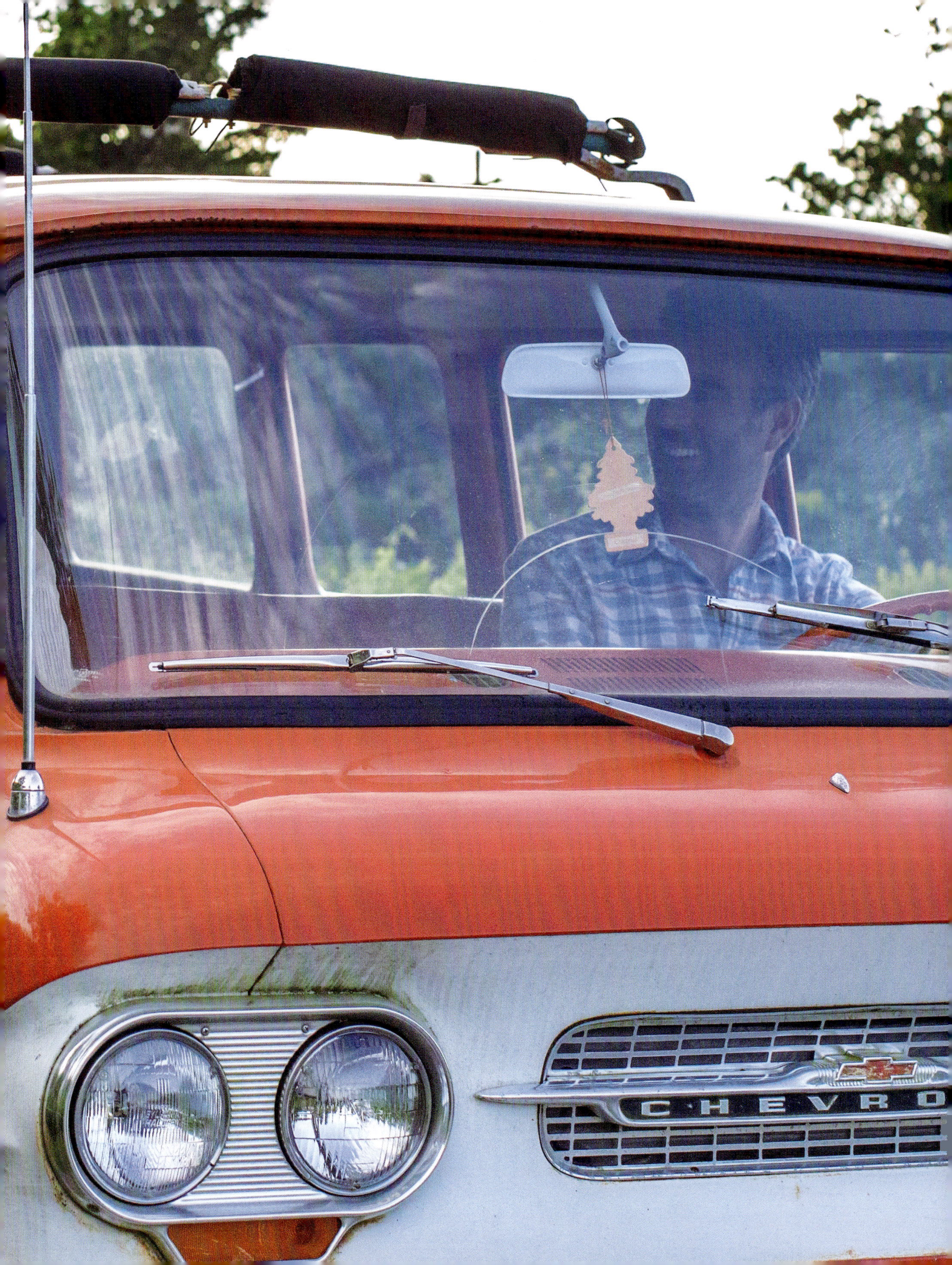
CHEVRO

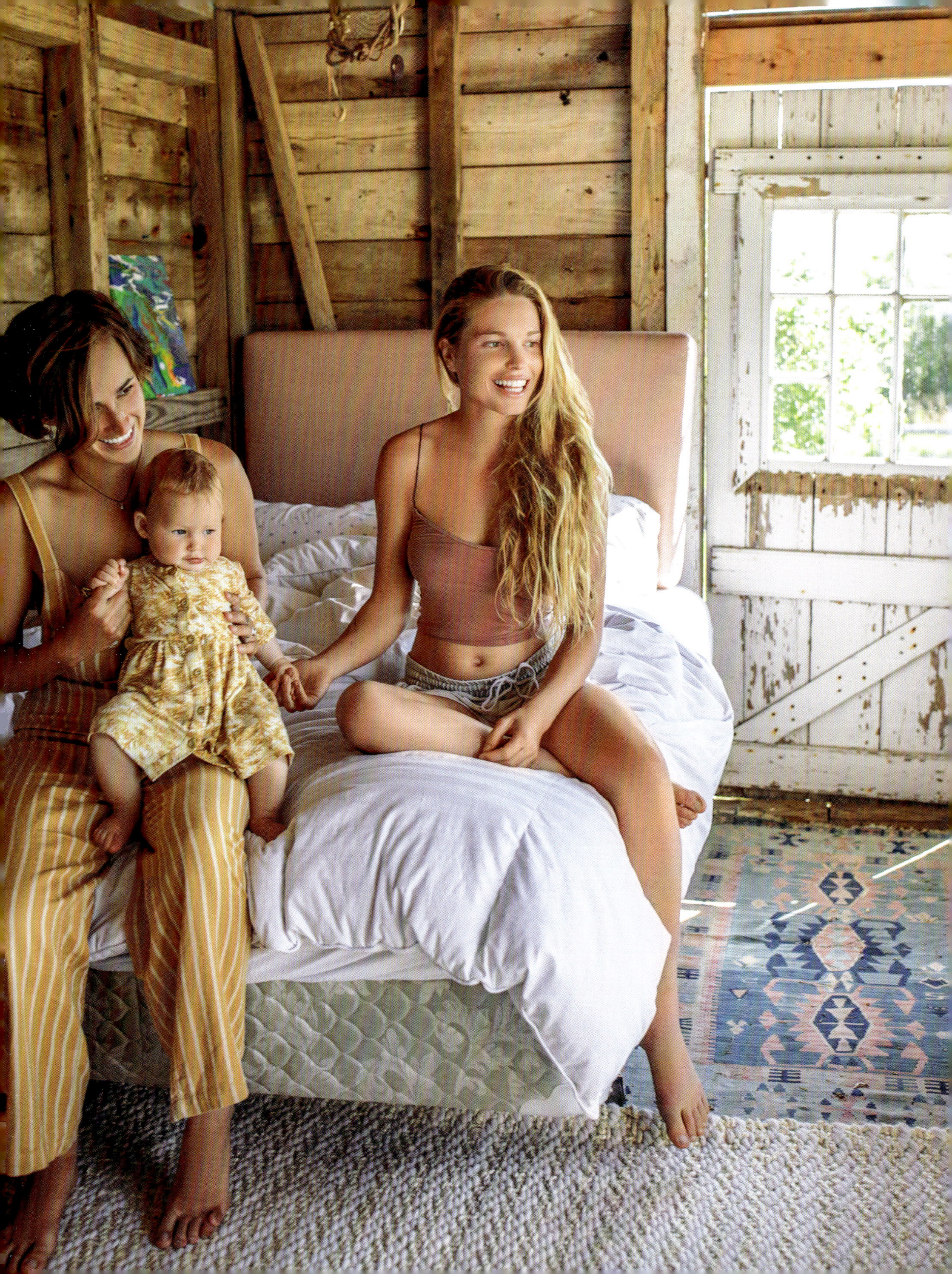

Islanders, washashores, and summer residents

For many, the island gripped them from their first visit, like New Yorker Betsy Hussey, Fashion Director at Calvin Klein, who spent the summers of her youth on Cape Cod but fell in love with Nantucket's island aesthetic as an adult and rented for many years before buying a small cottage. "It's been a dream," she says, from her minimalist office in Manhattan's garment district. "It's very stabilizing having that cottage. You feel totally different there, you feel ... far away."

Marcus Foley grew up in Jamaica and came to Nantucket one college summer with friends and felt an immediate connection because of the island lifestyle and, at the time, the Jamaican population of summer help. Now an artist, Marcus lives on-island with his wife and two boys, carving whales and other creations out of driftwood and selling them at the Farmers Market and via Instagram.

Sara Rossi found opportunity on Nantucket, a place she summered all her life. She and Taylor Ivey opened The Skinny Dip on Old South Wharf as a collective of independent brands rooted in the preppy aesthetic. The store took off and in just three years the duo has opened Skinny Dip locations in Charleston and Palm Beach: a testament to the Nantucket aesthetic beyond its shores (not to mention the island's power as a retail incubator).

Thomas L. Macy has spent his whole life summering on Orange Street, and now lives there half the year. His direct relative, many generations ago, Thomas H. Macy, was one of Nantucket's first European settlers arriving in 1659. Tom is a fifth-generation Macy to live on Nantucket and he spends his time reading, boating, and at the Nantucket Yacht Club and Wharf Rats club swapping sailing stories with the island's old-timers.

Both summer residents and islanders speak of the magic of Nantucket. Not just the beauty and charm but the embracing community and the plentiful support for the arts. These people, and others we'll meet, are of disparate backgrounds who shape the distinct American style on Nantucket island. These people are the island, its champions, caretakers, investors, creators, craftspeople. They include business owners and CEOs, chefs and servers, builders and gardeners, designers and makers, sailors, and even rebels. And more often than not, they're friends, too. Welcome to Nantucket.

"There's a freedom in Nantucket's isolation that's pretty glorious."

—**John S. Johnson, arts patron and summer resident**

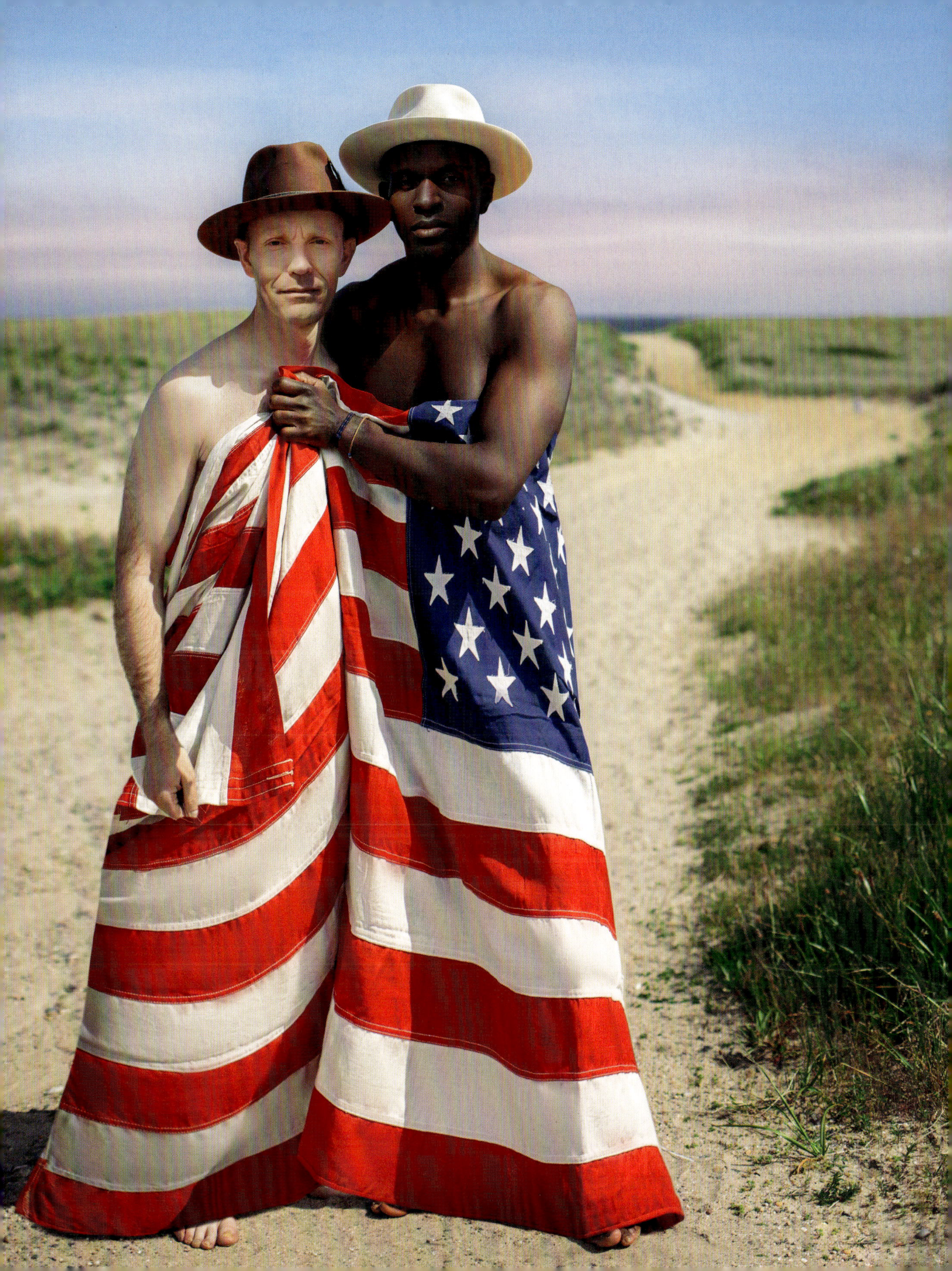

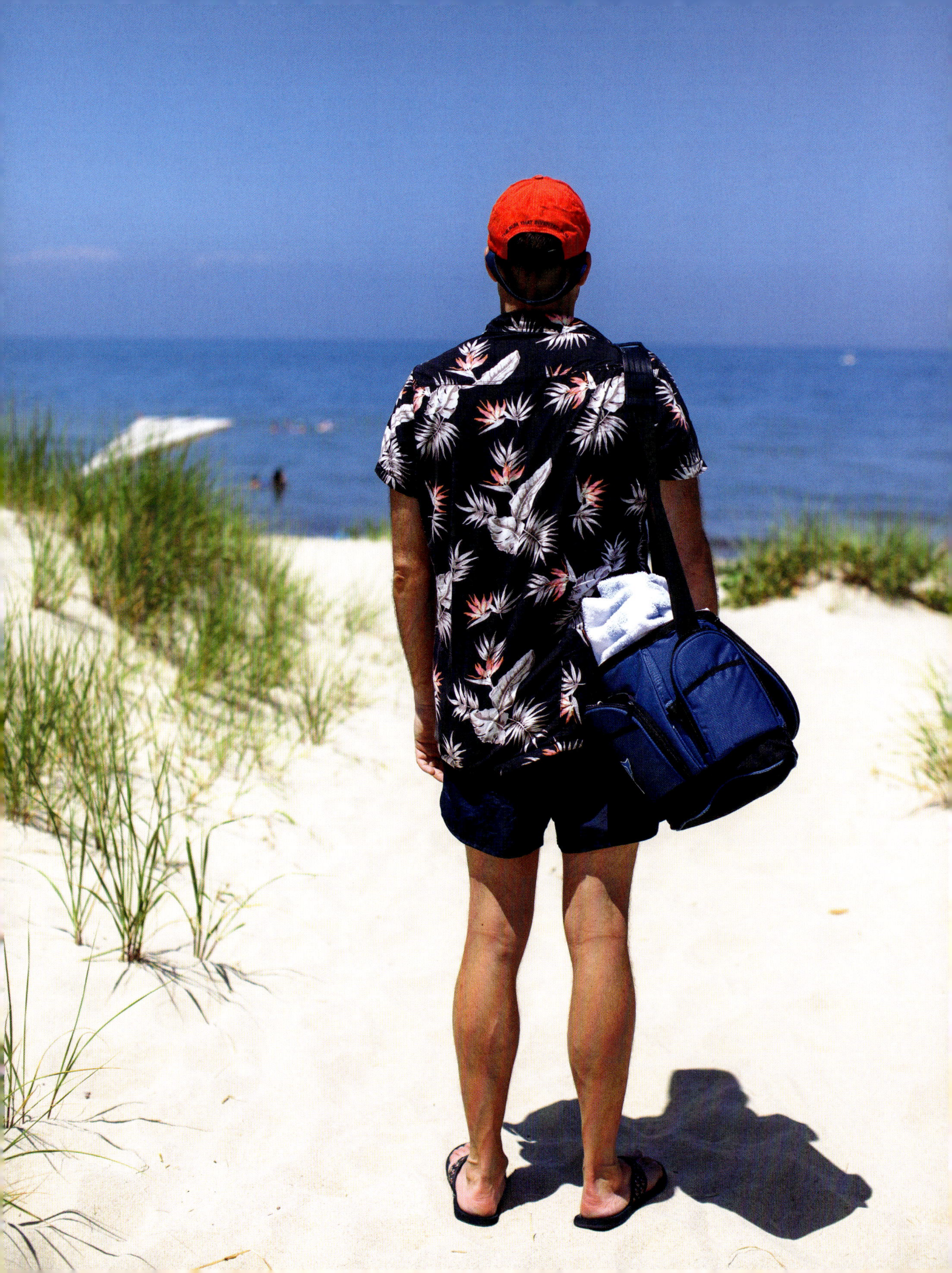

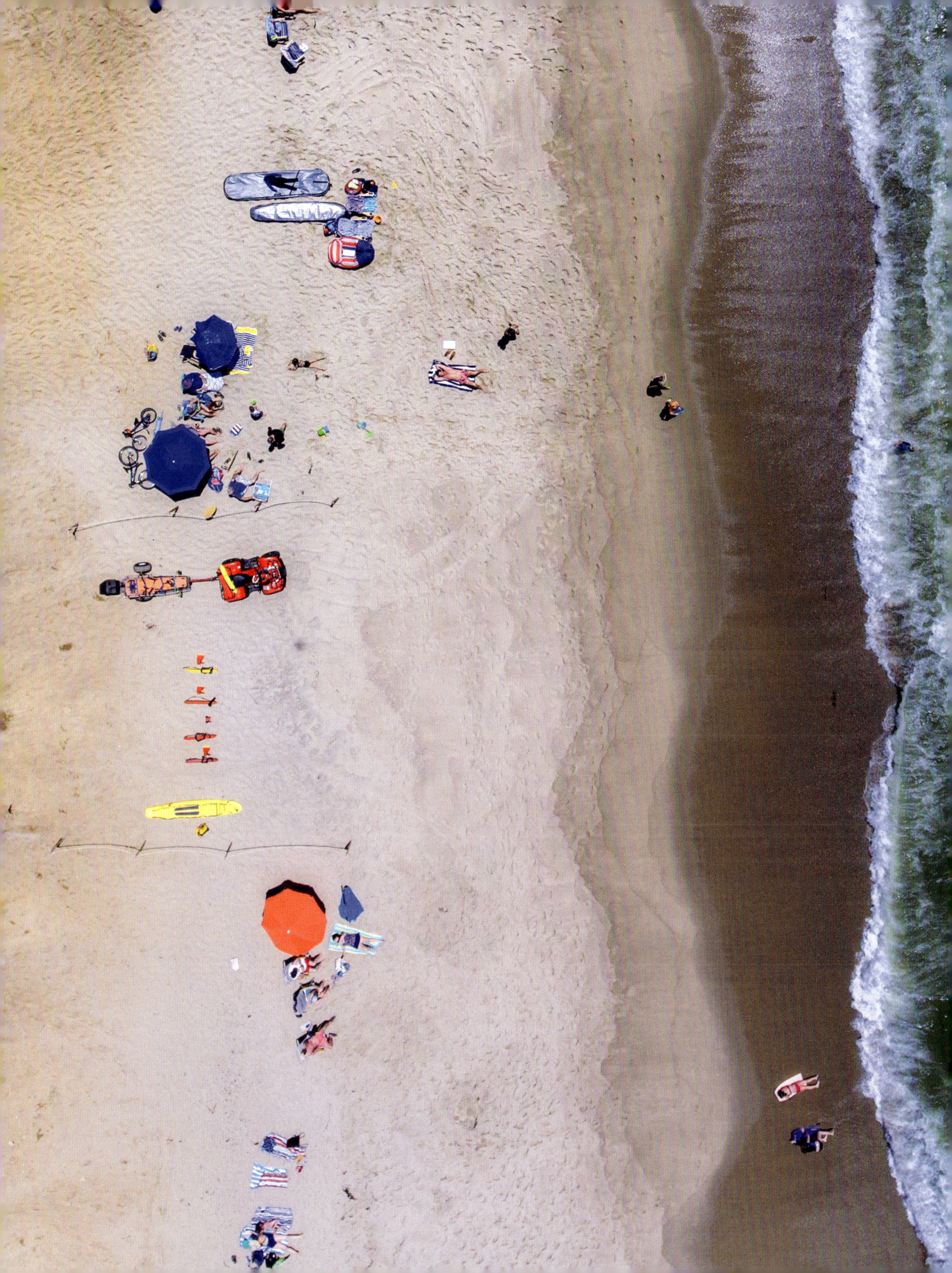

Jill Kargman, writer, actress, and creator of the television show **Odd Mom Out**

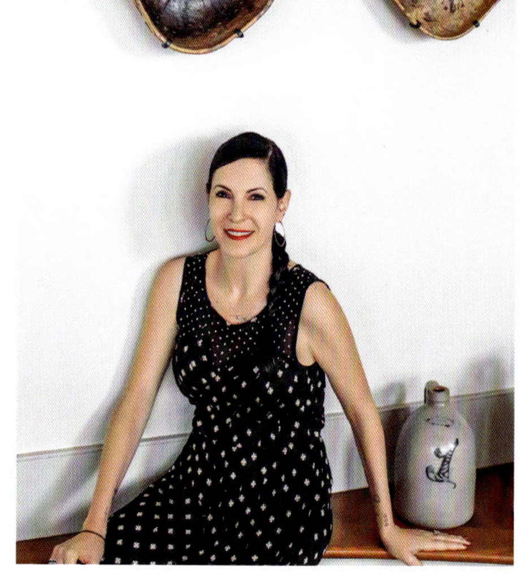

YEARS ON NANTUCKET: *Forty-five! I came at ten days old in a baby burrito swaddle; the first place I ever traveled outside Manhattan.*

ISLAND HOME: *My parent's house in town. I don't know how to drive so I like being right in the action.*

MODE OF TRANSPORT: *Feet!*

FAVORITE BEACH: *Cliffside for the umbrellas, chairs, and bathrooms! There are no waves but also no lawsuits from my umbrella flying out and impaling someone.*

SUMMER UNIFORM: *Long black flowy dress. I'm more Sicilian widow than Vineyard Vines.*

_ IS BETTER ON NANTUCKET: *Ice cream*

GREATEST EXTRAVAGANCE: *Going out to eat in Tucky's many restaurants I love.*

DEFINE NANTUCKET STYLE? *For everyone else I'd say preppy AF.*

MOST DAYS ON NANTUCKET I ... *walk to the hub and get my iced espresso with vanilla syrup and half and half.*

CLASSIC NANTUCKET IS ... *my dad's Nantucket Reds from Murray's.*

FAVORITE THING/SPOT ON NANTUCKET? *Parchment, my fave store. Heidi has great taste and I love all the paper, ribbons, place cards, and colorful tapes.*

COMMON MISCONCEPTION ABOUT NANTUCKET? *That there are zero Jews here.*

NANTUCKET HISTORICAL FIGURE/EVENT THAT SPEAKS TO YOU? *I love that when the whale oil industry dried up overnight, and essentially froze the economy, it also froze time. There are so many historic homes because people couldn't afford to redo them so it's a treasure trove of architectural masterpieces.*

NECESSITY ON NANTUCKET: *Flip-flops*

IDEAL DAY: *Brunch at Downyflake Donut with zero line, walk around town, late afternoon beach with sunset, drinks at Club Car, dinner at Black-Eyed Susan's.*

MOST TREASURED EXPERIENCE/THING ON-ISLAND: *My third date with my husband Harry!*

_ IS SO NANTUCKET: *ACK merch*

THING YOU ONLY WEAR/DO ON NANTUCKET: *Large hats*

BEST PART OF ISLAND LIFE: *Being isolated from assholes.*

FIVE THINGS THAT INSPIRE YOU ABOUT NANTUCKET: *Cobblestones, fog, creepy vibes in the fall, lighting of the Christmas trees the day after Thanksgiving, and historic houses.*

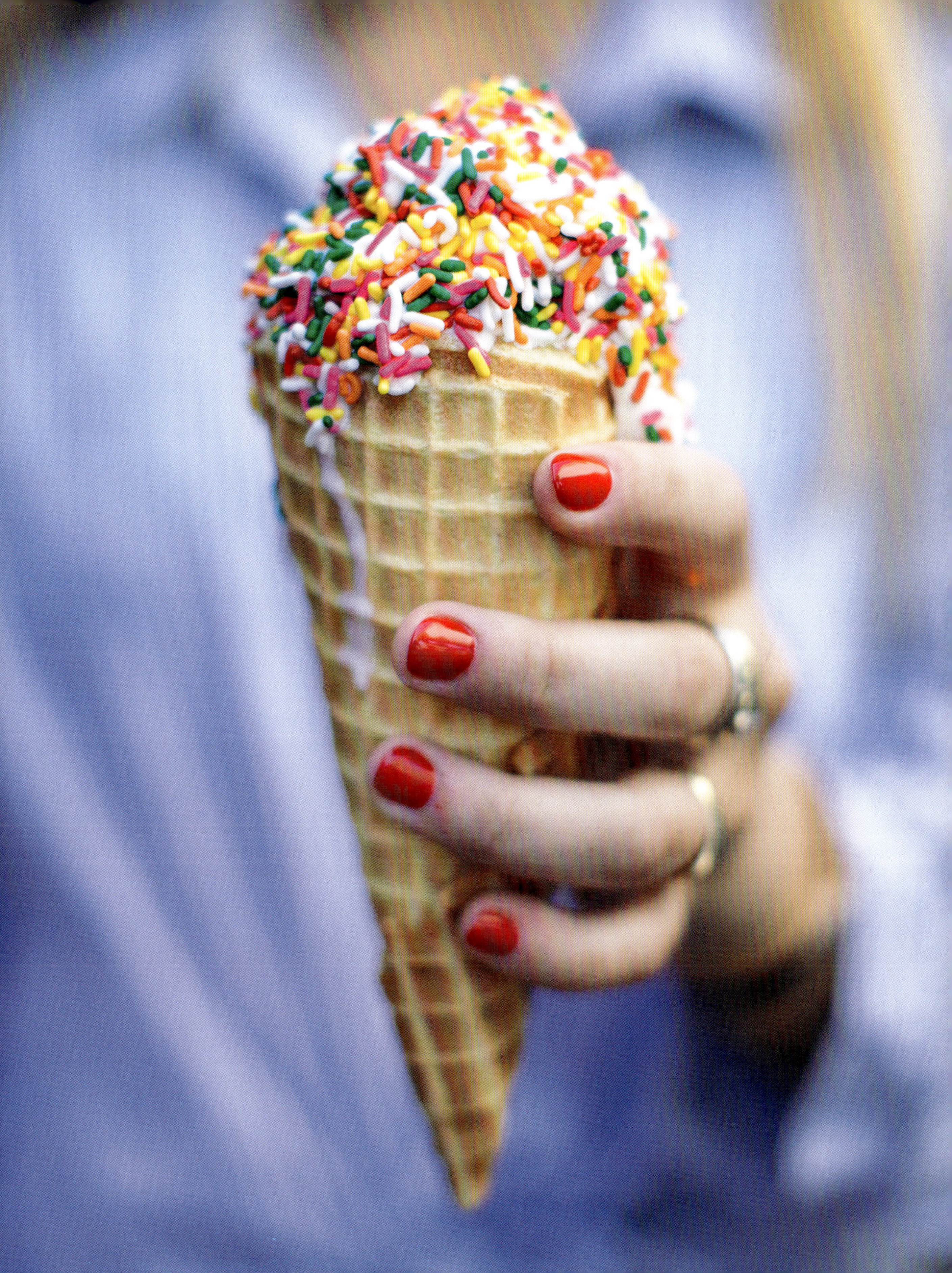

REBELLIOUS STOCK: WHALERS, QUAKERS, ARTISANS, ENTREPRENEURS

The island has always been a talisman for ambition. Those lucky enough to hear legend of its opportunities or peek at its possibilities still need a healthy dose of rebel to pull off life, and work, on this 30-mile-out spit. It's one of the throughlines of Nantucket history. From the whalers of the eighteenth century to the entrepreneurs and foreign-born workforce of today. Who washes up on Nantucket is a fascinating group; a true mixture of those who epitomize capitalism and those who are bohemian enough to live out of the mainstream. The island offers possibility for the ambitious willing to take the risk, and willing to work for it.

Once you get to talking with washashores you notice a common theme. It may be desire for independence, as it was for the Quakers, or to start a business, or embark on an adventure; whatever the reason the island represents opportunity to separate from the mainland, make money and live with less convention, without a rat race, strip malls, pollution, crime, or stop lights. With nature, history, community and possibility. Surfers can run a school and take off to Costa Rica for the winter. Artisans can sell their work to tourists from all over the world and hole up in their studios with the quiet and headspace to create in the off-season. Restaurateurs can pack them in over the summer then shutter in the winter and seek inspiration in far-flung lands. Creatives and entrepreneurs use the off-season to energize and refuel off-island with Nantucket's seasonal lifestyle. And the island's many influential summer visitors offer ideal exposure for brands and businesses looking for a launchpad.

While the rest of the country is taking summer Fridays and barbecuing with family and friends, most Nantucket islanders are working nonstop in what is their condensed ninety-day earning period. Nantucketers with island-based businesses do not get a break during the summer, not even weekends off—and have to be savvy enough to manage seasonal businesses with drastic differences of crushing summers and dormant winters. Budgeting, staffing, housing, planning, and managing expectations of the elite resident and traveler are not for the casual business owner. But hard work can yield an idyllic life on this island incubator. So much so that some talk of their children's hesitance to leave. Who could blame them when they are surrounded by such beauty, nature, and the fun of seasonal friends enjoying their carefree vacations each summer, along with the influence and potential the summer folks bring to island ideas and institutions.

The Nantucket Cottage hospital foundation was able to raise $120 million in three seasons thanks to the generosity of islanders and many affluent summer residents. Between the Nantucket Golf Club and Nantucket Yacht Club they reward five Nantucket High School seniors full, four-year tuition to the college of their dreams. The Nantucket Boys & Girls Club is operating in a brand new, multimillion-dollar facility thanks to island generosity. The possibilities and perks are there for those willing to hear the island's siren call.

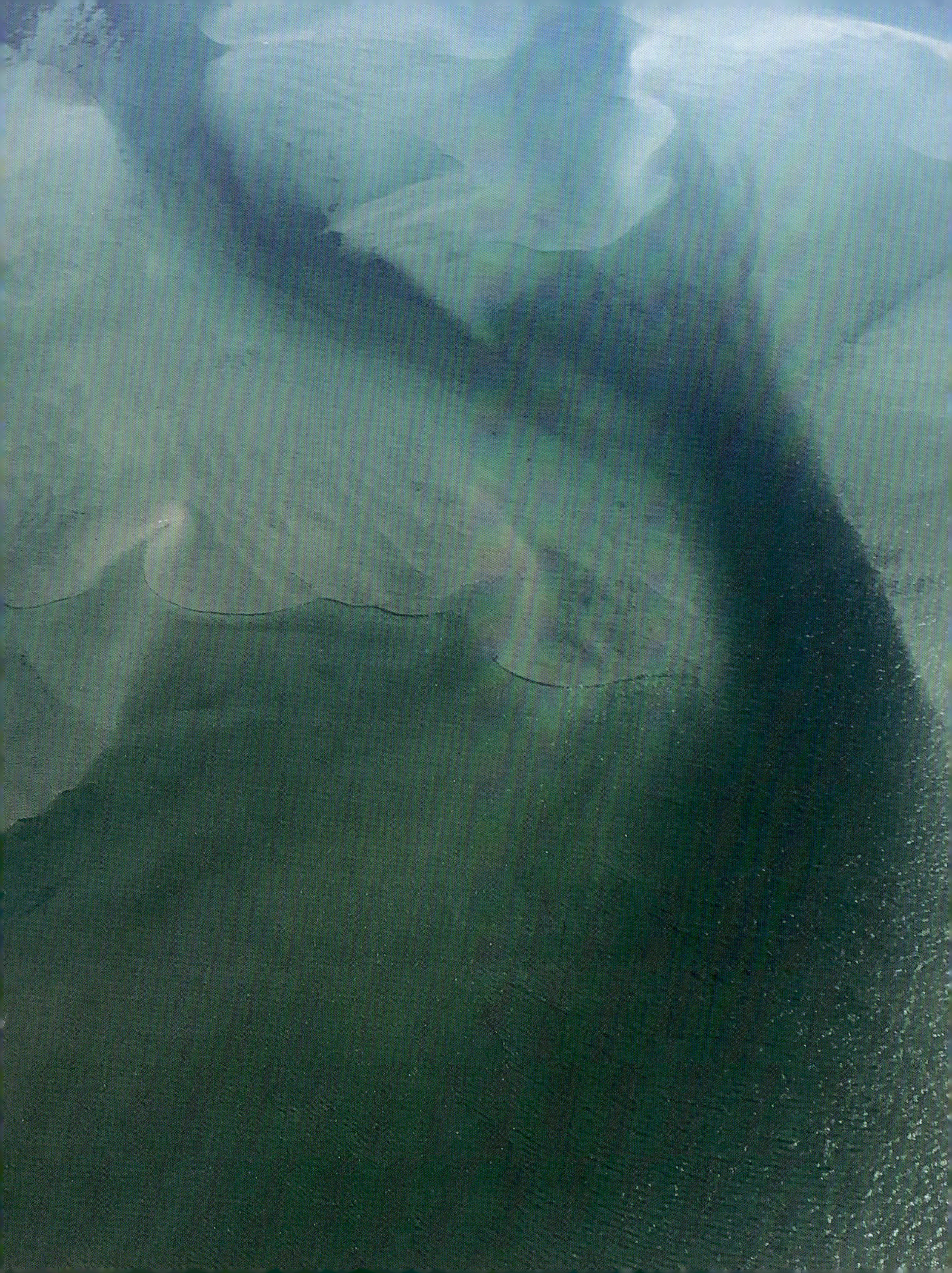

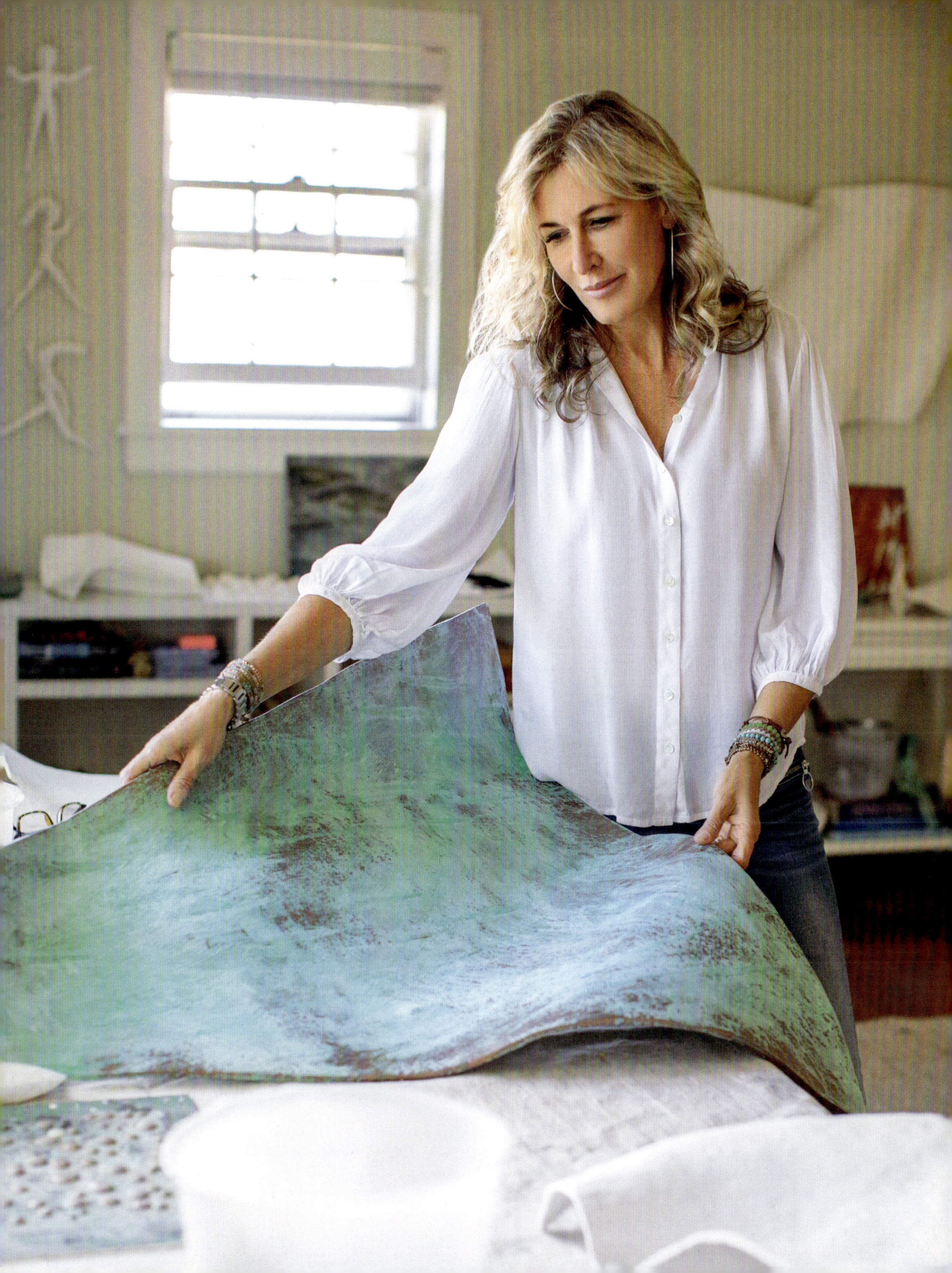

"When you are a summer person you really just date the Grey Lady. You think you know her but you only know her at her best, when she's ready to step out into the world. She's dolled up and looking really beautiful, like Nantucket looks in the summer: there's roses and romance and hydrangeas and wildflowers, and the beaches are perfect, everybody's got a smile. But you don't really know Nantucket until you've lived here year-round and, in a way, you marry her. You see her in all her modes. But then, it turns out the worst: the blizzards and hurricanes, blackouts, and no boats for four days, and the harbor is frozen and the Navy has to send ice breakers to rescue people with food, and there's no power, no phone service, no internet—those things that might seem like the worst turn out to be the best of her. That's when you feel like you are really part of a community: people go door to door and knock to make sure everybody is okay and everybody just bands together like you dream about; where it's us against the world."

—John Shea, actor-director and fifty-year resident

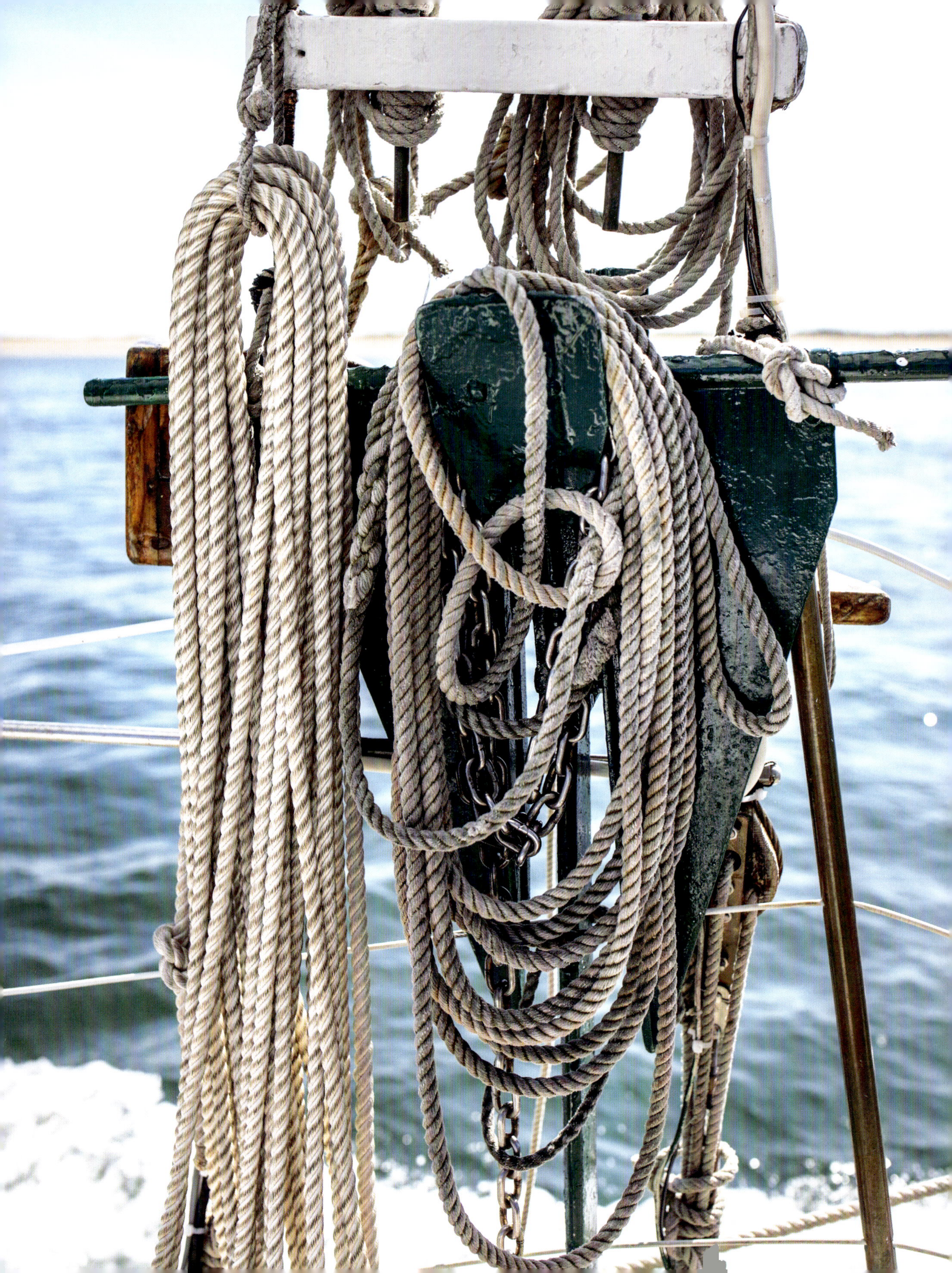

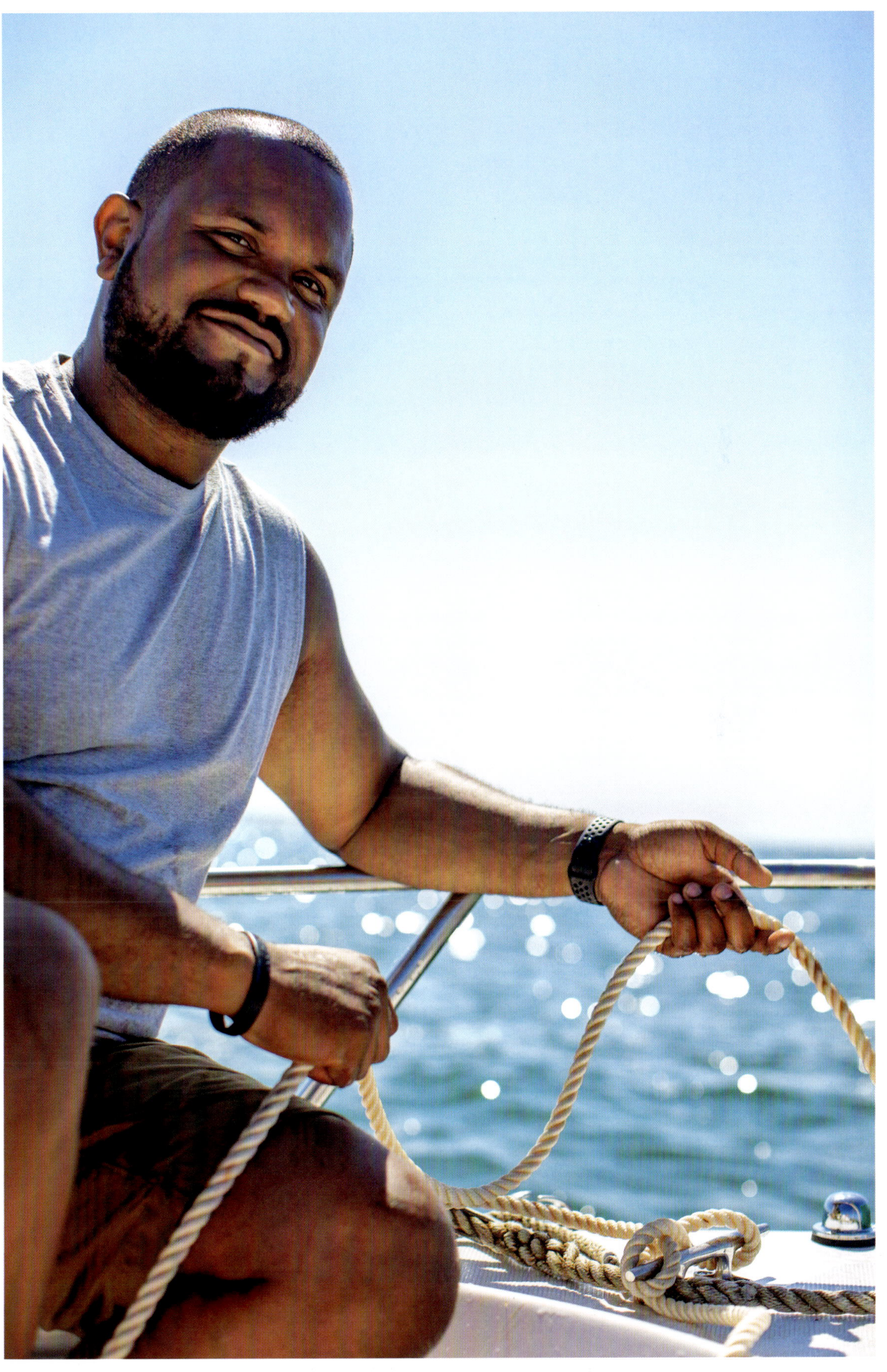

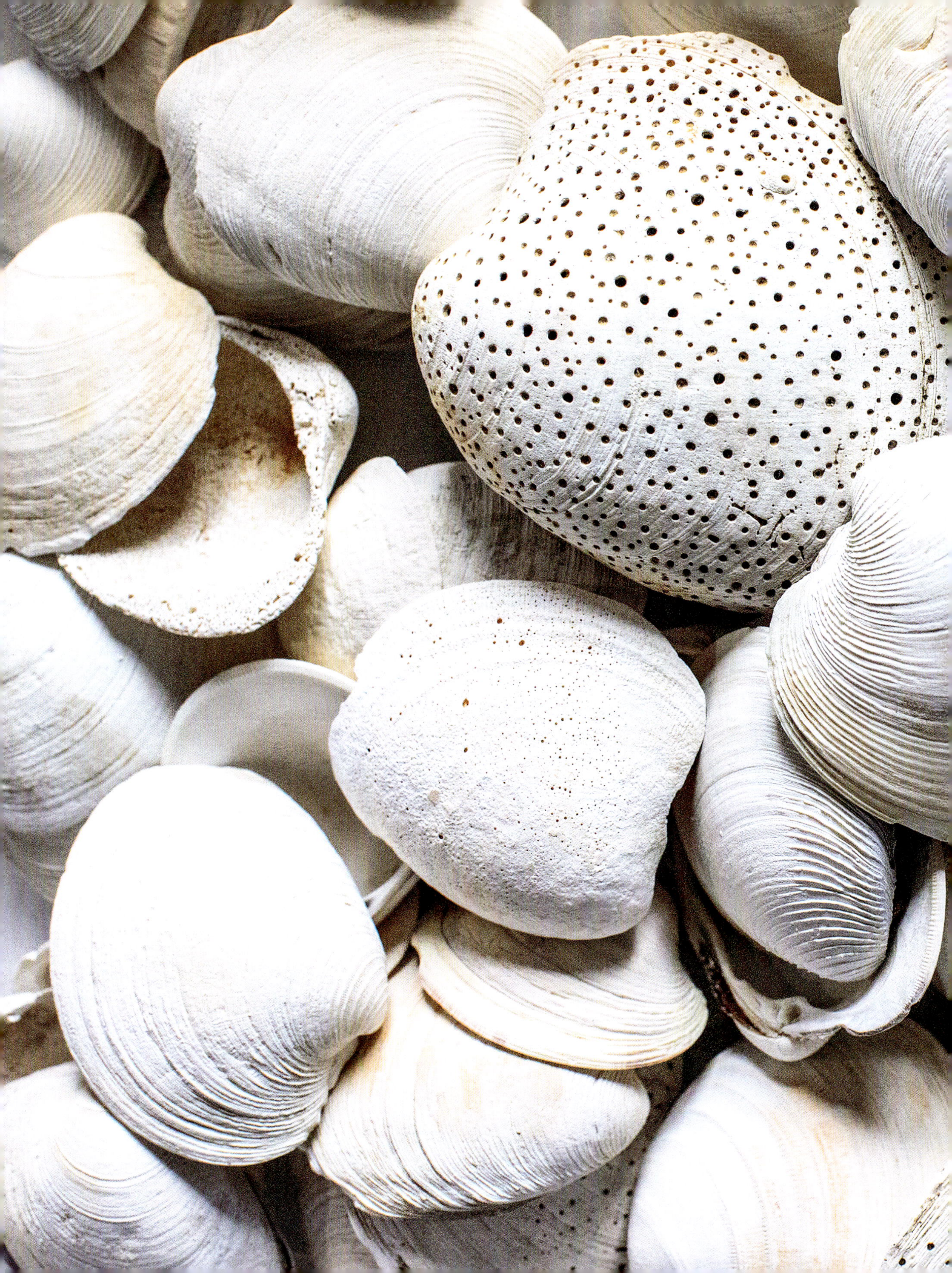

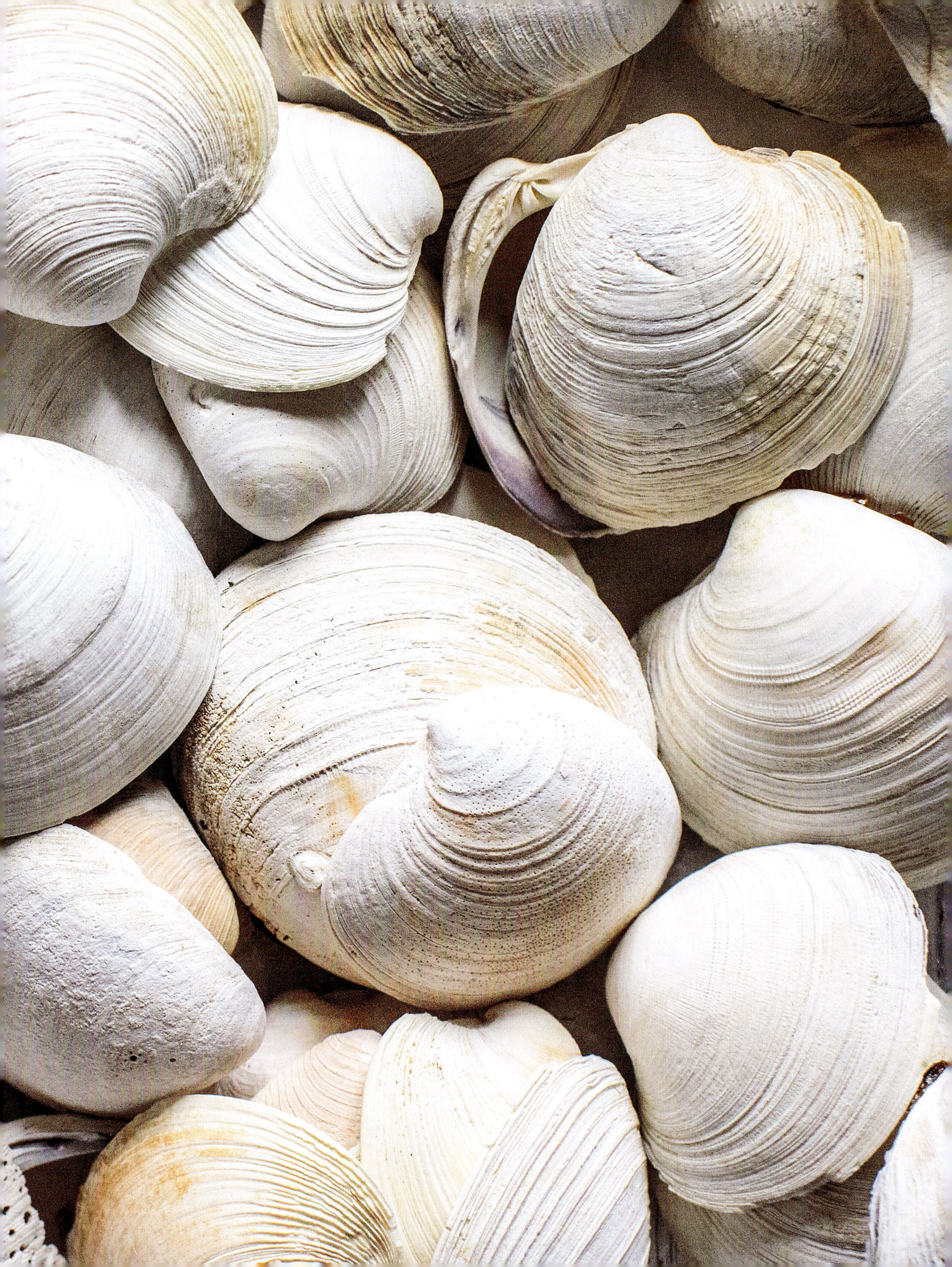

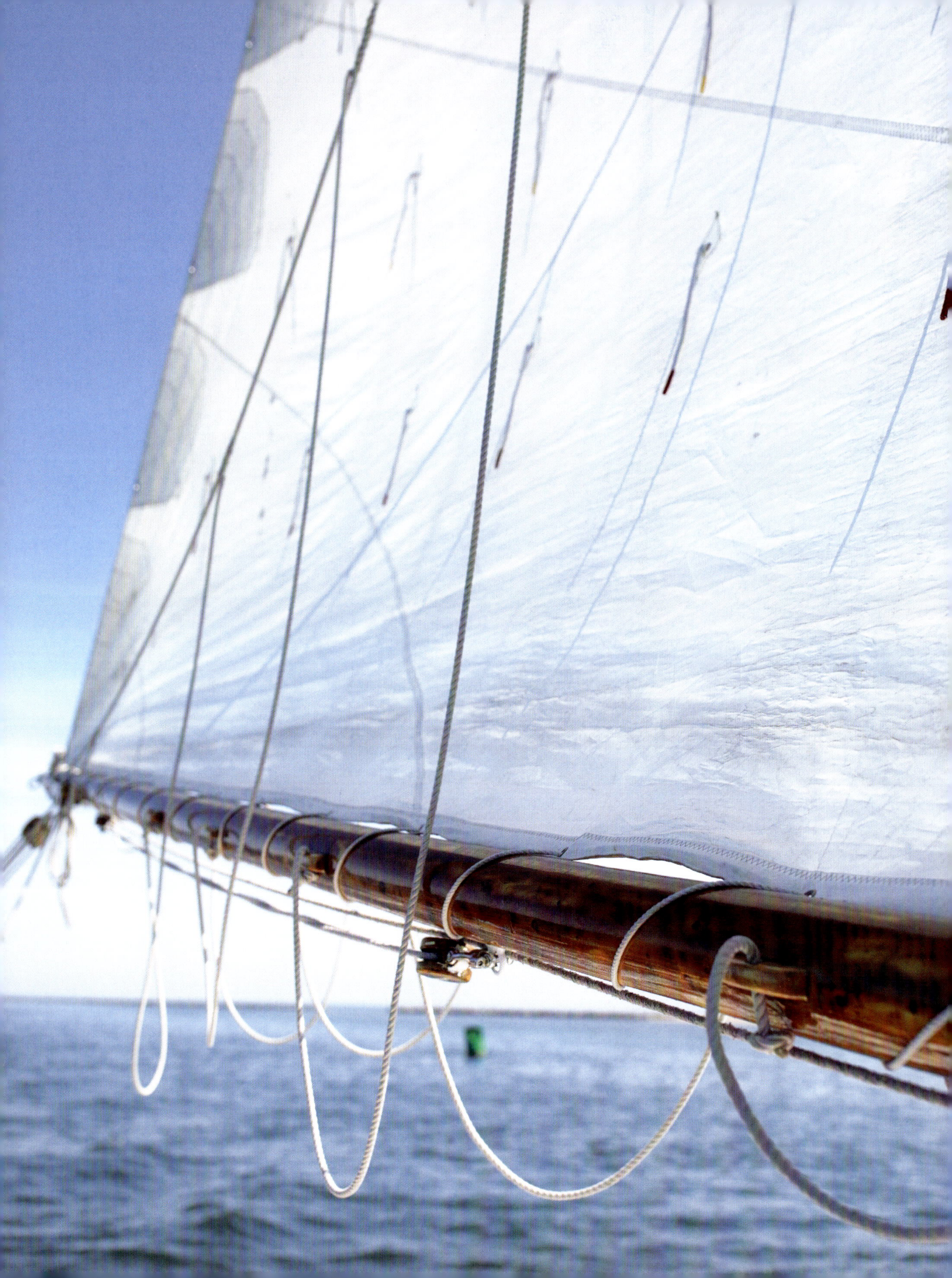

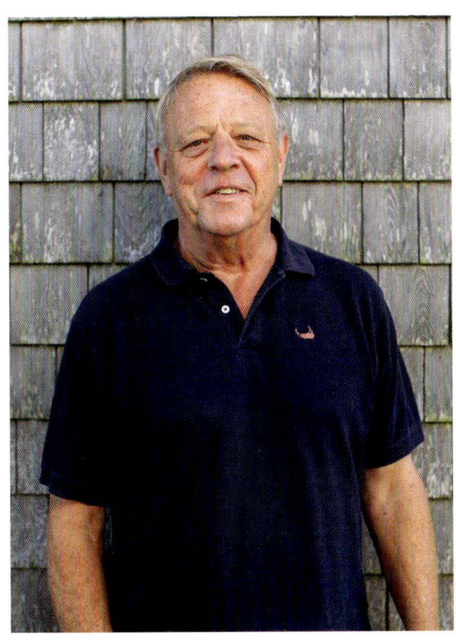

Thomas L. Macy, lifelong resident and descendant of founding Nantucket settler

YEARS ON NANTUCKET: *Sixty-seven summers, and the last eleven as my primary residence*

ISLAND HOME: *A 221-year-old house on Orange Street downtown.*

MODE OF TRANSPORT: *Subaru Forester, which I don't use much, a bicycle, and a little boat.*

FAVORITE BEACH: *Ladies Beach or Great Point, which is a 10-mile drive out on sand to the point.*

SUMMER UNIFORM: *Shorts and a polo shirt or khakis and a collared shirt.*

_ IS BETTER ON NANTUCKET: *Fog*

GREATEST EXTRAVAGANCE: *Owning a home on Nantucket.*

NANTUCKET HISTORICAL FIGURE/EVENT THAT SPEAKS TO YOU: *Thomas H. Macy, my ancestor whose name I bear. He was a rugged individualist. He got sick and tired of the Puritans and got together with eight or nine others and came to Nantucket in 1659. He was the one to prove you could make it through the winter, basically living in a sand cave. The Wampanoag were nice to him and he was a real advocate for them; he insisted they be paid for the island.*

BOOK: "In The Heart of the Sea" *by Nathaniel Philbrick. That account strikes a nerve about the filthy work of whaling captains. A rough business, but they made Nantucket.*

CHILDHOOD MEMORY: *At eight years old we'd bike around the island with friends without a care in the world. No television, beach picnics at night, and reading—reading filled our days.*

Page 15: Griffin Gailliot, Mary Mottershead, Maddy Grayson, Cabell Grayson, Lila Gailliot, Kip and Jocelyn Gailliot, Teddy Gailliot; Page 19: Gary Kohner; Page 21: Jarret O'Connor; Page 25: Server at 167 RAW; Page 31: Aiden Bourke; Pages 33 and 43: Daisy Chaussee; Page 36: Lifeguard at Surfside Beach; Page 38: Carly Heitlinger; Page 39: Katherine Gougin and Henry Michaelis; Page 44: Carly Heitlinger; Page 46: Debi Lilly; Page 48: Hallie Bletcher; Page 49: 4 Pilgrim Ct., Tomaiolo Development and Fishers Island Real Estate; Page 50: Scott and Darcy Creech Marelli; Page 55: Jonathan Nimerfroh; Page 57: Dean Dellas, Brett Sousa, Christine Bloom, Gwen "Bunny" Hyde; Pages 58–59: Donick, Amadi, Kim and Otis Cary; Page 60: Samuel, Owen, Cindy and Lee Milazzo; Page 62: Kendrick Monaco, Lilakai Shaw, Caroline Powers; Page 65: Joshua Moore and Odini Gogo; Page 66: David Anderson; Page 69: Juice Bar ice cream cone; Page 73: Melissa MacLeod; Page 77: Diony A. Gil

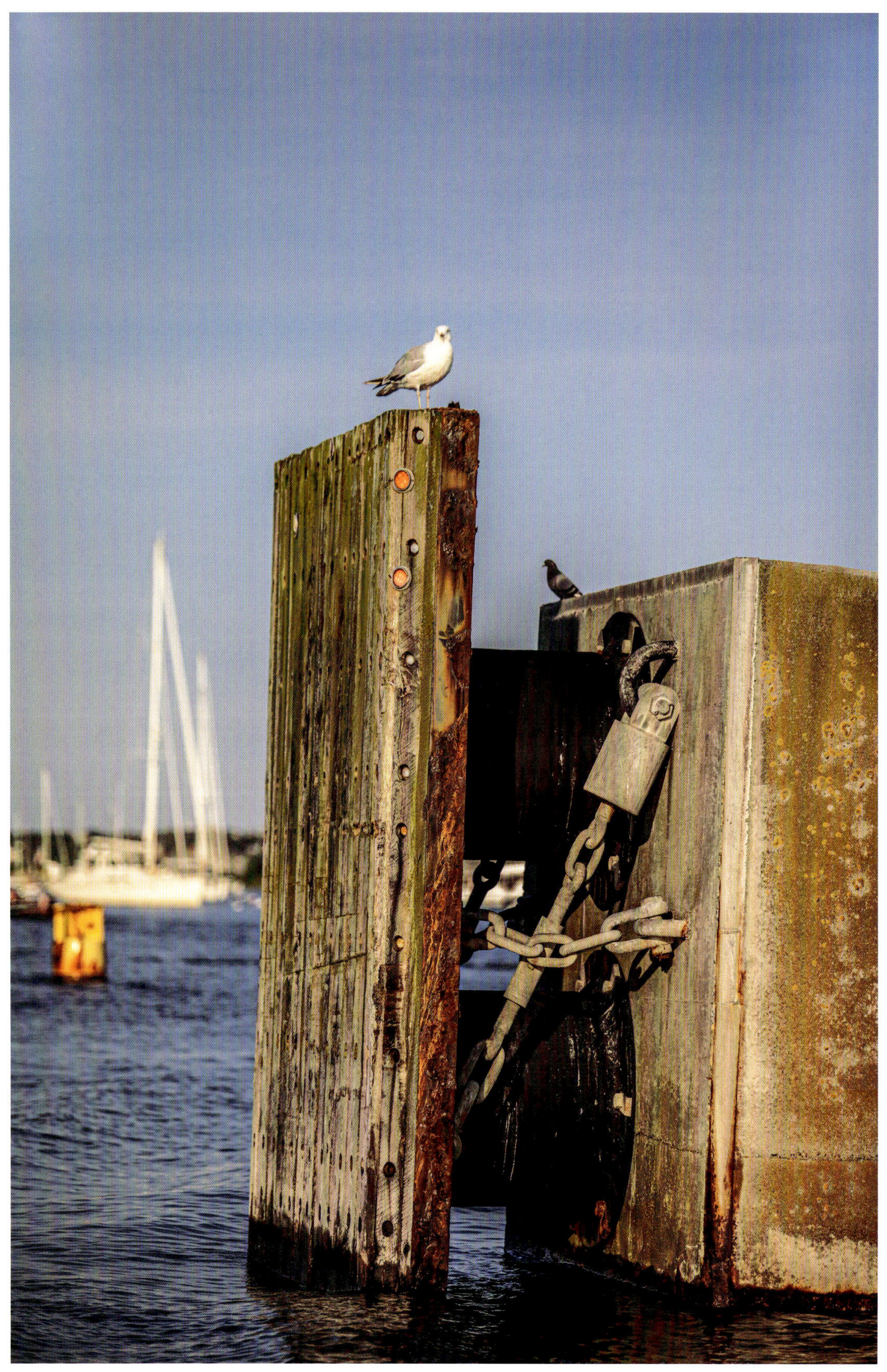

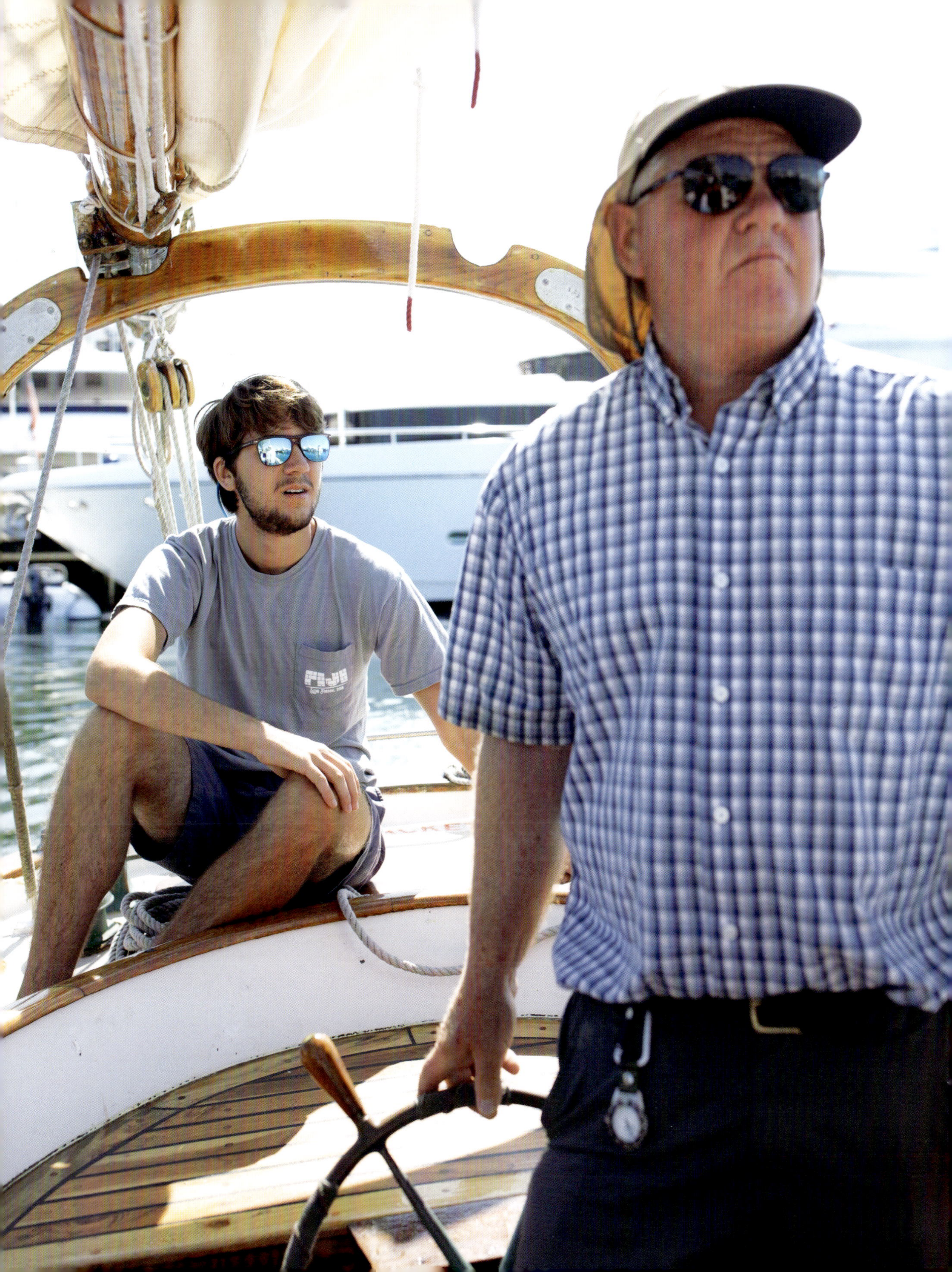

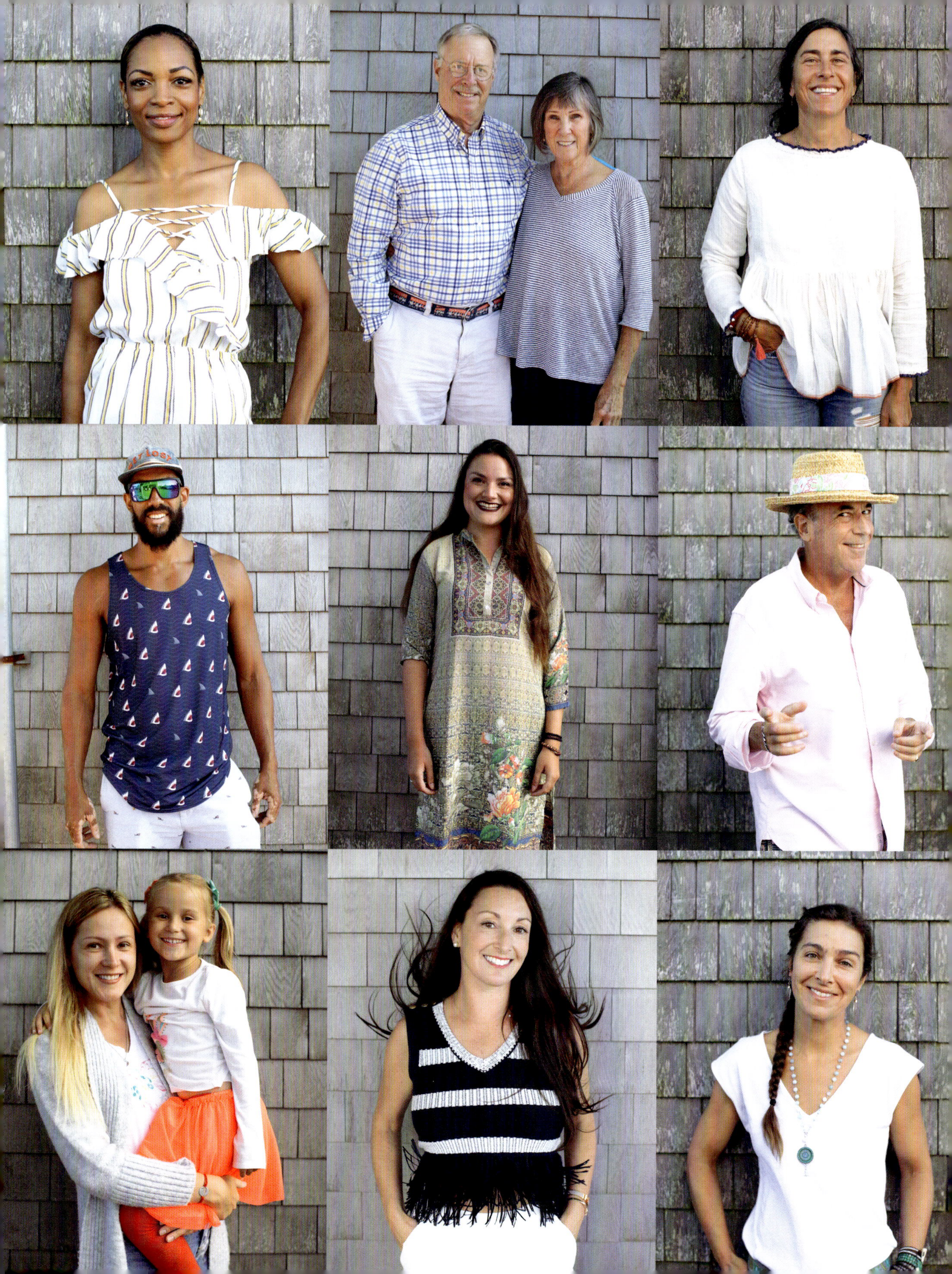

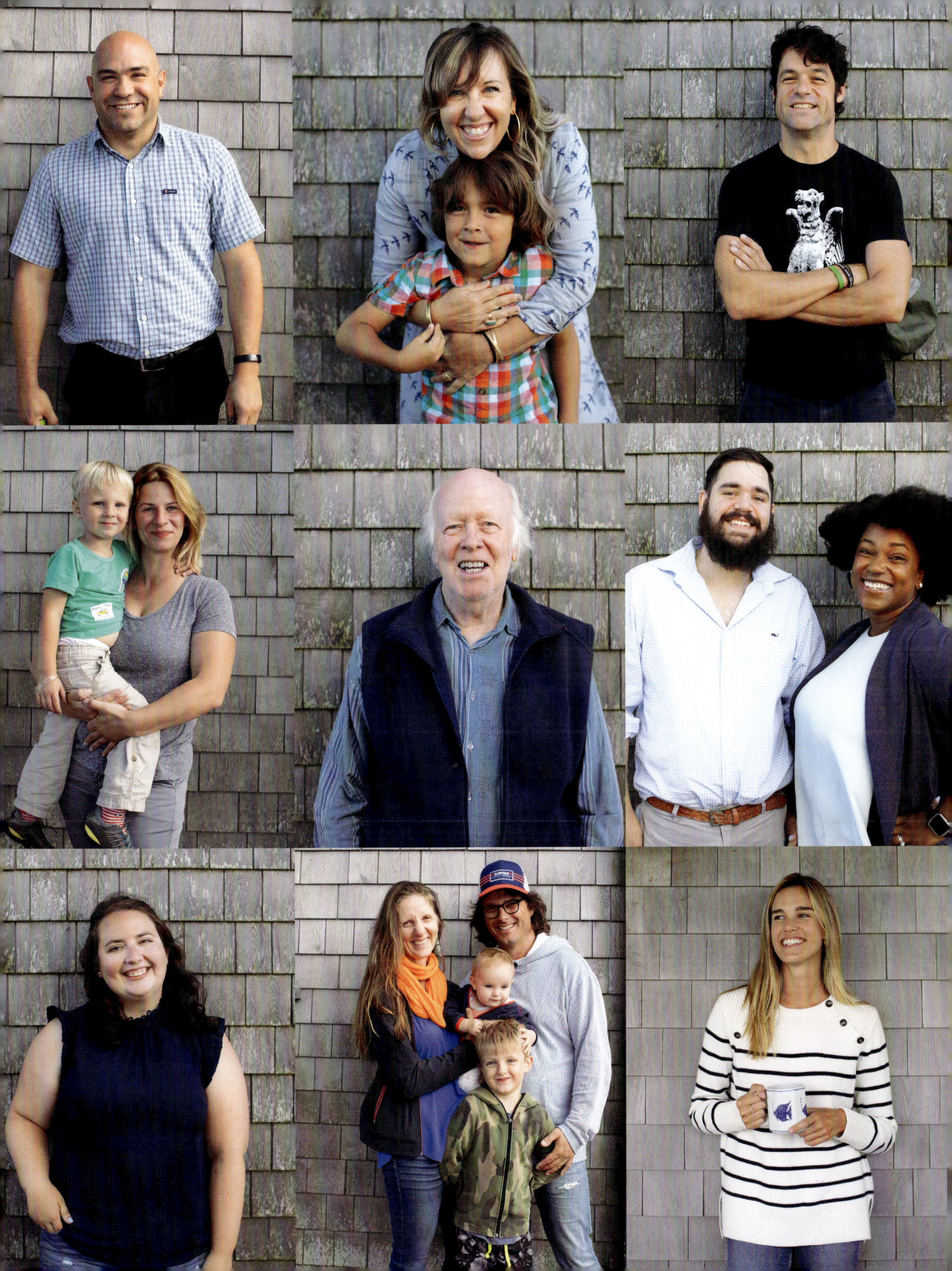

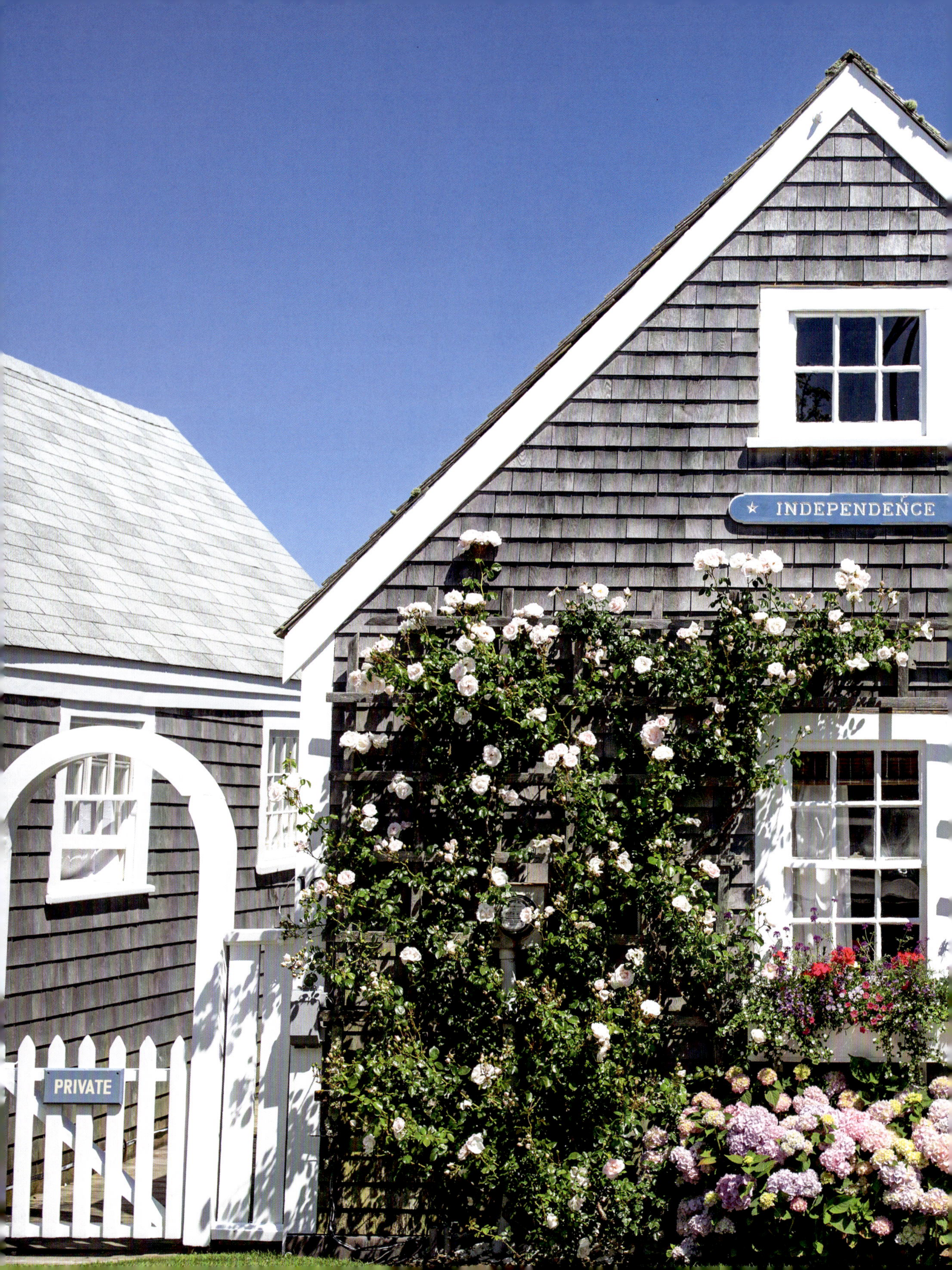
INDEPENDENCE
PRIVATE

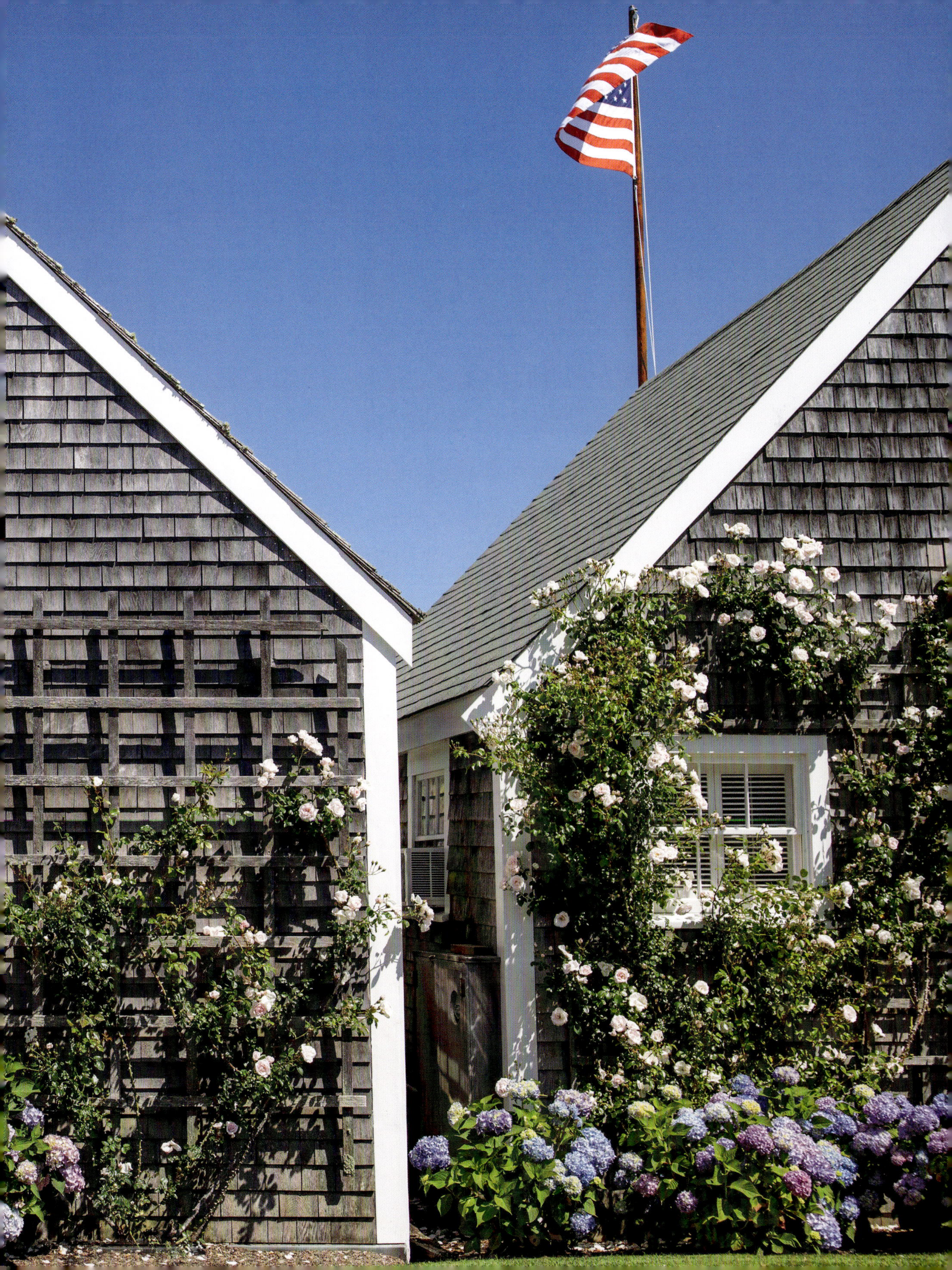

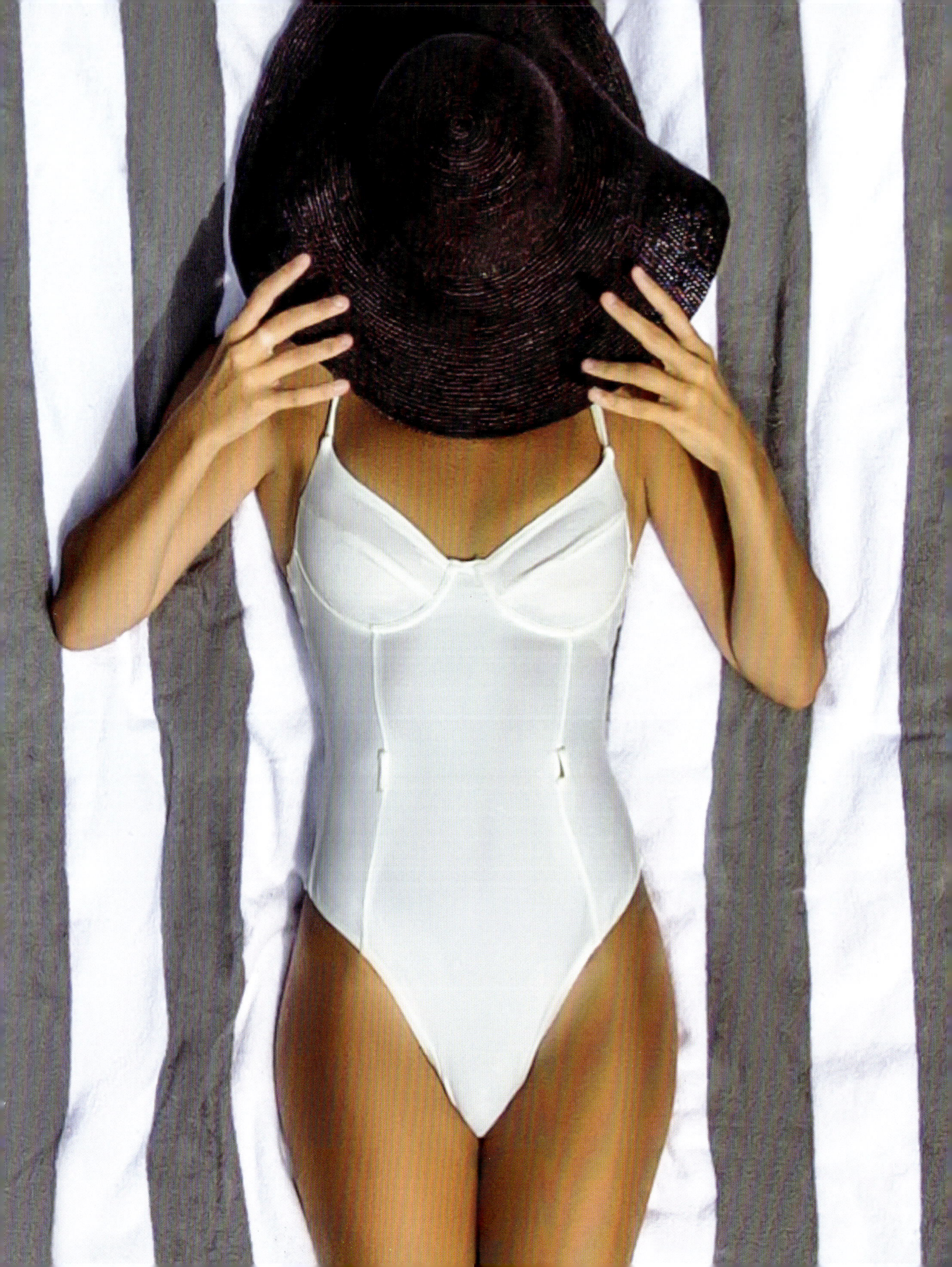

HISTORY OF INDEPENDENT WOMEN

In the nineteenth century, Center Street was dubbed Petticoat Row because of the dominance of women-owned businesses and that legacy carries on. Young female entrepreneurs speak of a close-knit support system of women-owned businesses as being essential to helping them get their ideas off the ground.

Today, countless successful businesses on-island are women owned: Elizabeth Winship, Bess Clarke, Stephanie Hall and Rebecca Peraner of Nantucket Looms; and Colleen Darby Wurts of the internationally sourced giftwares store Atlantic; Darcy Creech of Peter Beaton Hat Studio; Amanda Tanner from Nomad, the rustic-modern clothing and home shop; Julie Biondi from The Lovely, often voted best "dress" store on-island; Remy Stressenger of Remy; Lisa Soeder of the Martin House Inn; Angela Raynor of The Pearl and Boarding House restaurants; watercolor artist Meredith Hanson of Meredith Hanson Designs; Erin Wilson of Salty Soul t-shirts; Melanie Gowan Designs; Steph Sproule of Bodega homegoods; Beth English of Current Vintage, where you can find wine and vintage pieces; Avis Skinner of Vis-A-Vis; gallery owner Susan Hostetler; Leah of Aunt Leah's Fudge; and so many more.

Throughout history Nantucket bred fierce, independent women born out of both necessity and Quakerism. The tone was set during the height of the whaling days of the mid-eighteenth century when whalers spent two or three years at a time out to sea with mere months back in between. That left women tending, not only to their homes and families, but to much of the economy of the island, which was booming. Something called "Mariner's Power of Attorney" gave many Nantucket women rights normally denied to women of the time, such as the right to sell property during the absence of a husband, father, brother, or even male friend. Whaling was dangerous and many times the men did not return at all.

Quakerism, too, played an essential role in empowering women. Nantucket-born Lucretia Coffin Mott, who helped to launch the women's suffrage movement at the 1848 Seneca Falls Convention, and was an outspoken anti-slavery advocate, was raised with the Quaker belief in equal rights for all under God. Maria Mitchell, America's first female astronomer who became world-famous after her 1847 discovery of a comet, grew up on Quaker-influenced Nantucket where women were expected to learn and work and lead, during a time when women elsewhere were relegated to domestic life. The pioneering women of Nantucket helped pave the way for other women's independence and learning.

"I'll haste to wed a sailor,
and send him off to sea;
For a life of independence,
is the pleasant life for me."

—**Eliza Brock, whaling captain's wife, 1856**

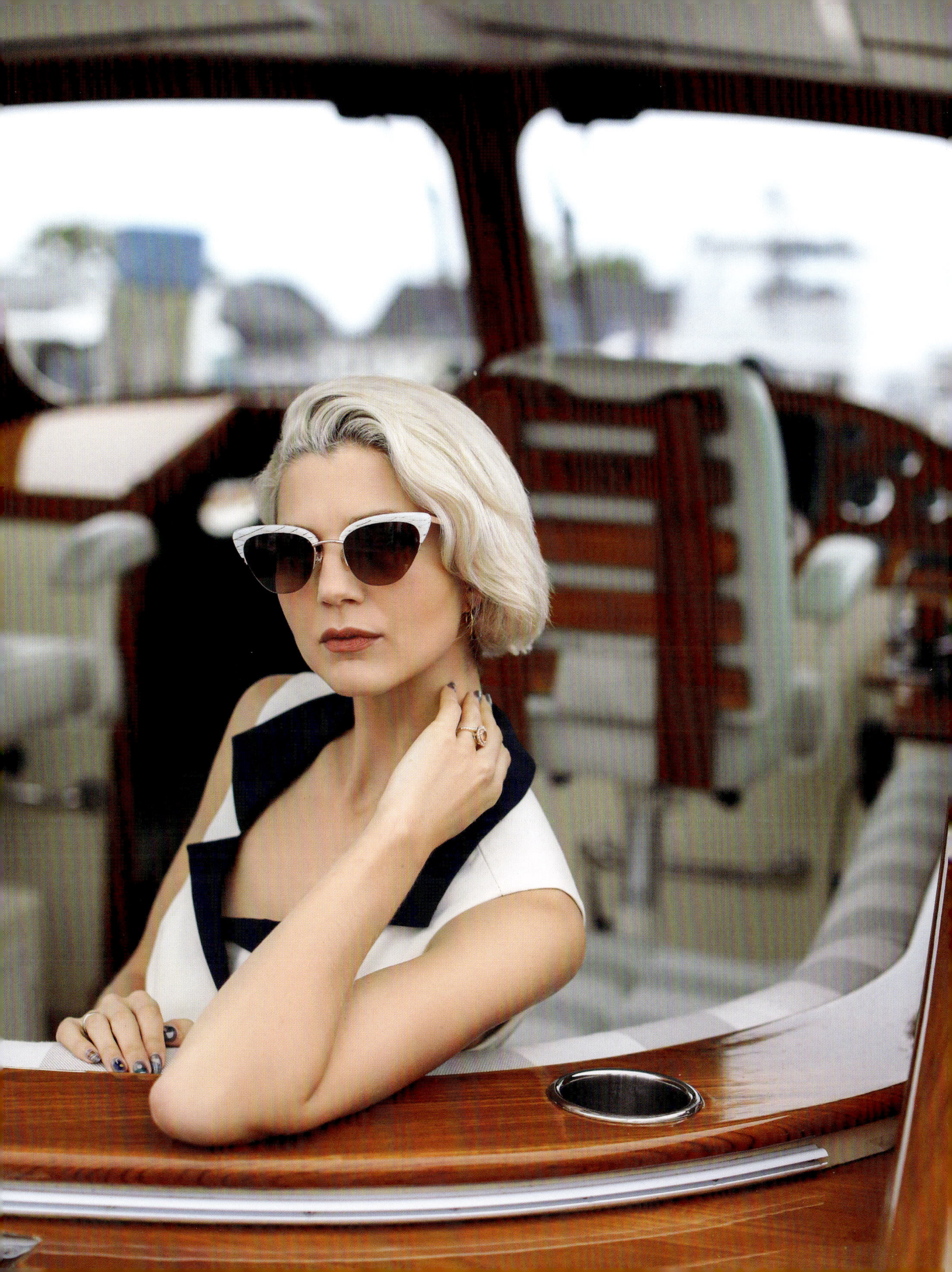

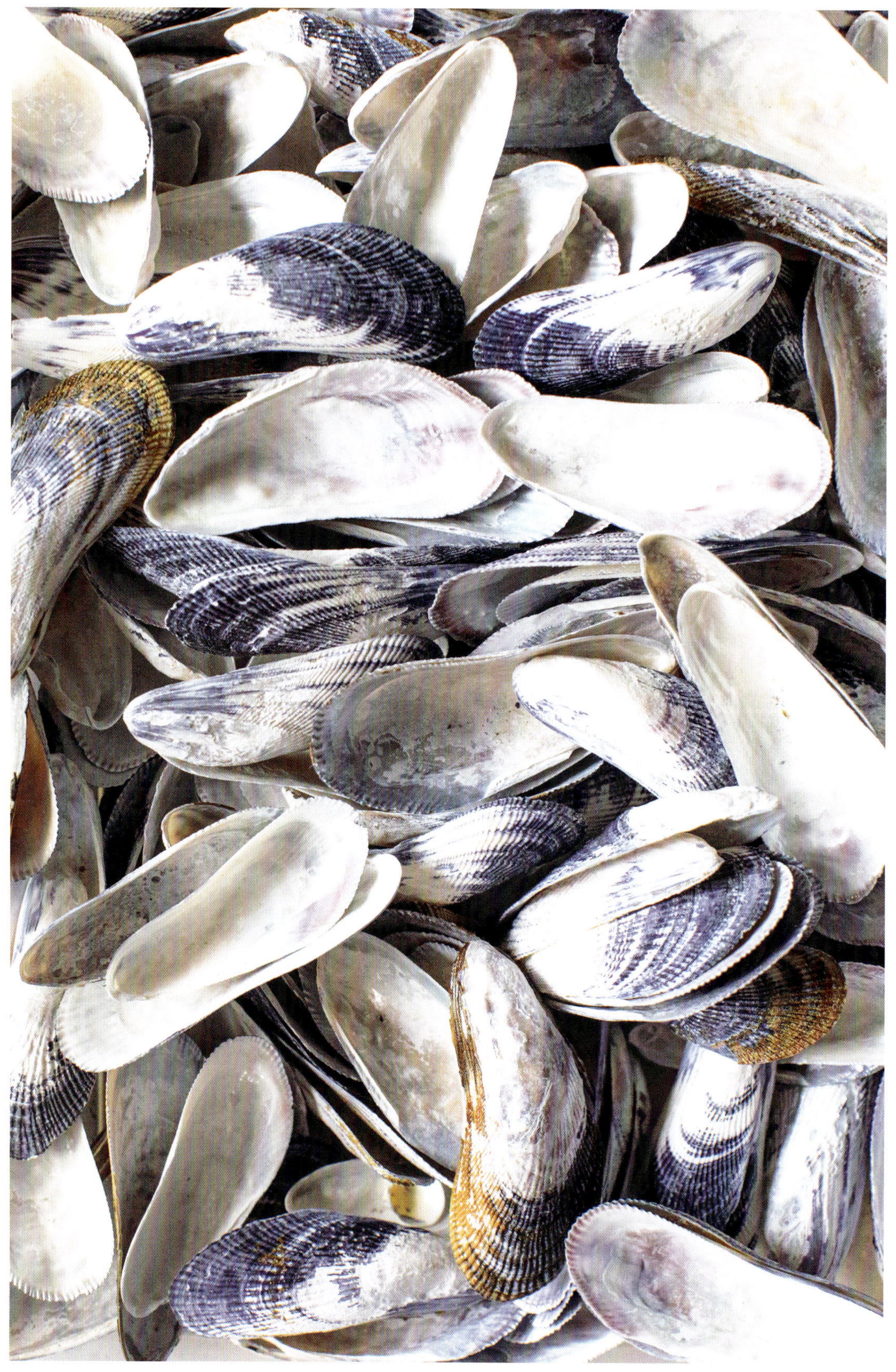

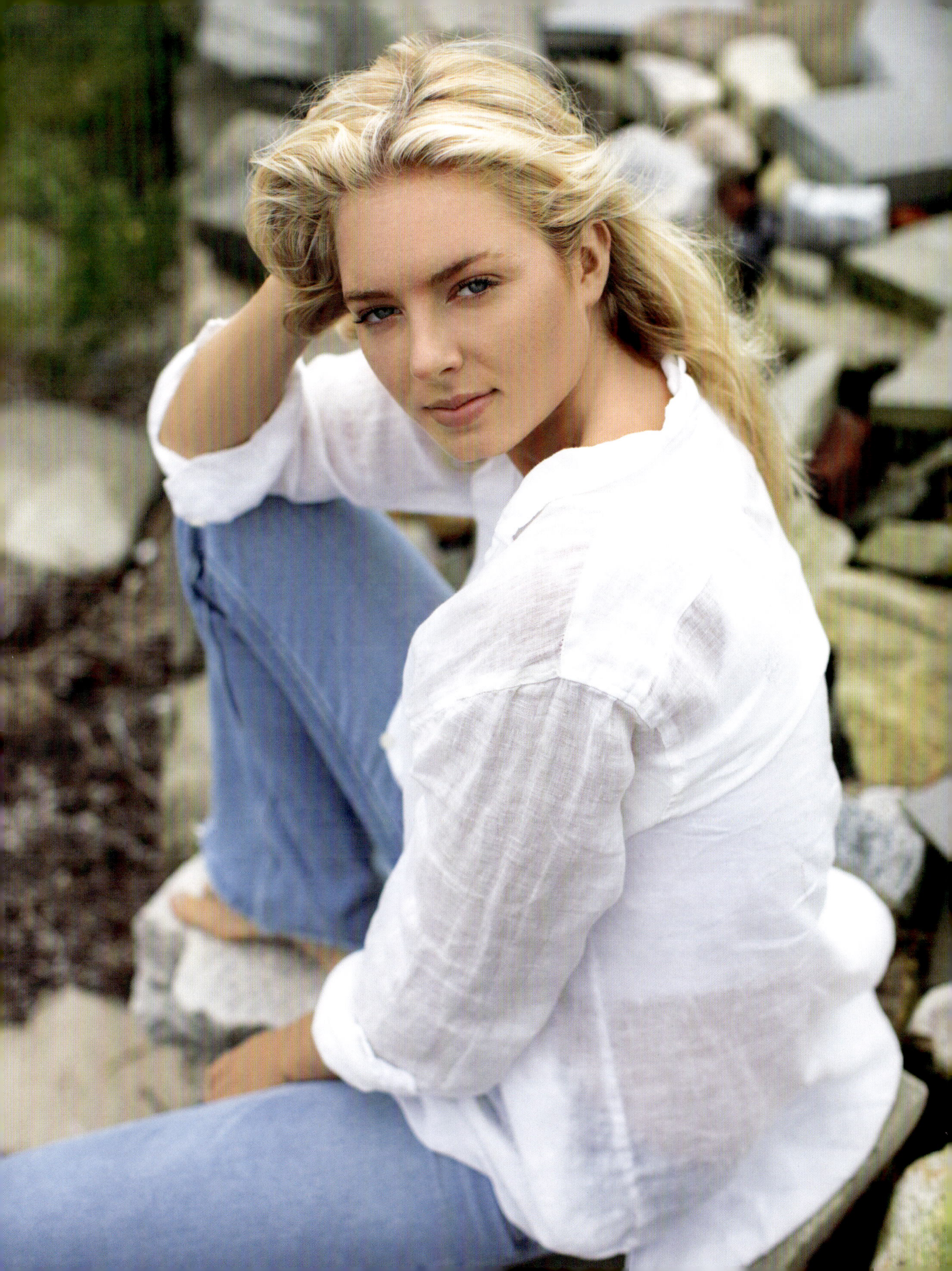

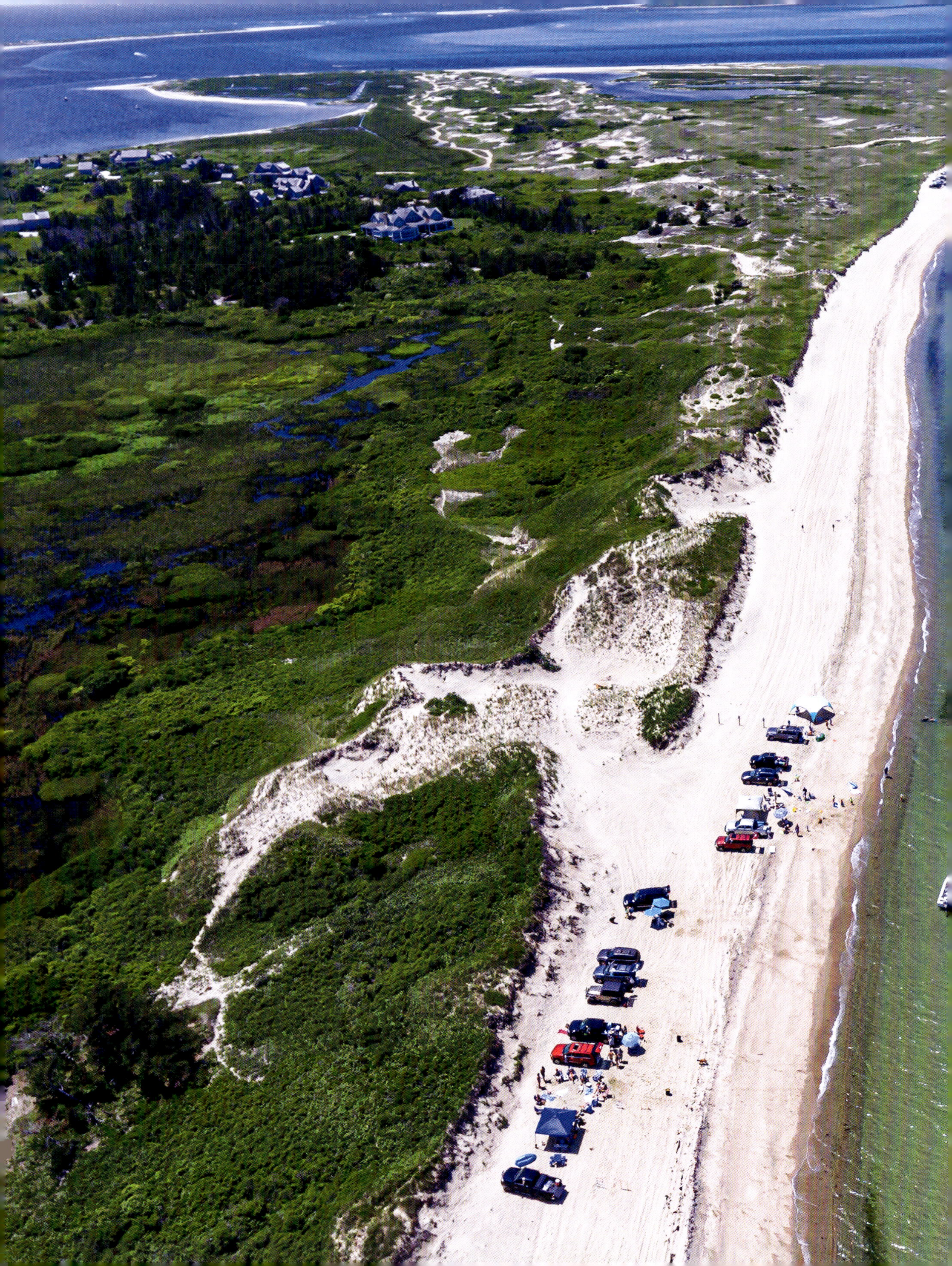

Angela Raynor, proprietor of Boarding House and The Pearl restaurants

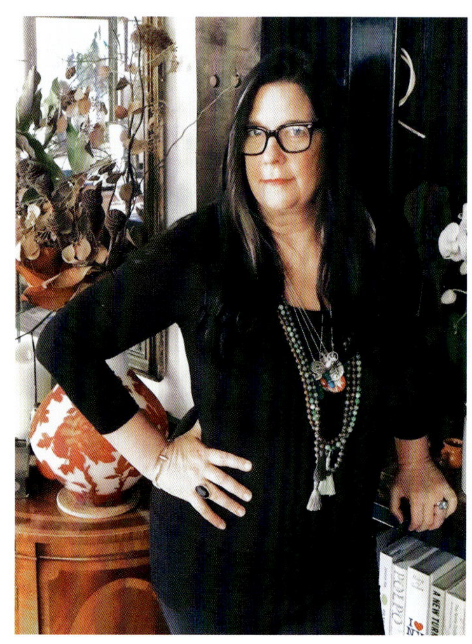

YEARS ON NANTUCKET: *Thirty-five*

ISLAND HOME: *"LoveFarm," our home, test-kitchen, and gathering incubator, abutting the magical state forest.*

MODE OF TRANSPORT: *Vintage dune buggy that belonged to my father whenever possible, otherwise my mud-caked jeep.*

FAVORITE BEACH: *Smooth Hummocks*

_ IS BETTER ON NANTUCKET: *The moonlight*

GREATEST EXTRAVAGANCE: *Taking the winter off.*

DEFINE YOUR NANTUCKET STYLE: *I gravitate toward craftsmanship—bespoke or hand-made items that hold intention and energy of the maker—anything with an echo speaks to me.*

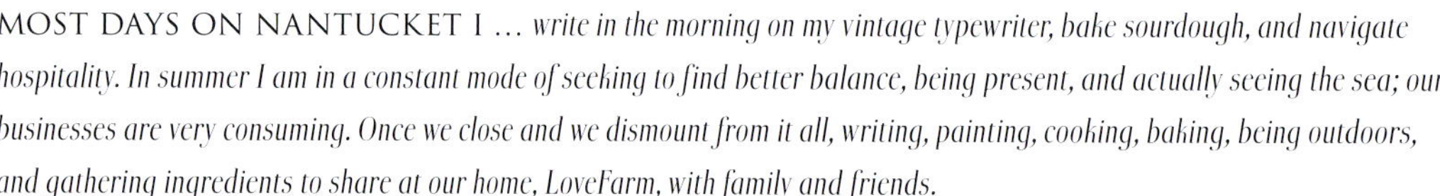

MOST DAYS ON NANTUCKET I … *write in the morning on my vintage typewriter, bake sourdough, and navigate hospitality. In summer I am in a constant mode of seeking to find better balance, being present, and actually seeing the sea; our businesses are very consuming. Once we close and we dismount from it all, writing, painting, cooking, baking, being outdoors, and gathering ingredients to share at our home, LoveFarm, with family and friends.*

NECESSITY ON NANTUCKET: *Kindness, patience, and gratitude. We are an island community and need each other.*

IDEAL DAY: *Write in the morning and paint. Bake sourdough. To have my family home and friends free to gather at the beach, swim, surf, laugh, and be together. Gather food from Pumpkin Pond and Washashore Farms, fish and seafood, and watch the sunset. Then cook with everyone, spend hours at the table, play vinyl, play cards or the name game, settle in and talk all night.*

MOST TREASURED EXPERIENCE ON-ISLAND: *Having both of our children be born here and my parents settling here to share life with us before my dad died.*

BEST PART OF ISLAND LIFE: *The light, the beauty, the people. Cellular shifts happen on the island to people; collaborations, connections, and possibilities for true alchemy unfold.*

CHALLENGE OF ISLAND LIFE: *Erosion, both physical and emotional, that comes with change.*

FIVE THINGS THAT INSPIRE YOU ABOUT NANTUCKET: *Sunsets. Sunrises. The "magic hour" light. The resiliency of the people who live here year-round. The stars.*

LOCAL SECRET: *The off-season is magical.*

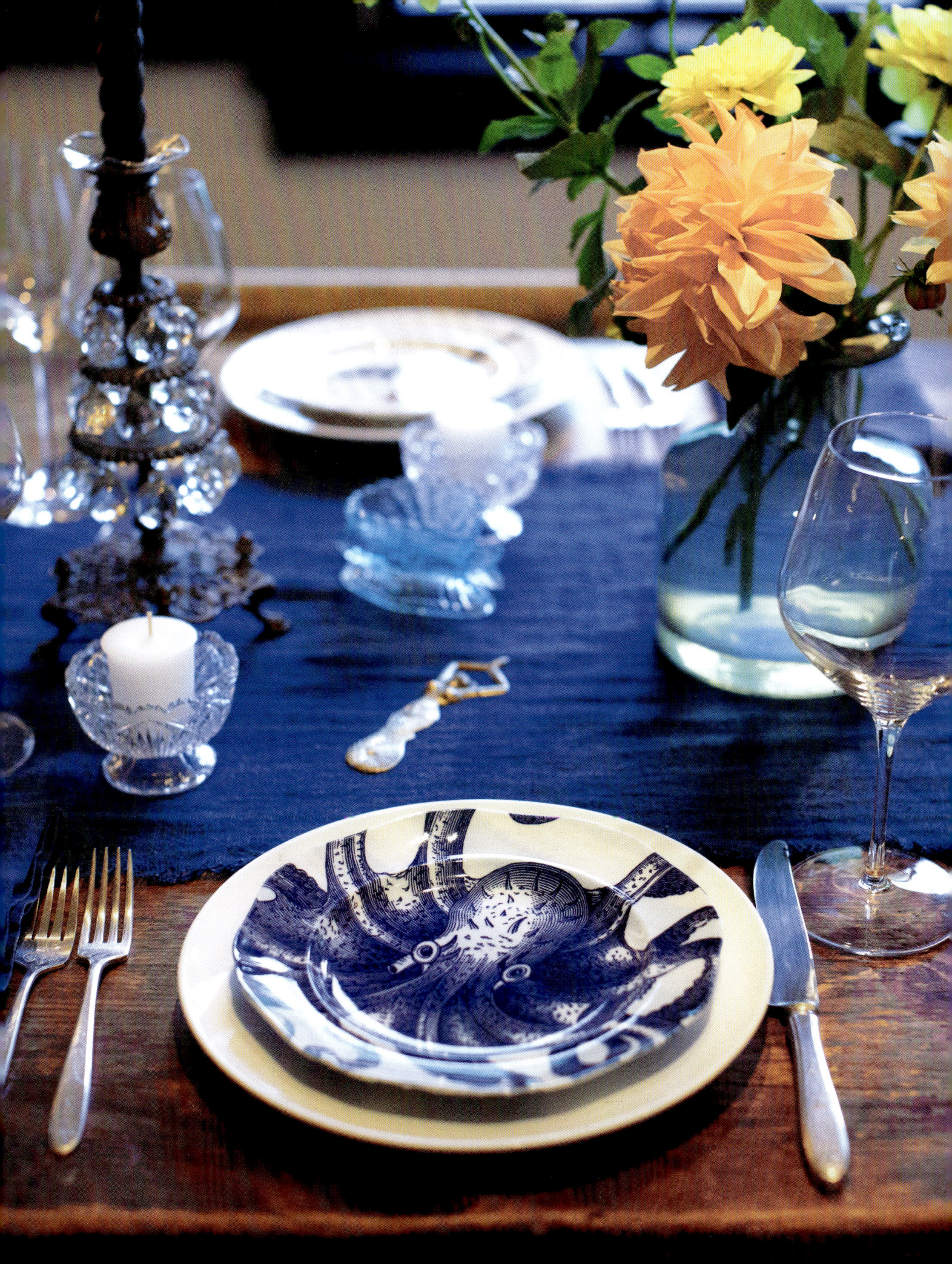

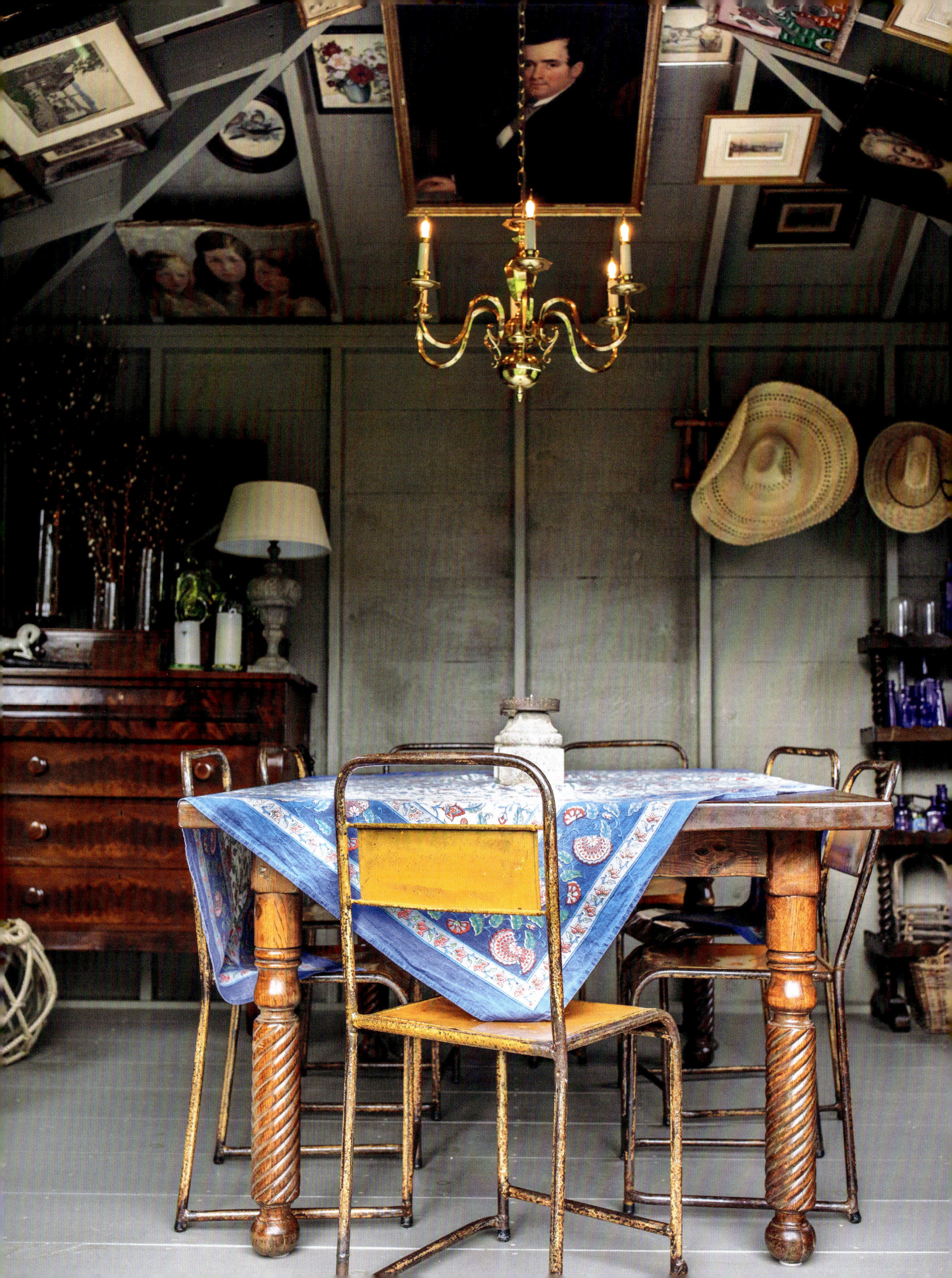

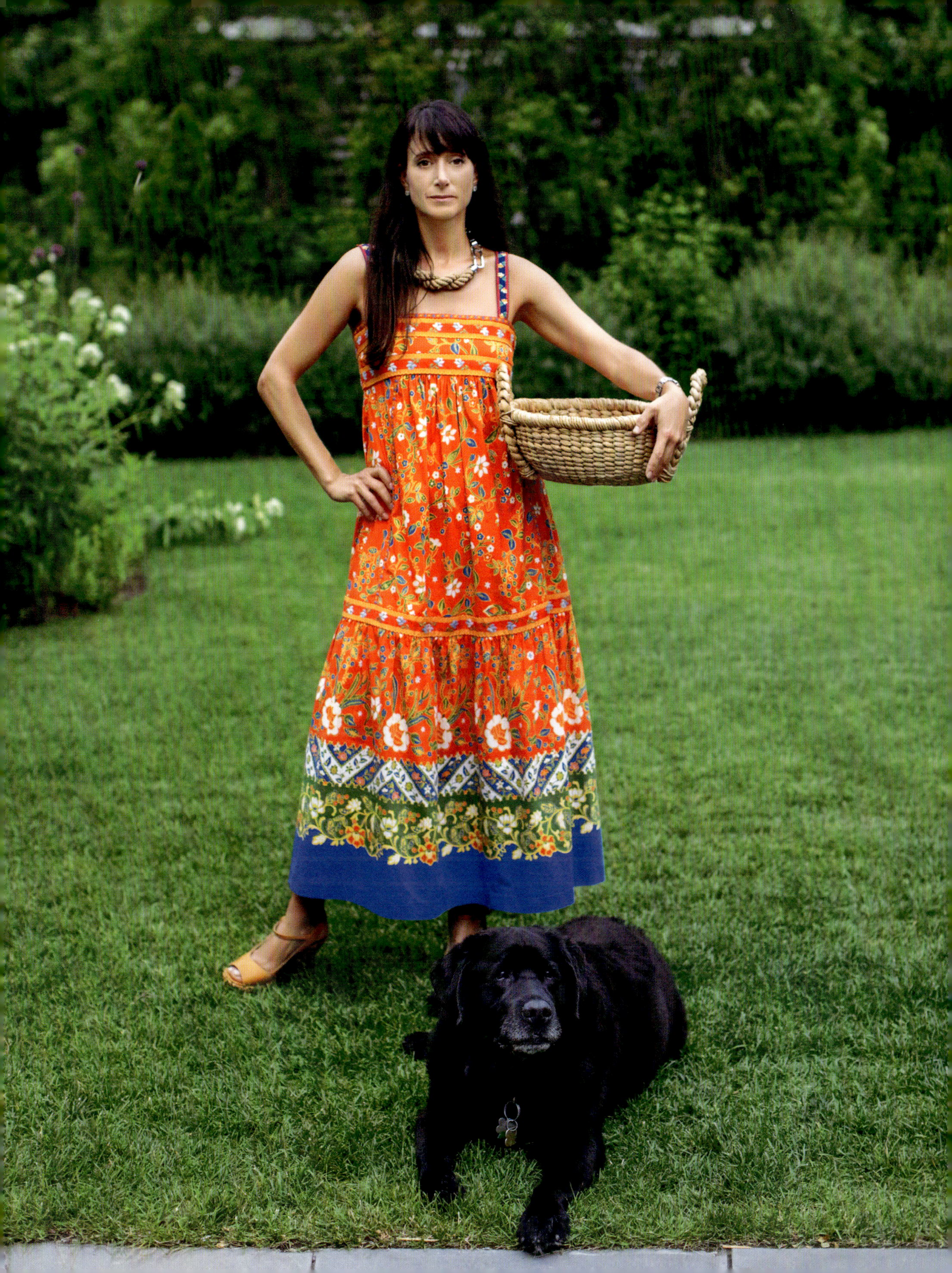

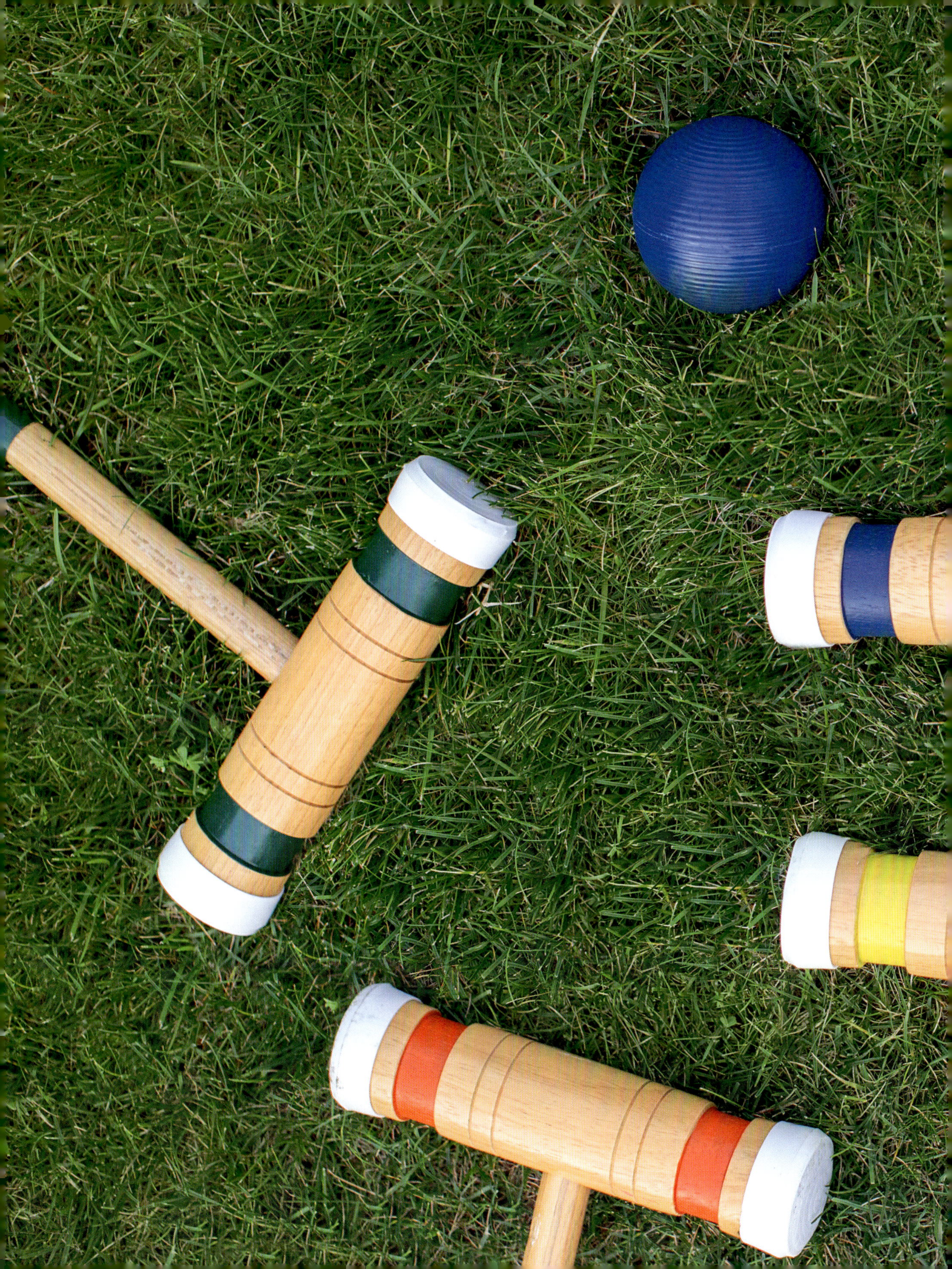

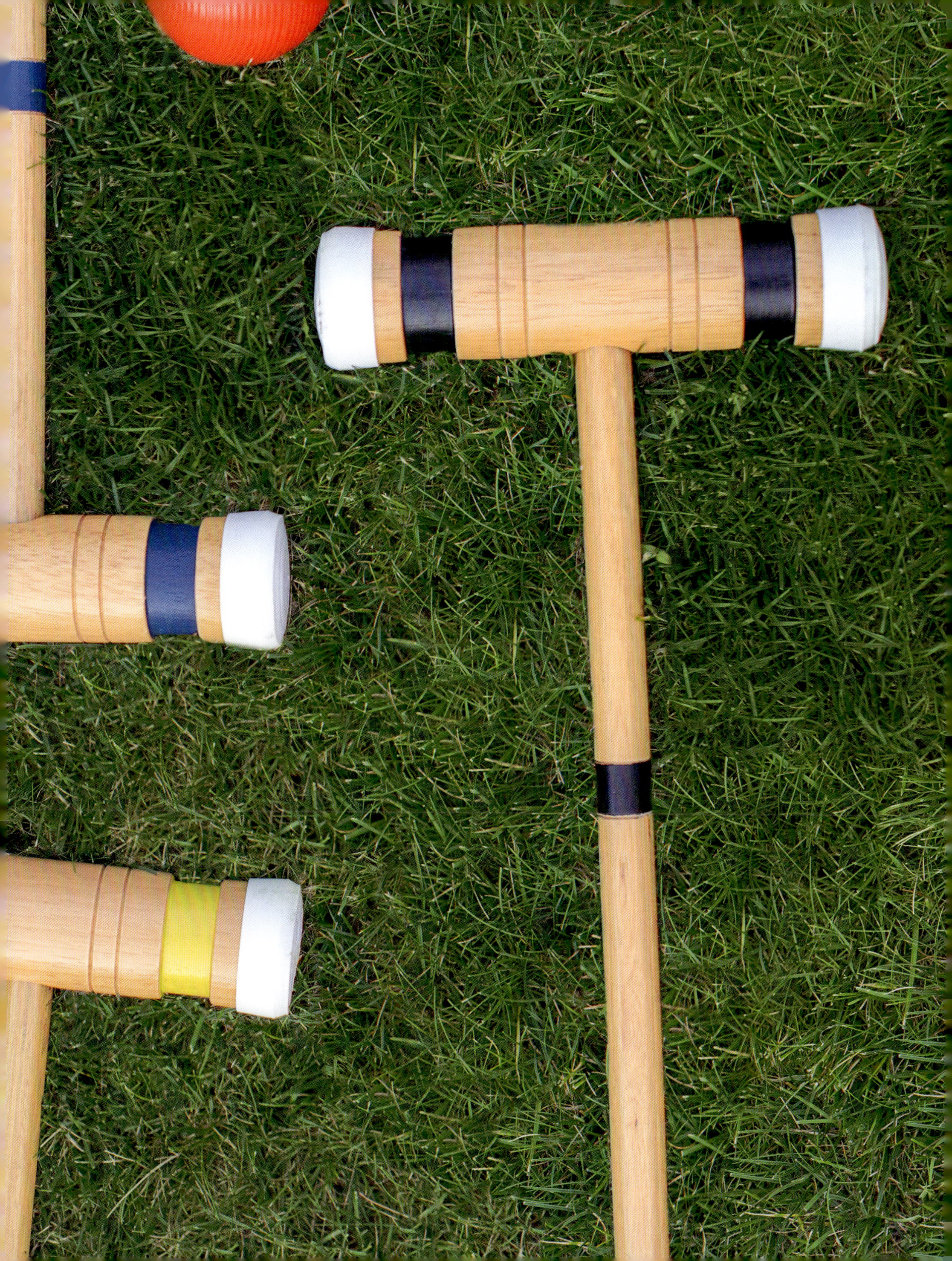

FINDING INSPIRATION: ACTORS, ARTISTS, AUTHORS, CREATIVES

The isolation of island life and the wild beauty that surrounds you on Nantucket are natural magnets for the many actors, artists, authors, and other creatives. And the added bonus of being able to find backing or gain exposure to influential inhabitants can make Nantucket life fruitful for creatives.

Nantucket has a long history of attracting creatives. Around the turn of the last century, when theaters would close down for the summer, a group of the Broadway community would descend upon Nantucket's Siasconset (or 'Sconset) neighborhood to live in beach cottages and stage productions by the sea. The "Actors Colony" as they became known, eventually built the 'Sconset Casino for performances and recreation. The tradition continues across Nantucket's theater groups, such as Theatre Workshop of Nantucket, Dreamland Stage Company, and White Heron Theatre Company. In some cases idle summering teenagers can work on productions with professionals—an opportunity they wouldn't likely have at home. Nantucket's small size begets access.

Thanks to arts patrons, several incubators ensure artists continue discovering and being inspired by the island. Philanthropist and arts advocate, John S. Johnson, founder of BuzzFeed, son of sculptor Seward Johnson (and great-grandson of Robert Wood Johnson, co-founder of Johnson & Johnson) founded an artists colony and screenwriters colony operating out of a family compound with a 200-year-old barn. Johnson brings in artists from around the world for his colonies, which are run by local creatives, where colonists attend events and interact over dinners with Nantucket's many creative practitioners. "The island is still chock-full of interesting people," he says.

It's easy to find inspiration on Nantucket, says printmaker Eric Holch. "Go to Newport, Rhode Island, and drive the backroads and you'll go past Jiffy Lubes and gas stations. Here it's still unspoiled." Holch, who left New Canaan, Connecticut, and a successful advertising career to pursue his side project making art, pulls direct inspiration from island life: its sailboat races, beaches, gardens, and lighthouses.

Landscape painter Illya Kagan, the son of famed furniture designer Vladimir Kagan and needlework artist Erica Wilson, also sees the island as muse. In Kagan's case, it's the unique topography, which includes poetic natural elements such as acres of moors, rolling plains patched with wild grasses, long stretches of open beach, and a particular, rounded cobblestone that gives Nantucket Town an unmistakable aura of the past.

Beyond the direct visual inspiration, many island artists thrive off the natural surroundings, and report that the solitude of winter provides ideal time in the studio, or for creative development, while island summers bring influential backers and patrons.

"For friends of mine living on the island, anyone with any kind of creative practice, I think there's a freedom in Nantucket's isolation that's pretty glorious," says Johnson. "Then what is so cool is you have that freedom combined with the stimulation of connection in the summer when there's this great influx of people and you're going to a dinner

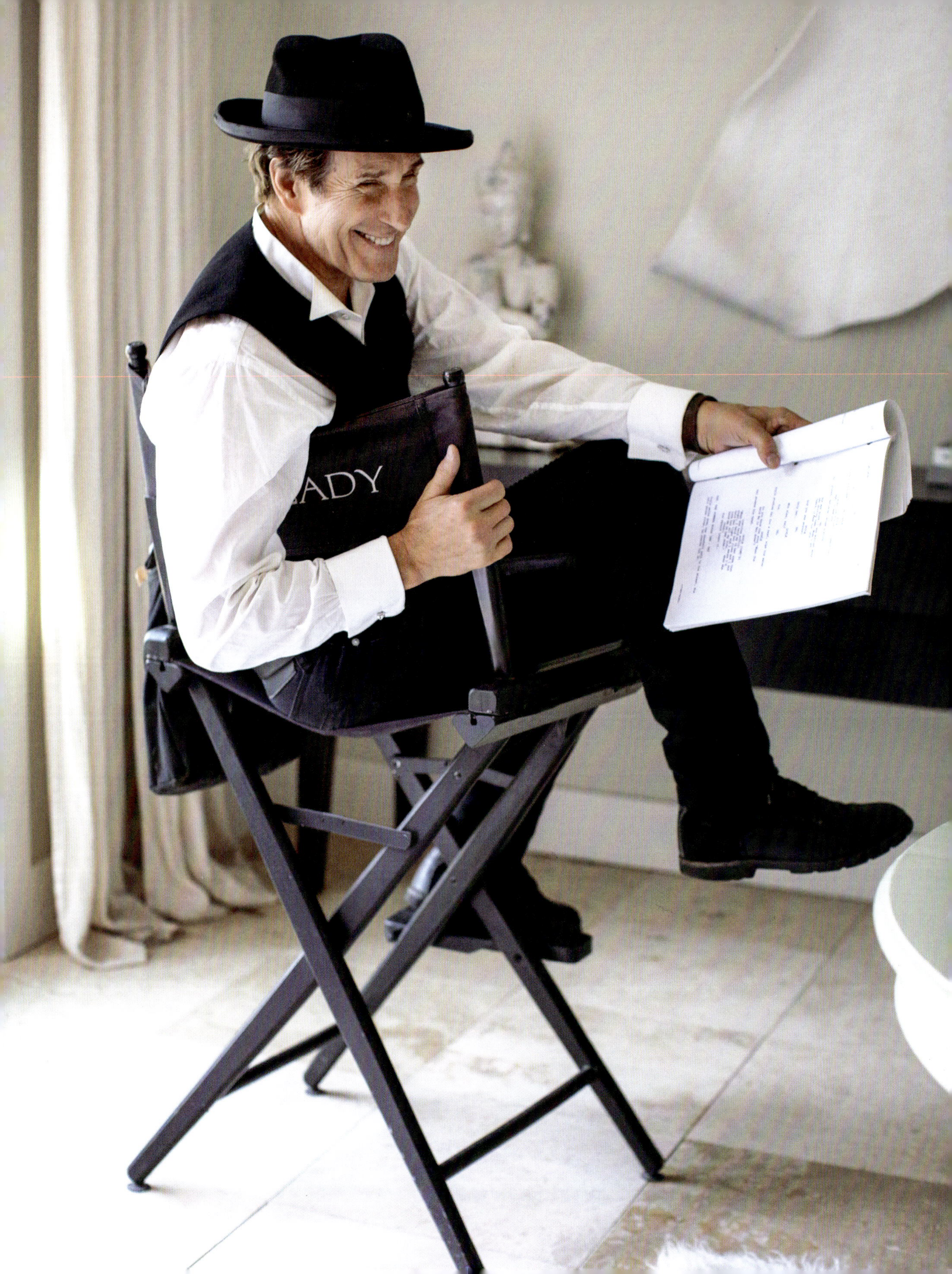
ADY

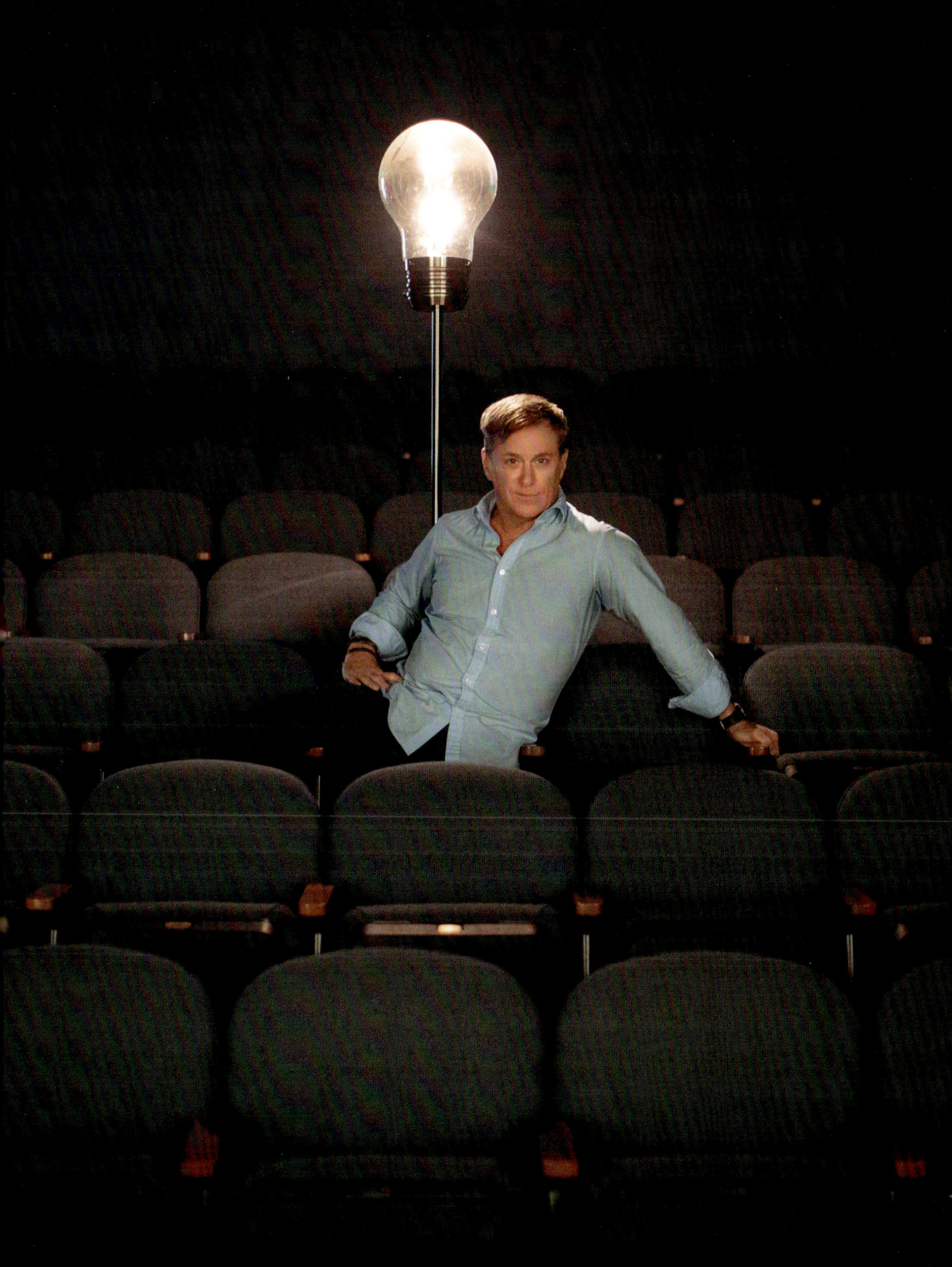

party meeting somebody interesting, or seeing somebody downtown that's a friend of a friend. There aren't a ton of places where you can have both of those things."

The world still comes to Nantucket, or at least its powerful creatives and captains of industry. Summer visitors last year have included many Fortune 100 CEOs, politicians like Joe Biden, and even the Hollywood set: Gwyneth Paltrow, and Drew Barrymore. Its summer residents include Ambassador Elizabeth Bagley, former Google CEO Eric Schmidt and philanthropist Wendy Schmidt, the late Jack Welch (former GE CEO) and journalist/philanthropist Suzy Welch, architect Graham Gund, Chanel Vice-Chairman Arie Kopelman, New England Patriots coach Bill Belichick, actor Jerry Stiller, and many others. The year-round population has some of its own creative fame: **New York Times** best-selling author Elin Hilderbrand has penned her twenty-six romance novels (most set on Nantucket) from beaches and poolsides. Nathaniel Philbrick writes historical nonfiction rooted on Nantucket's history, his National Book Award–winning **In the Heart of the Sea** was recently turned into a movie directed by Ron Howard.

Even when the island doesn't foster wider fame it can bring exposure. For Nantucket musician and music producer Floyd Kellogg, when big-name artists come to record or play at the island's iconic club, The Chicken Box, but don't want to incur the expense of bringing their whole band, Floyd often stands in. He's had the opportunity to play with members of the Red Hot Chili Peppers, Florence and the Machine, G. Love & Special Sauce, and others. Being a big fish in a small pond does have its advantages, especially when New York is now just a Jetblue flight away.

Actor-director John Shea, known for his many roles in television and movies, including **Gossip Girl** and **Lois & Clark**, and award-winning work on Broadway, has maintained a fifty-year love affair with the island. Shea originally came as a college student, later returning as a Yale School of Drama graduate and young hippie, and for the last decade living year-round with his artist-wife Melissa MacLeod and their two children. Shea enjoys appearing in island productions—notably Orson Welles's **Moby Dick—Rehearsed**, which he performs annually under a 50-foot sperm whale skeleton suspended from the rafters at the Nantucket Whaling Museum—but also regularly travels off-island for work and inspiration.

"In mid-winter we retreat, Nantucket people love to travel," says Shea. "Friends of mine will say, 'I was skiing in the Swiss alps, I was just in Sri Lanka, or I was scuba diving in Turks and Caicos, or I was riding horseback in Patagonia.' They're doing crazy things like this all over the world all the time. And if you're a restaurateur you're bringing menus and recipes and spices that you found in a souk in Morocco and you're adding it to your ingredients. And if you're a painter or a photographer you're bringing back images from around the world. If you are a writer you're inspired by what you just experienced when you were on a pilgrimage in India. That kind of thing also makes the island really rich culturally."

"This has always been a haven for people who are writers, artists, dreamers. I think there's a renaissance moment that this island provides for people. They can connect to a different time and space."

—Angela Raynor, proprietor of Boarding House and The Pearl restaurants

Illya Kagan, artist and island resident

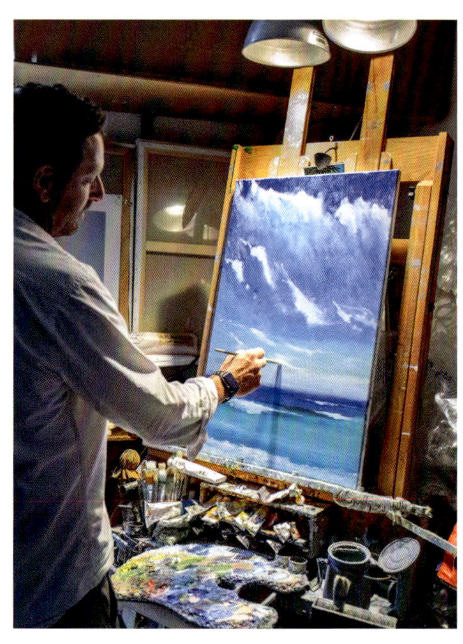

YEARS ON NANTUCKET: *Fifty summers, and year-round since I graduated college in '91.*

ISLAND HOME: *West Chester Street in town.*

MODE OF TRANSPORT: *Walk (or '72 MGB)*

FAVORITE BEACH: *Madequecham*

SUMMER UNIFORM: *Cargo shorts and a t-shirt.*

_ IS BETTER ON NANTUCKET: *Everything*

GREATEST EXTRAVAGANCE: *Sailboat*

DEFINE NANTUCKET STYLE: *Shabby chic*

MOST DAYS ON NANTUCKET I ... *paint.*

CLASSIC NANTUCKET IS ... *biking through the Moors at Altar Rock.*

FAVORITE THING/SPOT ON NANTUCKET: *Afternoons on Coatue [National Wildlife Refuge].*

COMMON MISCONCEPTION ABOUT NANTUCKET: *That it's the Hamptons.*

NANTUCKET HISTORICAL FIGURE THAT SPEAKS TO YOU: *Anne Ramsdell Congdon (especially her landscape paintings from early/mid-1900s).*

NECESSITY ON NANTUCKET: *Flip-flops*

IDEAL DAY: *Surf, sail, paint.*

MOST TREASURED EXPERIENCE/THING ON-ISLAND: *Sailboat races at First Point with family and friends.*

THING YOU ONLY DO ON NANTUCKET: *Cross-country skiing on the beach after winter storms.*

BEST PART OF ISLAND LIFE: *Knowing everyone (best and worst).*

LOCAL SECRET: *Not telling.*

ON NANTUCKET YOU NEVER ... *honk.*

WHAT SPEAKS TO YOU ABOUT THE ISLAND? *Being removed from the rest of the world by 30 miles of Nantucket sound.*

FAVORITE ISLAND MEMORY: *Family mornings at Miacomet (first with my parents, and now with my kids) followed by breakfast at Bartlett's Farm.*

_ IS SO NANTUCKET: *Sunset beach barbecues*

NANTUCKET HISTORICAL FIGURE/EVENT THAT SPEAKS TO YOU: *Anne Ramsdell Congdon (especially her landscape paintings from early/mid-1900s).*

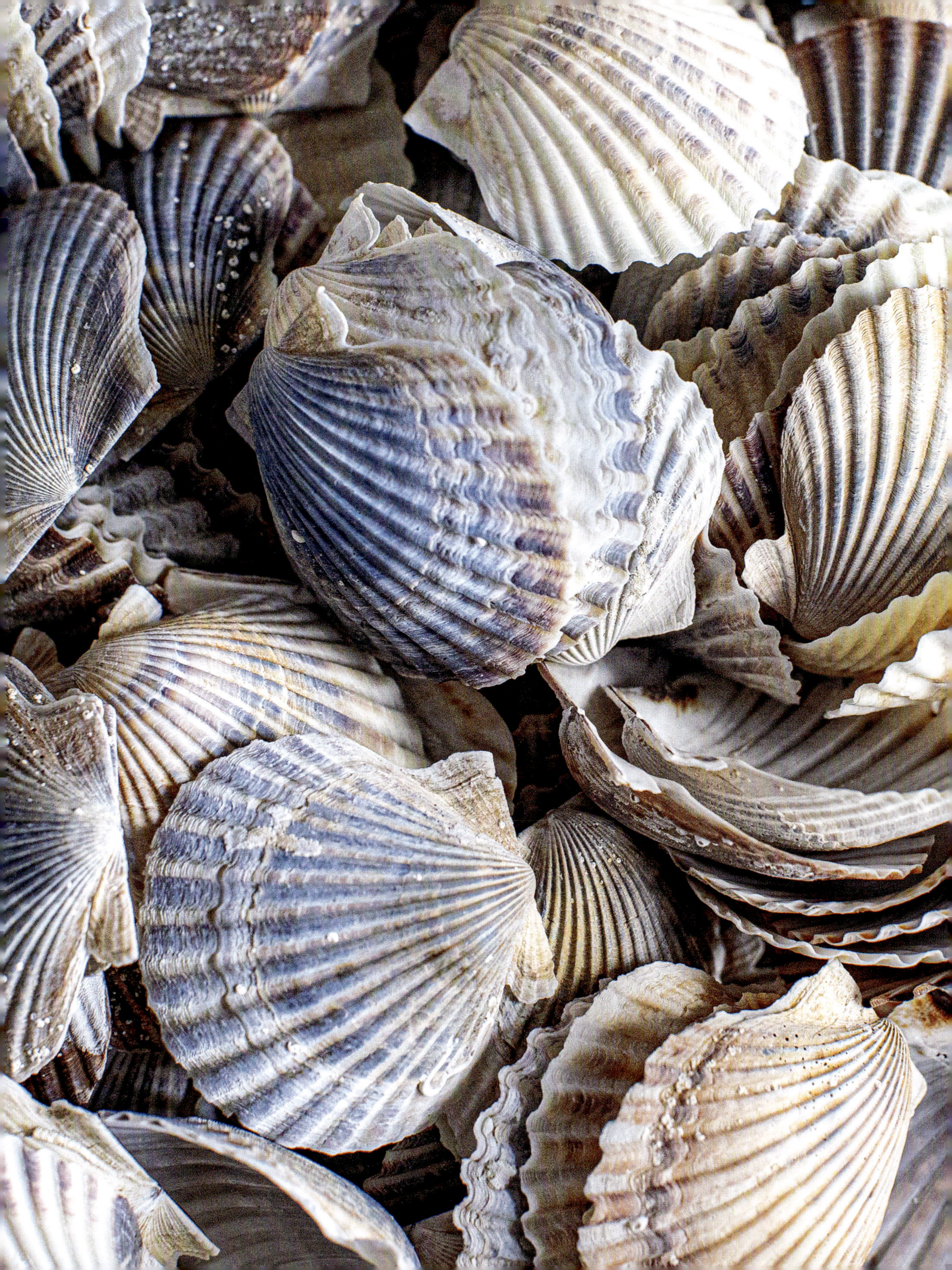

"When you live here and are used to eight or nine or ten months of peace and quiet, summer seems like a big party, almost a raucous intrusion on tranquility. I look at it as a filmmaker: like it's a Hollywood backlot where they haven't called the extras yet. Then suddenly someone calls action and it's filled with life in the summer."

—John Shea, actor-director and fifty-year resident

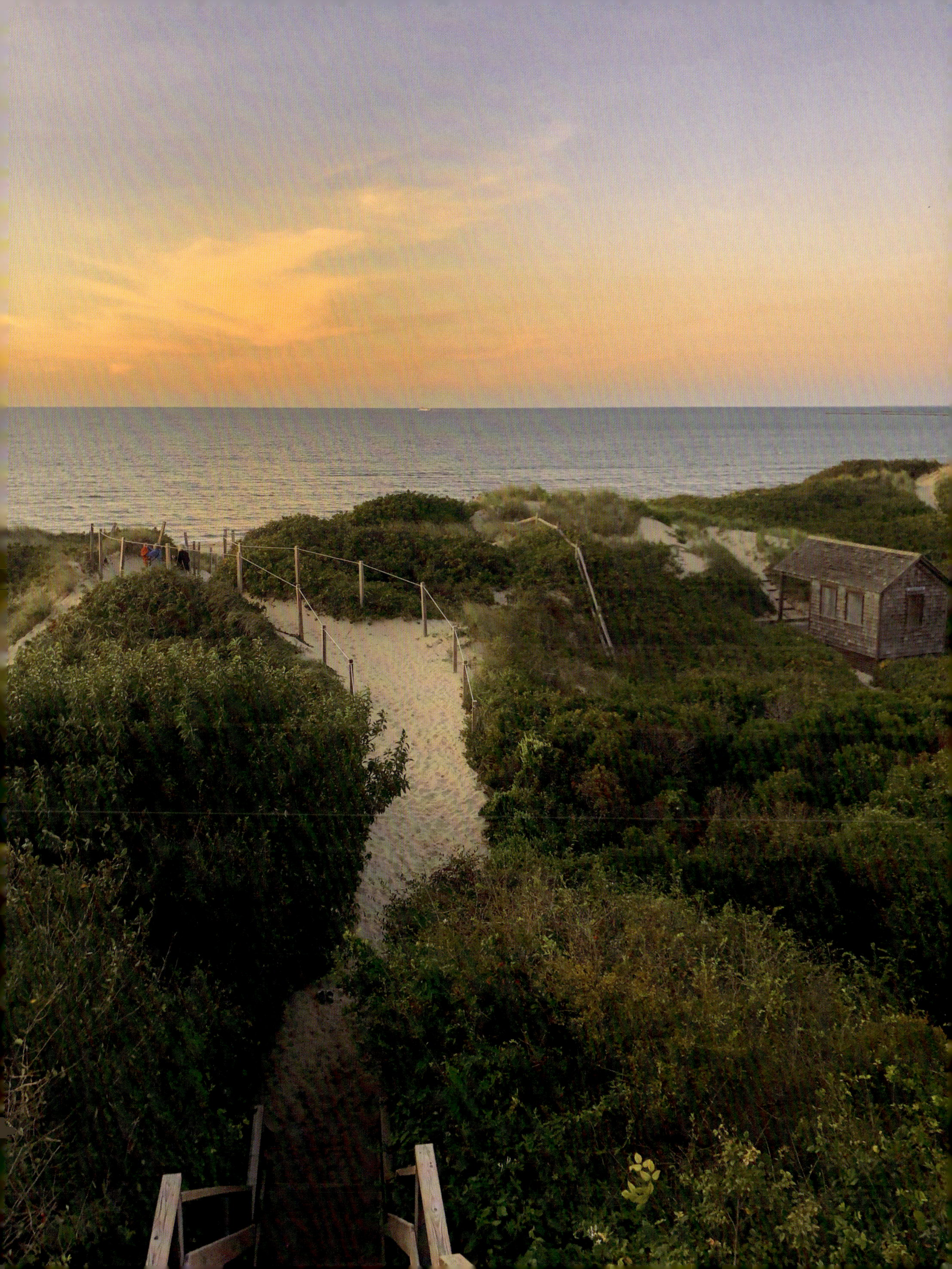

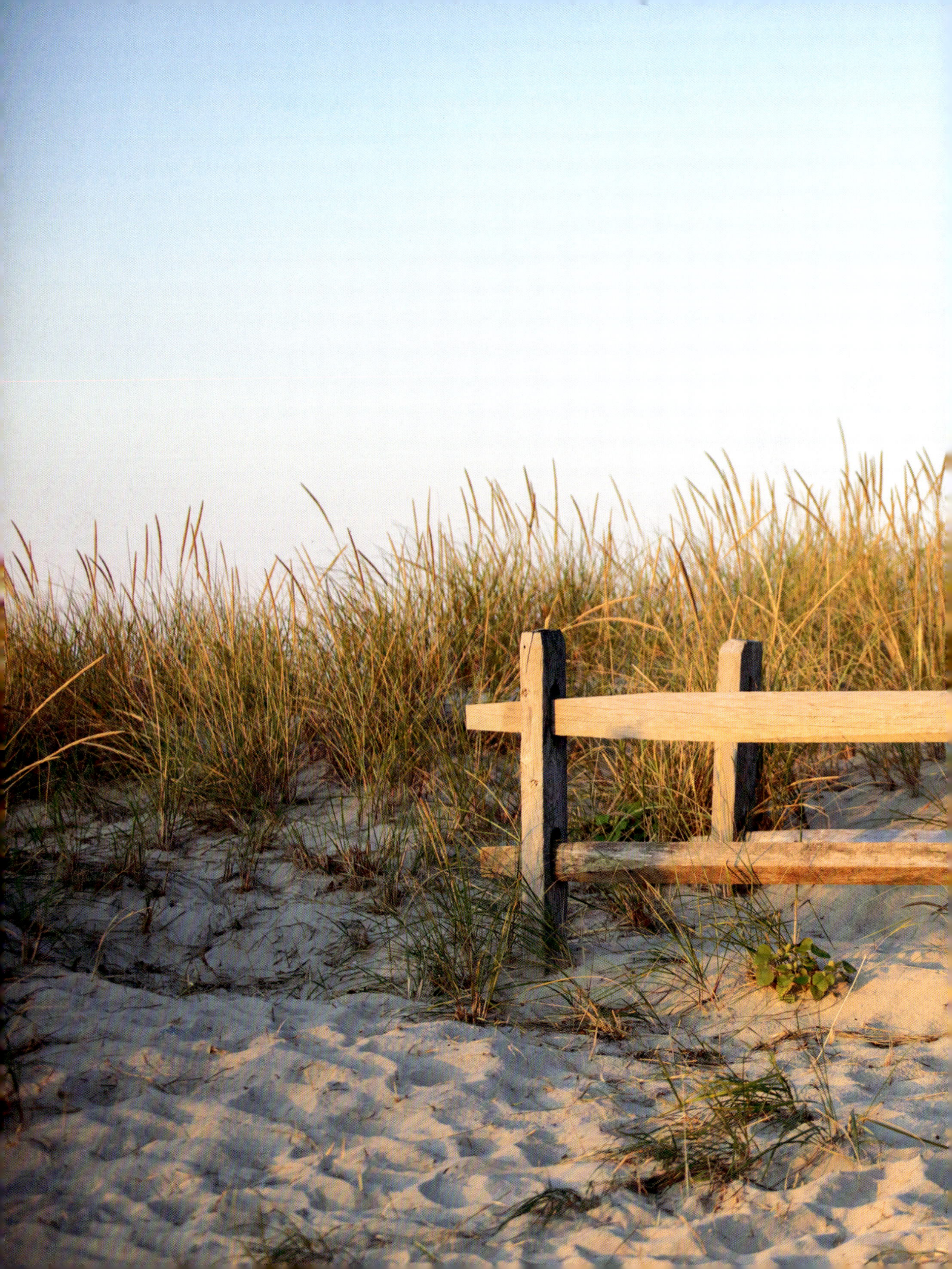

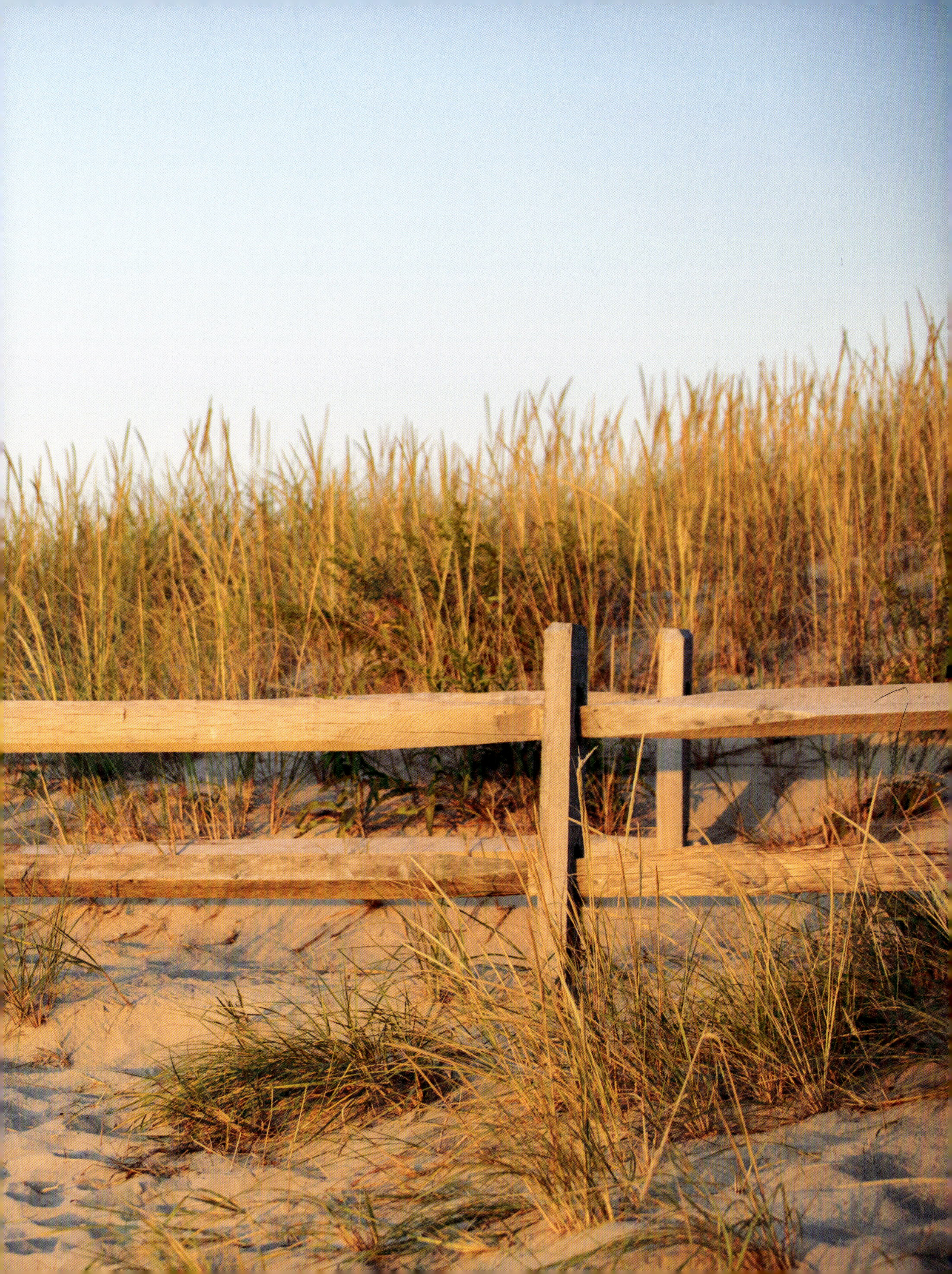

CLASSIC AMERICAN STYLE

From an outside perspective, Nantucket Style is often defined as the preppiest of the prep, setting the tone for that East Coast look that one can achieve only with money and success. However, despite the island's nautical tropes and pastel-flowered color-scheme, clothing essentials have changed over the years as a reflection of year-round island life, and an influx of new visitors.

For many summer people, evenings are often devoted to family barbecues, dining at chic restaurants in town, charitable social events, or dinners at private clubs. In town on a summer evening, you can still see throwbacks to a bygone era. During high season, July and August, Nantucket Town is a flurry of color and print. People dress to impress, and nothing seems too over-the-top. In fact, it can be nearly impossible to find a spot where casual beach attire and flip-flops pass for evening wear.

A few very-Nantucket looks can still be spotted: a straw hat, usually with grosgrain ribbon, from the Peter Beaton Hat Studio; a pastel cashmere poncho from Island Cashmere, and a Nantucket Friendship basket purse, sometimes even all at once. Long-time Nantucket families

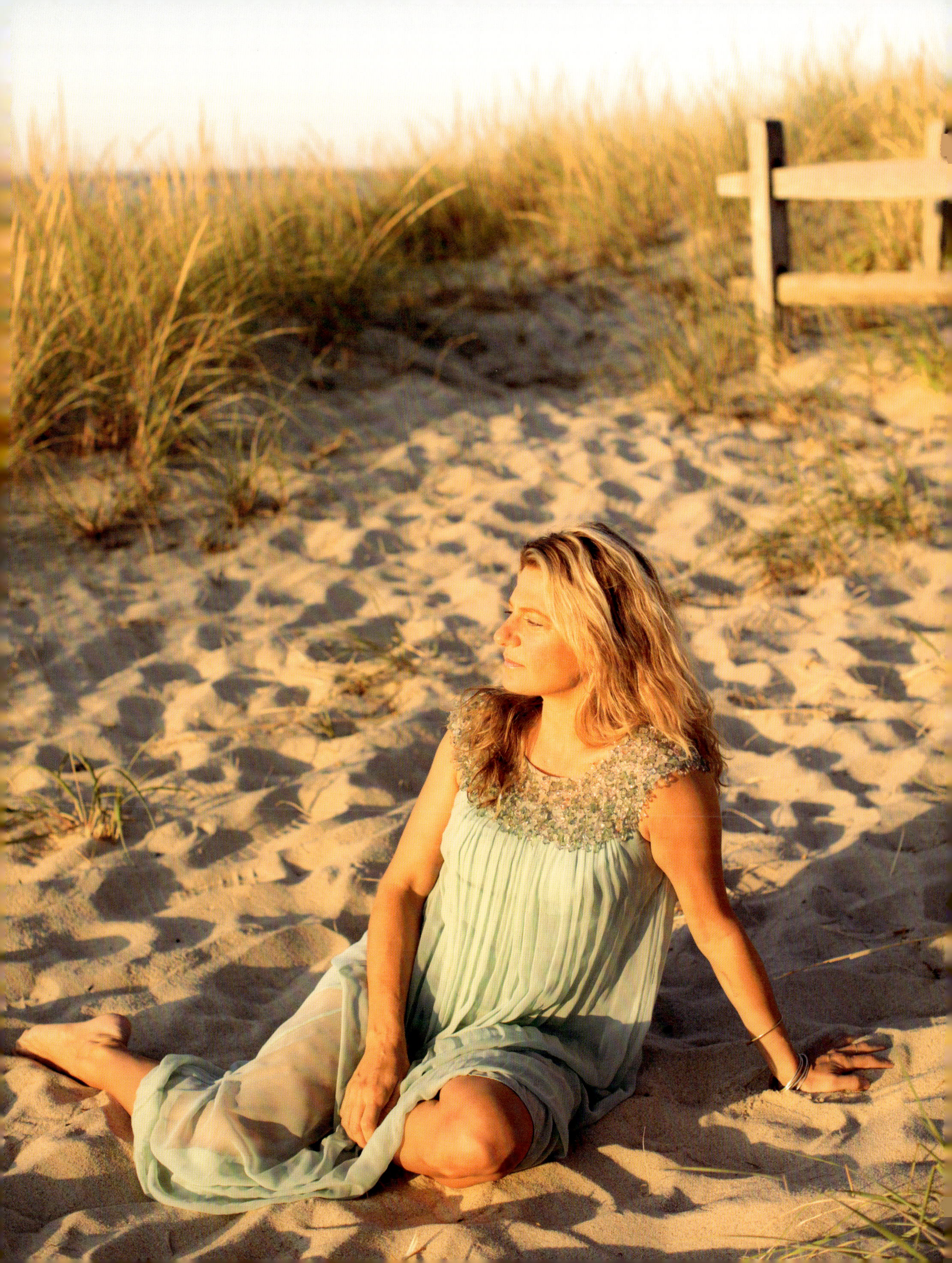

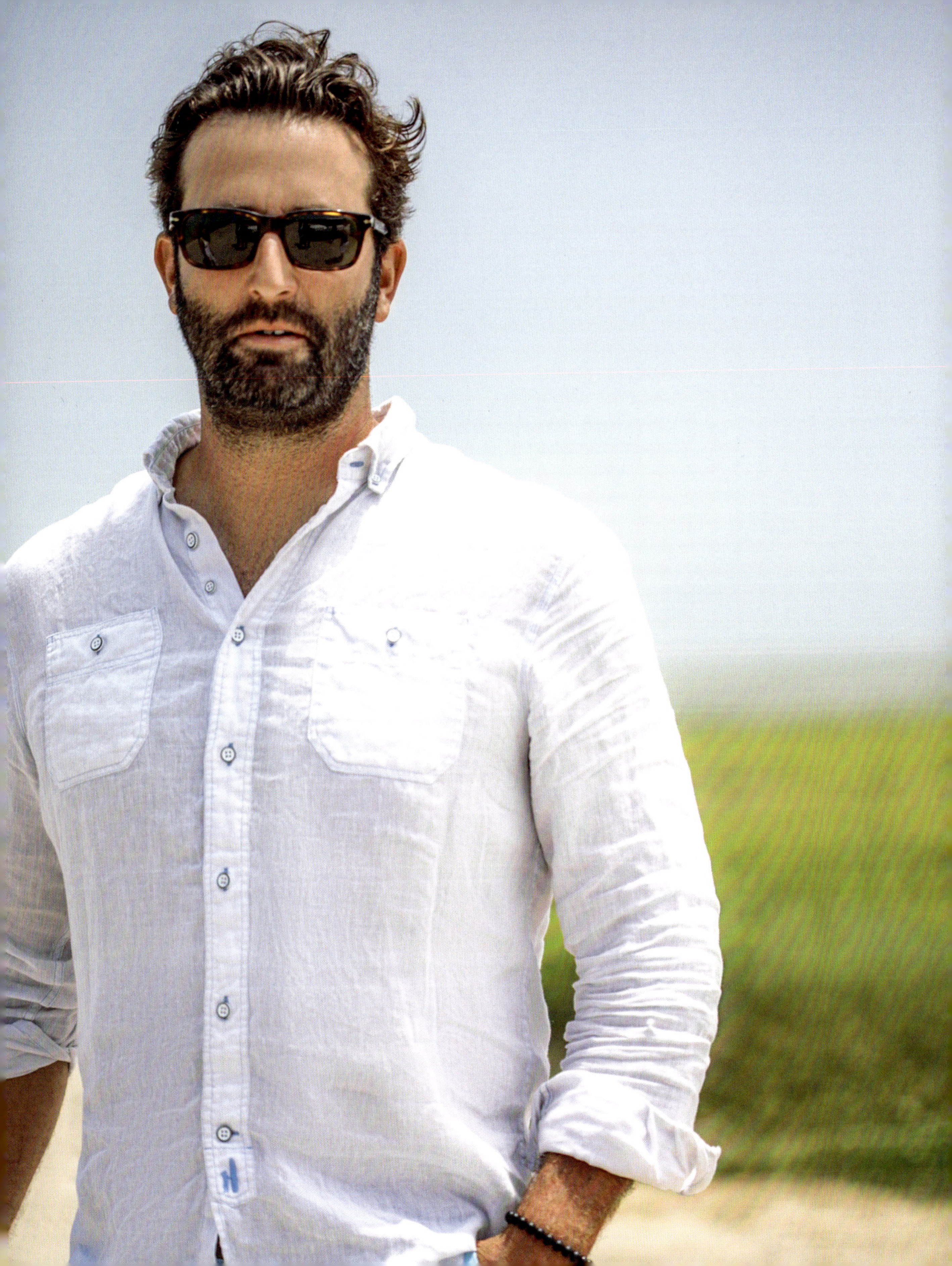

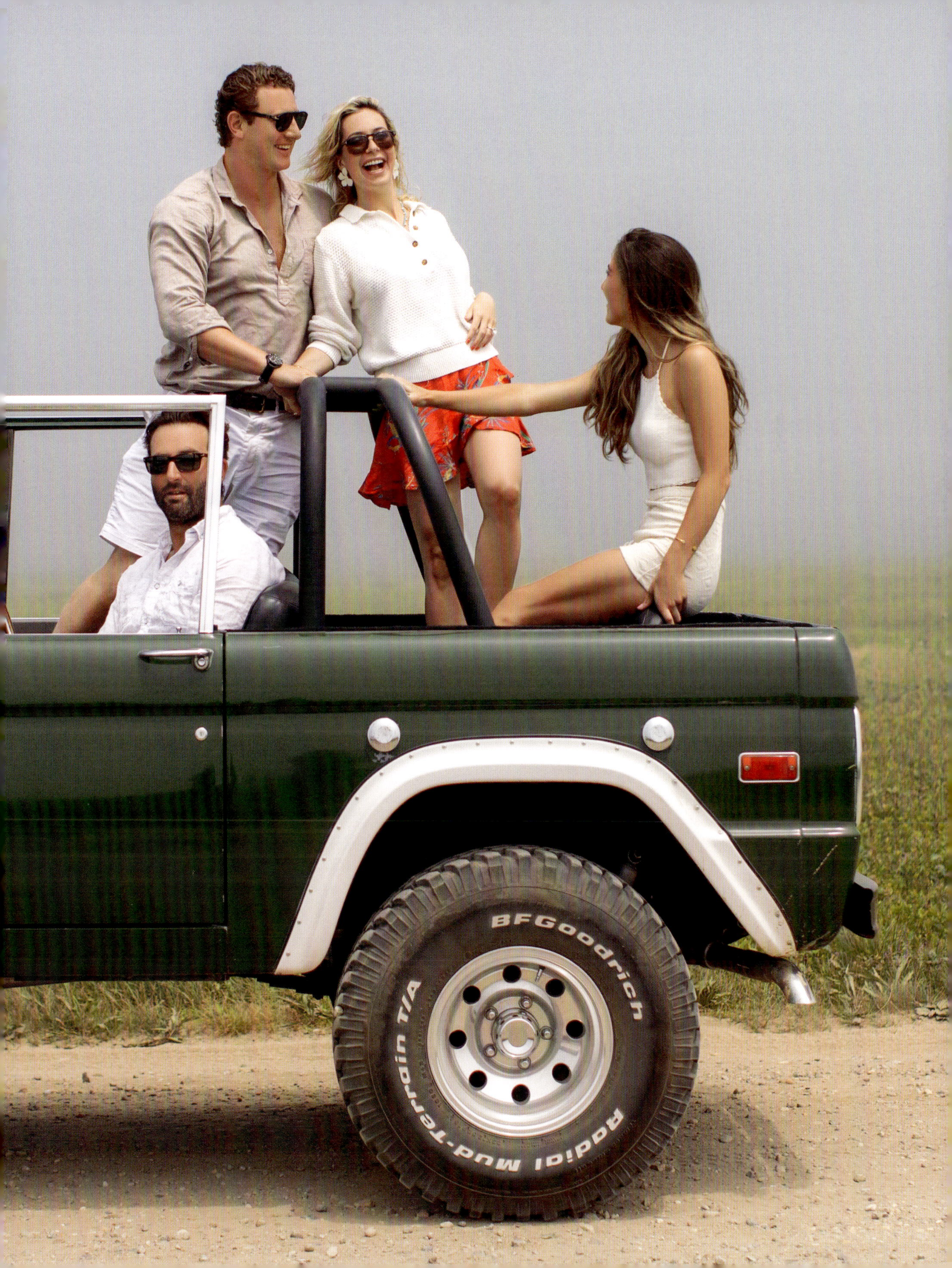
BFGoodrich
Radial Mud-Terrain T/A

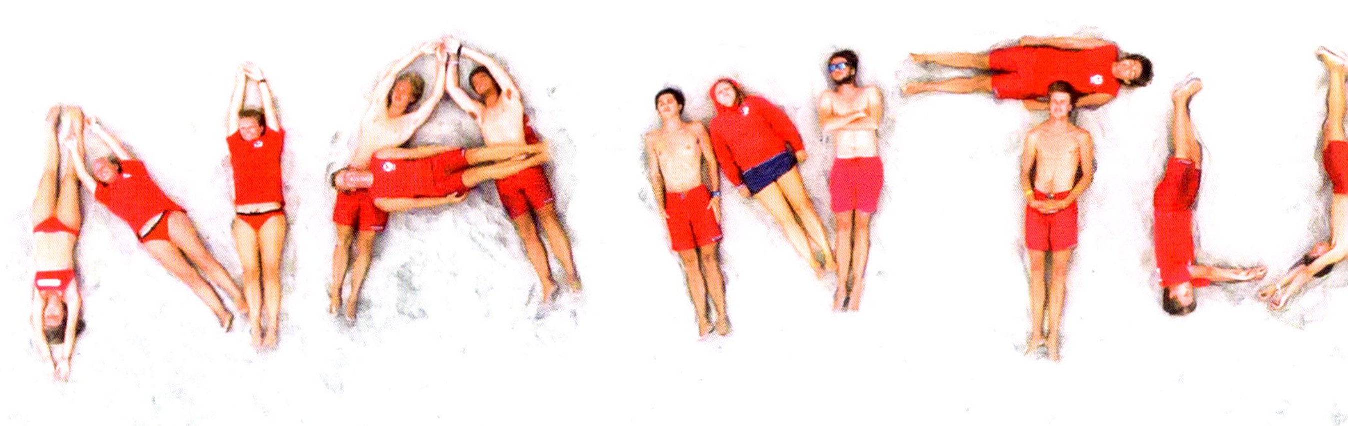

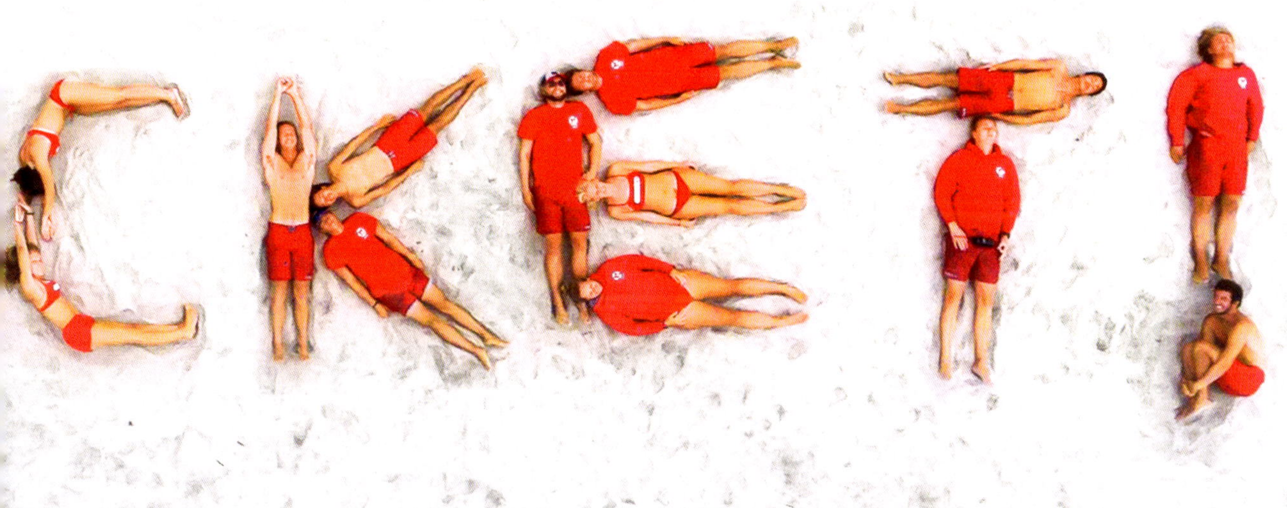
CKET!

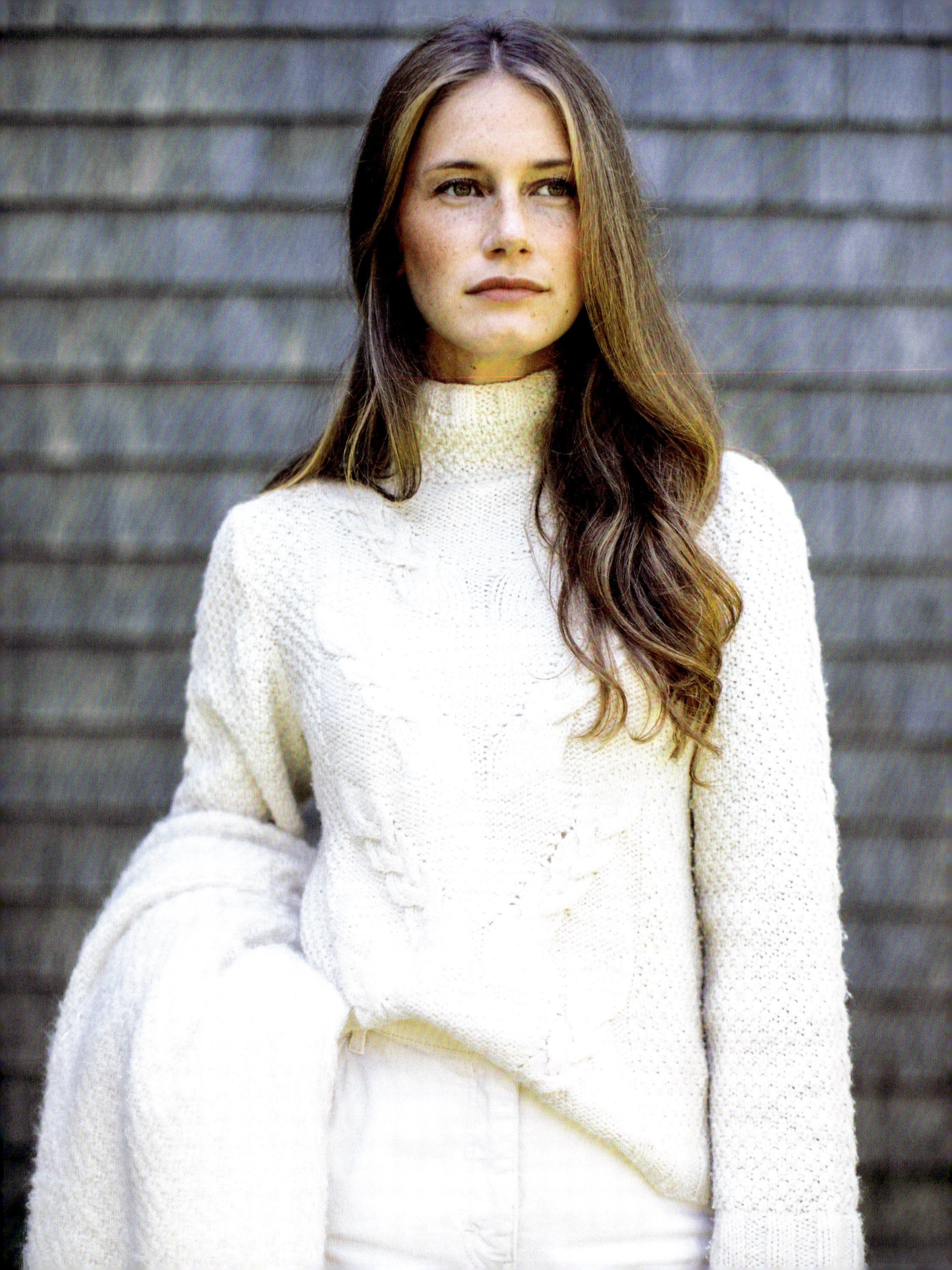

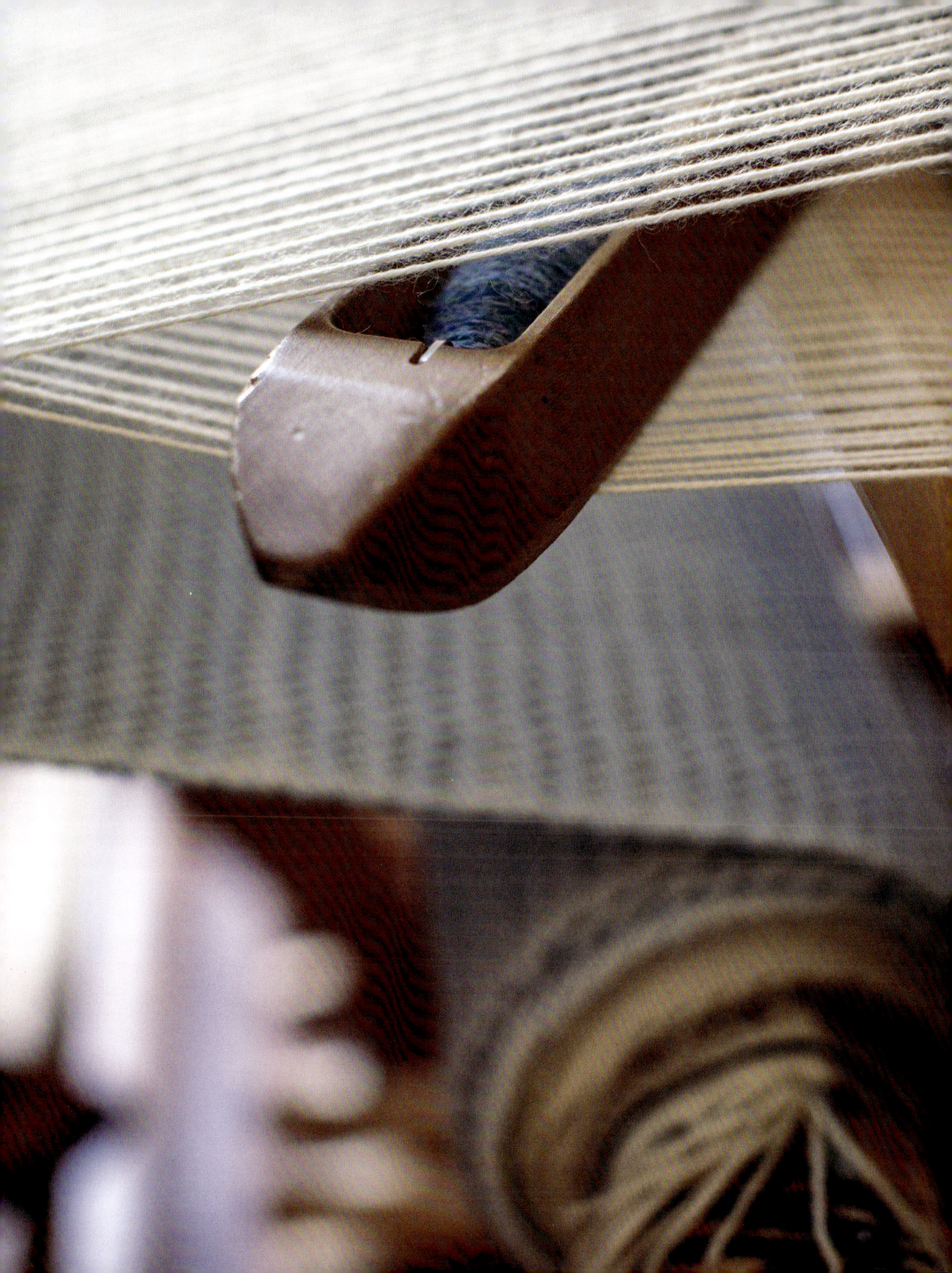

often pass down Nantucket basket purses with carved ivory pieces on top, and name plates inside the lid indicating the owner.

The time-tested staple of the island for men, the ubiquitous uniform of Nantucket Reds pants from Murray's Toggery Shop, white button-down shirt, navy blazer, Sperry top siders and needlepoint belt (often made from a pattern from Erica Wilson's needlepoint shop on Main Street) are still a favorite and flank the cobblestone streets of town. Lilly Pulitzer dresses, J. McLaughlin and CK Bradley clothing and accessories, Jack Rogers sandals, and pearls were once as common for women, but style is shifting with time, and those preppy bastions are now diluted by the addition of a more cosmopolitan look. The uber preppy are both celebrated and simultaneously poked fun at, and have garnered the character names of "Becky" and "Chad." Yet there is a sense of fun in the unabashed preppiness that's acceptable on Nantucket. Young men dig deep in the family coffers for loud pants, and Beth English's popular Current Vintage wine and clothing shop sells racks of vintage '60s and '70s Pulitzer, Missoni, and more in bold pastel prints. The immensely popular Hospital Thrift Shop presents an ideal spot to snag a classic island find. If ever there was a place to embrace your prep, even if tongue-in-cheek, it's Nantucket.

During the day, lifestyle informs fashion on the island. The beach plays a large role in what people wear, and activities like tennis, sailing, clamming, scalloping, and biking all play a part. Practical New England weather gear, and rain slickers remain essential for the wind and fog that can roll in at a moment's notice.

A classic Nantucket beach sight has always been old men in faded shirts and swim trunks, a completely weather-worn L.L.Bean bag, whose straps barely hold on. That is the surest sign of hearty New England stock. Now that the island is more easily accessible by ferry and plane, newer families come to the island, too, with less of an adherence to the classic New England prep look, and more and more the newest and latest trends make their way across the beach.

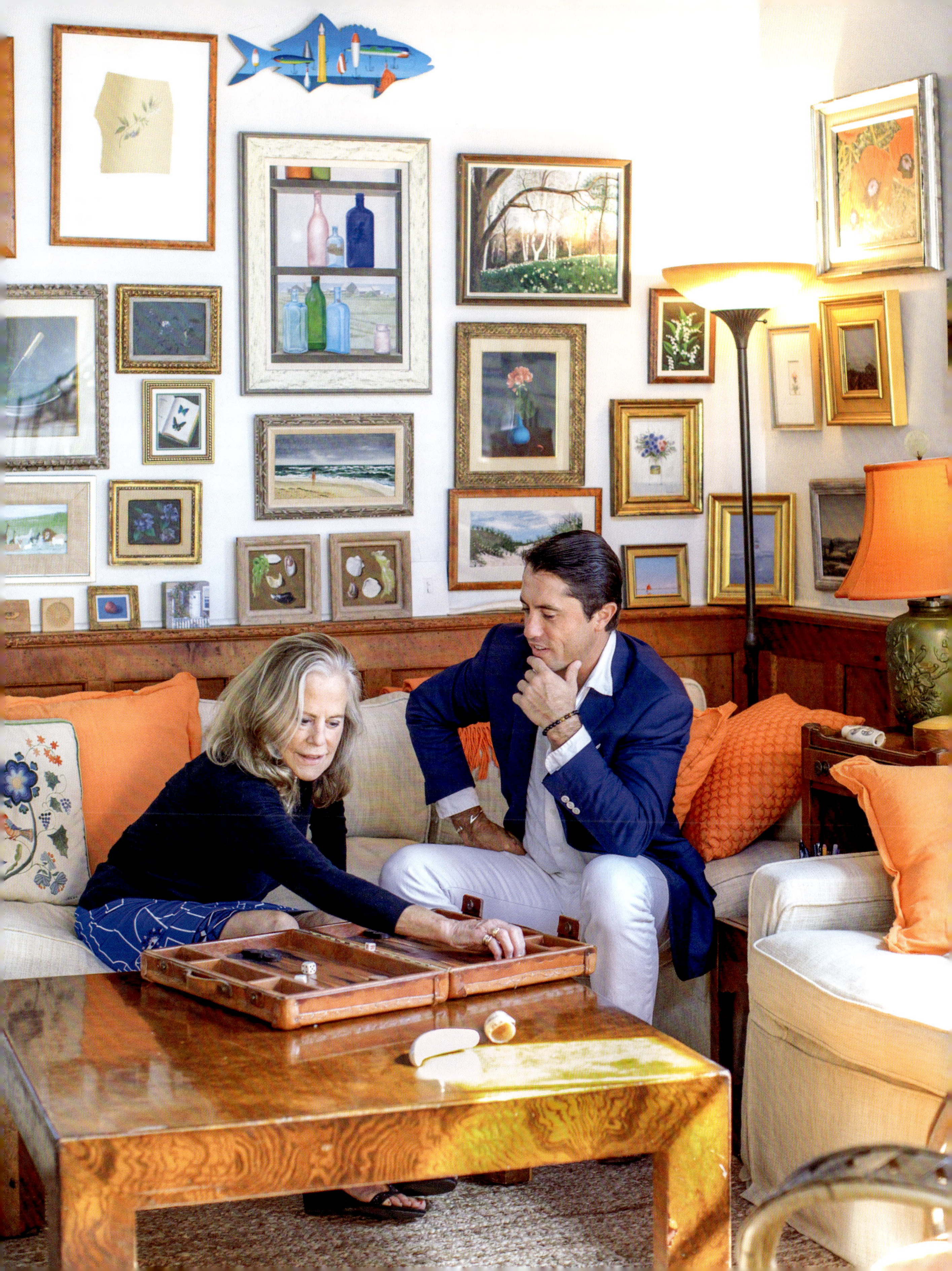

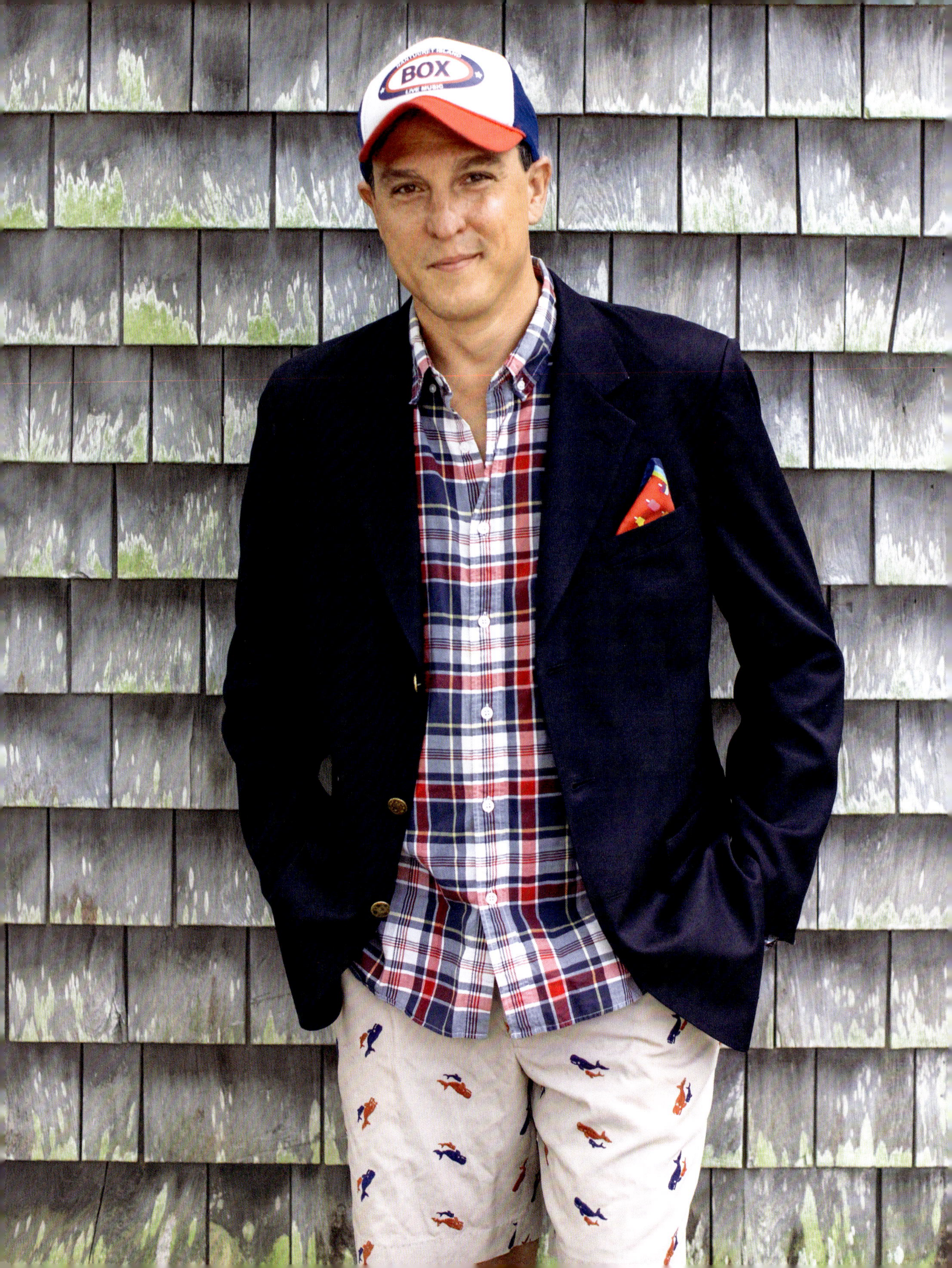
BOX

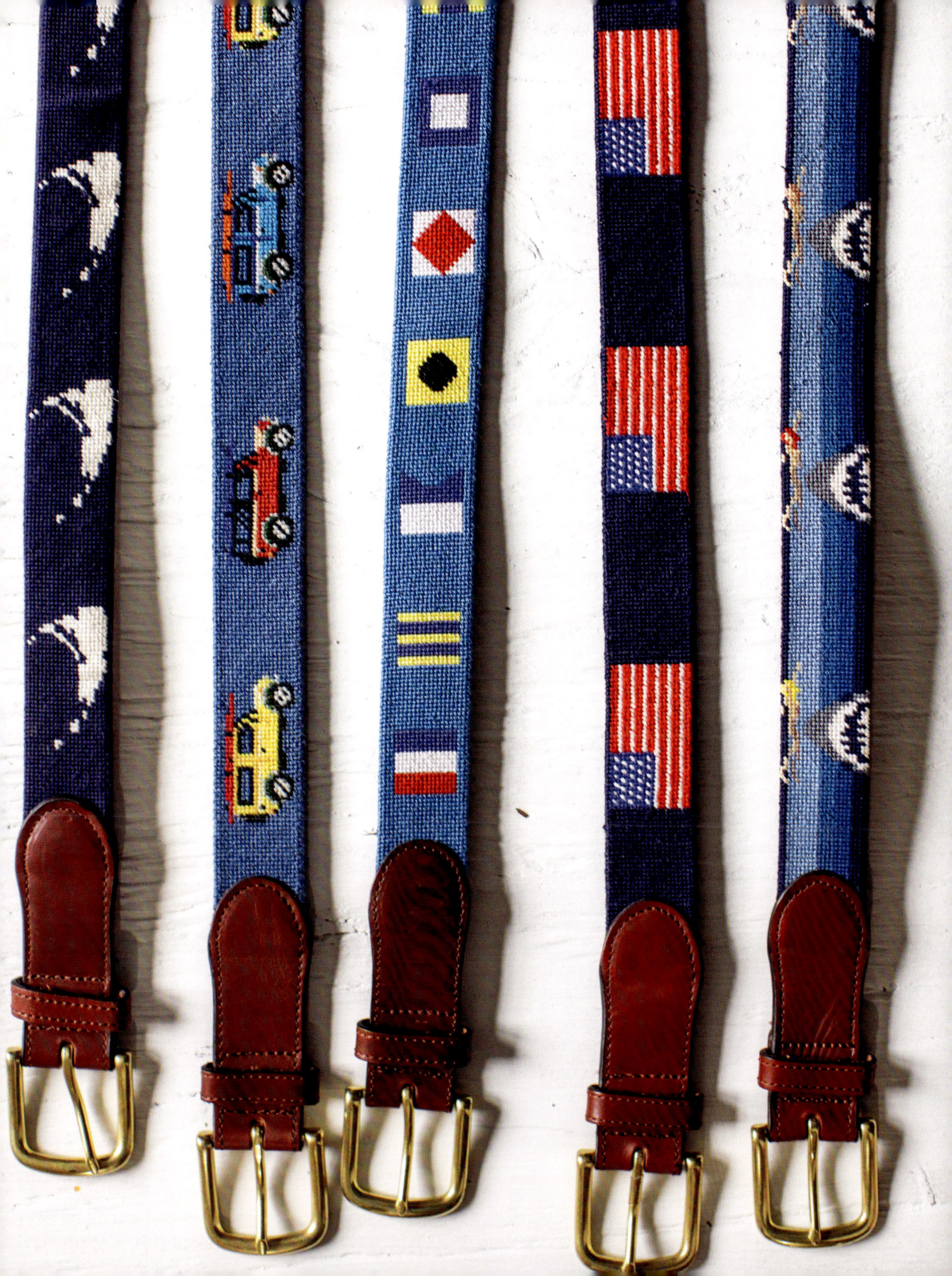

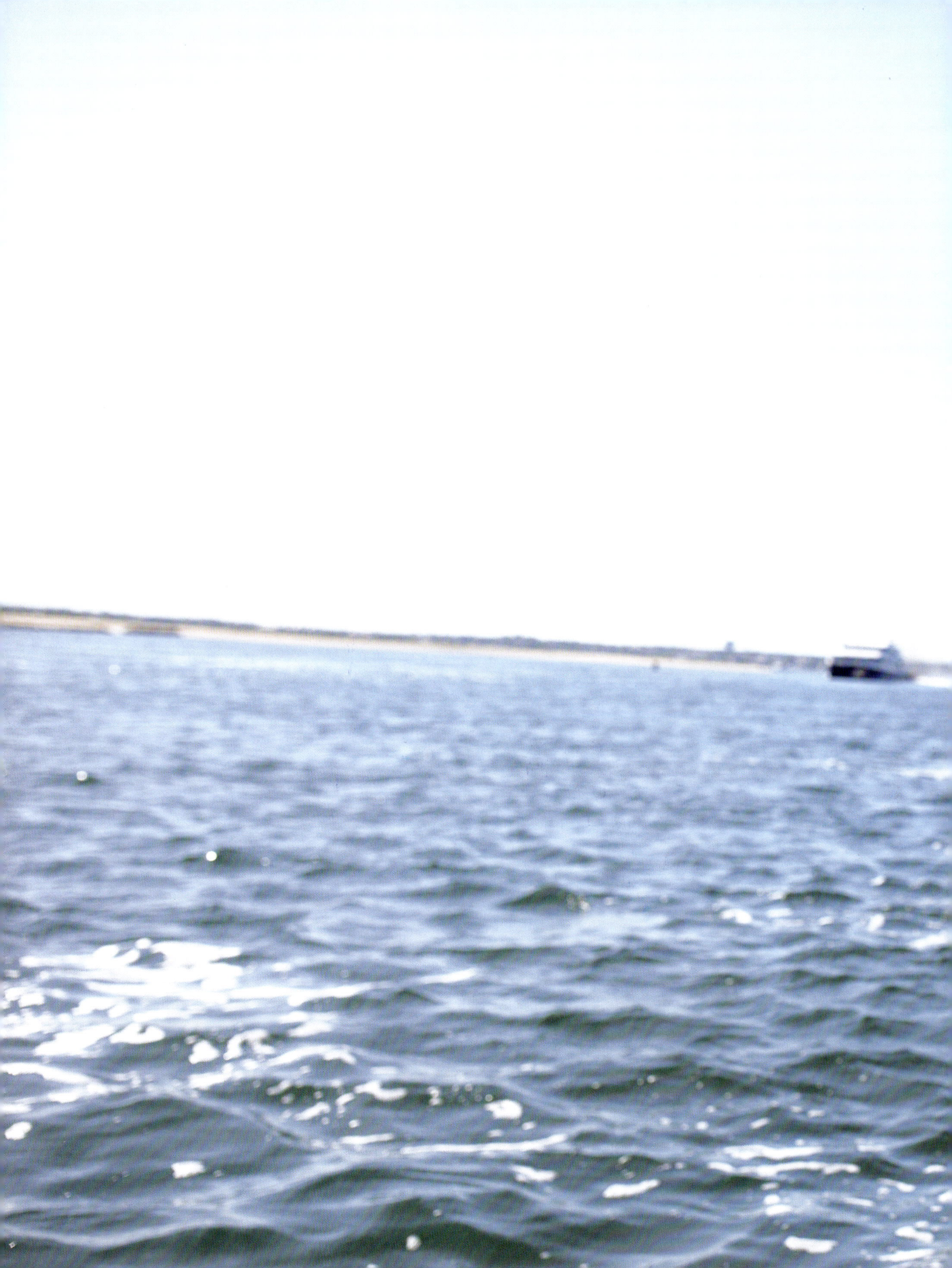

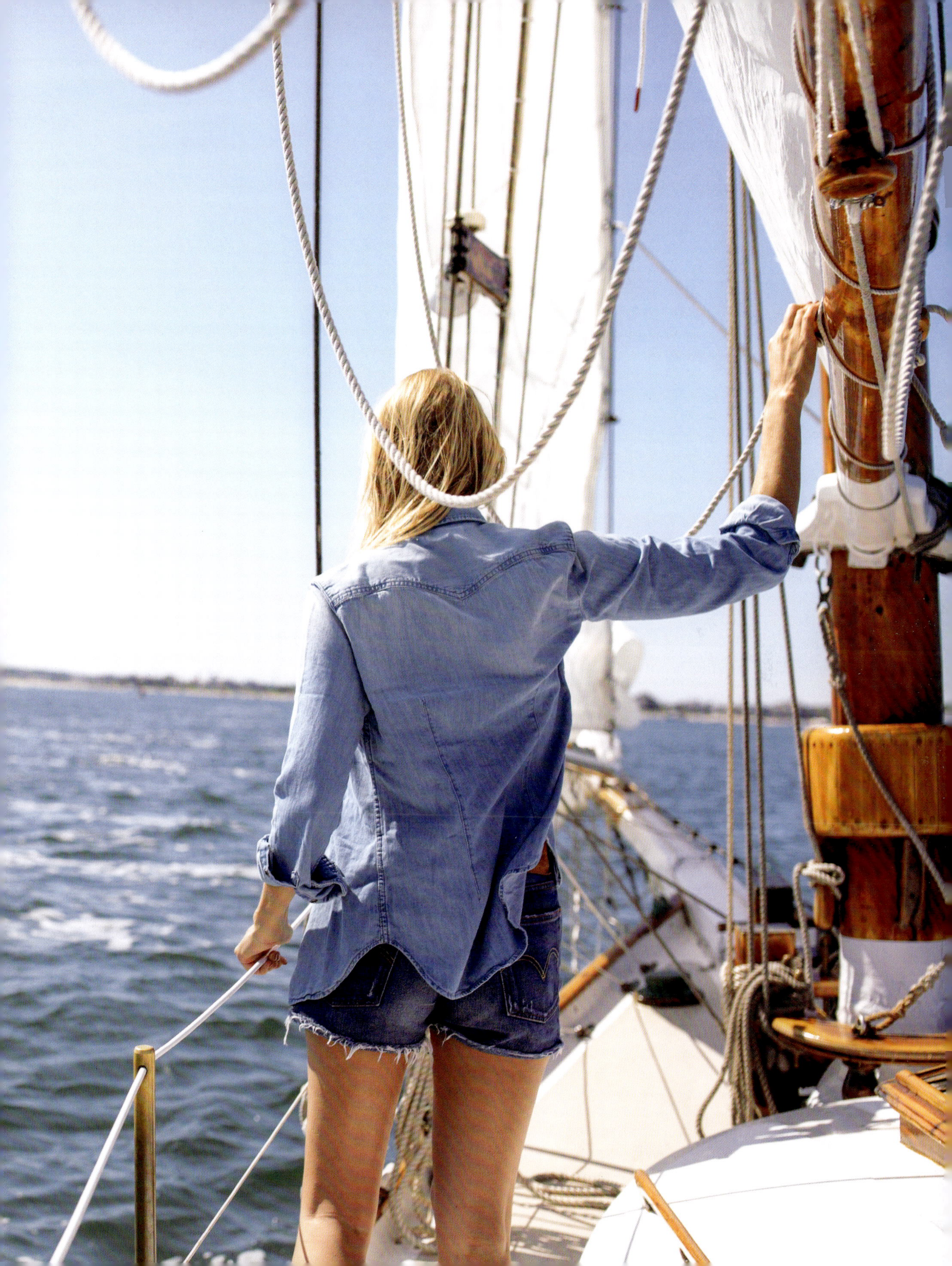

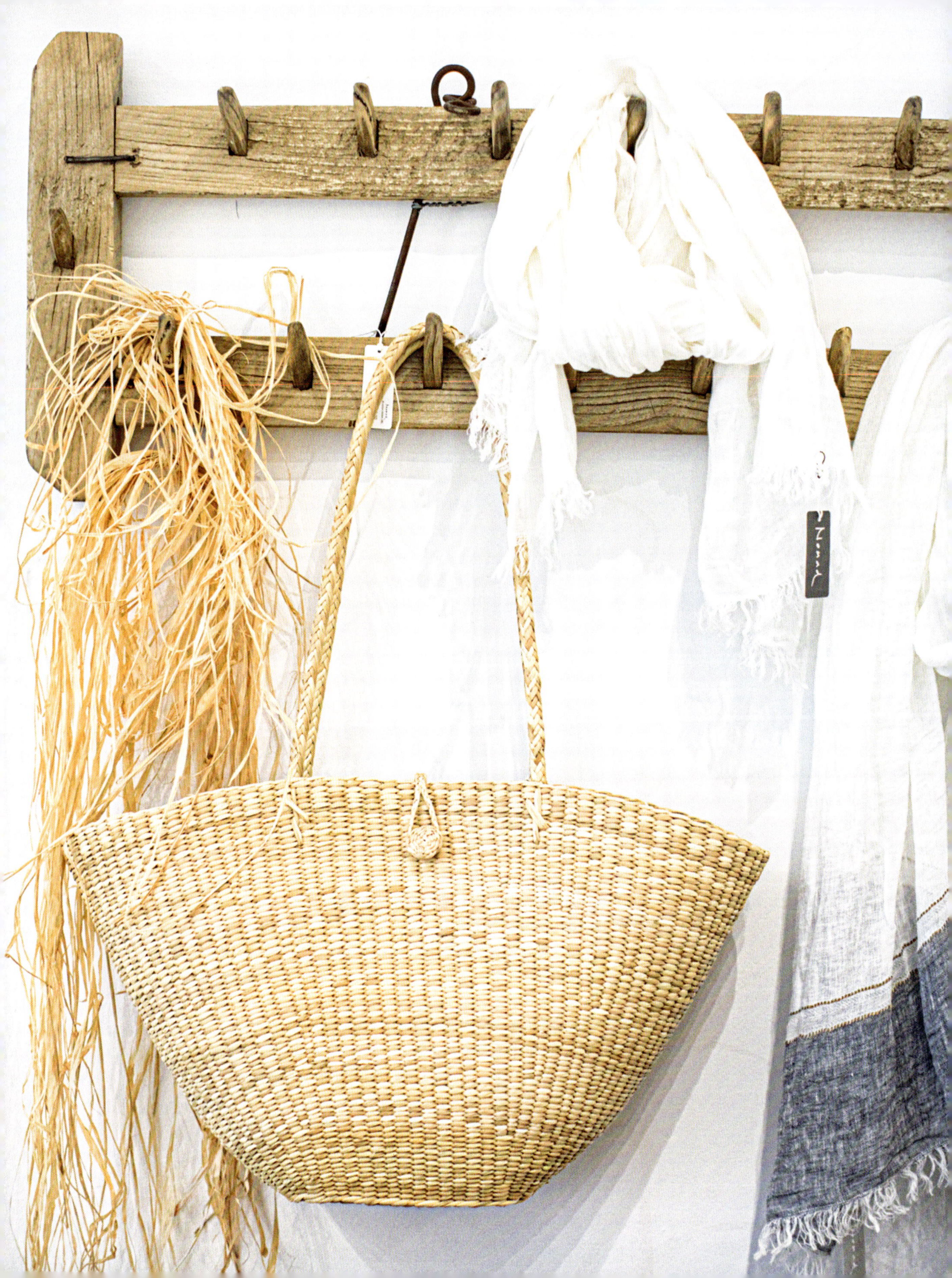

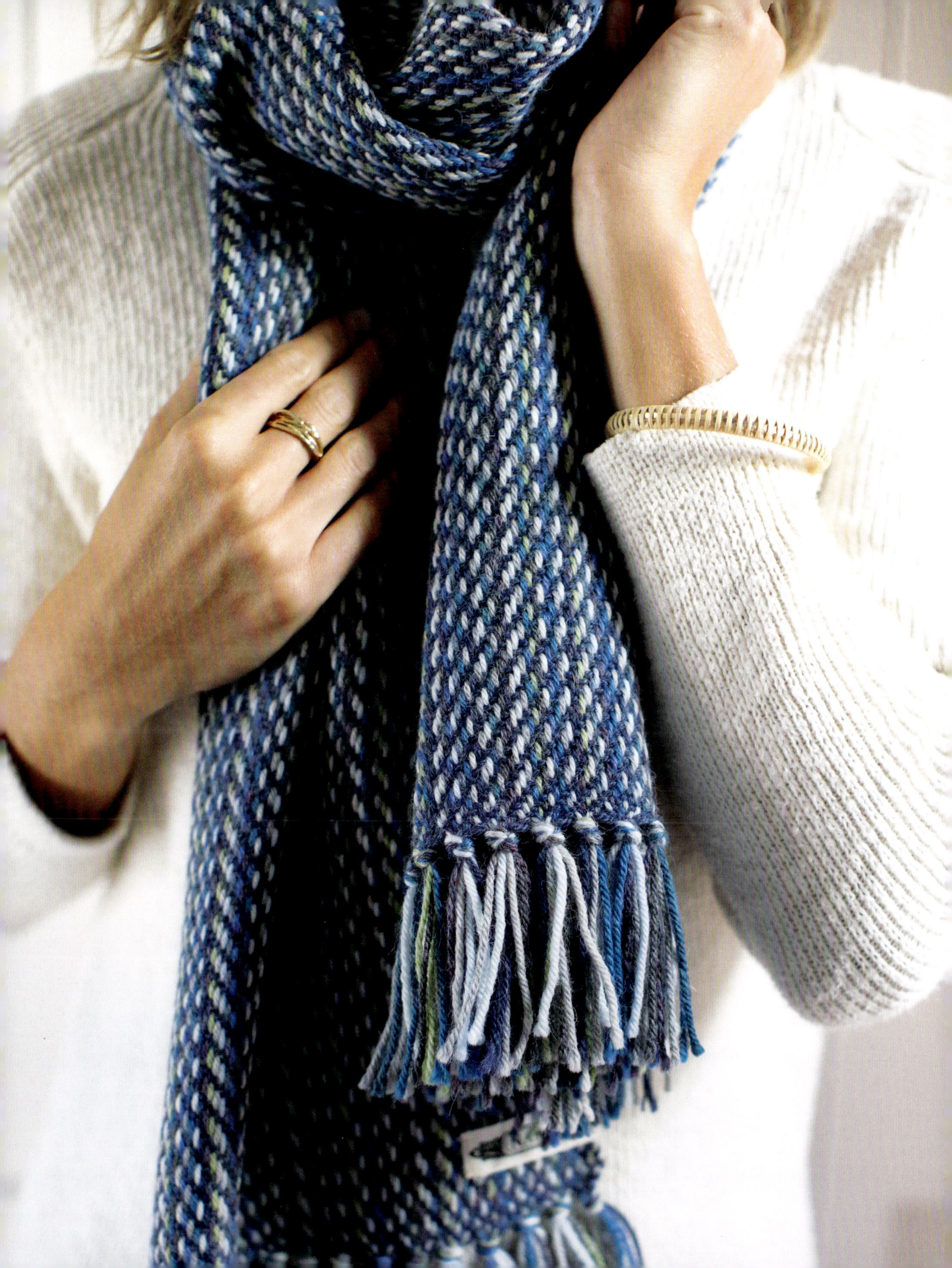

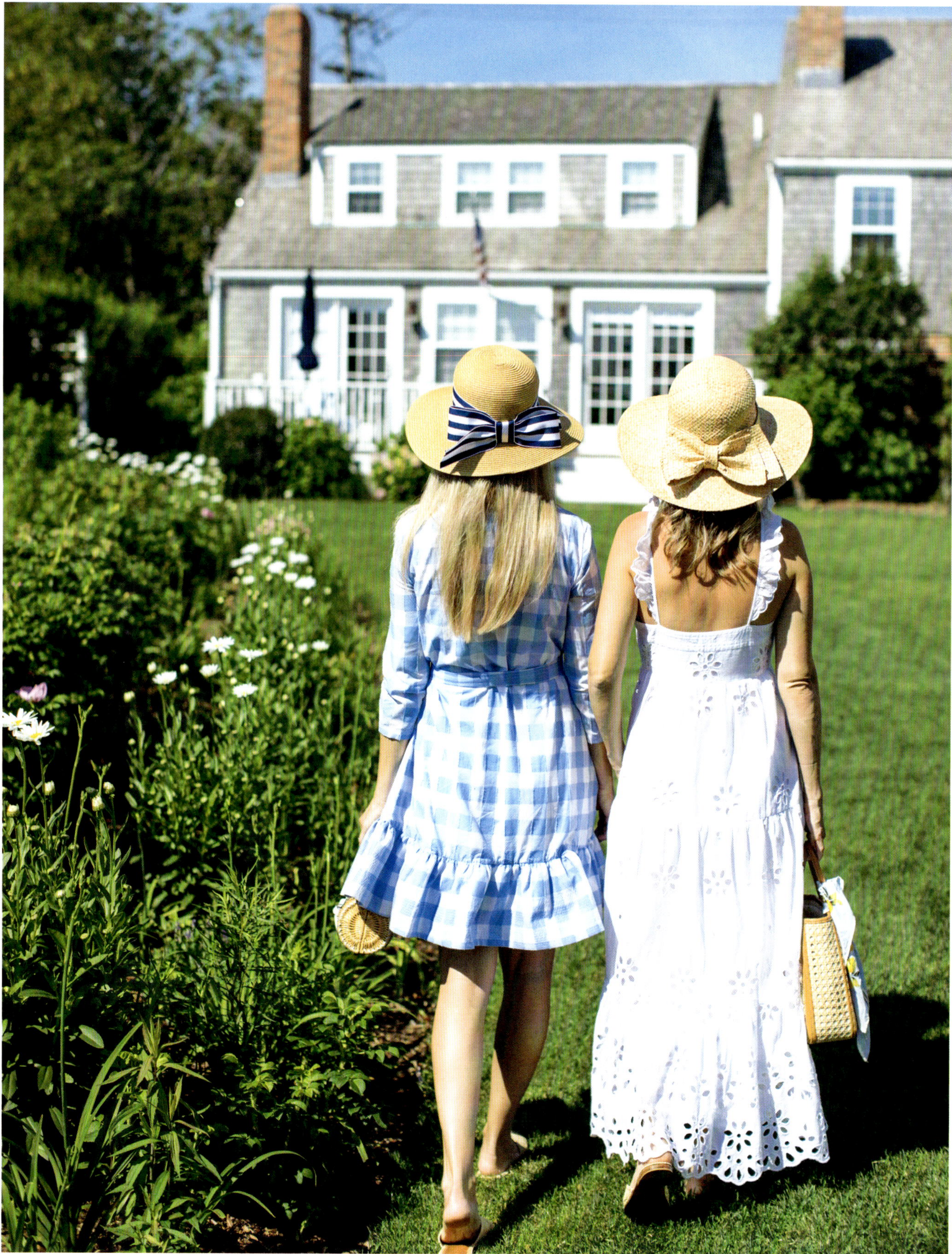

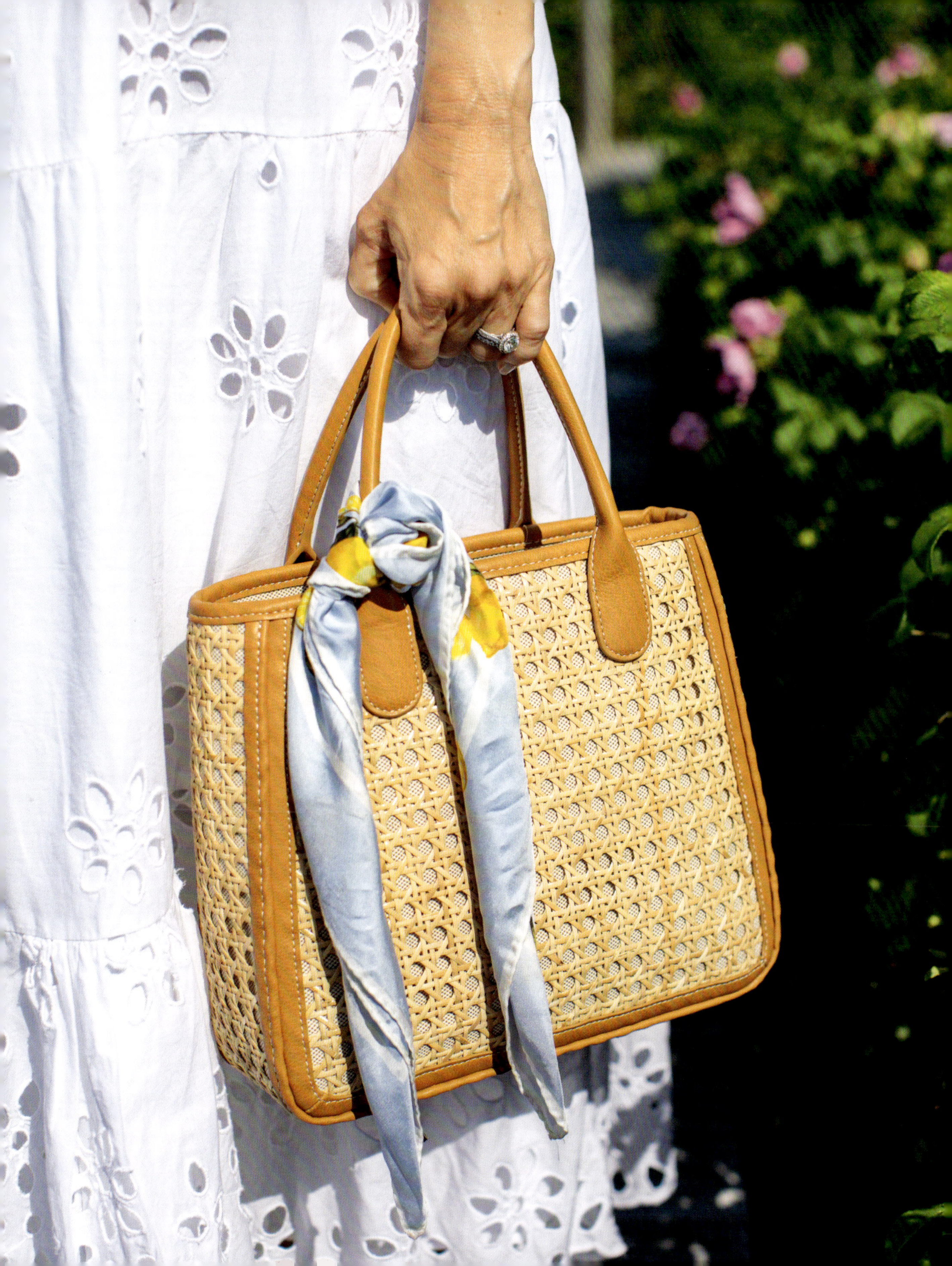

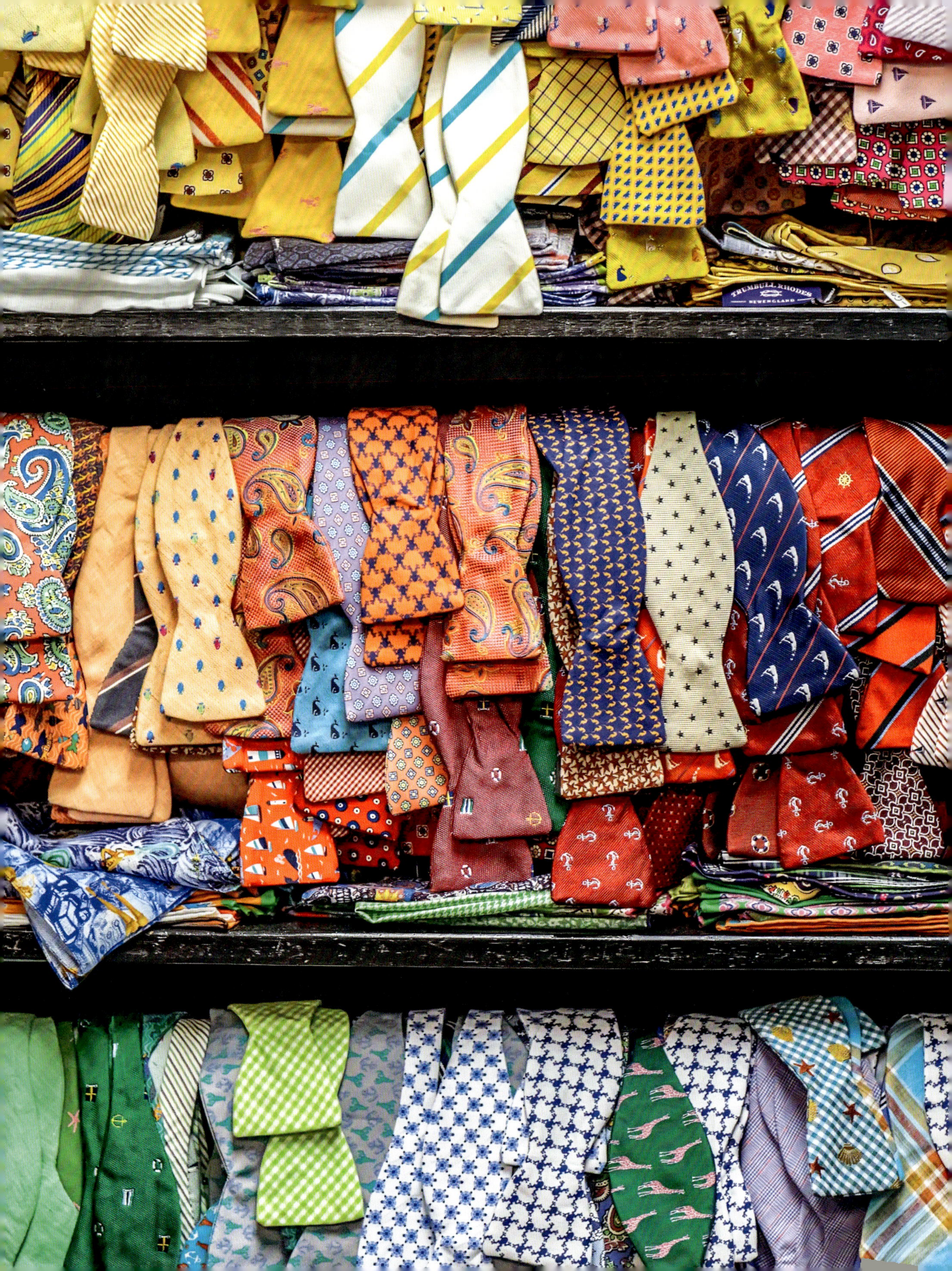
TRUMBULL RHODES
NEW ENGLAND

Nantucket Style has always been something of its own. "You have '60s, '70s, '80s preppy New England," John S. Johnson remembers, "but way before that you have the Quakers who have this simplicity that can veer into the austere and then in those whaling days from what I understand it was so cosmopolitan. Melville captures this in **Moby-Dick**. You had people from the South Seas walking around in whatever they packed, or maybe a mishmash."

Yet there is one sure sign of a tourist: women in ambitious heels. Every Nantucket regular knows that Nantucket cobblestone and heels don't mix. Islanders opt for flat sandals or summer wedges, which also happen to be superior for tented charity events held outdoors.

"Classic Nantucket is a cottage where you opened up the front door and swept out the back door. Beautiful old houses with window boxes that were askew. About embracing the imperfection."

—**Liz Winship, Nantucket Looms owner 1993–2013**

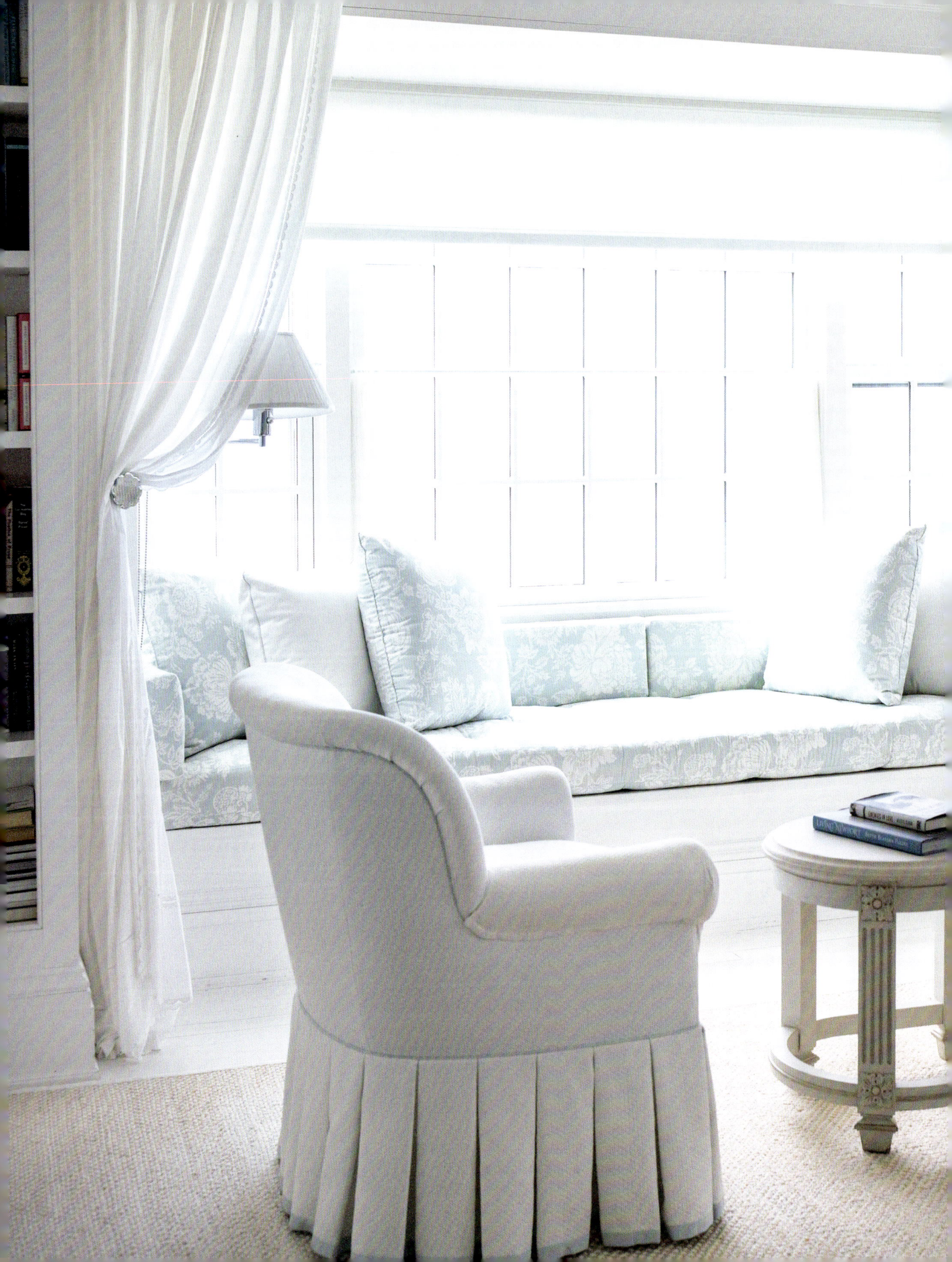

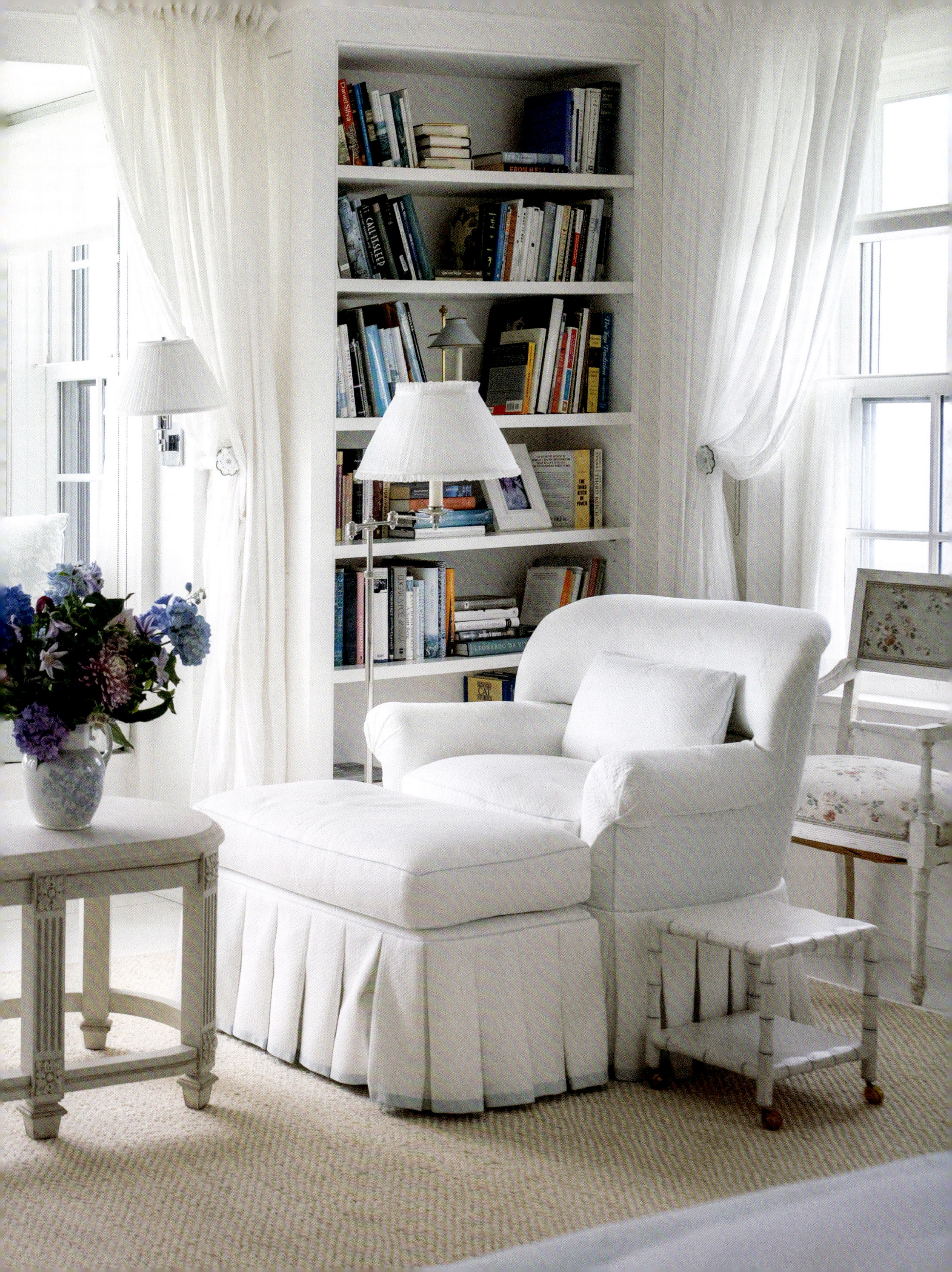
Daniel Silva
FROM HELL
CALL IT SLEEP
THE FIRST WORD
The Yoga Tradition
THE THIRD REICH IN POWER
THIRD REICH
LEONARDO DA VI
CAT STORIES

Liz Winship,

Nantucket Looms owner 1993–2013

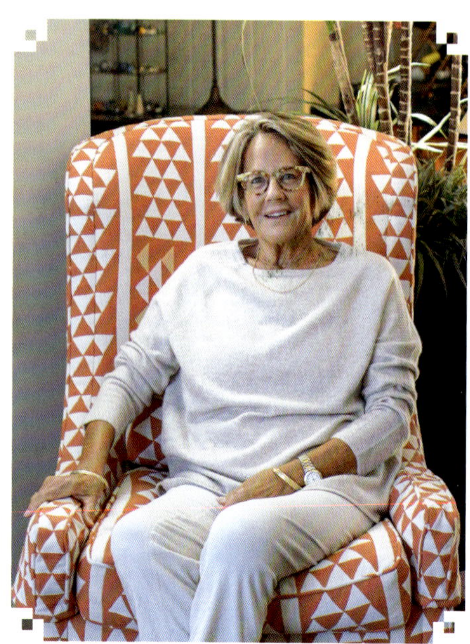

YEARS ON NANTUCKET: *Fifty*

ISLAND HOME: *Our 3-acre compound by the south shore with my husband, two daughters, and their families. We call it "The Ponderosa." We have a pond, sheep, ducks, and chickens.*

MODE OF TRANSPORT: *A little Fiat.*

FAVORITE BEACH: *"Fat Ladies" beach on the south shore.*

SUMMER UNIFORM: *A good old classic: A crisp, blue-striped linen or cotton shirt and a pair of white pants and a Susan Lister Locke signet ring she gave me for my fiftieth [birthday] with [Nantucket Looms founder] Bill Euler's crest on it.*

GREATEST EXTRAVAGANCE: *To have the Ponderosa and to have my family here with the pool and the acreage.*

NANTUCKET STYLE IS ... *eclectic, although there's a code.*

FAVORITE THING/SPOT ON NANTUCKET: *I love to go out to Great Point and picnic with friends, especially in the off-season.*

COMMON MISCONCEPTION ABOUT NANTUCKET: *That it's just for summer folks. It really isn't just a wealthy man's playground. People do really live and go to work and school here. We have a pretty special year-round community, too. There's an amazing support system here. This is a very, very philanthropic island.*

NECESSITY ON NANTUCKET: *Friends. I think that's how you're able to make it on an island.*

IDEAL DAY: *When I was working it was a Sunday when we'd get up early, meet friends, and spend the whole day at the beach in the summer. Give me the ocean and that sky. It just revives me. Now, it's to read by the pool.*

MY ISLAND SOCIAL LIFE REVOLVES AROUND ... *It used to revolve a lot around my work. I used to joke that [being at the store] was like being at a cocktail party without a cocktail. Now, I volunteer, I give my time to the Hospital Thrift Shop and I'm on the board of the hospital.*

_ IS SO NANTUCKET: *Nantucket Looms chaise throws. It's been our signature for more than fifty years.*

BEST PART OF ISLAND LIFE: *That it's not accessible. You have to want to be here. If you want fast food and fast lifestyle that's not Nantucket.*

THREE WORDS THAT DESCRIBE YOUR ISLAND LIFE: *Peace, love, happiness.*

NOTABLE CELEBRITY RUN-IN: *The first week I worked at Looms I met Princess Grace and Prince Rainier of Monaco. It was 1974. I remember she had on a Nantucket sweatshirt and a turban.*

ISLAND ARTISTS WORTH KNOWING: *There are so many amazing artisans. Painter Joanna Kane, I'm a real patron of her work. Paul LaPaglia, his was the first painting I ever bought at Looms when I was twenty-six years old. Painter David Lazarus and painter Robert Stark III and jewelry maker Susan Lister Locke. All still great artisans on this island. Rebecca Peraner, the master weaver at the Looms, she's just incredible. Karol Lindquist is the best lightship basket maker on the island. Susan Boardman does incredible needlepoint narratives. Mark Sutherland restores figureheads for boats and makes amazing boat models.*

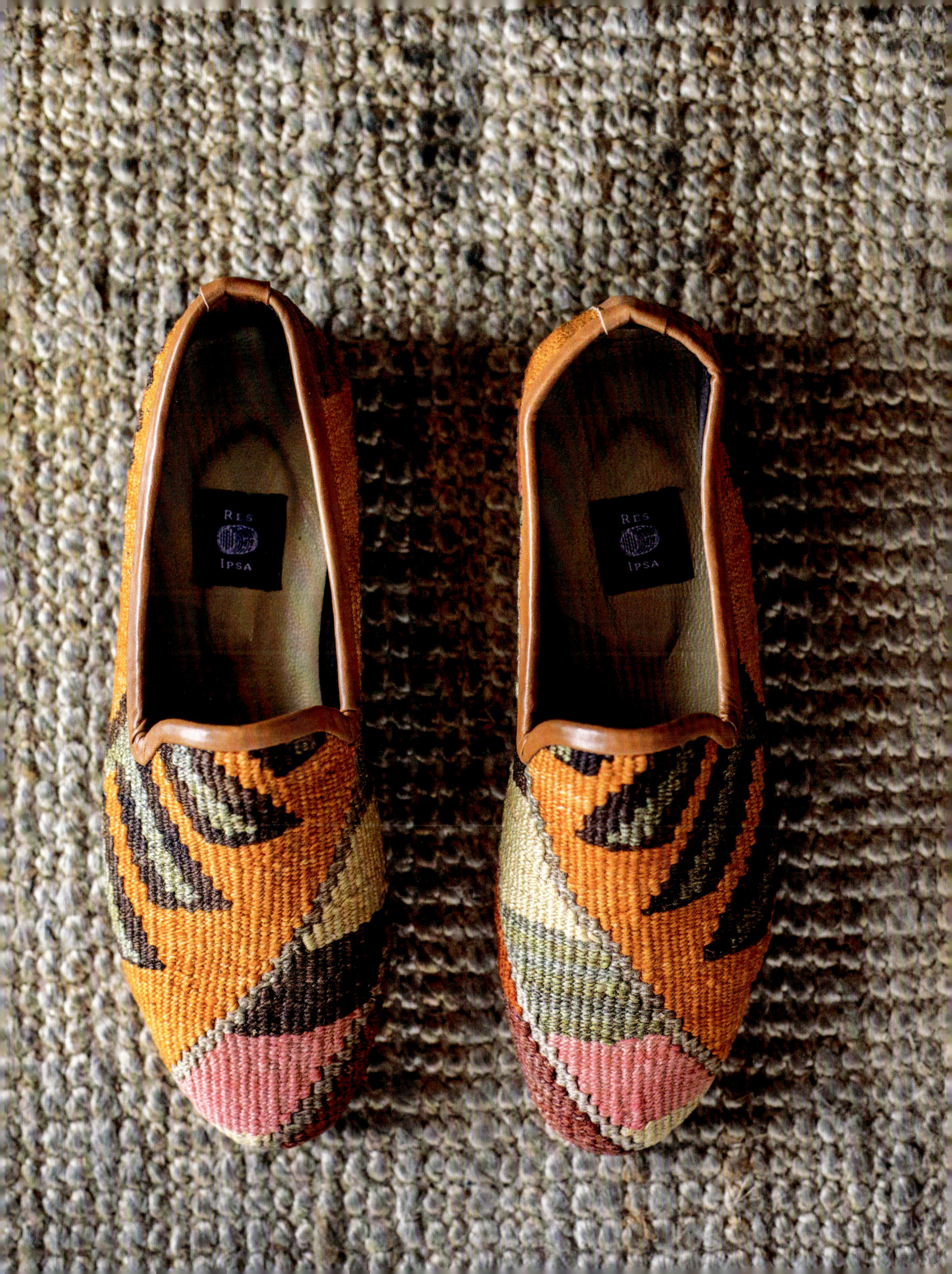
Res Ipsa
Res Ipsa

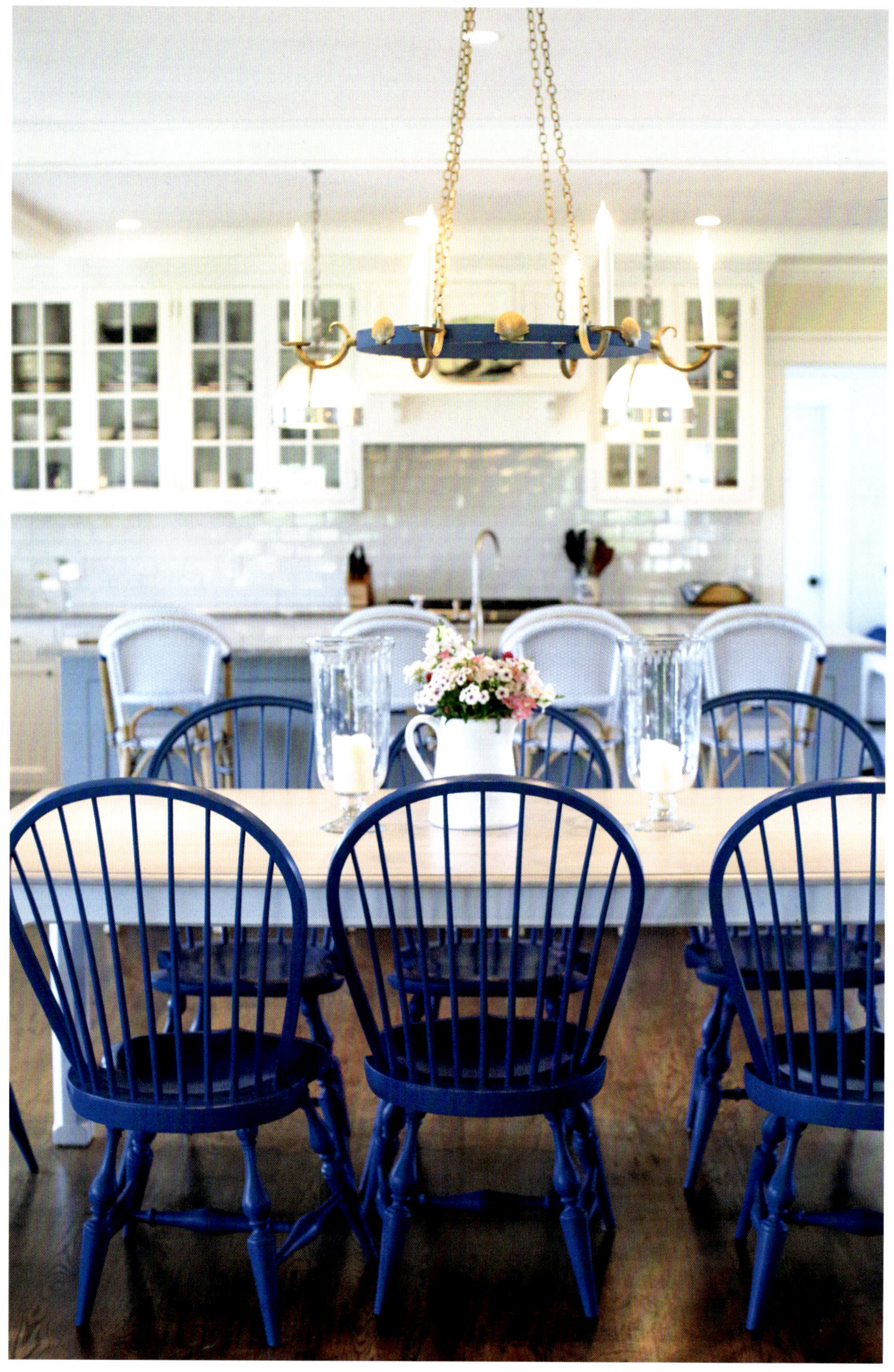

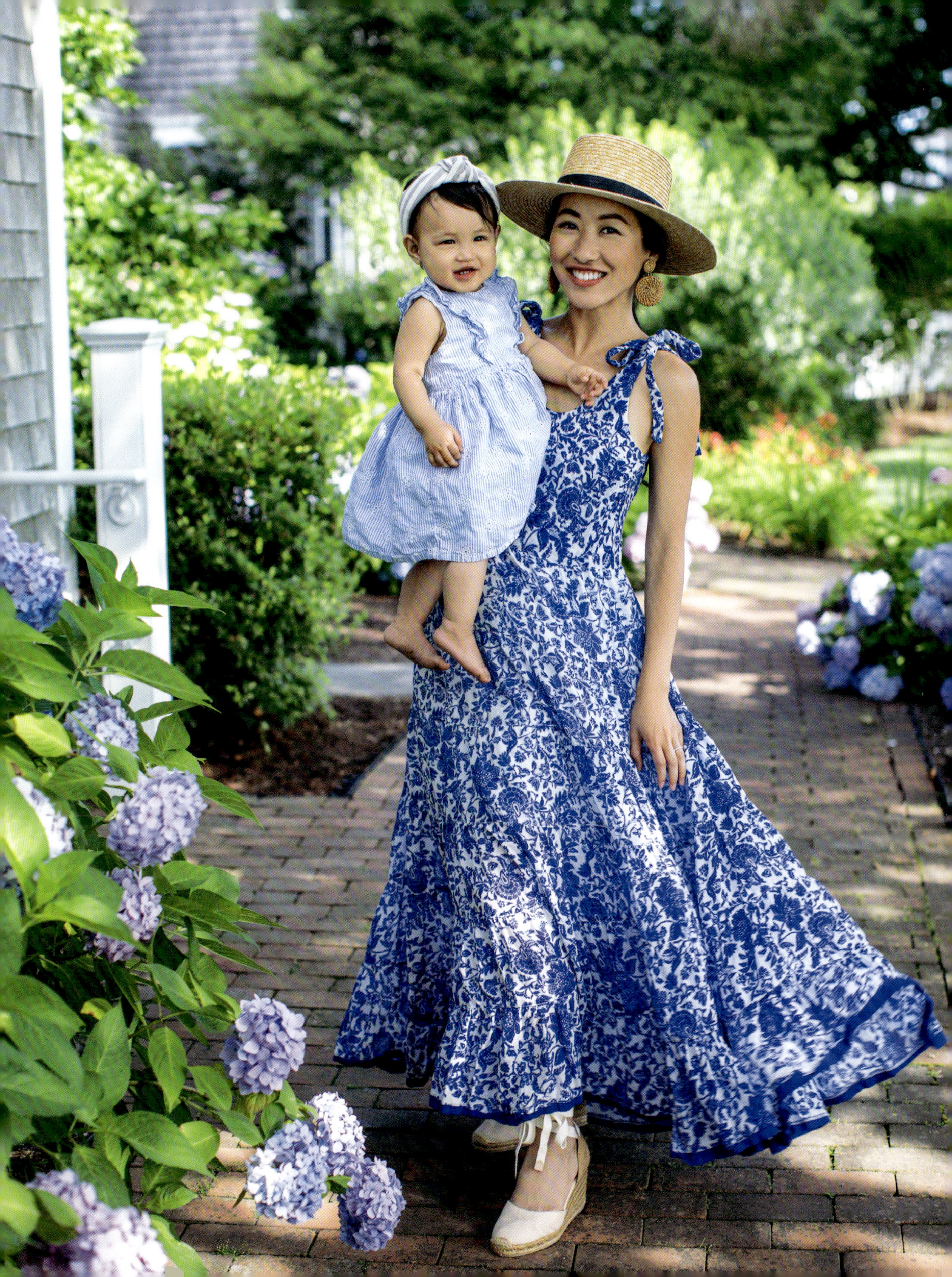

Jocelyn M. Gailliot,

founder and CEO of Tuckernuck retailer

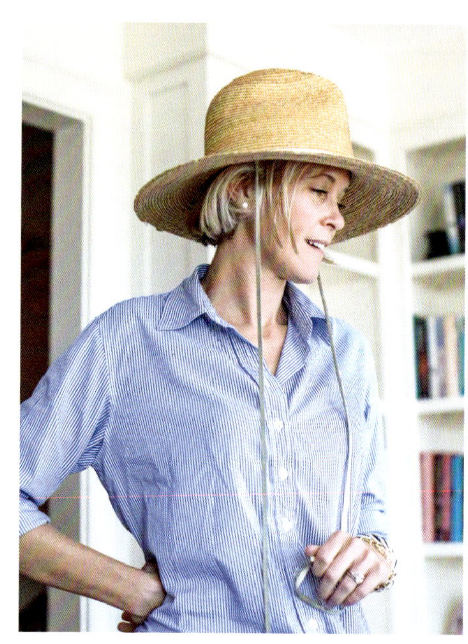

YEARS ON NANTUCKET: *Thirty-eight years (every year since I was four weeks old).*

ISLAND HOME: *Cliff Road and 'Sconset*

MODE OF TRANSPORT: *Slow ferry (preferably the Eagle)*

FOUR WORDS THAT DESCRIBE YOUR ISLAND LIFE: *Adventurous, sporty, carefree, inspired.*

FAVORITE BEACH: *Fisherman's and Water Tower.*

SUMMER UNIFORM: *Either tennis whites; cutoffs, stripes and Tretorns; or a sundress.*

_ IS BETTER ON NANTUCKET: *Sunsets*

GREATEST EXTRAVAGANCE: *Antique Nantucket basket from my dad and a Nantucket charm bracelet he's been building since I was a little girl.*

DEFINE NANTUCKET STYLE: *Chic and with purpose.*

MOST DAYS ON NANTUCKET I … *play some tennis, visit a beach, work on a puzzle, take a bike ride with the kids, or an alfresco dinner at home with my family that usually includes something locally caught or picked.*

CLASSIC NANTUCKET IS … *Murray's Toggery and The Sunken Ship (From Nantucket Reds to waders and knot bracelets, those shops cover it all).*

FAVORITE THING/SPOT ON NANTUCKET? *Sunset beach bonfires with family and friends at Eel Point.*

COMMON MISCONCEPTION ABOUT NANTUCKET? *That it's fancy.*

NANTUCKET HISTORY THAT SPEAKS TO YOU: *From the great fire to the countless shipwrecks off the shoals, to Herman Melville, Nantucket is rich in important history. I often wander the cobblestone streets and back roads imagining the bustling energy from the eighteenth and nineteenth centuries. It's through the beautiful architecture that you can feel and see the soul of the island's rich history.*

NECESSITY ON NANTUCKET: *Be up for anything, and a sunhat.*

IDEAL DAY: *A friendly tennis match in the morning, a stroll into town, a boat ride to Coatue for clamming and a beach picnic with the kids, pitstop for fresh corn at Moors End Farm, and then home in time for a big sunset barbecue on our deck, followed by a rousing game of cards or charades.*

MOST TREASURED EXPERIENCE ON-ISLAND: *Learning how to ride a bike, seeing my first shooting star, getting married, bodysurfing with my brothers, off-roading at Great Point with my dad (can't do that anymore), my first turkey plunge, teaching my kids to ride a bike, my kids' baptisms in 'Sconset, movies at the old Dreamland, beach bonfires, Something Natural bread, late-night sing-alongs with the piano man at the Club Car and Summer House, scalloping, throwing pennies from the ferry, special time with my family and friends—there are too many to count.*

LOCAL SECRET: *Movies at the Casino; Black and White frappé from The Pharmacy; fresh produce from Moors End Farm.*

ON NANTUCKET YOU NEVER … *wear high heels unless it's a comfortable wedge.*

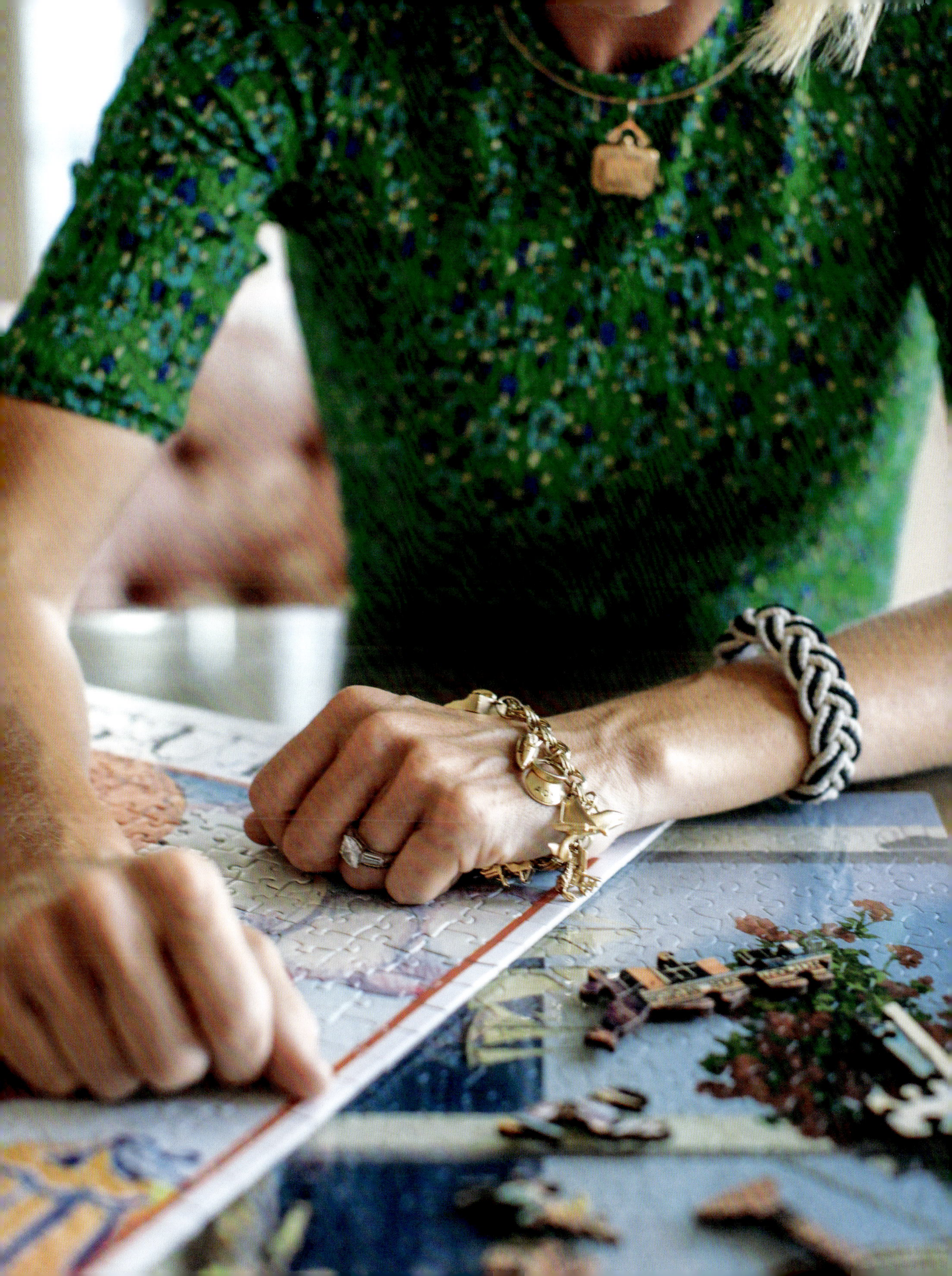

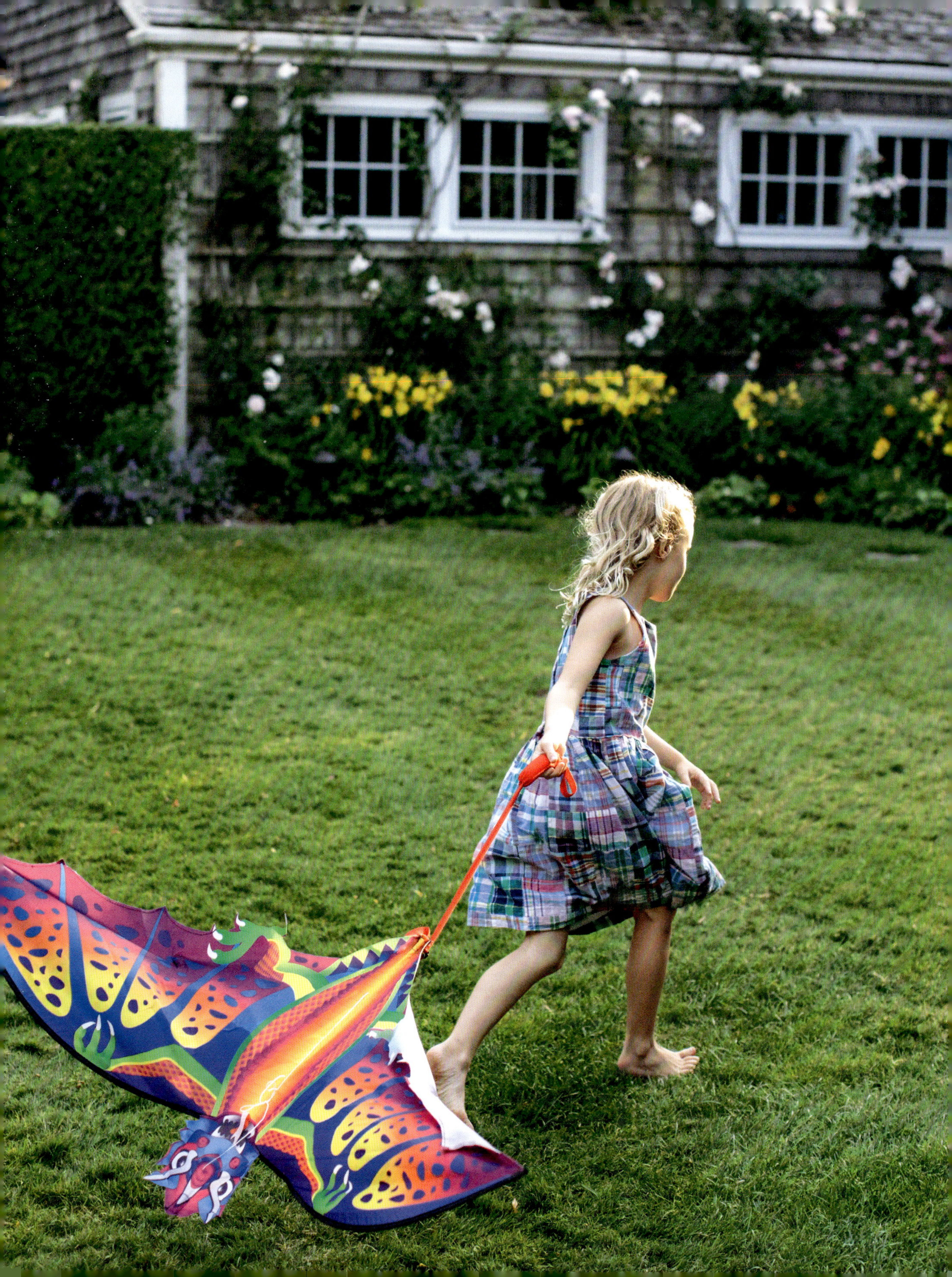

SUMMER LOVE

Nostalgia runs high for the summers of one's youth, but on Nantucket it can hit a fever pitch. Maybe it's natural for a place with such strong multi-generational ties to summer life on its shores, so far from "real life" back home. A place that embodies the sweet freedom of youth, its summer romances and beach bonfires, screen doors, sandy floors, strawberry picking, and Fourth of Julys. Here we are on this idyllic little island guarded by 30 miles of sea.

And for much of Nantucket's history that created a real barrier for contact with the outside world. It's still not easy to hold on to a good internet connection, but island summers today offer a fraction of the disconnection they used to supply—or journey they used to require. Earning that island summer is quite a bit easier, but just as sweet.

It wasn't always the island that attracted visitors, sometimes they were simply looking to get away. Far away. One longtime summer resident says his mother ferried them to Nantucket for fear of polio that was said to spread in the hot city summers. "She was running away from

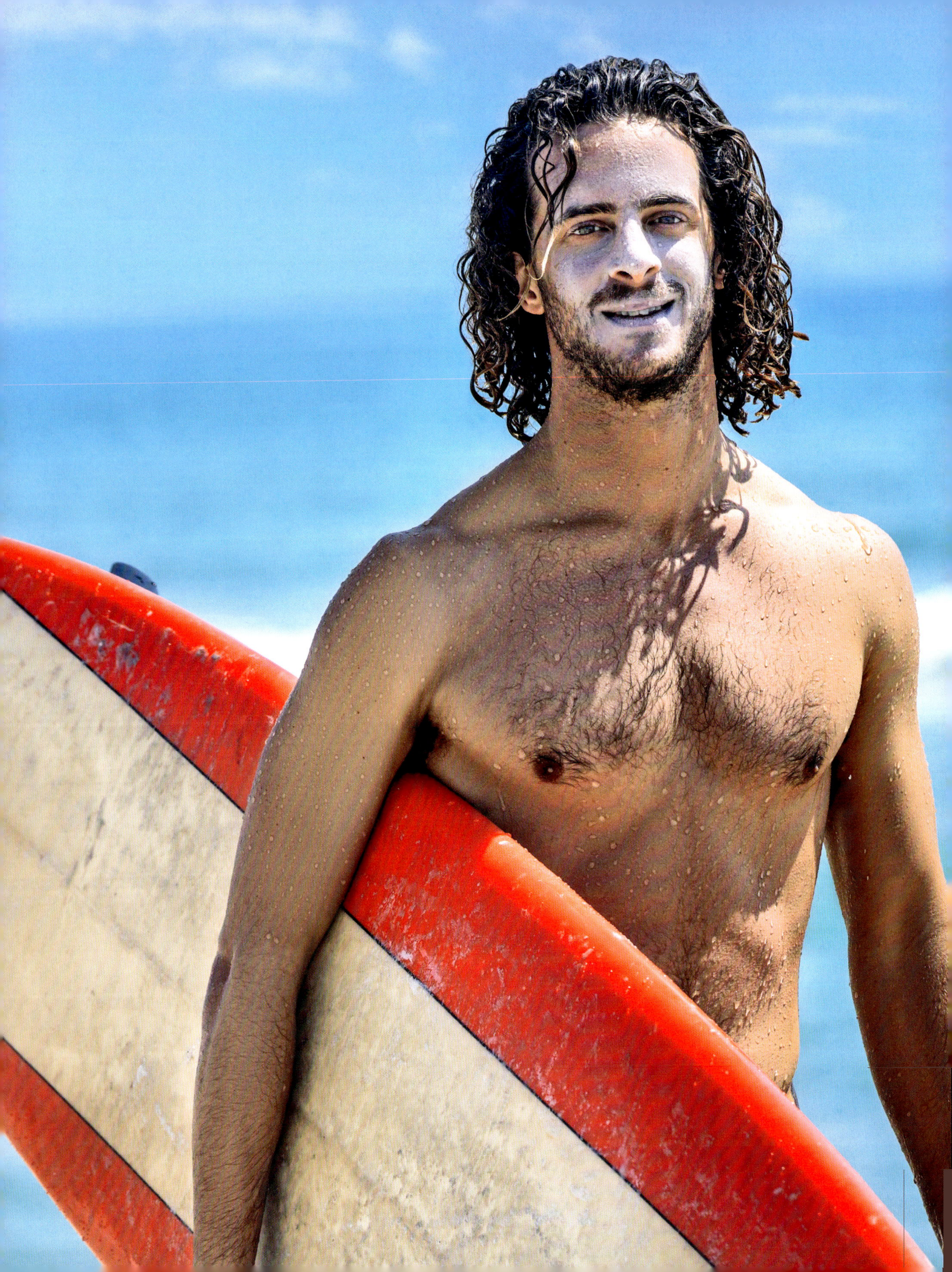

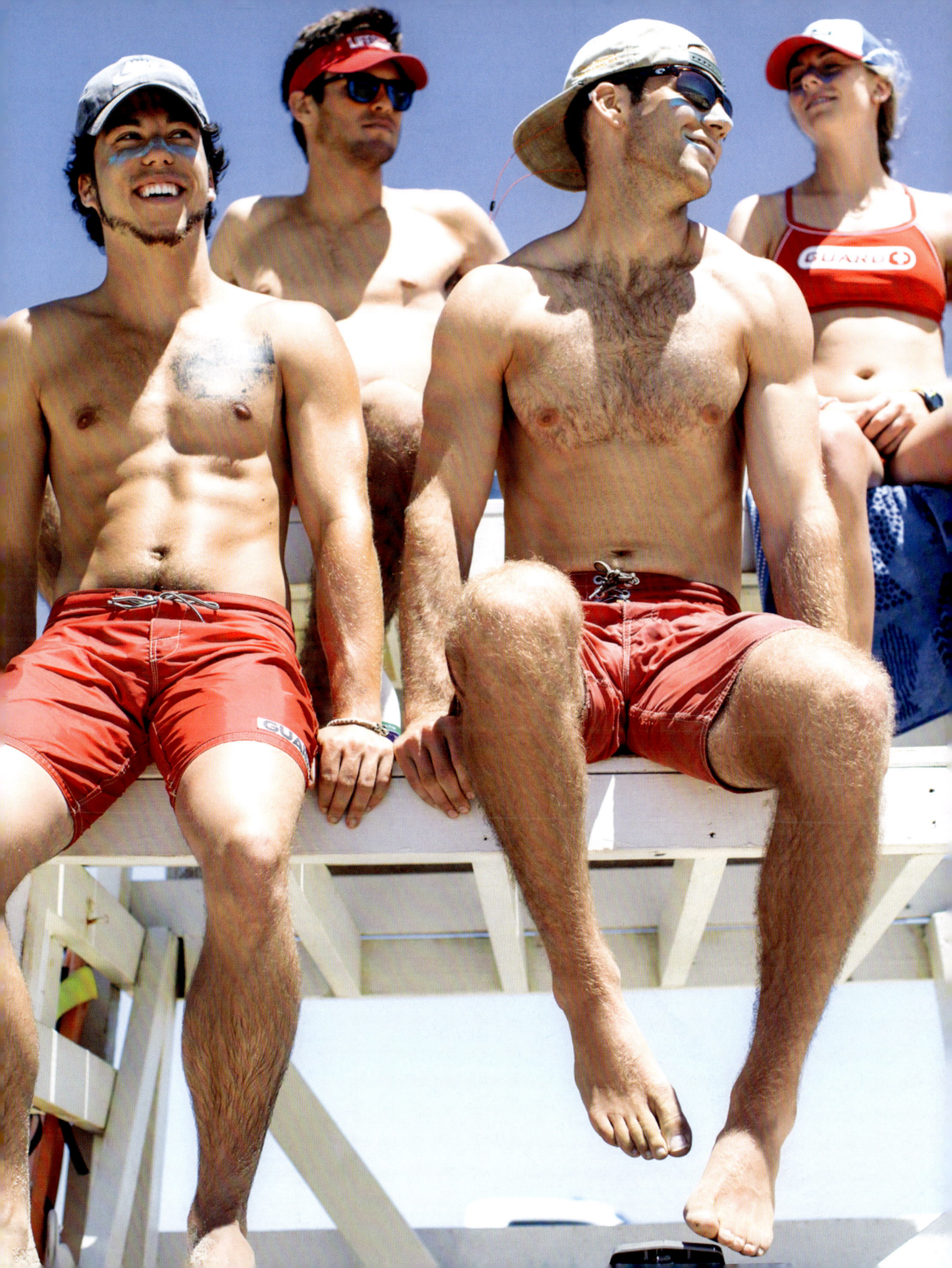
GUARD

something rather than running to something," he says. More than one resident mentioned parents or grandparents who staked a claim for the family on anonymous summers on Nantucket after losing money.

Prior to the 1980s tourism boom, and the advent of the fast ferry in 1995, which cut the trip from Cape Cod to Nantucket to an hour, an arduous journey was required to arrive.

"It took them a week, I think, to get there," islander Edward Sanford says recounting the journey his grandfather and family would take to arrive from Knoxville in the 1920s. "They would drive to New York, take an overnight steamer [for] eight hours to New Bedford, Massachusetts, then take another ferry four hours from New Bedford to Nantucket. And, of course, they'd be bringing their whole house staff; their nannies, the cooks. They would only use their White Lily flour that was made in Knoxville, Tennessee, so they would bring their 50-pound bags. I'm sure it was quite the caravan." And naturally, they would stay for the whole summer.

Lifelong summer resident Lissy Bryan remembers when a new ferry was introduced in the '60s that couldn't steer properly at a slow speed. "So when the fog rolled in it would be anchored out off the jetties waiting for the fog to move. There were lots of stories of people waiting six, seven, eight hours out on the boat for the fog to move."

Yet the journey is part of the draw, adding to the feeling of detachment from real life. "They don't call it the faraway island for nothing," says Bryan. "You almost feel like you've achieved something when you get here."

Patricia Anathan remembers when **The Inquirer** and **Mirror** newspaper would announce when families' arrived on-island for the summer. A time of barefoot bike rides, whiling away the hours as a child in the 1950s and '60s, wandering the island, sailing, sneaking off for cigarettes, or going to the beach. And though much more is happening on the island today, for a great many there can still be, blissfully, very little.

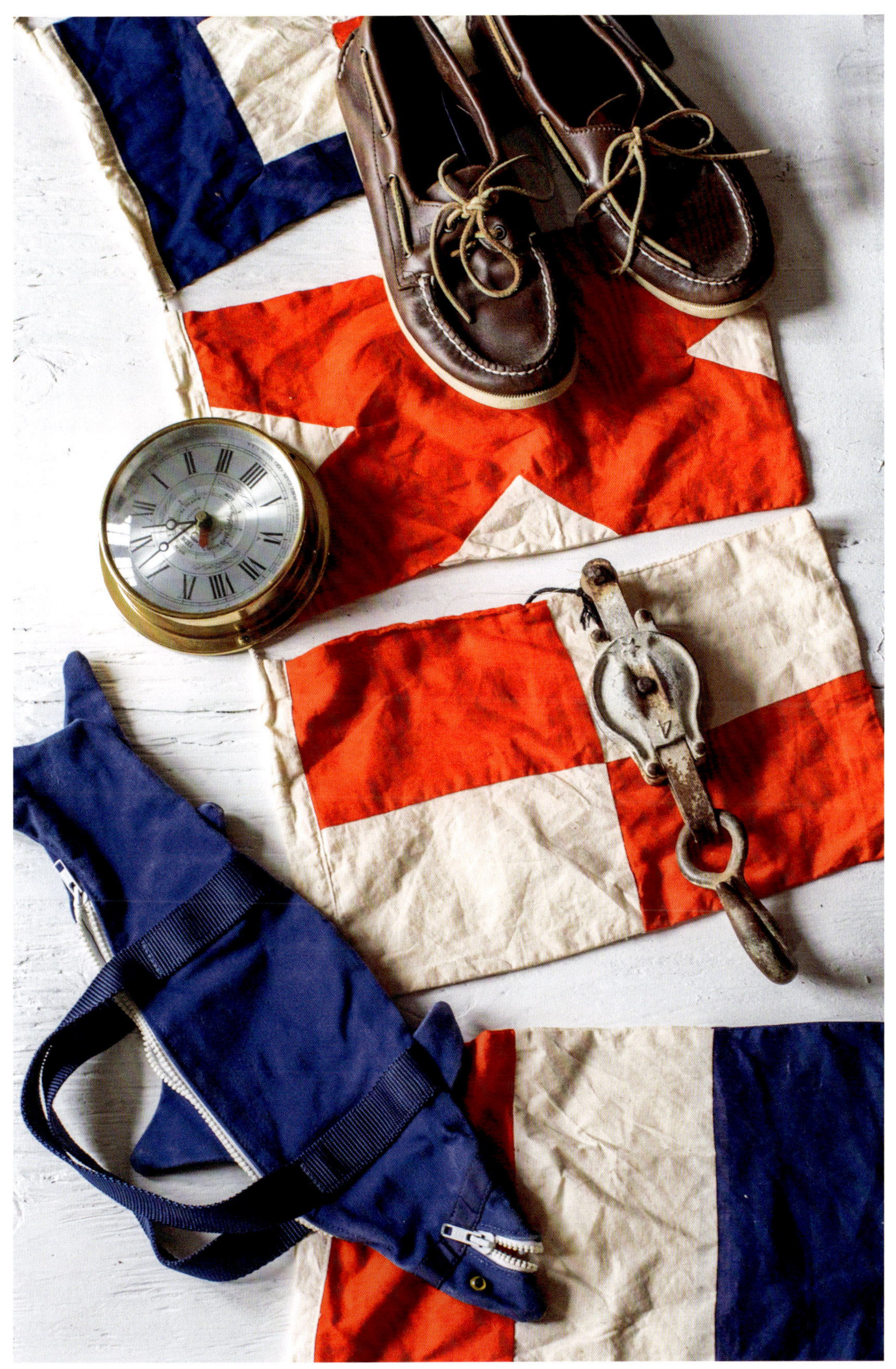

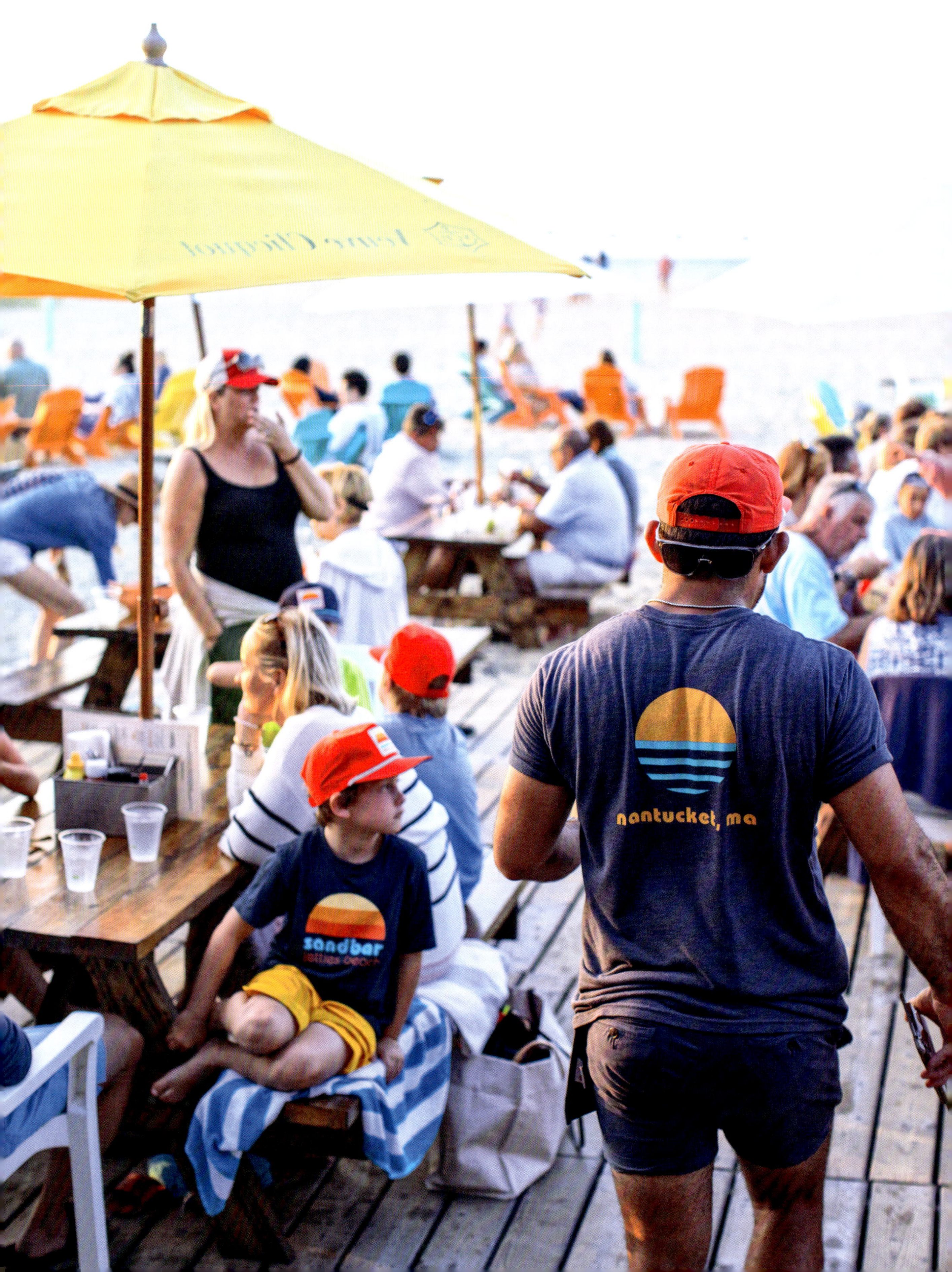
nantucket, ma
sandbar

Beyond the delicious freedom of youth, many talk about an openness they feel among people they meet. Even summer kids of the last few decades tell similar stories. Nina Colby, who grew up with three family homes in a row on Brant Point, which were filled with cousins and aunts, speaks of the strong friendships she made with islanders she met in sailing camps and summer jobs, the types of kids she wouldn't have met back home in Chicago, children of fishermen and builders, whom she still counts as close friends today.

Lulu Powers, a celebrity chef and author who has made a living entertaining others, says she loves the relaxed and egalitarian way of socializing on-island. "At a gathering it might be our friends who own a store, a corporate CEO, kids, and oh, your mom's in town? Great, bring her. House guests are always welcome. You end up meeting really interesting people."

The shared love of the island (and determination to be there) creates real connection and an air of possibility. In a world that's rapidly moving toward disconnection, the ability to let your guard down and connect with your inner child, or neighbor, is part of the island's alchemy.

"Everyone wants Nantucket to stay exactly like it was when they first fell in love with the island."

—**Jason Bridges, owner of Handlebar I and Nantucket Bike Tours**

Frisbie Family, Palm Beach real estate developers, owners of Harborview Nantucket hotel

YEARS ON NANTUCKET: *As a family, we've been coming since the 1970s.*

ISLAND HOME: *Brant Point*

MODE OF TRANSPORT: *Walking, biking, SUV'ing.*

FOUR WORDS THAT DESCRIBE YOUR ISLAND LIFE: *Familial, serene, idyllic, fun.*

FAVORITE BEACH: *Ladies Beach*

SUMMER UNIFORM: *For the ladies—white jeans, sweaters, Jack Rogers; for the guys—anything from Patagonia!*

_ IS BETTER ON NANTUCKET: *Just about everything*

DEFINE NANTUCKET STYLE: *Refined-casual*

MOST DAYS ON NANTUCKET WE … *spend the day with family—exercise, boating, fishing, biking, beaching, shopping, dining—always done best when family and close friends are included.*

FAVORITE THING/SPOT ON NANTUCKET? *Our family's deck on a sunny afternoon.*

MOST TREASURED EXPERIENCE/THING ON-ISLAND: *Being able to share this special place and build fond memories with our multi-generational family every summer.*

BEST PART OF ISLAND LIFE: *You can be as social as you want to be or as peaceful as you'd like—the island has so much to offer in so many ways.*

ON NANTUCKET YOU NEVER … *wear stilettos, or lock your car.*

FAVORITE ISLAND MEMORY: *Learning to fish, sail, and windsurf, and enjoying big family dinners after a busy, fun day of activities.*

Page 83: Captain Jim Genthner and son James of "The Endeavor"; Page 84: Row 1 (from left): Cavel Mattison, Sherry and Nelson Loucks, Amy Pallenberg; Row 2: Liam Mercer, Lubijcia Brigitte, Adam Dread; Row 3: Simona and Agne Lucas, Liza Gershman, Megan Anderson; Page 85: Row 1 (from left): Roberto Santamaria, Aubrey Sterk and Van, Floyd Kellogg; Row 2: Monika and Aaron Ruzgaite, Gene Mahon, Michael and Charity Grace Mofsen; Row 3: Bridget McGuiness, Ugne Aleknaite and Brandon Jellison and family, Lizzy Michler; Page 91: Samantha Angel; Page 93: Katherine Gougin; Page 99: Elizabeth Georgantas; Page 104: John Shea; Page 105: Kevin Flynn; Page 115: Sarah Fraunfelder; Page 116: Brett Sousa; Page 117: Brett Sousa, Dean Dellas, Gwen "Bunny" Hyde, Christine Bloom; Page 120: Molly Bennett; Page 121: Nantucket Looms; Page 123: Inez Hutton and D.W. Coffin; Page 124: Wally Marzano-Lesnevich; Page 130: Danielle Norcross and Beth Aschenbach; Page 139: Nori and Jean Wang; Page 142: Lila Gailliot; Page 144: Kelly Emery; Page 145: Tony Lacasse, Liam Carey, Marcus Gould, Alexis Kinney; Page 148: Sandbar at Jetties Beach; Page 151: (from left): Richard Frisbie, Kim Frisbie, (back row) Cody Crowell, Robert Frisbie, Sr., Robert Frisbie, Jr., (front row): Katie Frisbie Crowell, Ashley B.C. Frisbie and Robert Frisbie III, and Frances Frisbie; Pages 152–53: Cindy, Owen, Samuel and Lee Milazzo; Page 156: Jocelyn Gailliot and children; Page 161: Cathy B. Graham; Page 165: Paloma and Georgia Grace; Page 169: Westmore Club tennis players; Page 171: Doug Ellis; Page 180: Row 1 (from left): Marianne Felch, Sally Timpsom and Sarah Felch Lindvall; Sara Rossi; Row 2: Jean Rioux, Carl Lindvall, Wendy McCrae; Row 3: James Hutton, Karen Golov, Marguerite and J.J. Culpepper; Page 181: Row 1 (from left): Immanuel Chac, Taylor Ivey, Bob Felch; Row 2: Lillian Lindvall, Mary Hutton, Will Felch; Row 3: Bonnie Roseman, Hutton Lindvall, Lisa Soeder; Page 182: Meredith Hanson; Pages 186–87: Sunset dining on the water; Page 188: Dan Pronk; Page 189: Samantha Angelo; Page 192: New England Clambake at The Nantucket Hotel; Page 193: Molly Bennett

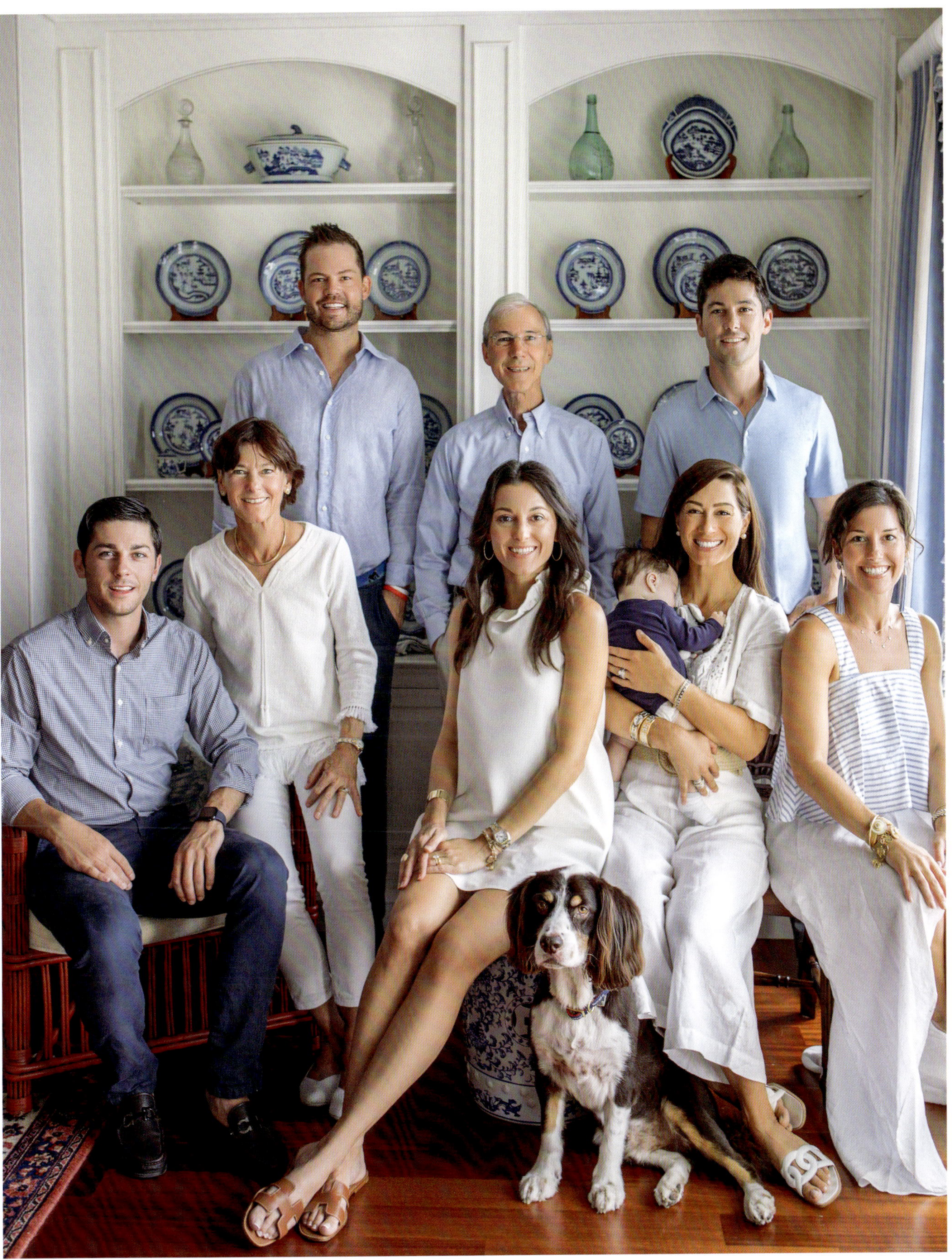

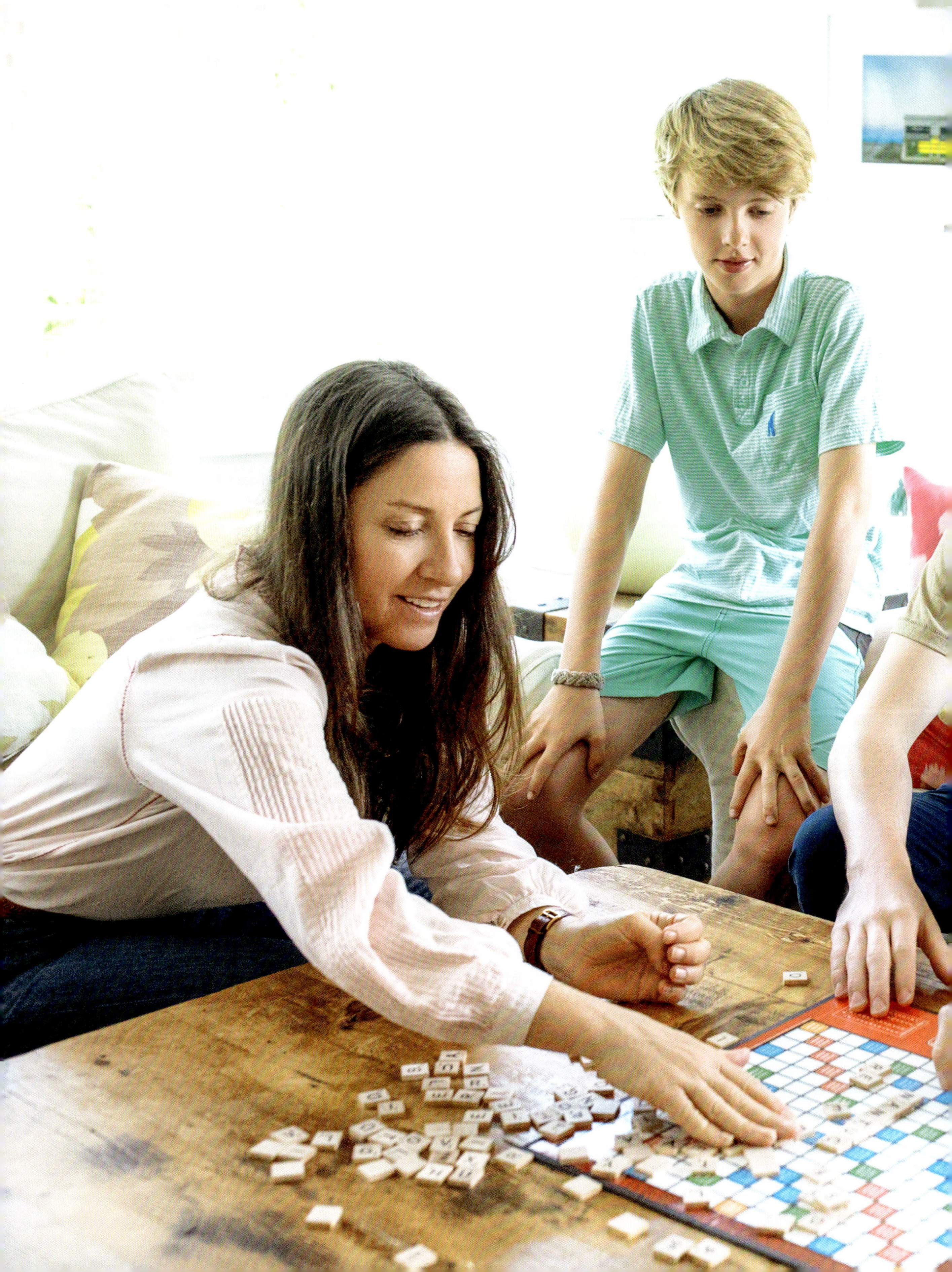

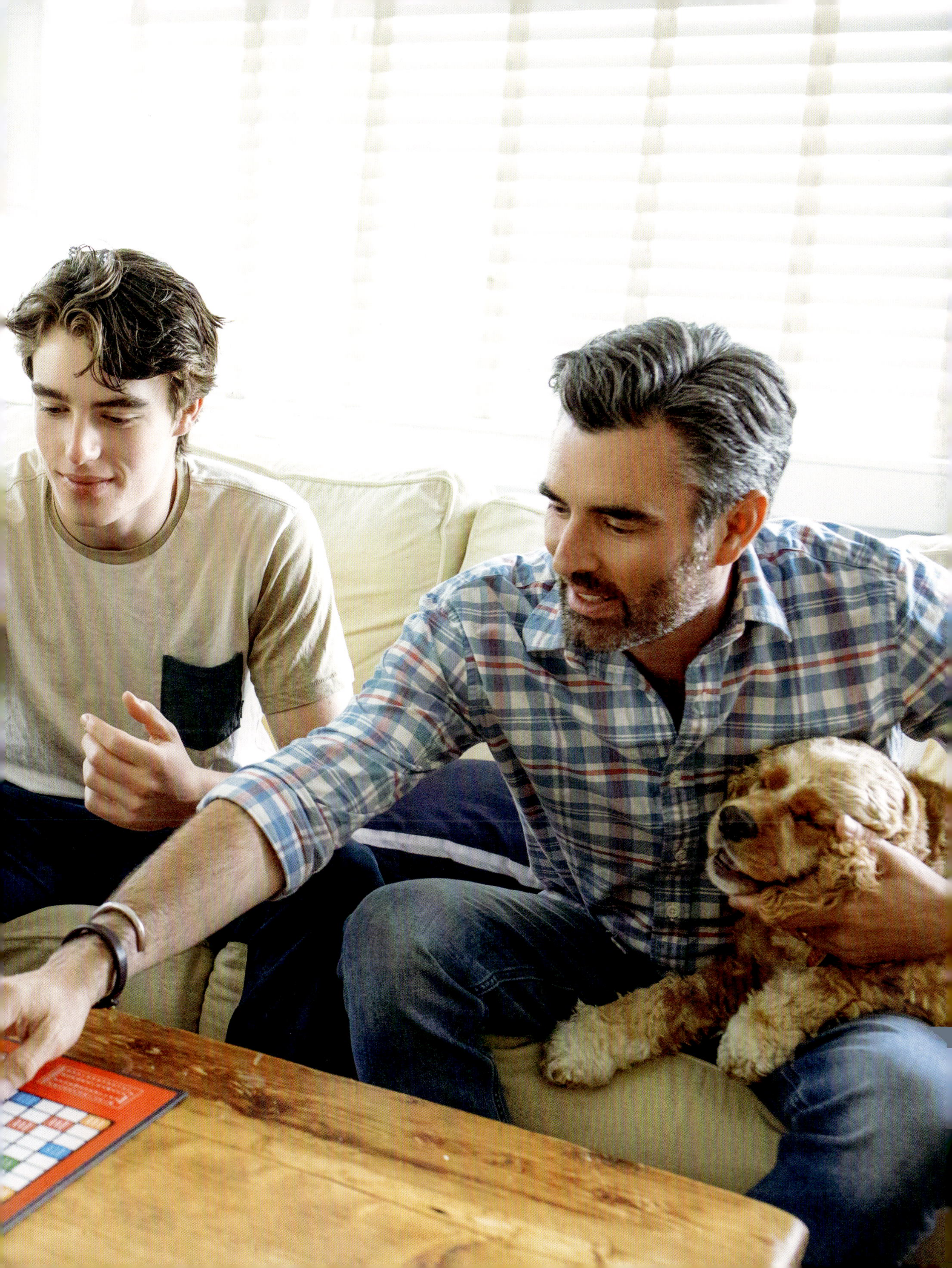

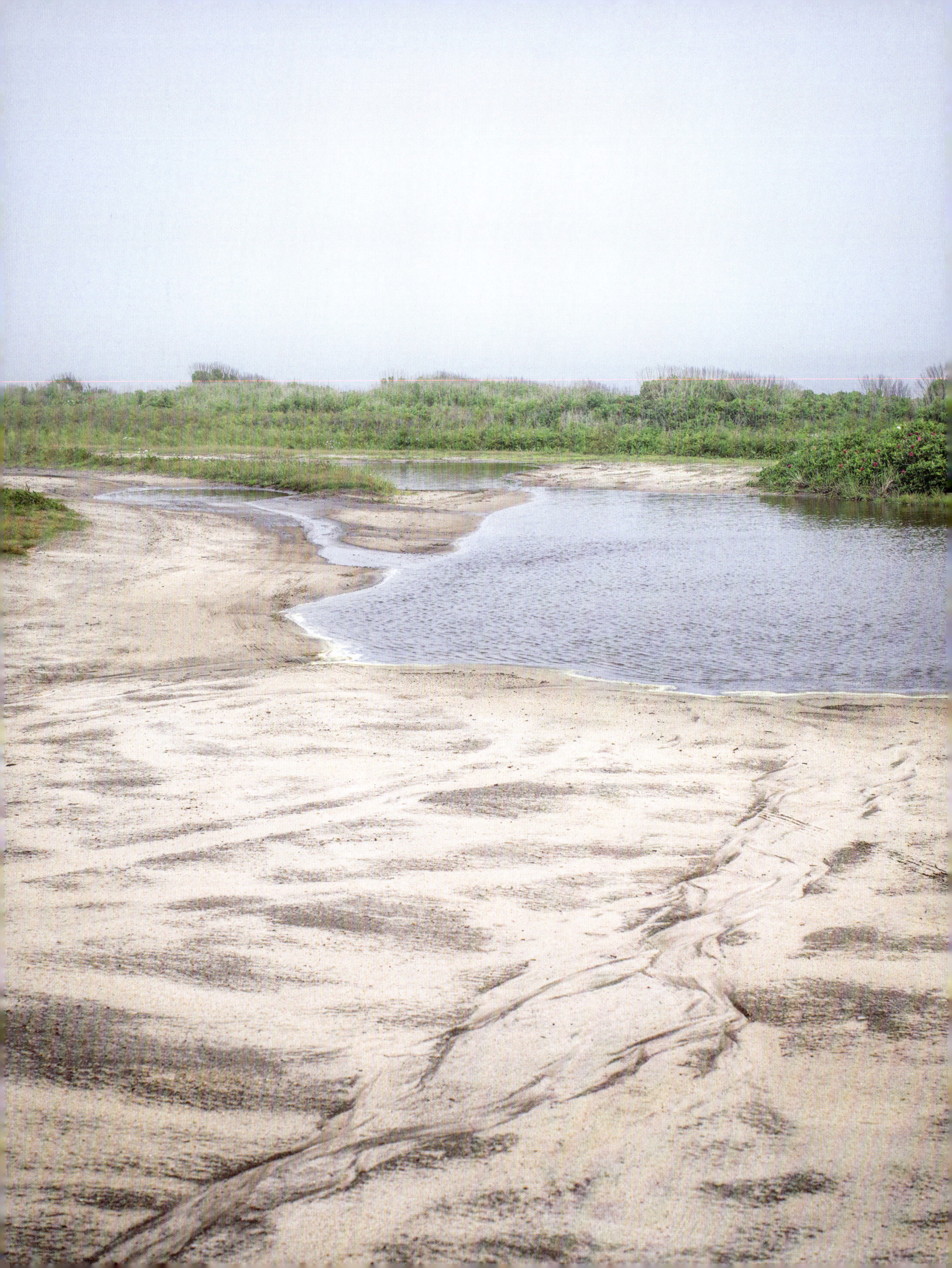

"Mother Nature has a filtration system. For some people, it's way too difficult to get here and they'll never return. It doesn't matter how large your jet, your ego, or anything else, if there's fog, sometimes there's just no getting here. It's an exercise in humility and patience and grace."

—Angela Raynor, proprietor of Boarding House and The Pearl restaurants

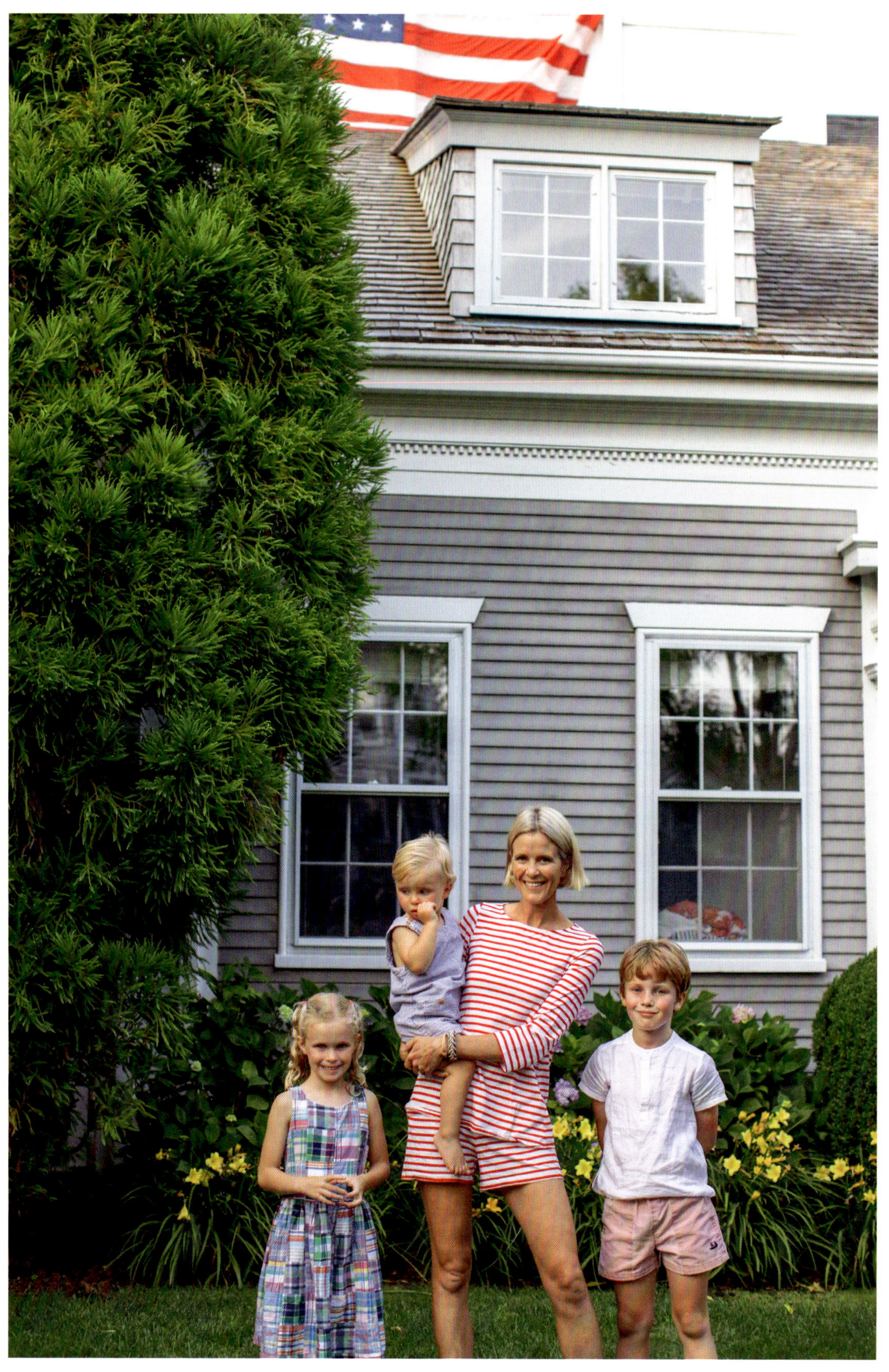

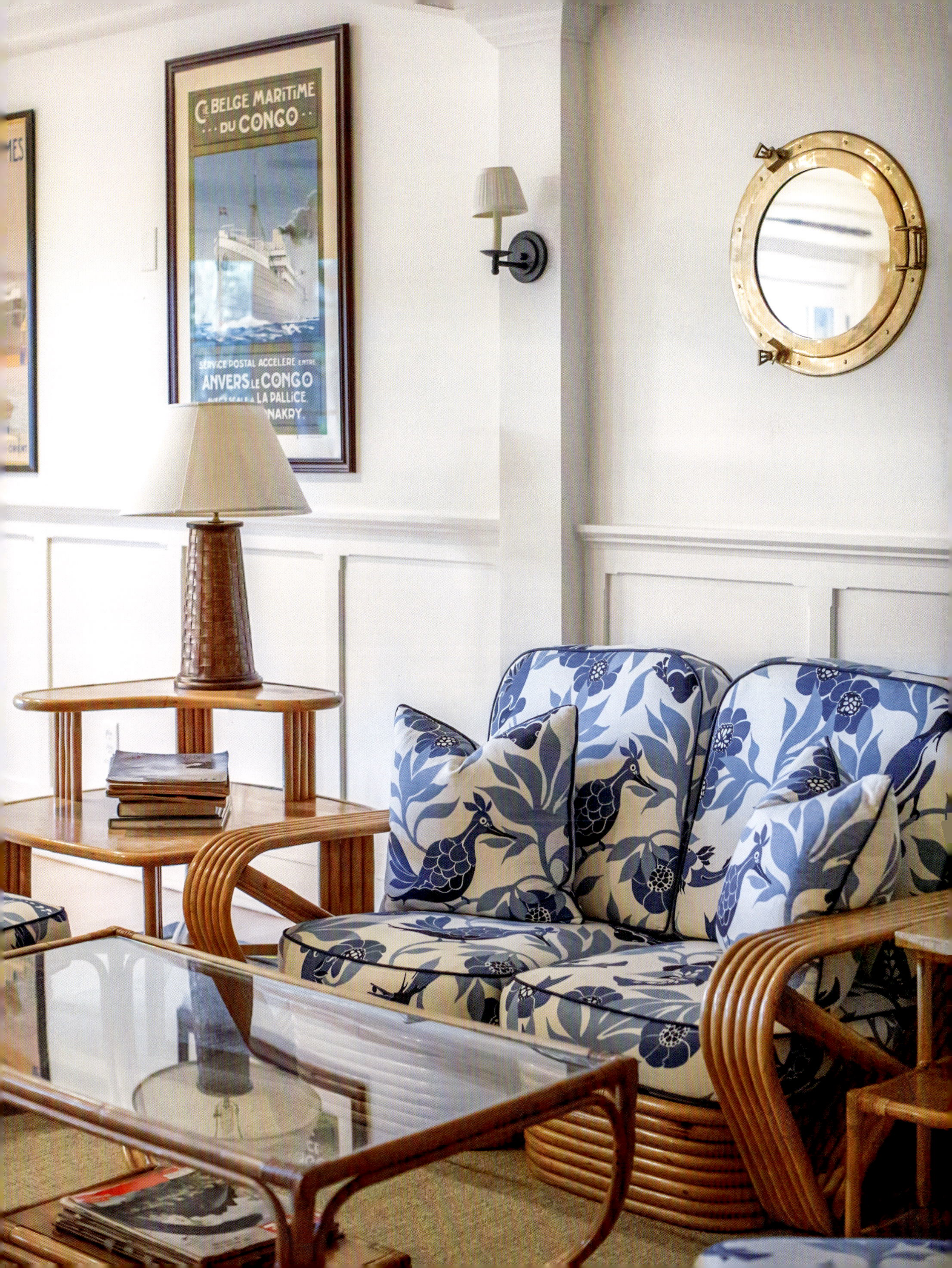
Cie BELGE MARITIME
DU CONGO
SERVICE POSTAL ACCELERE ENTRE
ANVERS LE CONGO
LA PALLICE

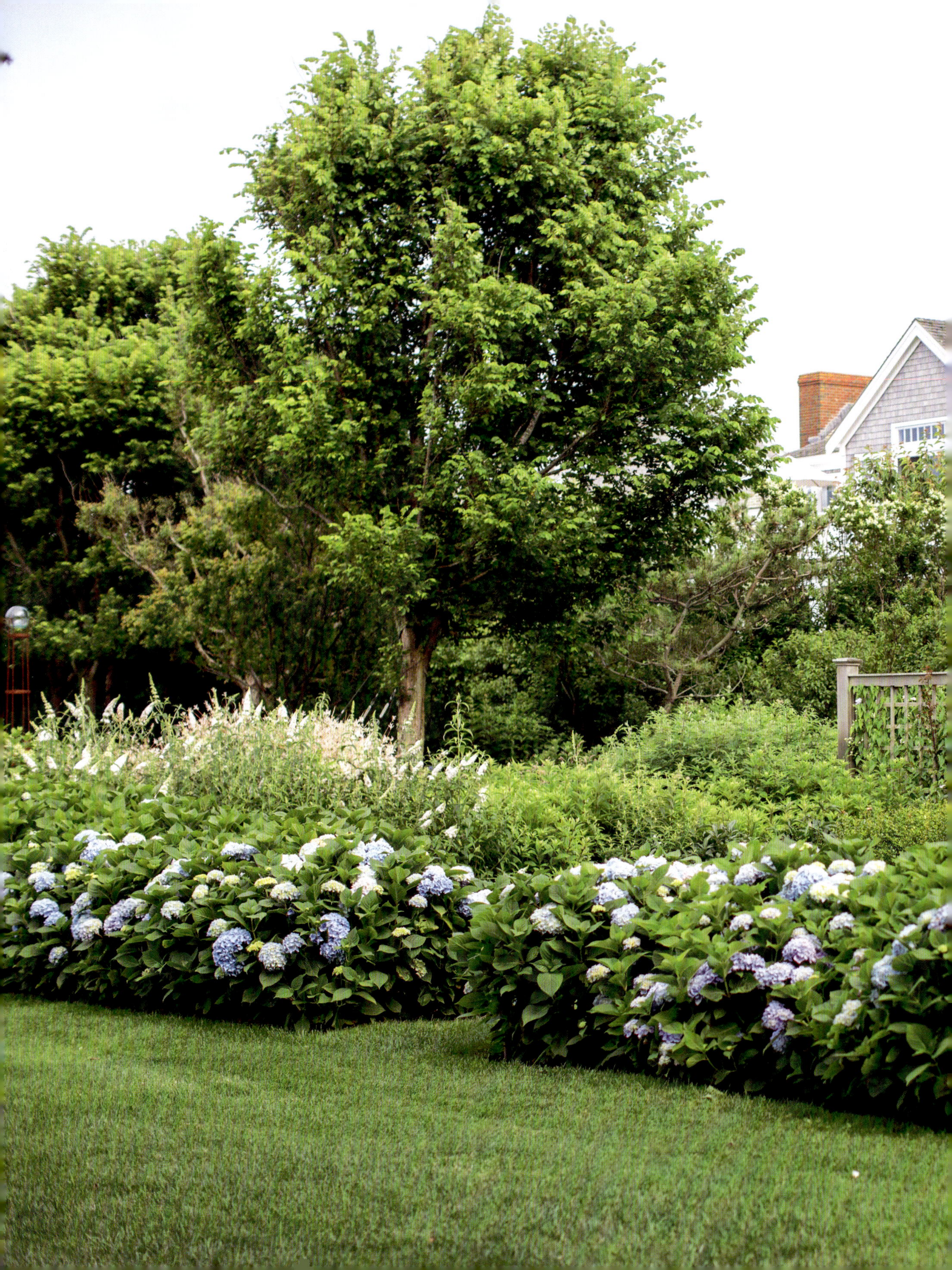

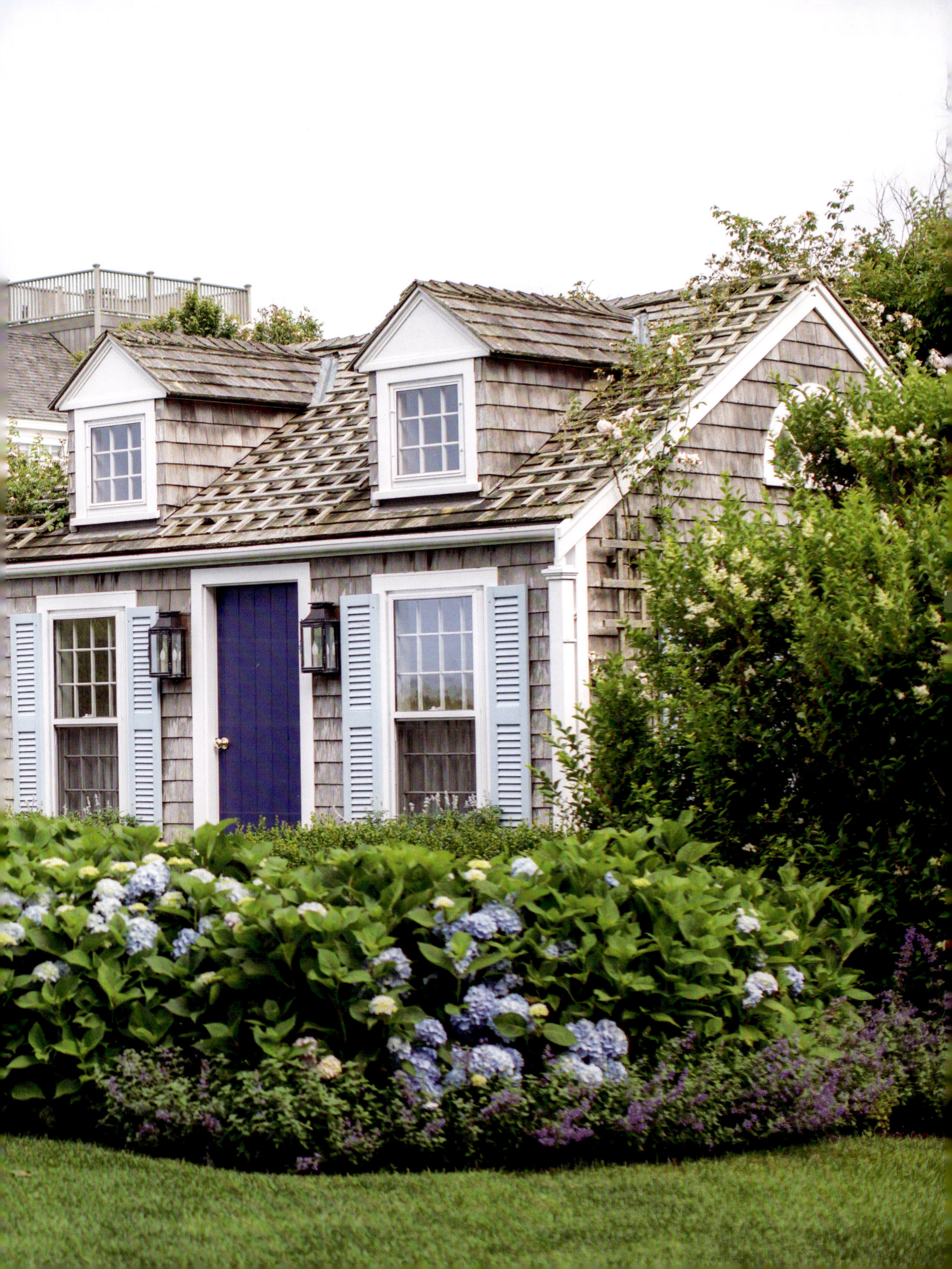

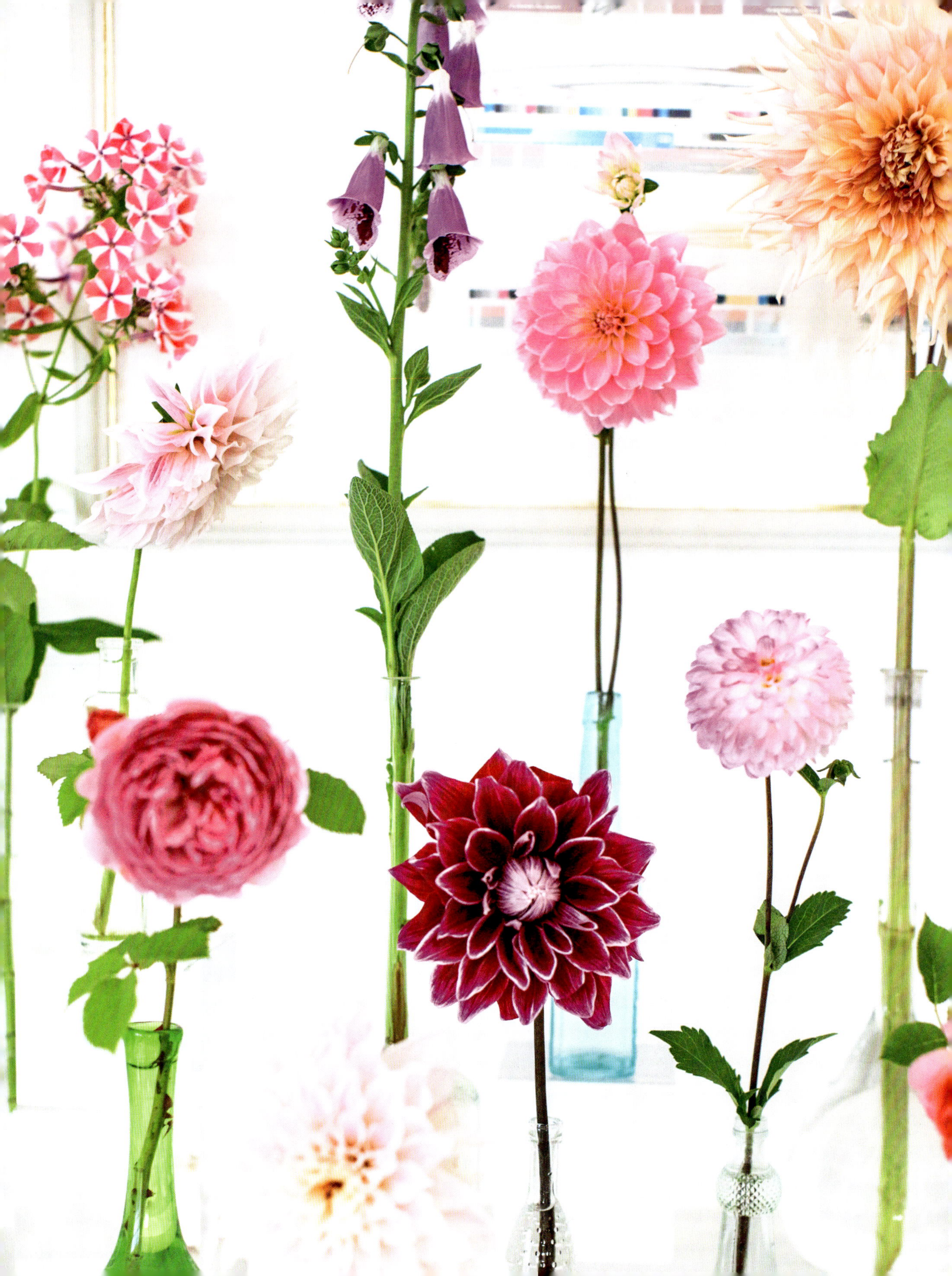

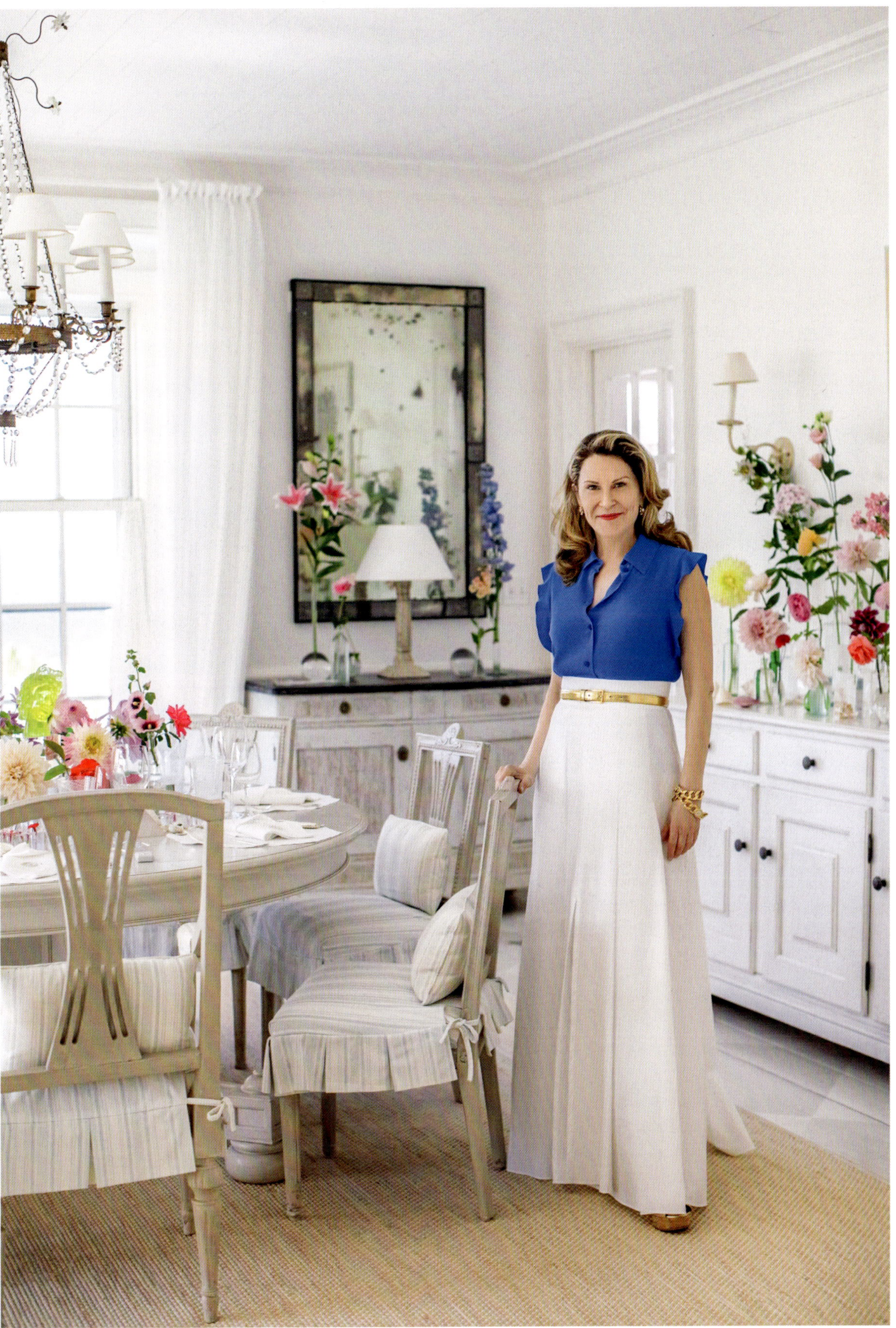

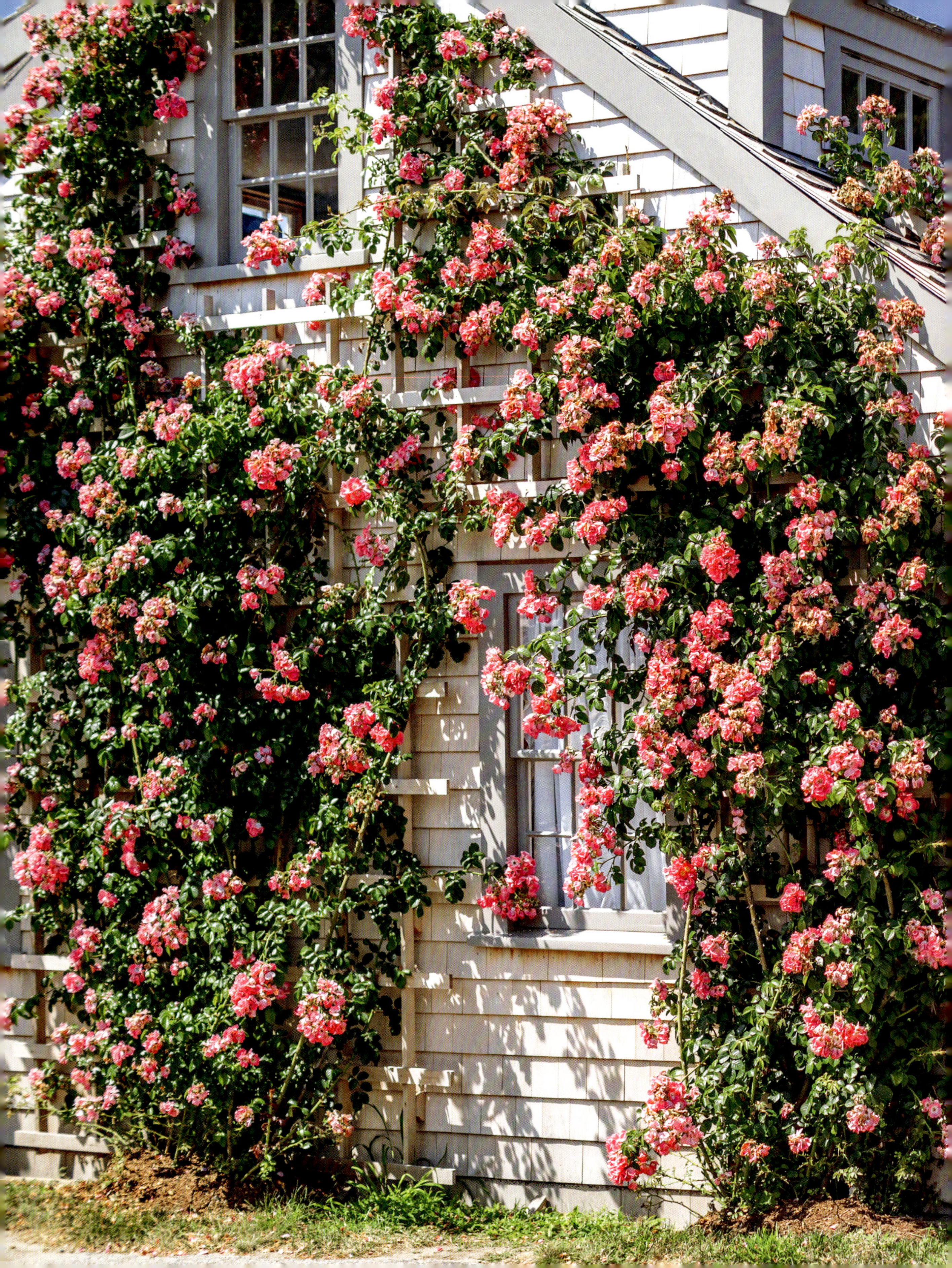

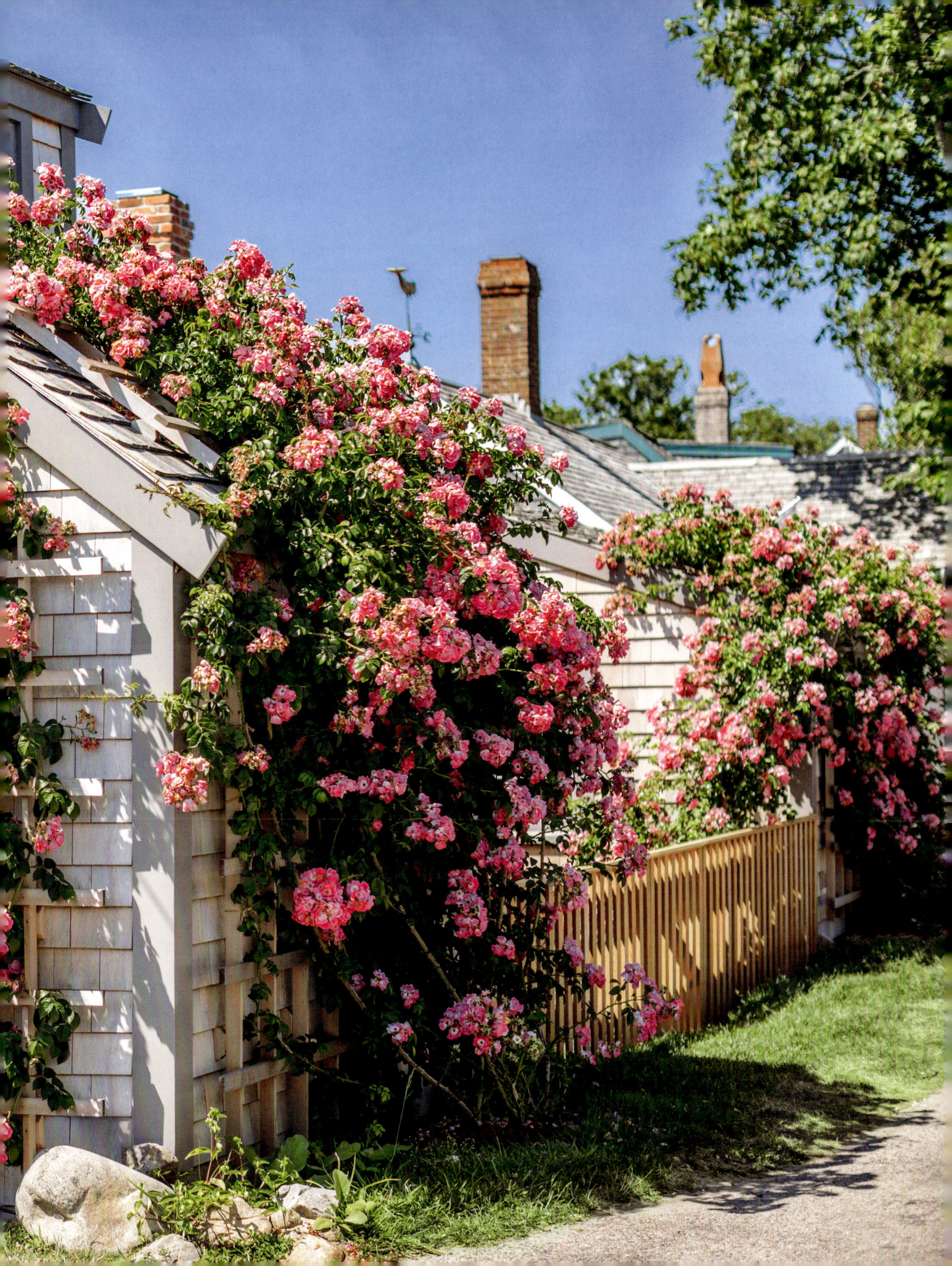

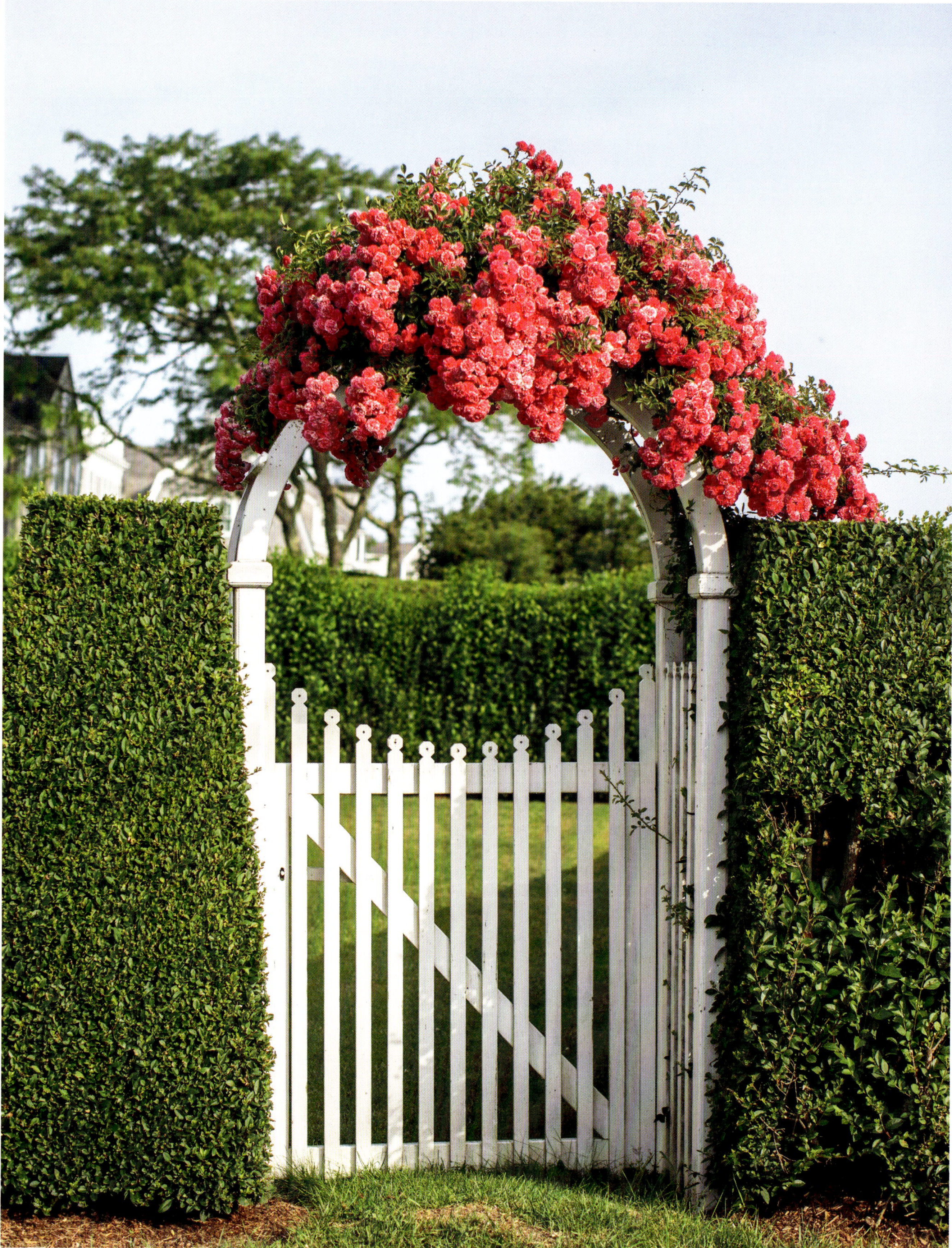

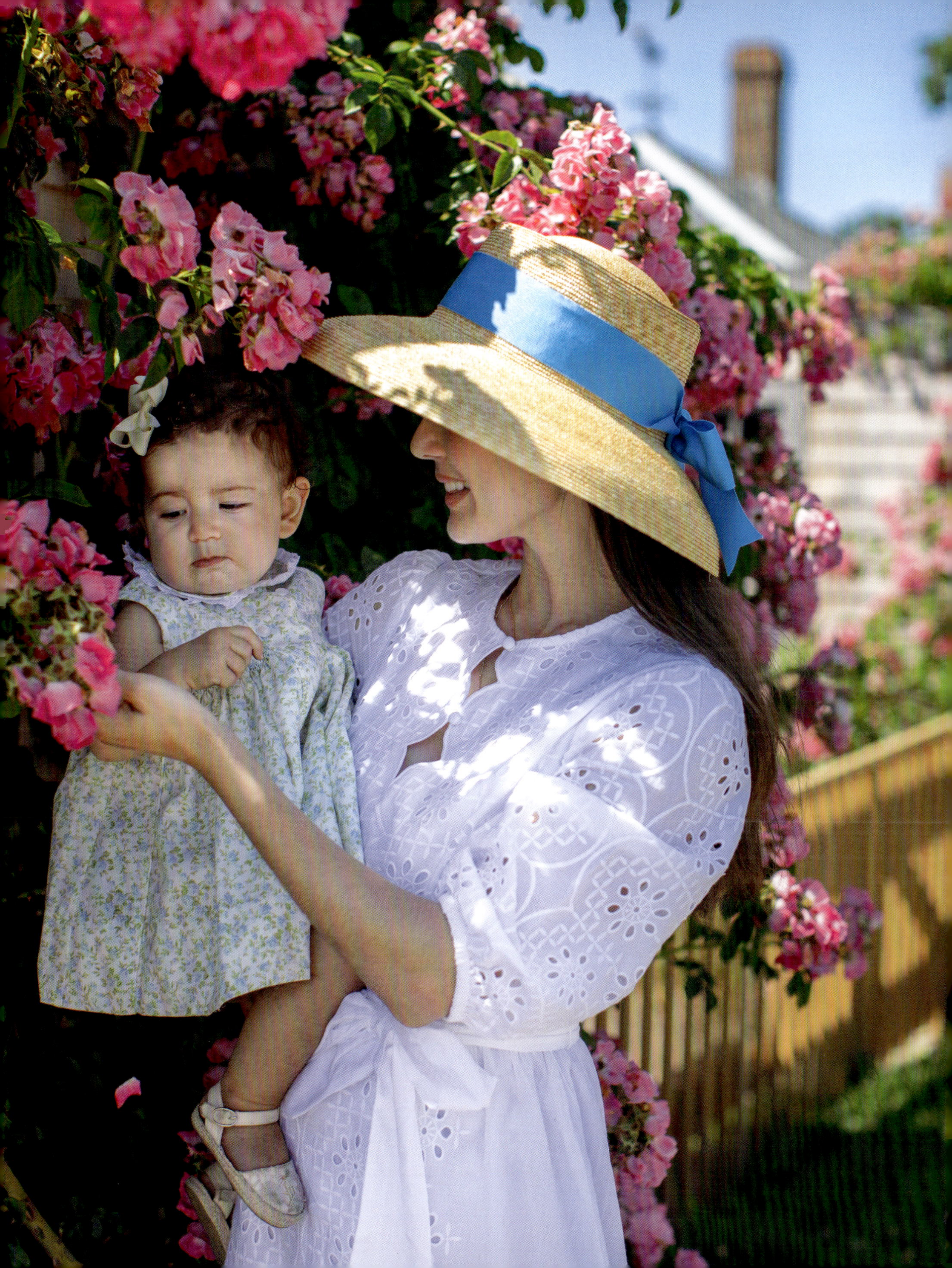

THE CLUB LIFE

Nantucket can often feel like a private club: fairly inaccessible, expensive, well-manicured, and traditional. Despite the seeming exclusivity of the island, and similar to American enclaves like Palm Beach, Aspen, or the Hamptons, Nantucket's private club scene is a strong part of the summer season's culture.

Patricia Anathan fondly remembers Nantucket entertaining during her childhood summers in the '50s and '60s. "It was simple living—father would go out clamming, my mother would organize a cocktail party, they would have cheese and crackers and clams, cigarettes, scotch." In those days people socialized at homes more than clubs. "A lot of socializing revolves around nonprofits now. Or we meet at the yacht club for dinner."

Some of the island's more popular clubs:

WESTMOOR CLUB (www.thewestmoorclub.com) Housed in a Colonial Revival mansion built in 1917 for Alice Claypoole Vanderbilt. Members enjoy yachting, tennis, squash, croquet, paddle tennis, pickleball, junior activities, wellness, fishing, dining, and two swimming pools.

NANTUCKET GOLF CLUB (www.nantucketgolfclub.org) Founded in 1998 by Trevor Rees-Jones, with one of the highest joining fees in the world at the time, members tout the club as the closest thing to a genuine British Isles course on American soil. Ranked in the top twenty golf courses in the United States.

SANKATY HEAD GOLF & BEACH CLUB (www.sankatyheadgc.com) Founded in 1923, designed by Emerson Armstrong, this is the first golf club on the island and one of the country's oldest extant links-style courses; it's ranked in the top ten in the United States. Known for its Caddy Camp, the last of its kind training young caddies. Families enjoy tennis and pool facilities at the Beach Club. In 2007 the Sankaty Head Lighthouse was moved to club property next to it to save it from erosion along the 'Sconset' Bluff, the club has been forced to move some of its cabanas as well. Membership is capped at 550, which has long made it in demand.

MIACOMET GOLF COURSE (www.miacometgolf.com) One of two public golf courses on Nantucket (see also Siaconset Golf Club). In 1956, Ralph P. Marble bought 400-acres of land on Nantucket's southern shore with the intention of raising cows for dairy production; instead, construction of a golf course began four years later.

SIASCONSET GOLF CLUB (www.siasconsetgolf.com) Laid out in 1899, Siasonset Golf Club is the oldest golf course still active on Nantucket. Called "Skinners" by the locals, it is considered the oldest privately owned golf course in the country still open to the public.

NANTUCKET YACHT CLUB (www.nantucketyachtclub.org) The organization which was to become the Nantucket Yacht Club was first chartered in 1890 as the Nantucket Athletic Club. By the summer of 1906 a second group had come together, calling themselves the Nantucket Yacht Club, whose purpose was to provide sailing and racing for the summer residents of Nantucket, their families, and friends.

GREAT HARBOR YACHT CLUB (www.ghyc.com) A private club that aims to be a "summer camp for grown-ups," it provides access to the harbor and waterfront dining. Offers sailing, tennis and squash, fishing, family activities, speaker series, book clubs, a spa, fitness, wellness, and more. A boastful 80 percent of members hold the title of CEO or own their own businesses.

SIASCONSET CASINO ASSOCIATION (www.sconsetcasino.com) Founded in 1899 when the Actors Colony pooled $3000 to build a "hall of amusement" with tennis courts, a bowling alley, and a stage. The short film **At the Sconset Casino** lovingly details the club's welcoming past: "Everybody could do everything and it didn't matter who you were." Still very much like that today, families fill the rooms throughout the season playing games, dining, and socializing.

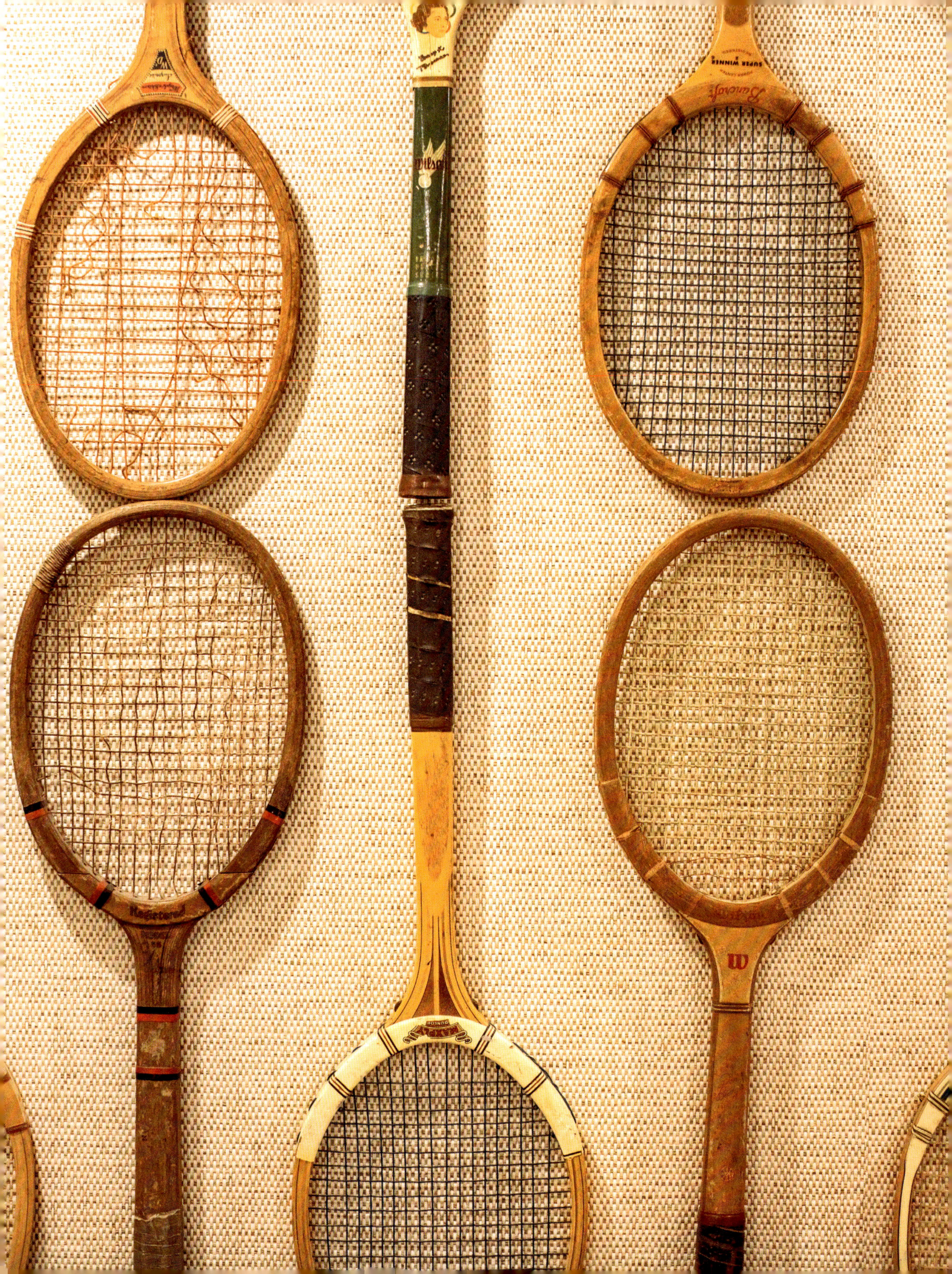
Registered
DUNLOP
MAXPLY

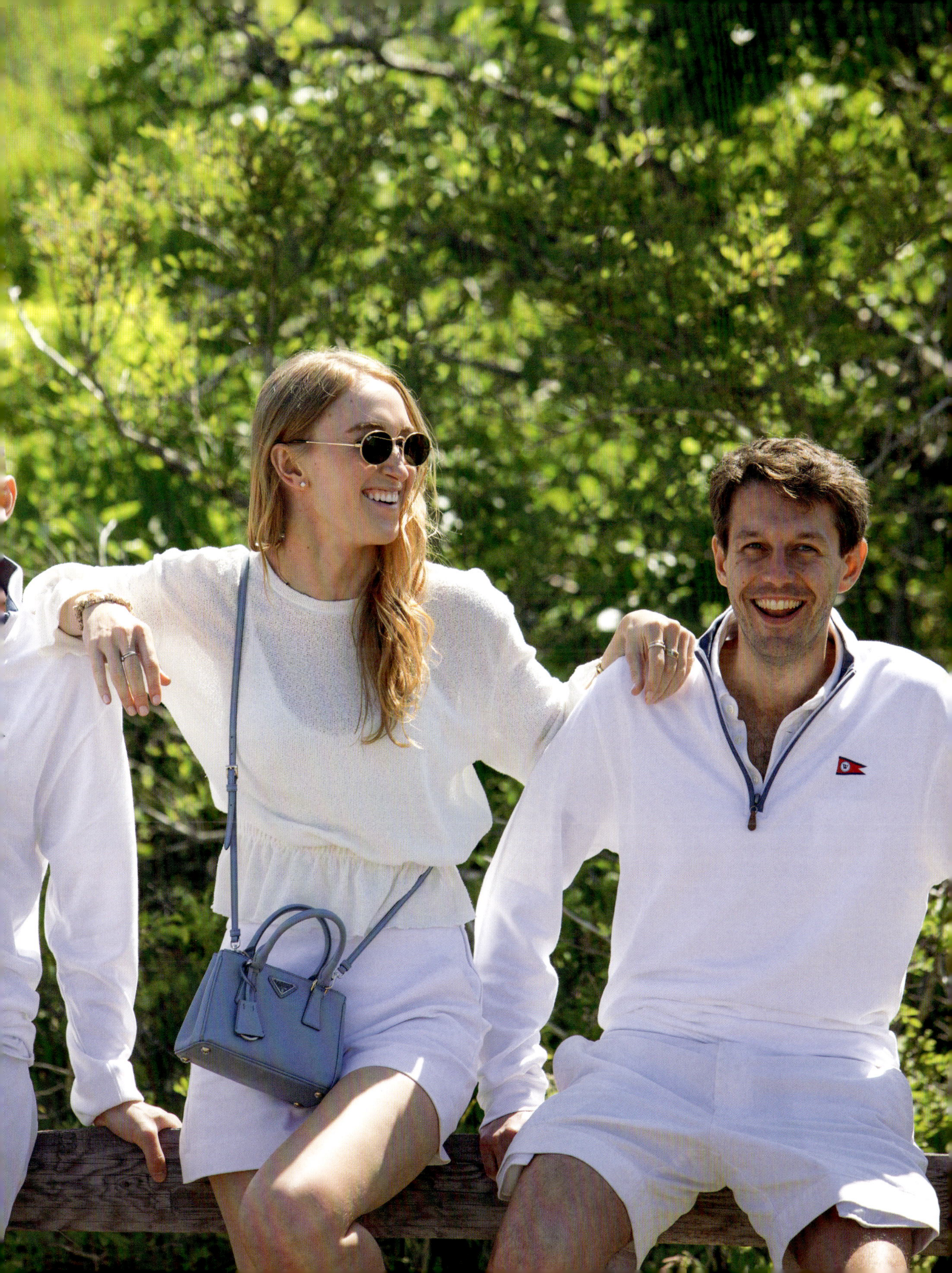

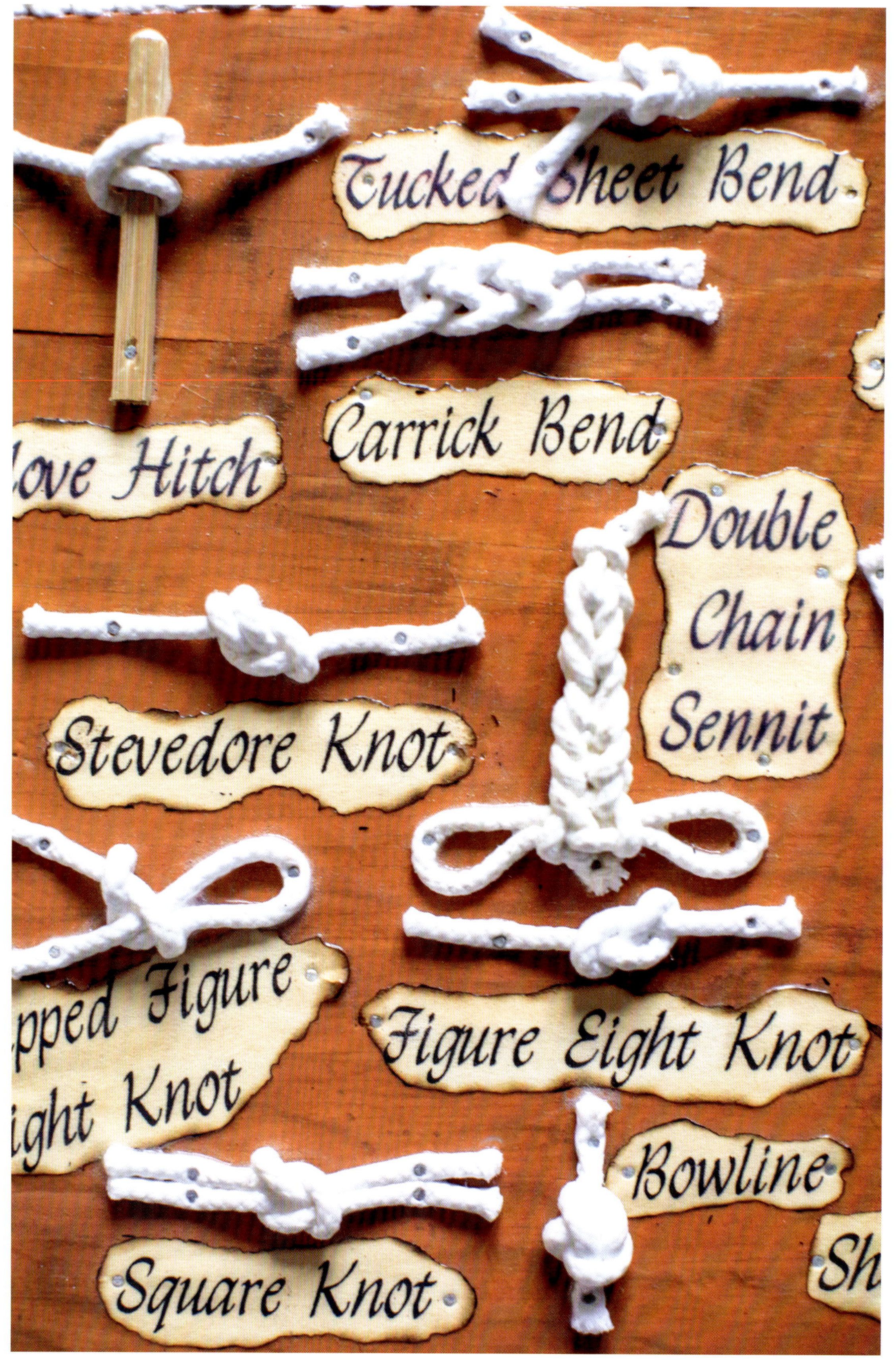
Tucked Sheet Bend
Hitch
Carrick Bend
Double Chain Sennit
Stevedore Knot
Figure
Knot
Figure Eight Knot
Bowline
Square Knot

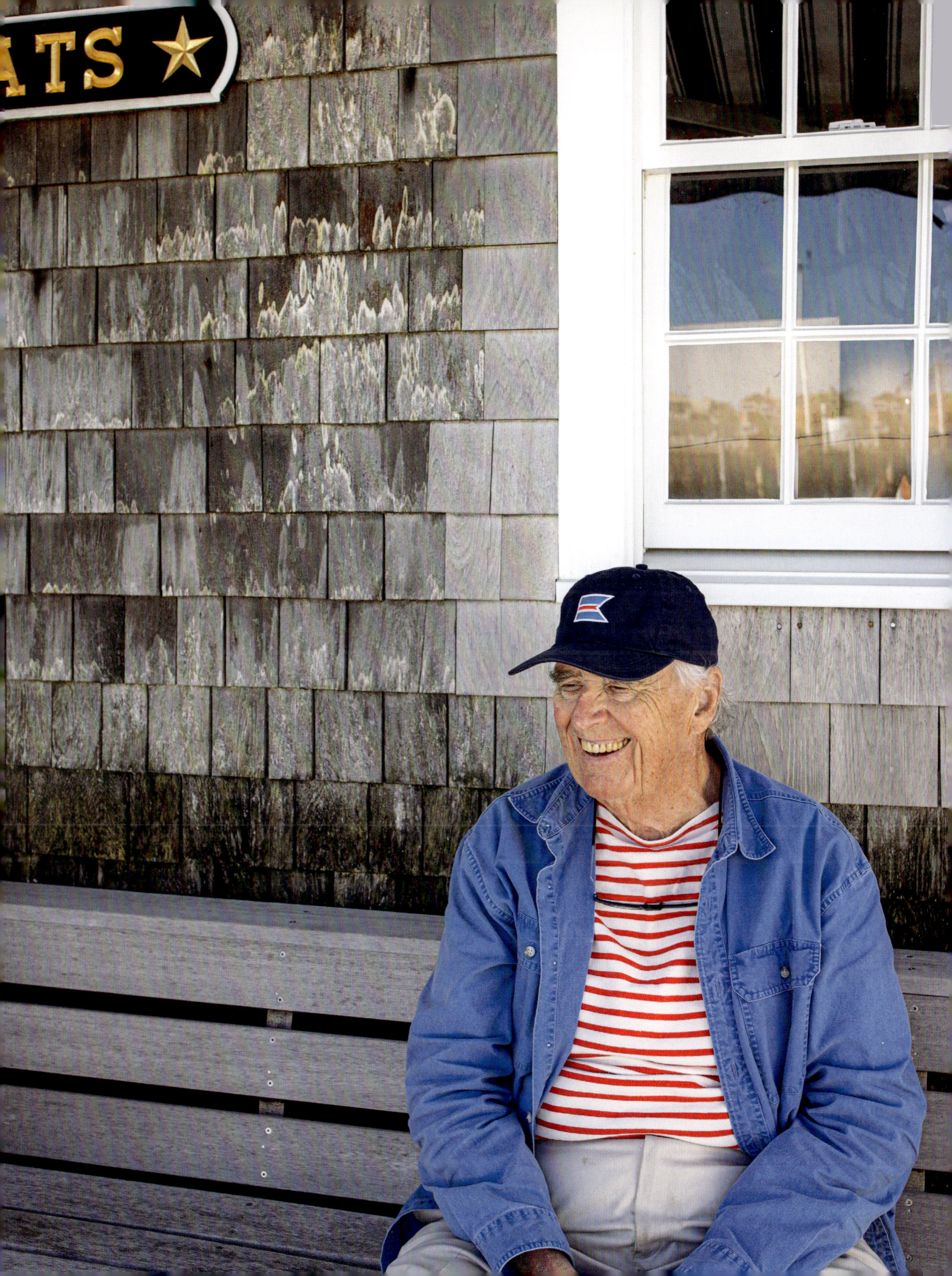
ATS

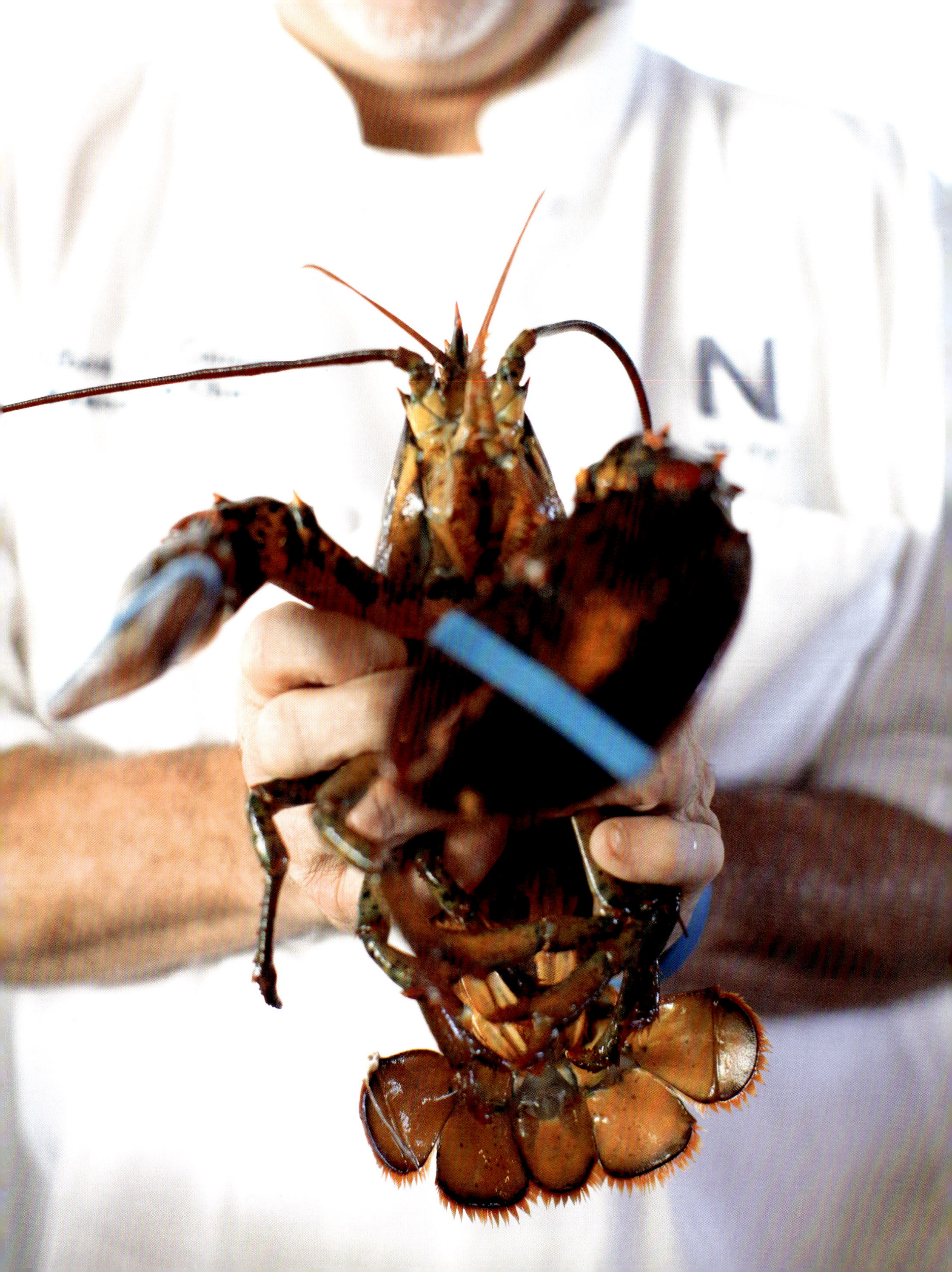
N

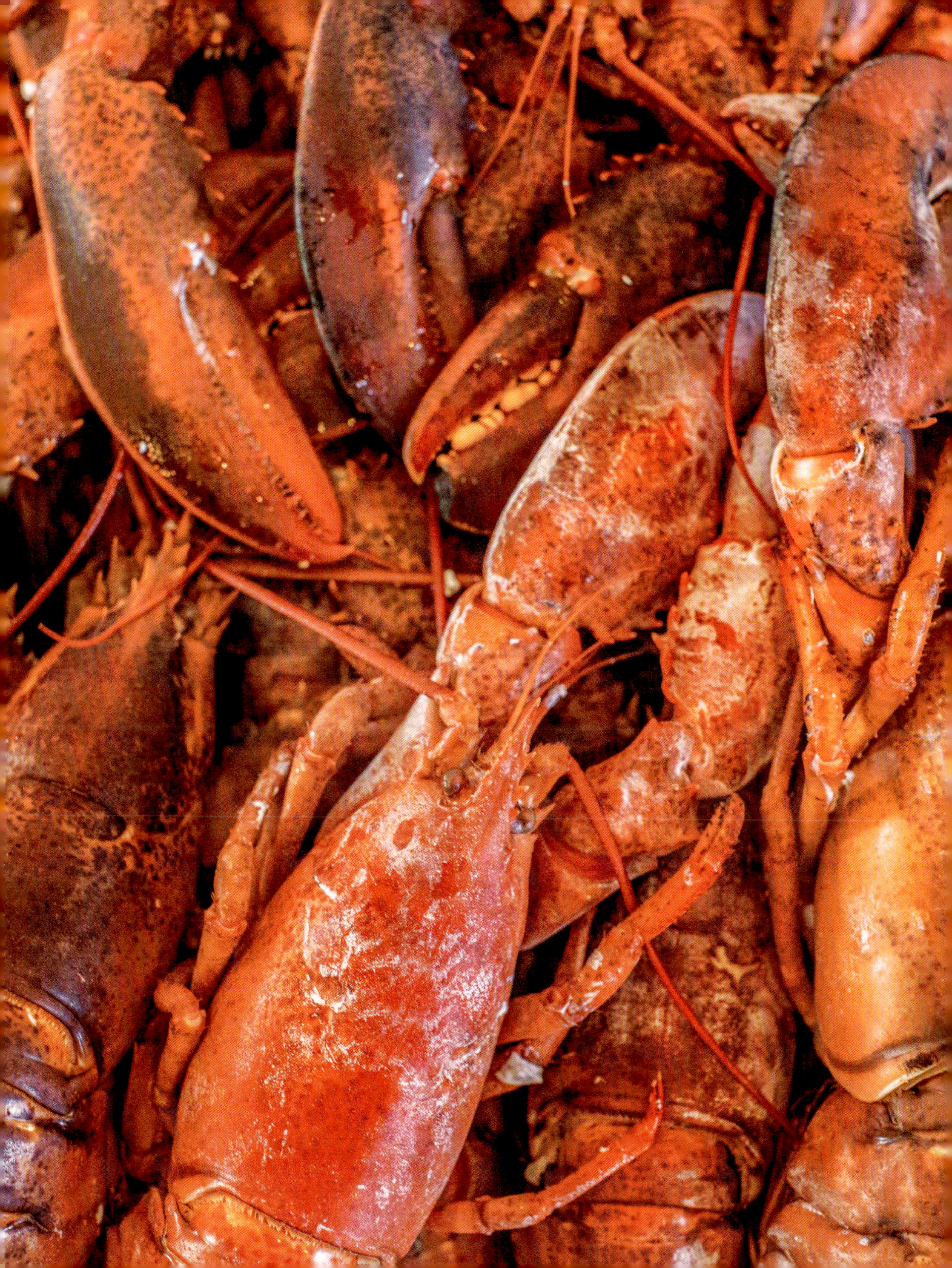

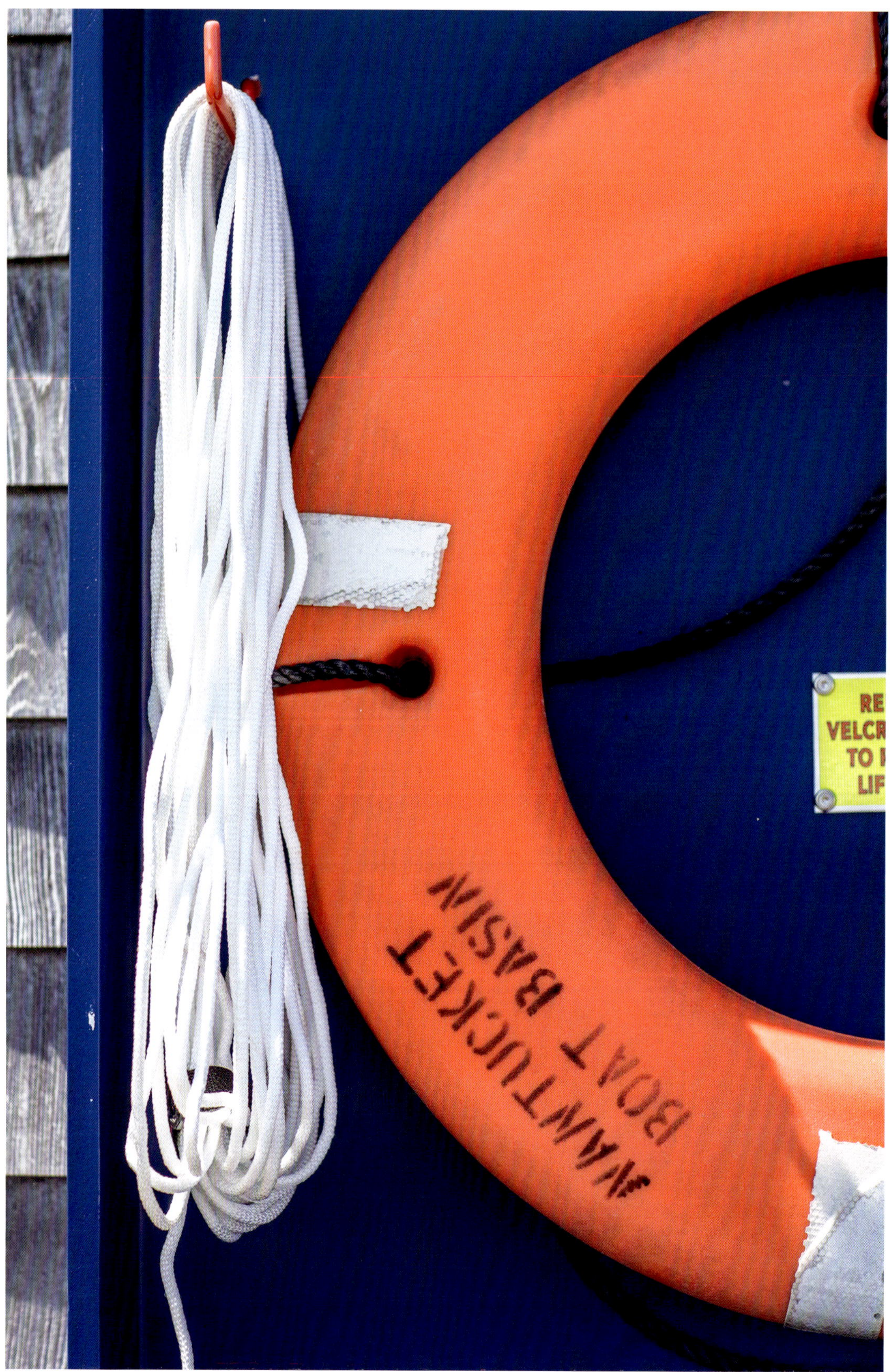
NANTUCKET
BOAT BASIN

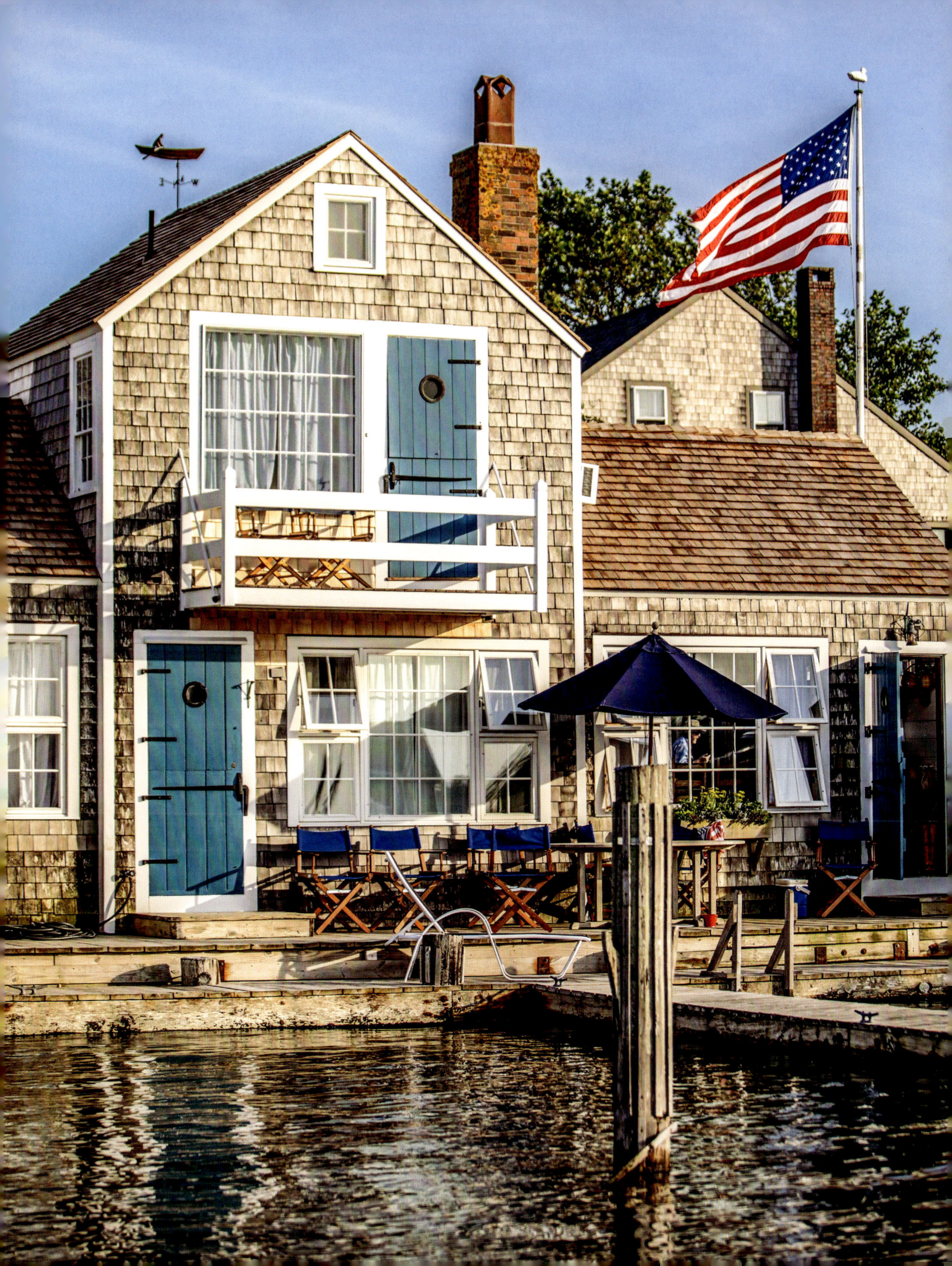

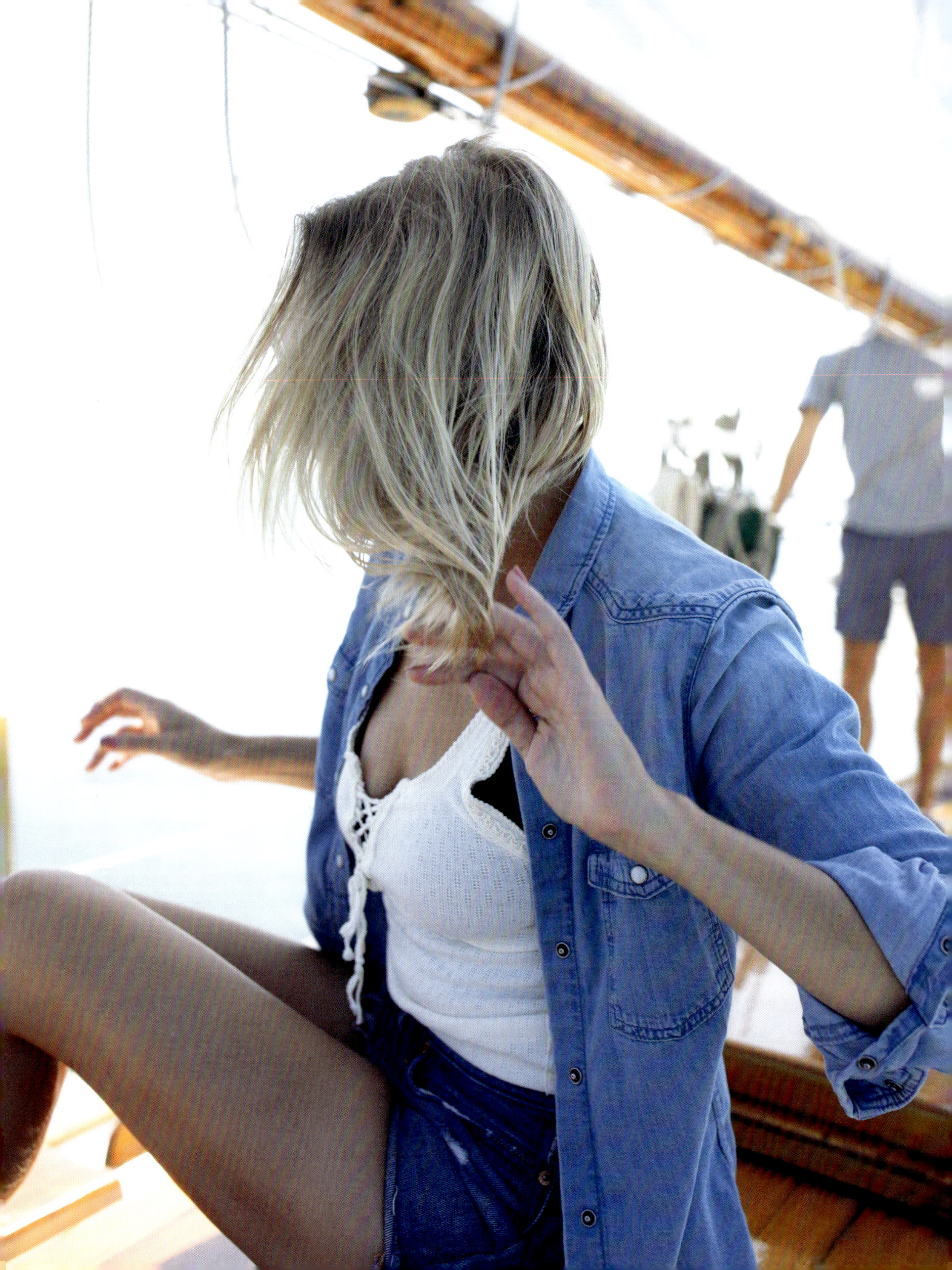

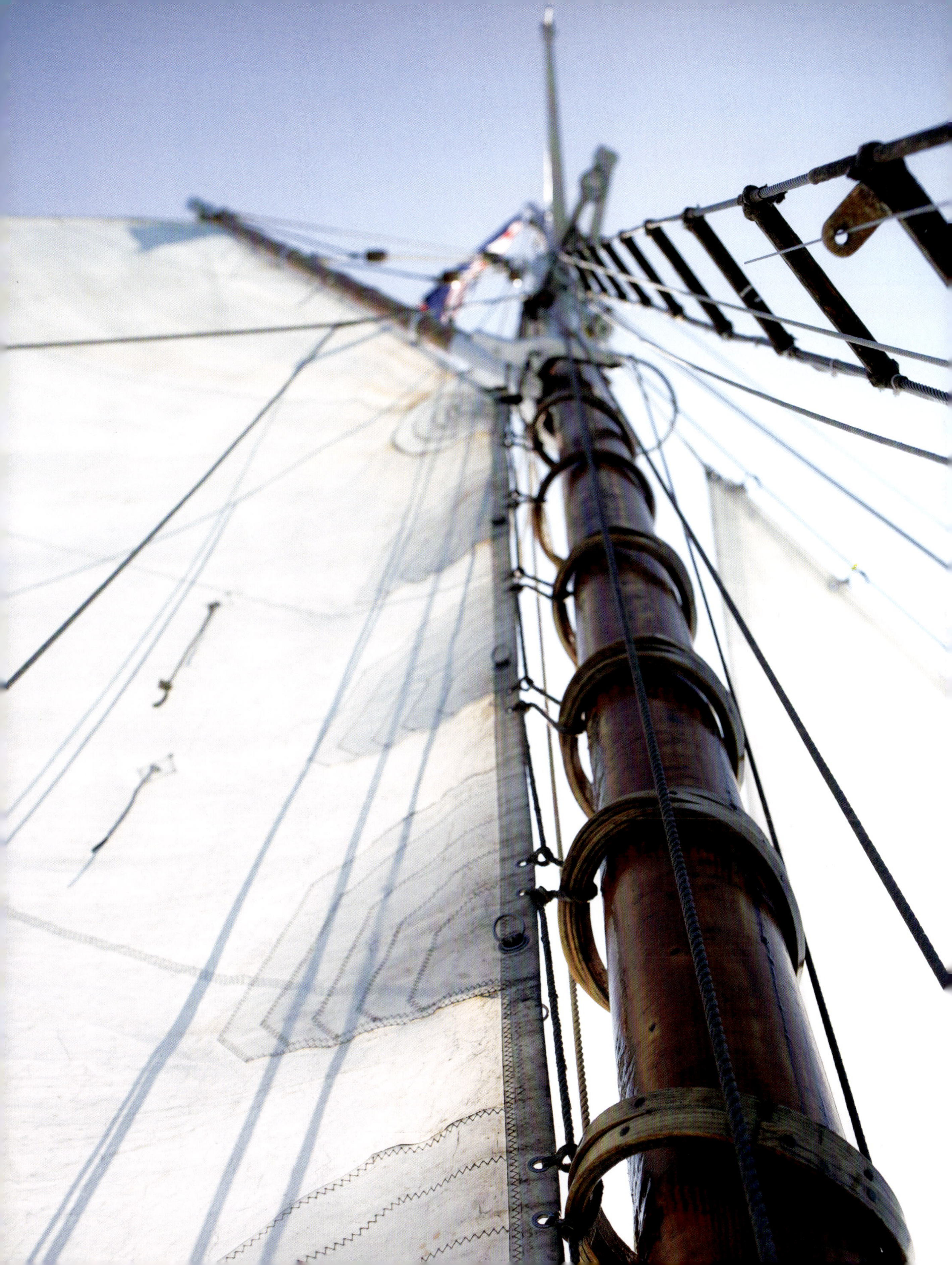

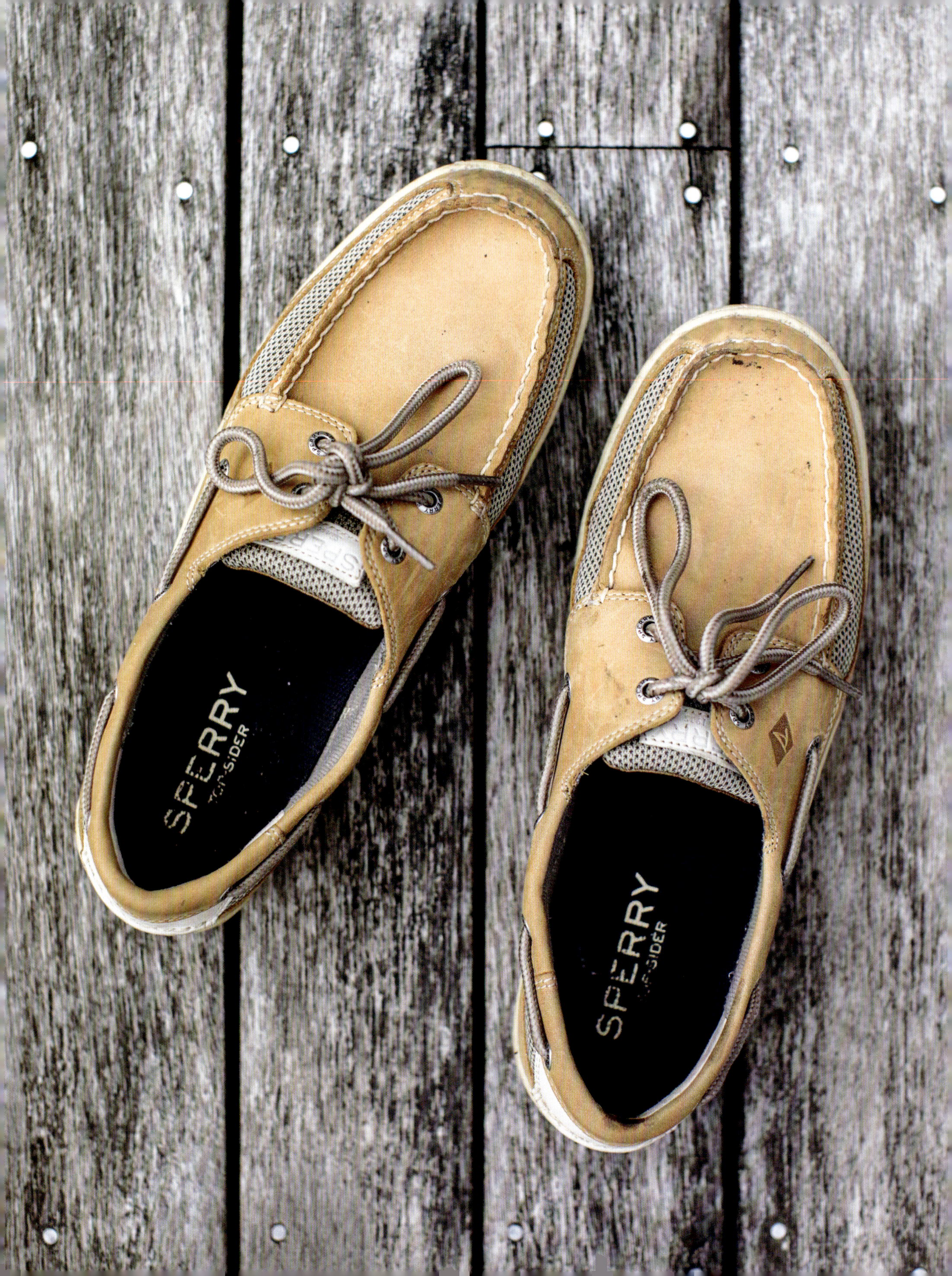
SPERRY
SPERRY

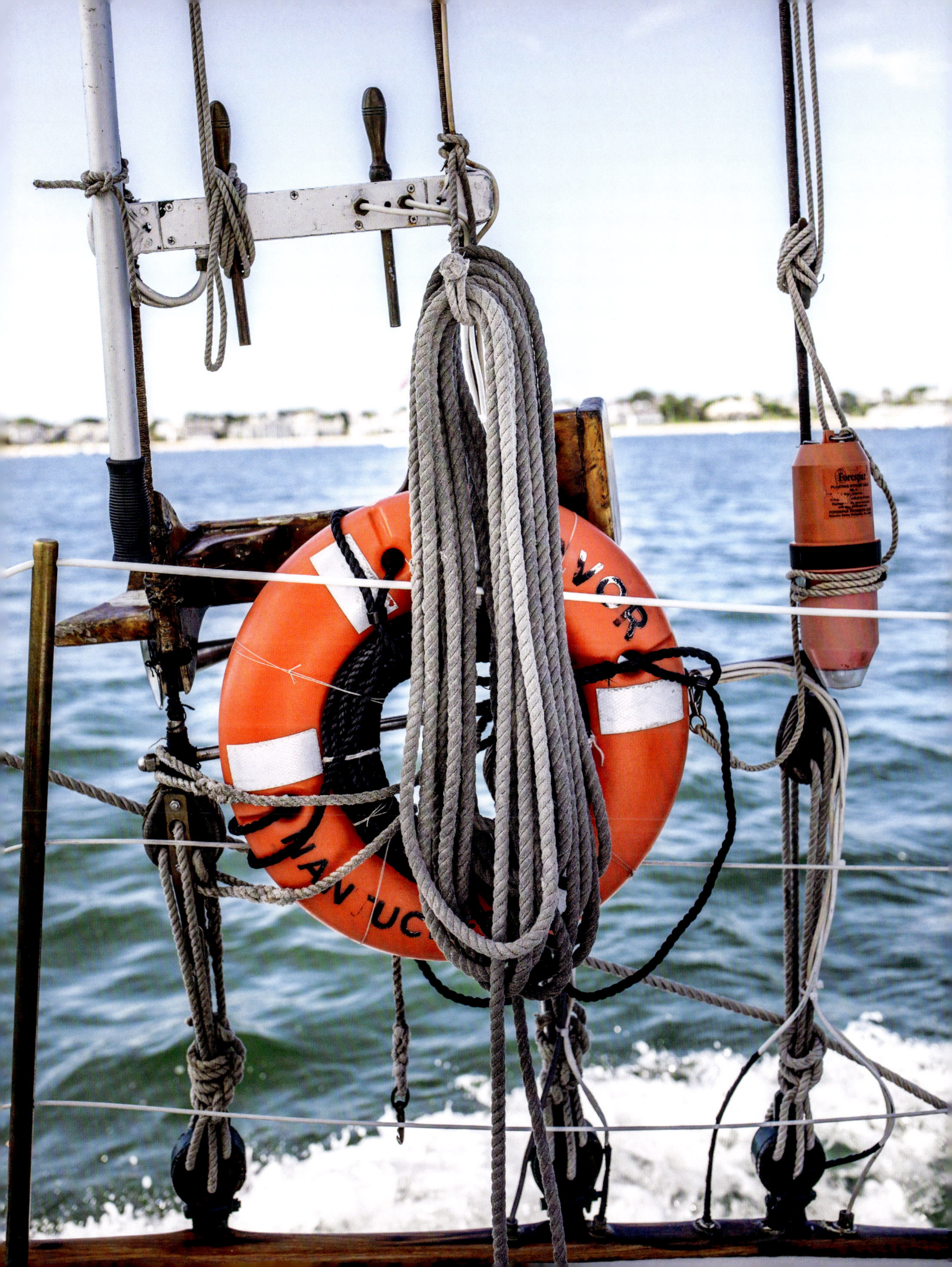
VOR
NANTUC

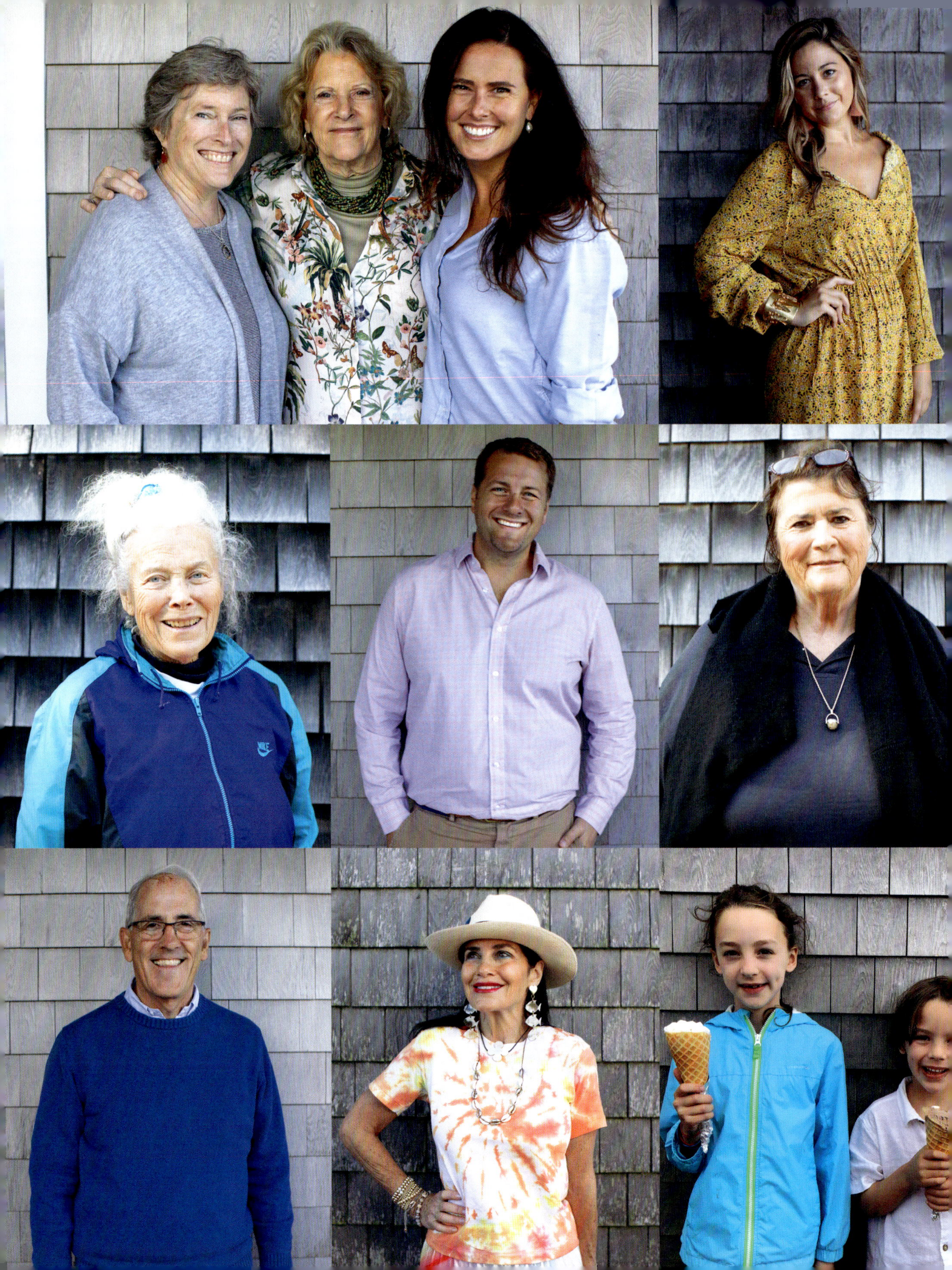

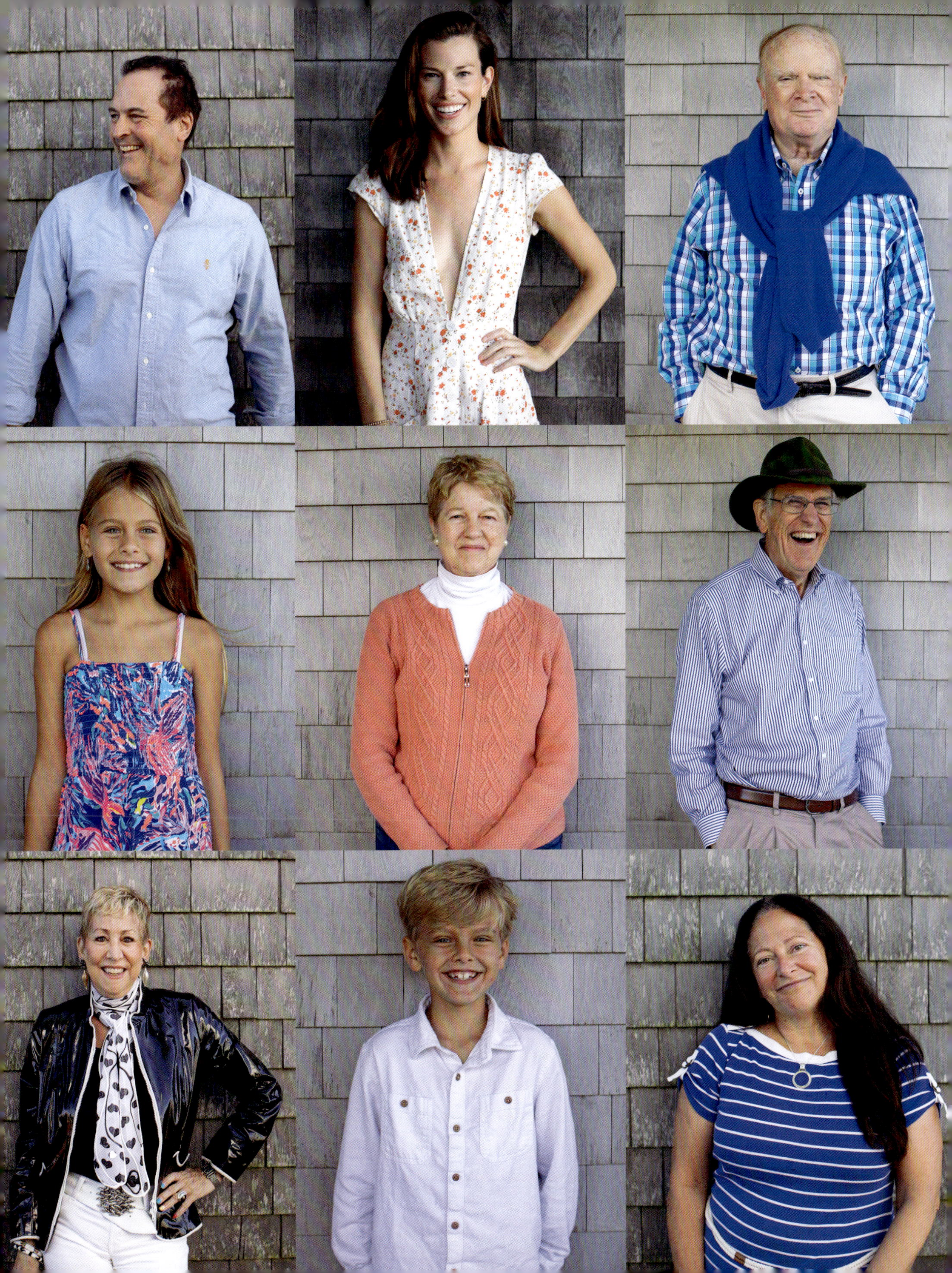

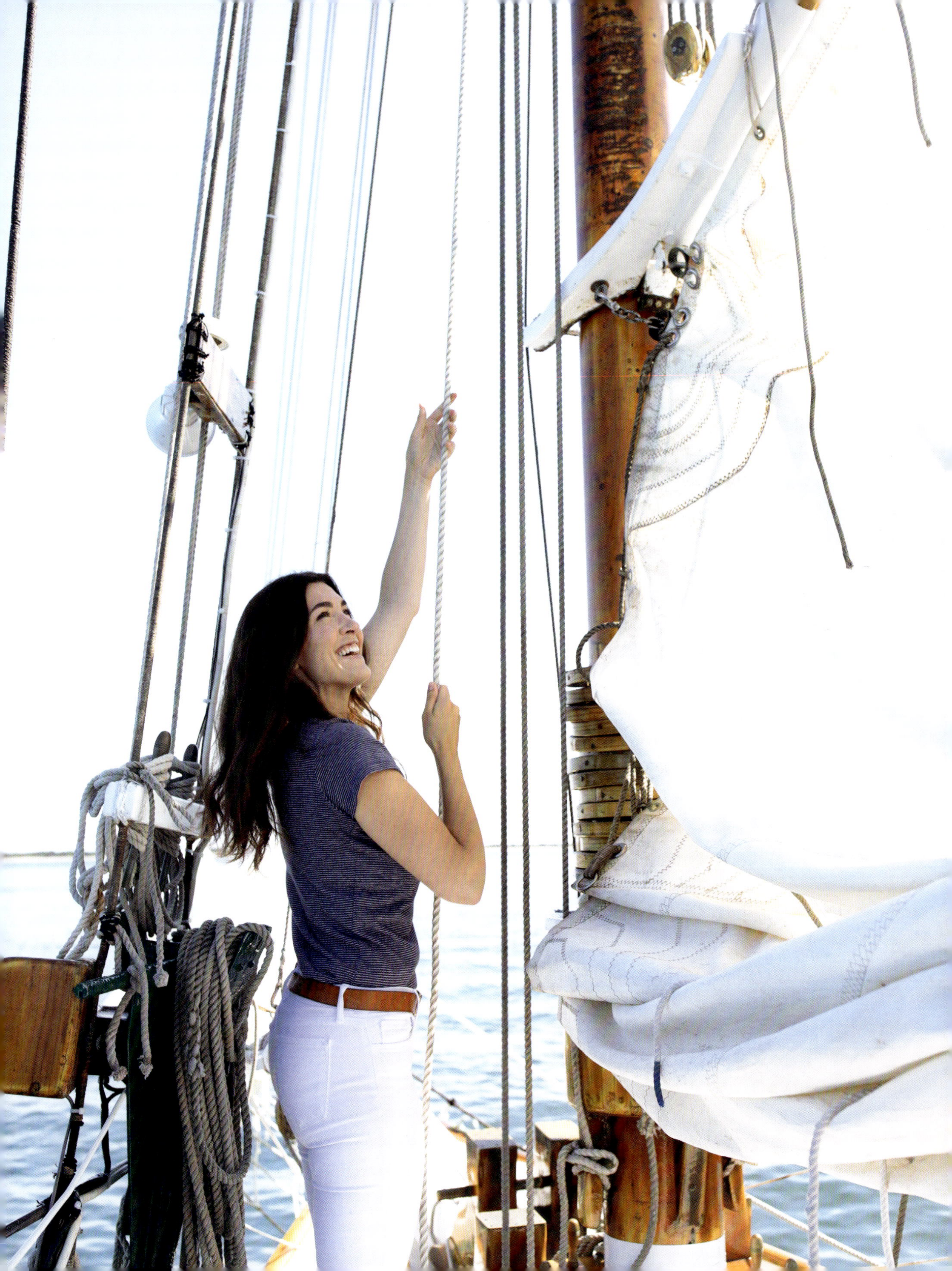

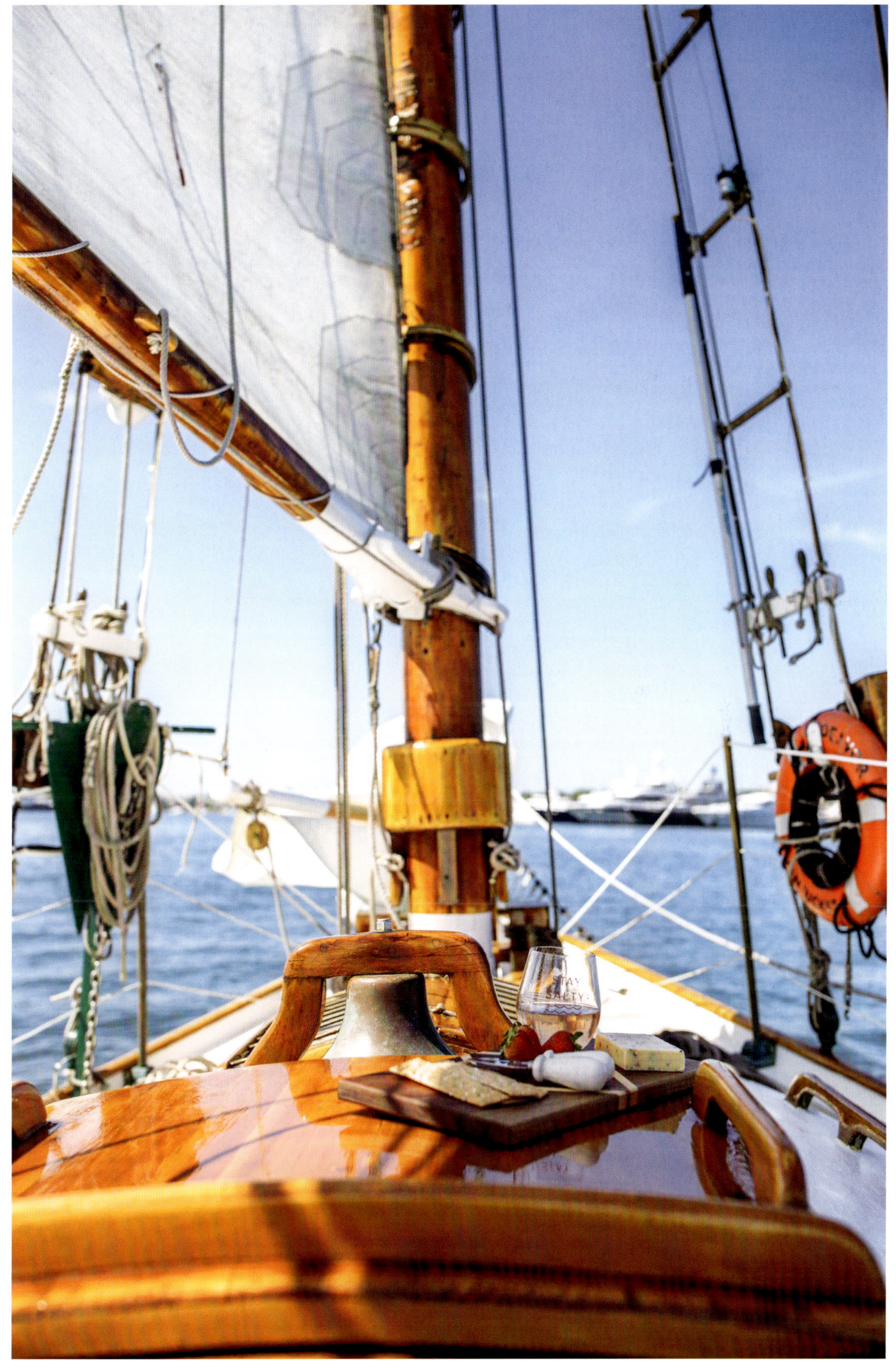
STAY
SALTY

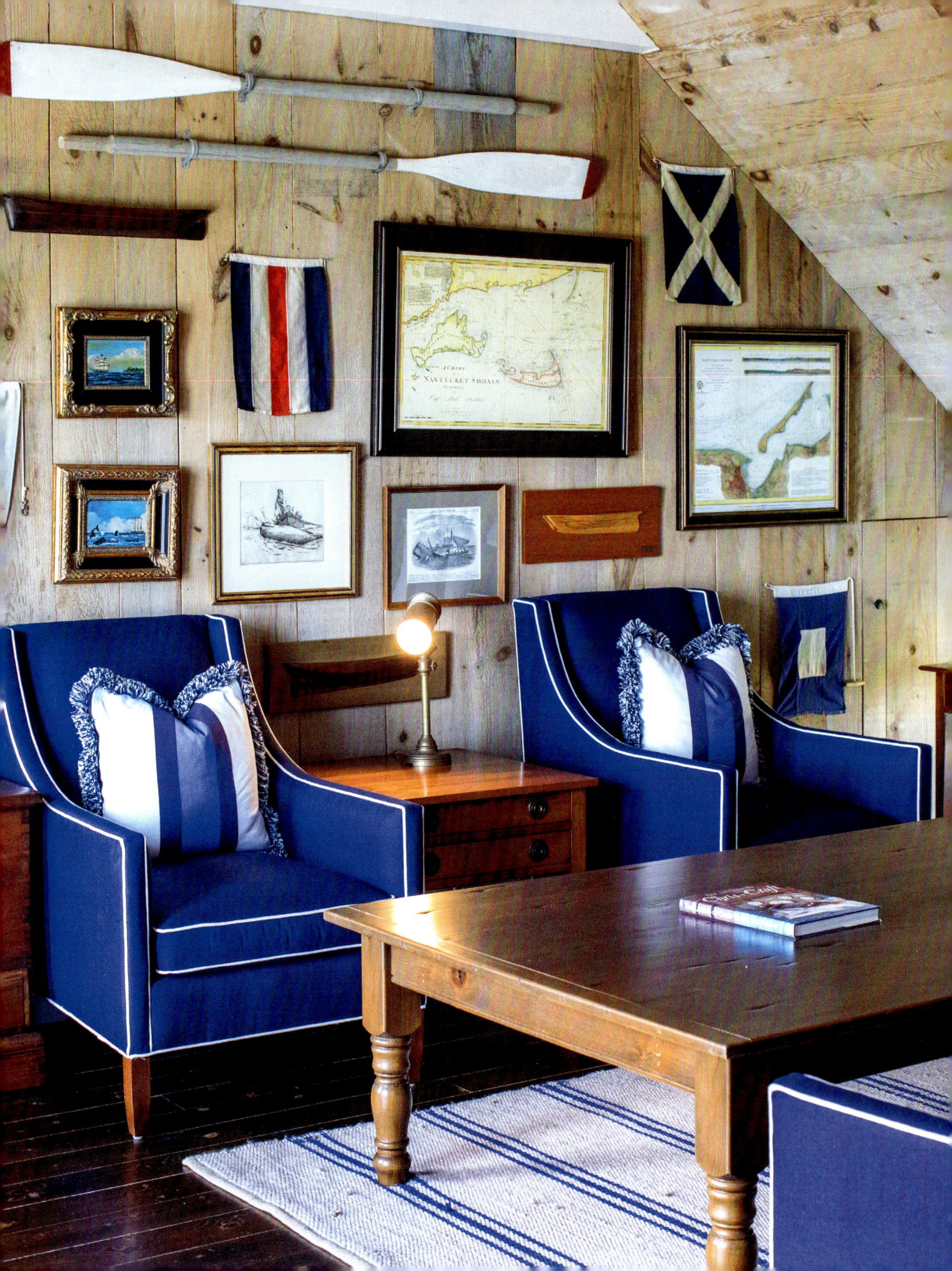
NANTUCKET SHOALS

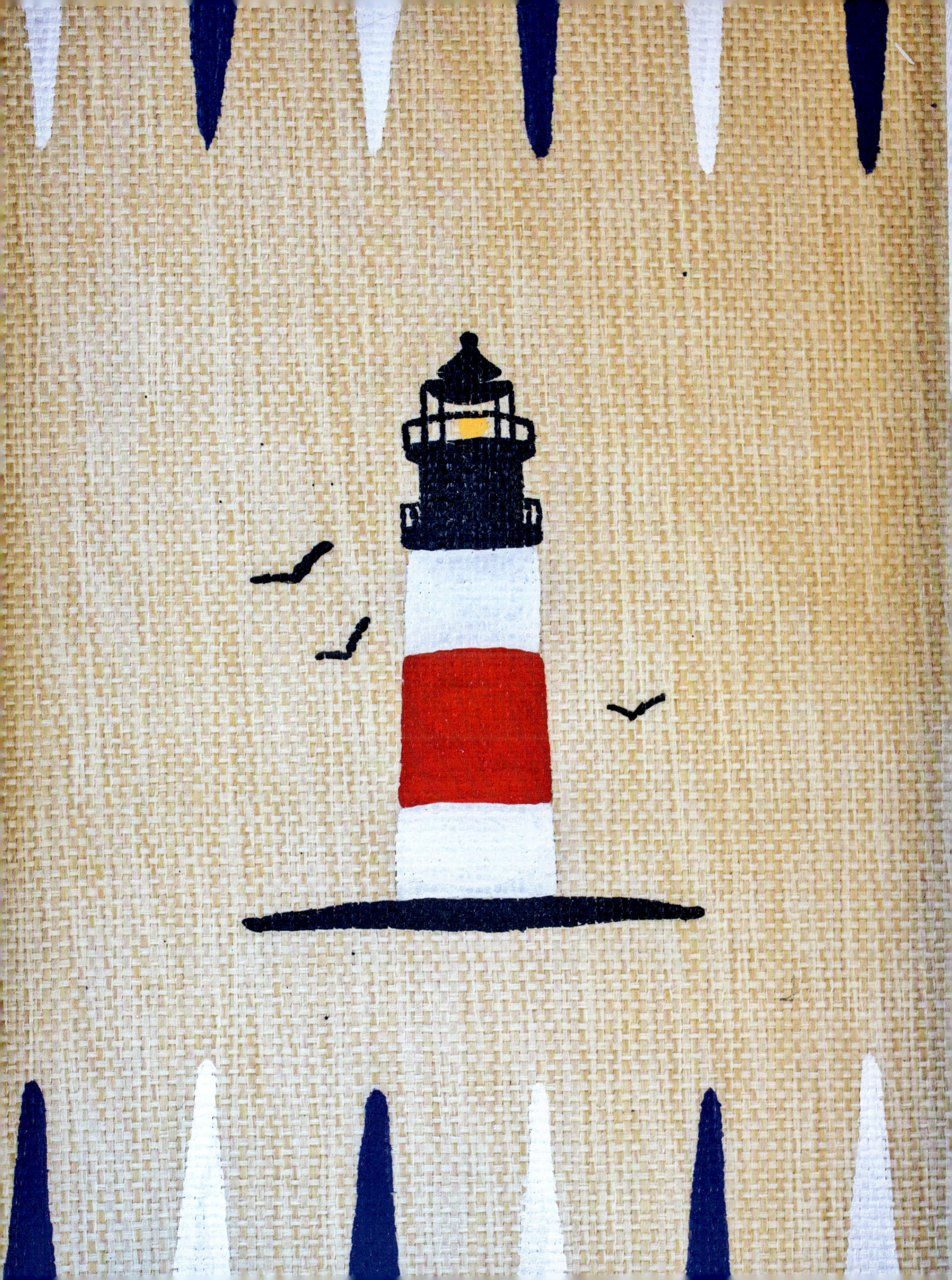

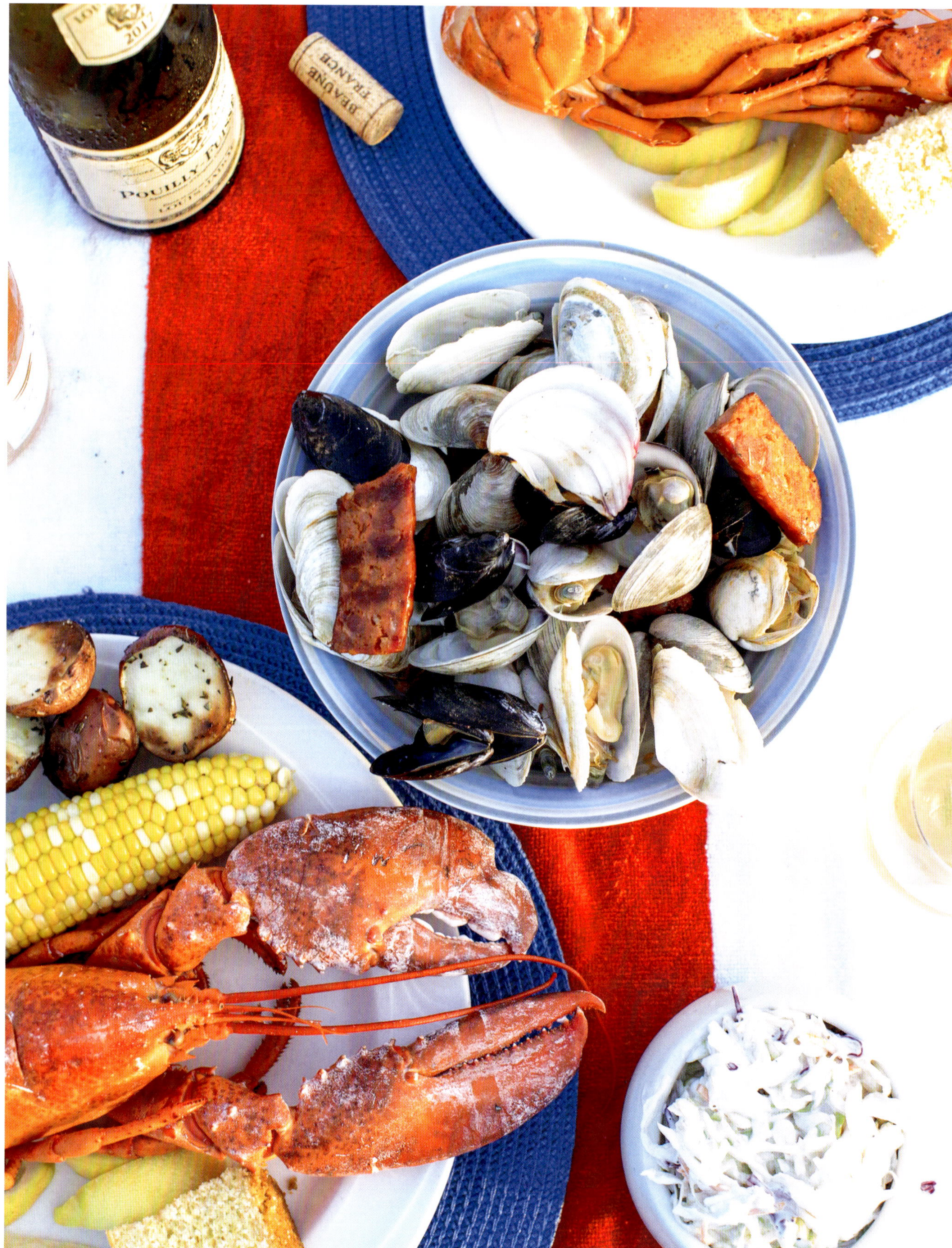
BEAUNE
FRANCE

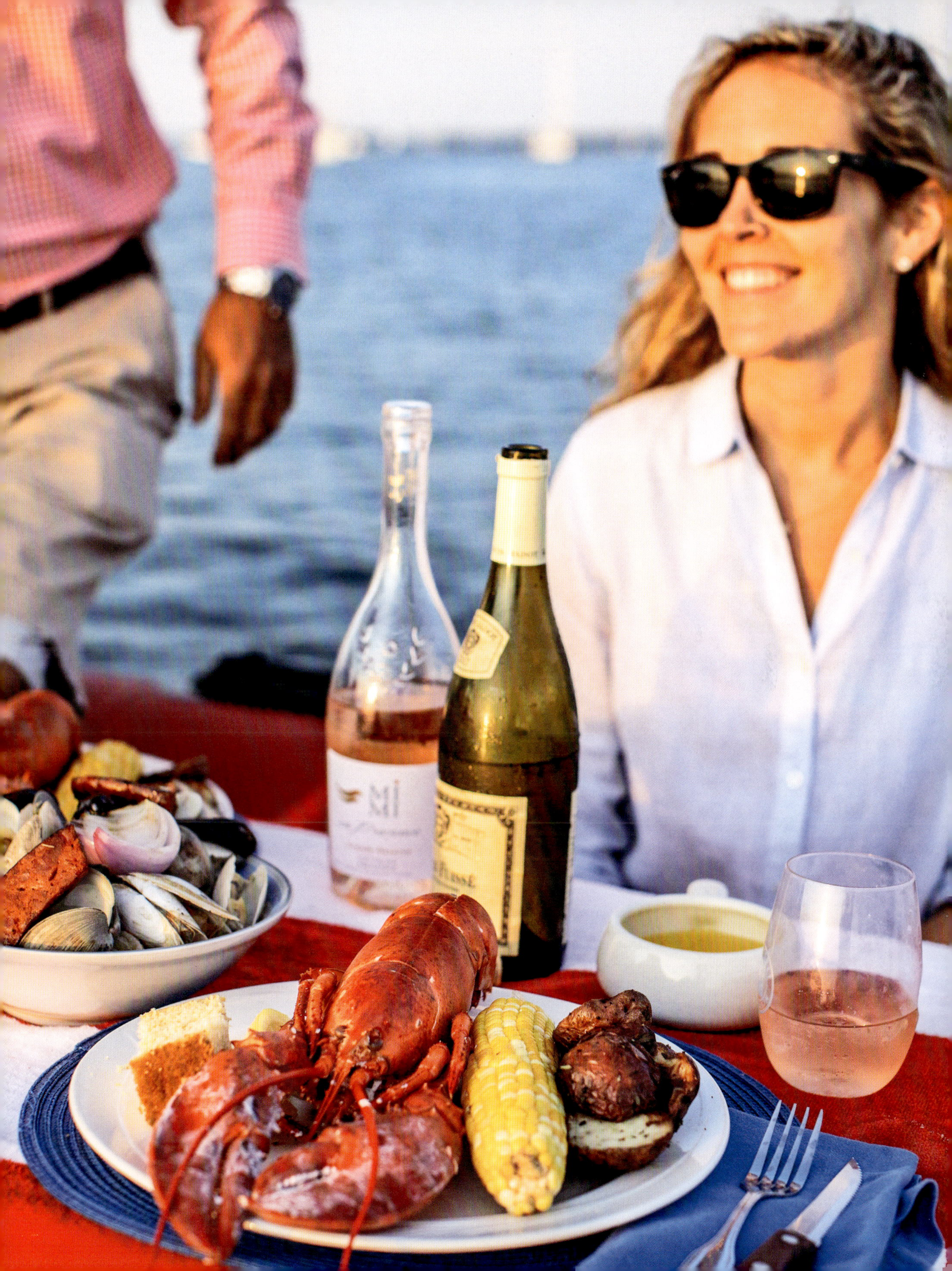

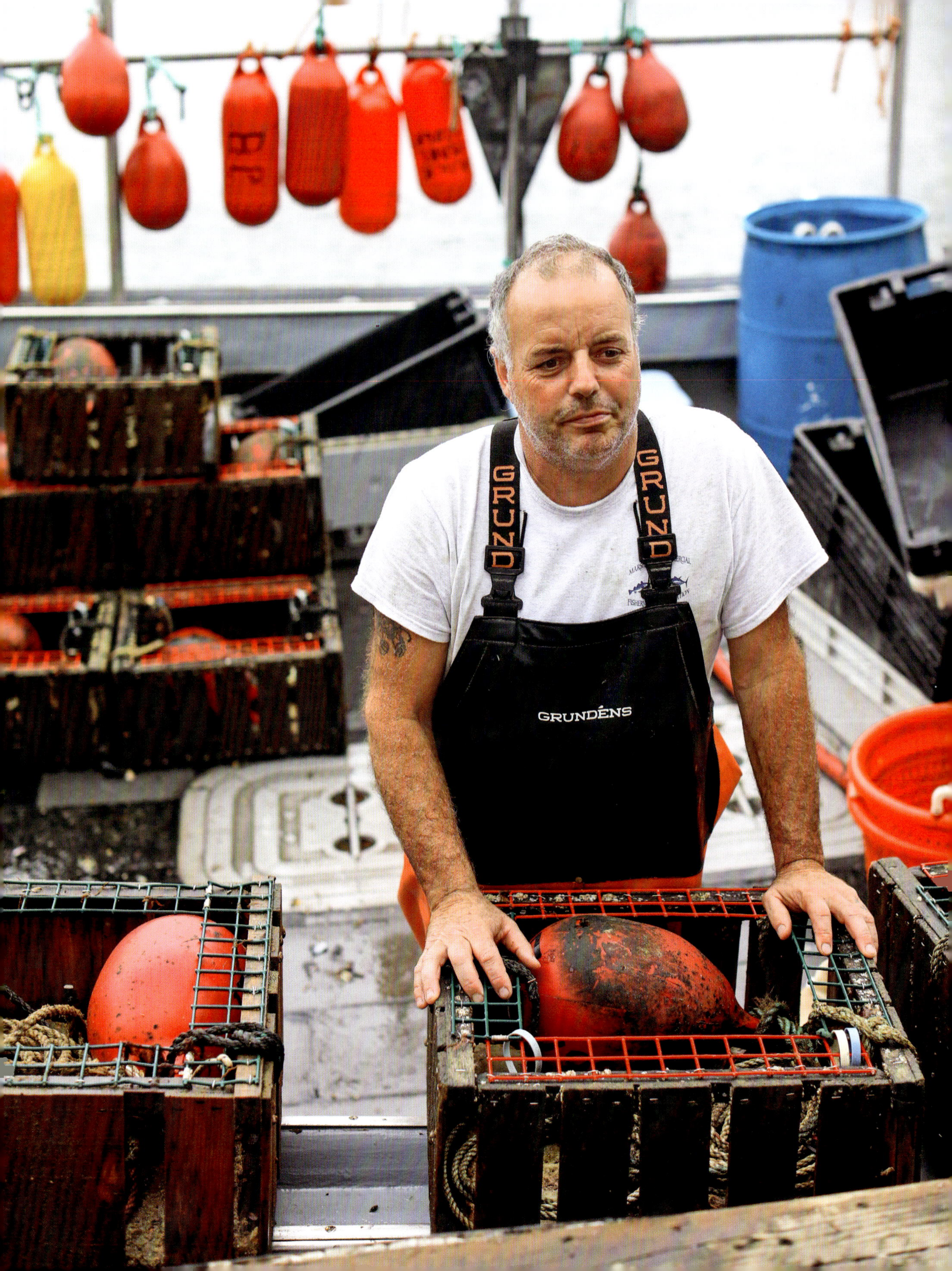
GRUND
GRUND
GRUNDÉNS

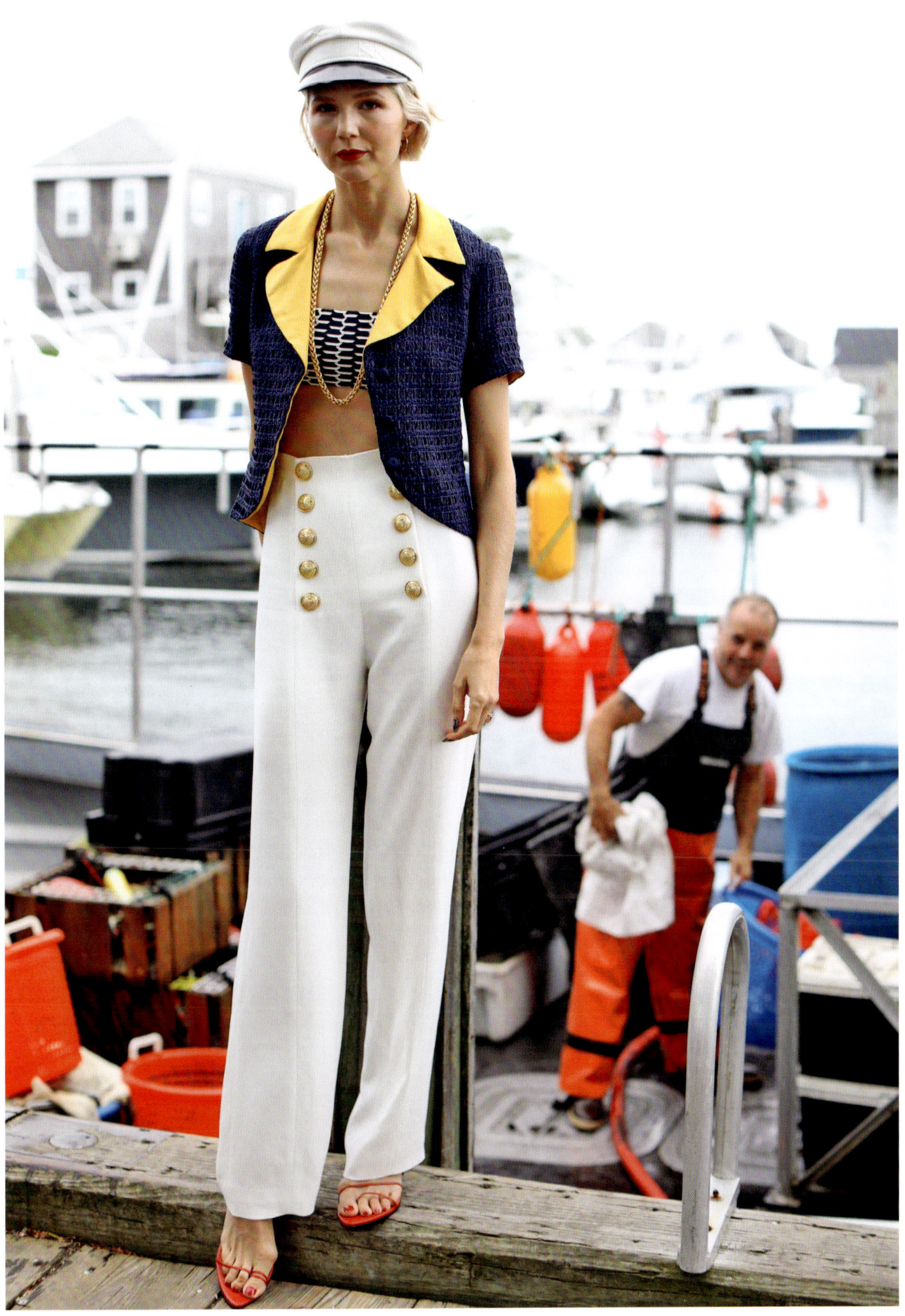

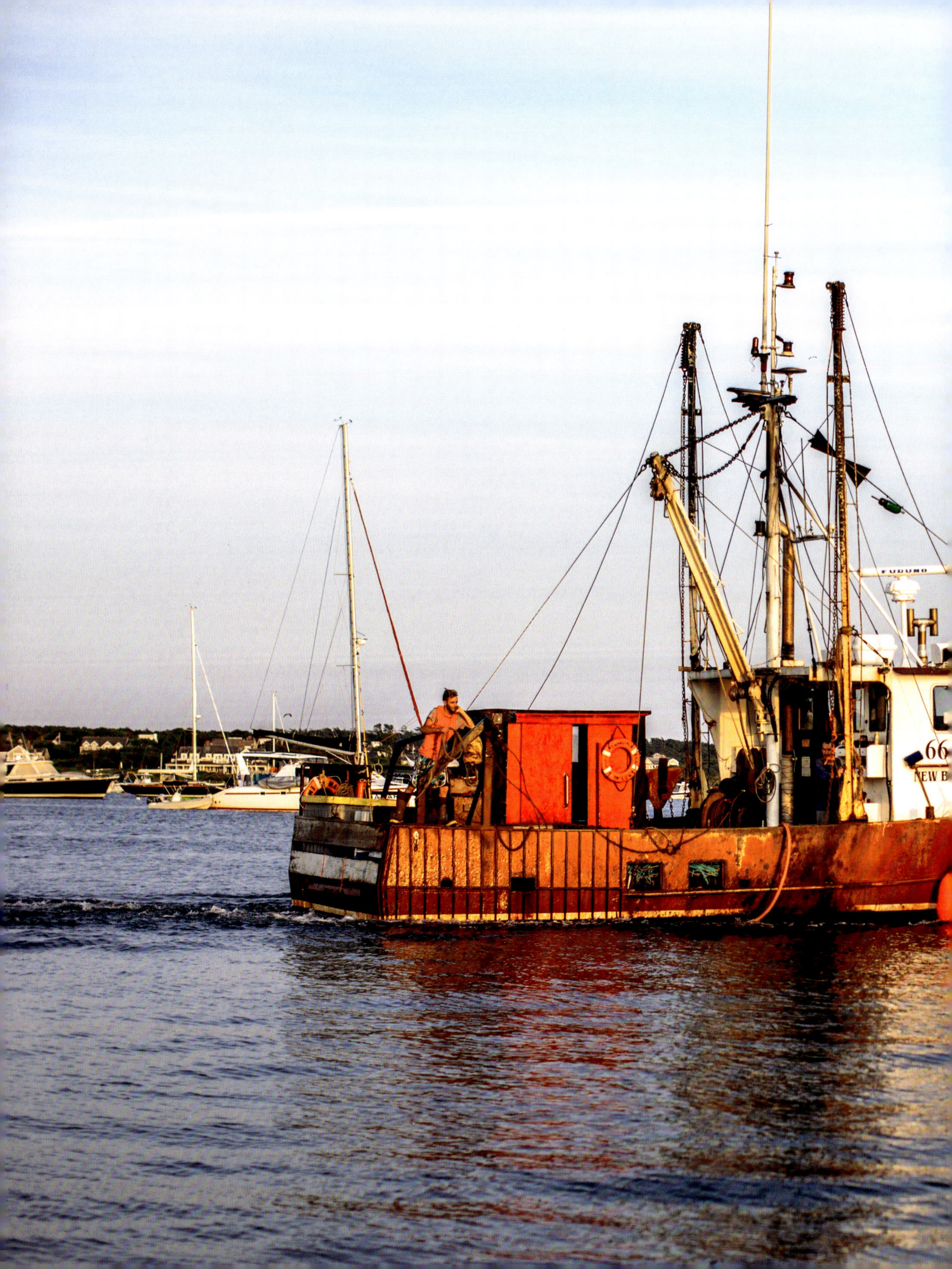

66

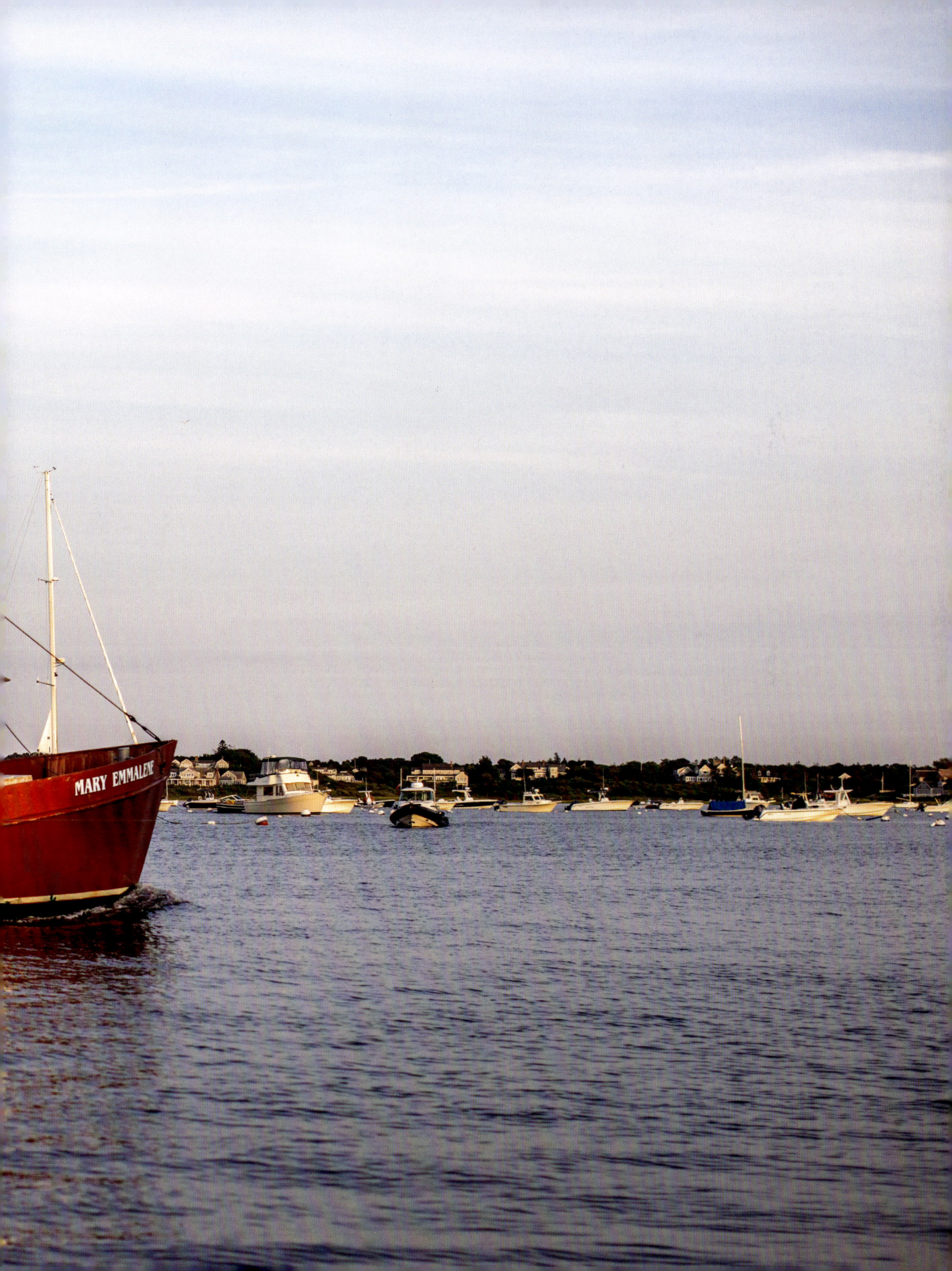
MARY EMMALENE

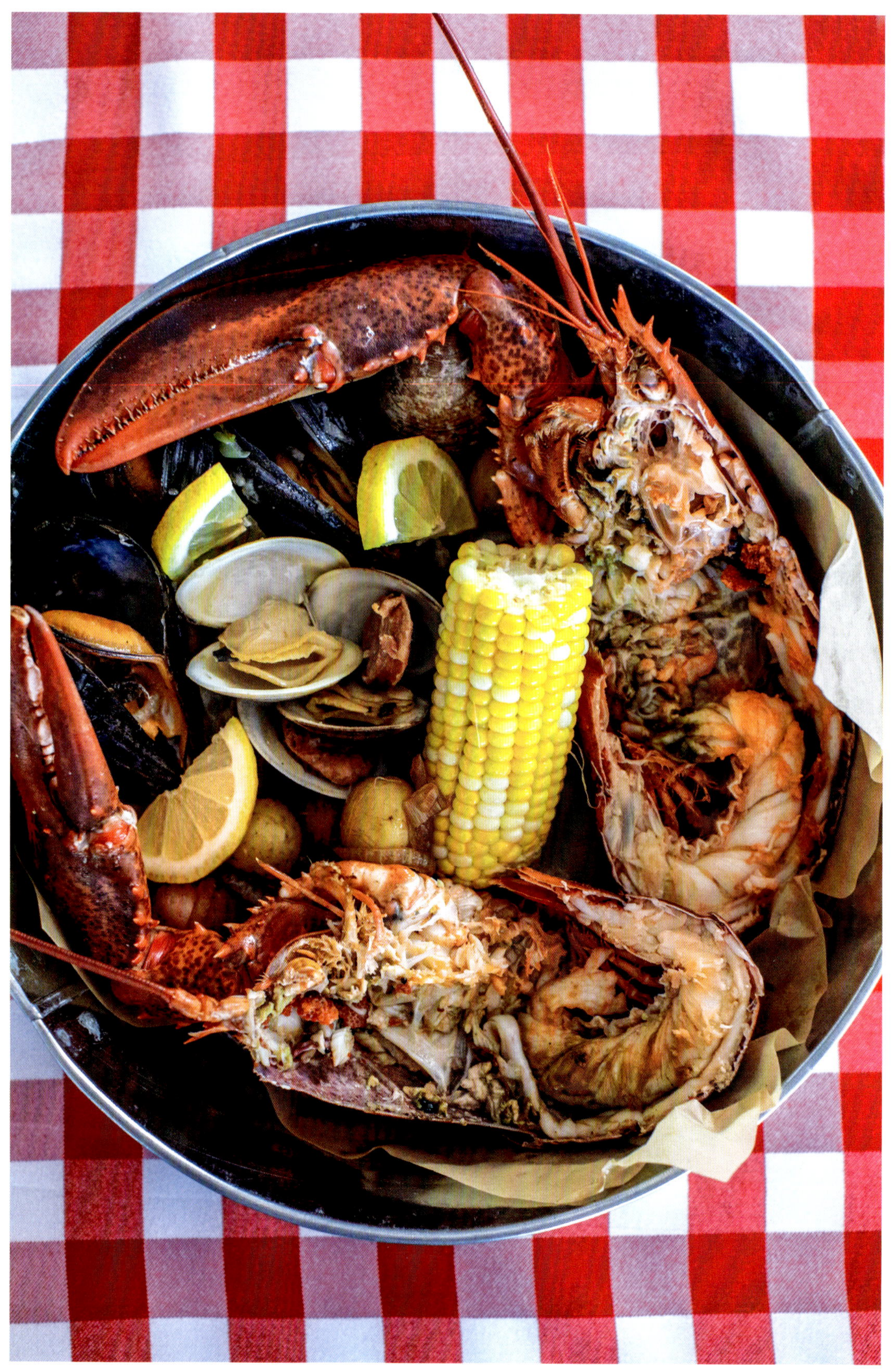

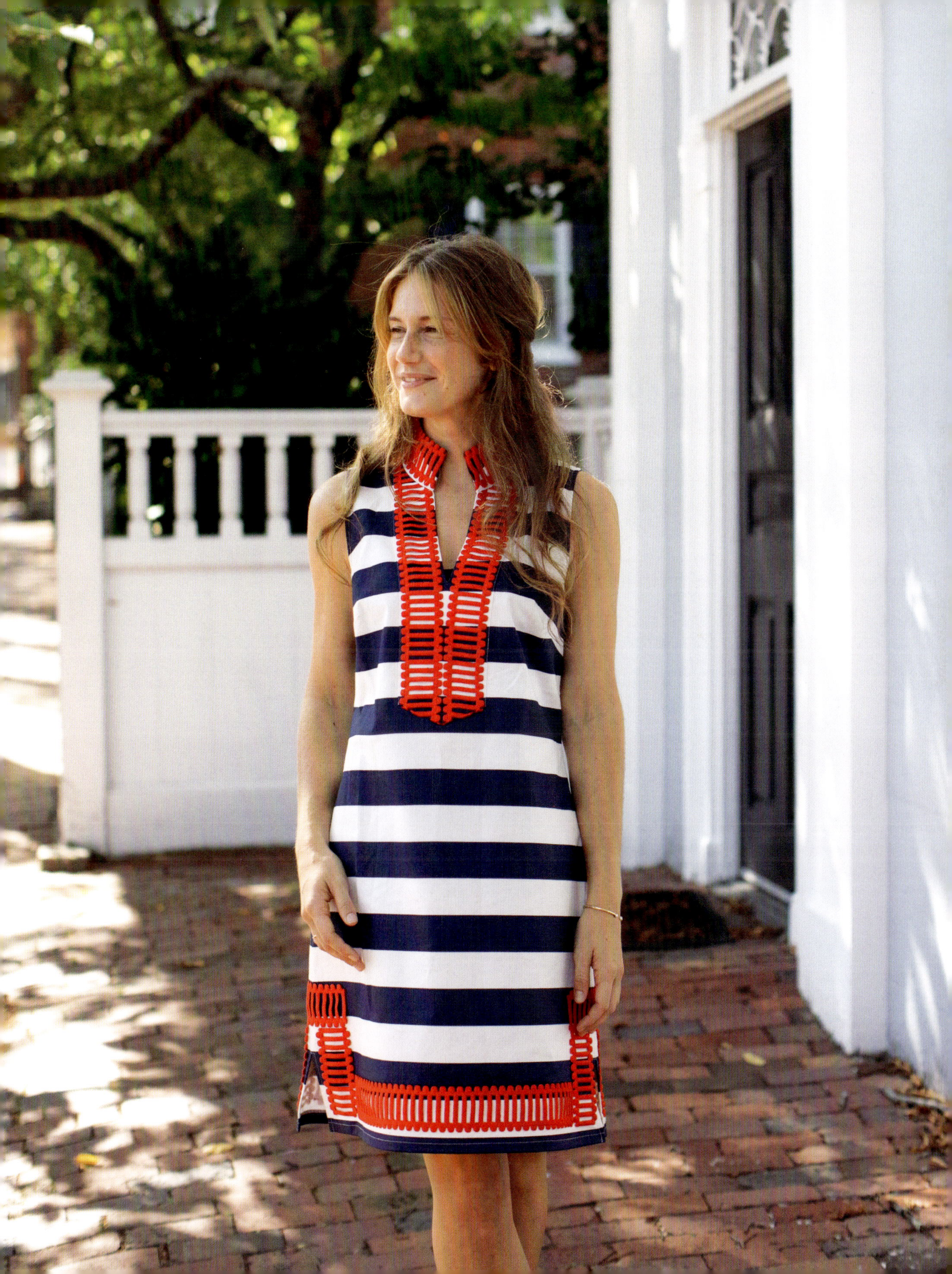

David M. Handy, founder and creative director, Handy & Dallaire Events

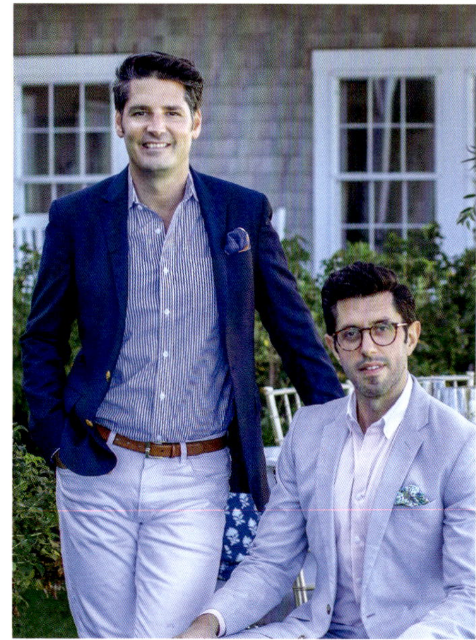

David (left) with husband and partner Donald Dallaire

YEARS ON NANTUCKET: *Seven*

MODE OF TRANSPORT: *I try to walk to slow down and take in the island.*

FAVORITE BEACH: *Driving out to Great Point.*

SUMMER UNIFORM: *White Levi's, blue blazer and loafers.*

ACCESSORY: *Vintage Hermès pocket square.*

_ IS BETTER ON NANTUCKET: *Summer*

GREATEST EXTRAVAGANCE: *Stubbs and Wootton shoe collection.*

IDEAL DAY: *Pool day then drinks on the patio at Cru.*

CLASSIC NANTUCKET IS … *lighthouse, anchors, chocolate-covered cranberries, and Main Street.*

FAVORITE THING/SPOT ON NANTUCKET? *Sunsets at the Galley.*

FAVORITE ISLAND ACTIVITY: *Clambakes on the beach with friends.*

COMMON NANTUCKET MISCONCEPTION: *That mopeds are a good idea on cobblestones.*

ISLAND EVENT: *Christmas Stroll is one of my favorites with everyone full of holiday cheer, supporting local businesses, and the wonderful Festival of Trees.*

NECESSITY ON NANTUCKET: *Reservations! So many amazing restaurants!*

IF ONLY EVERY VISITOR COULD … *experience the 60-second steak at The Pearl.*

ISLANDERS NEVER … *get confused at how to drive around the rotary.*

_ IS SO NANTUCKET: *Blue hydrangeas and Nantucket baskets*

Page 200: Erin Wilson; Page 204: John S. Johnson, Susan Short and their children Claire, Blossom, and Augustus; Page 210: design by Tara Young Earley; Page 212: Gail and Rafael Osana; Page 222: (Col. 1, top to bottom): Raymond Milnarik, Elin Hilderbrand, Thomas and Patricia Anathan, Jonny Arena; (Col. 2): Mackenzie Horan; Edward Sanford; (from left to right) Emily Millington, Kristen Kellogg, Georgie Morley, Meredith Hanson, Erin Wilson; Brooke Harlow and Sloane Palmer, Christopher Quidley; (Col. 3): Miguel Hernandez, Brigid Sullivan and Jock Gifford, Sloane Grover-Dodge, Starbuck Family, Mark and Gwenn Snider; (Col. 4): Stephen Danelian and Lulu Powers, Charlotte and Jamey Bridier, Alfie Sanford and Sandi Holland, Sarah, Sally and Lizzy Michler; Page 223: (Col. 1, top to bottom) Mitchell's Books, Sarah Lehn, Townsend Ambrecht and Ireland Mullin, interior designer (left) and client; (Col. 2): Stacey Leuliette, Daphne Mitchell and Cormac Collier, Edmond Tessier; (Col. 3): Deborah Gail Futter and William Cohen, Beverly Hall and David Lane Billings II; (Col. 4): Melanie R. Sabelhaus, Eric Holch, Elanor and Olivia Termaine, Sage Goldsmith Termaine

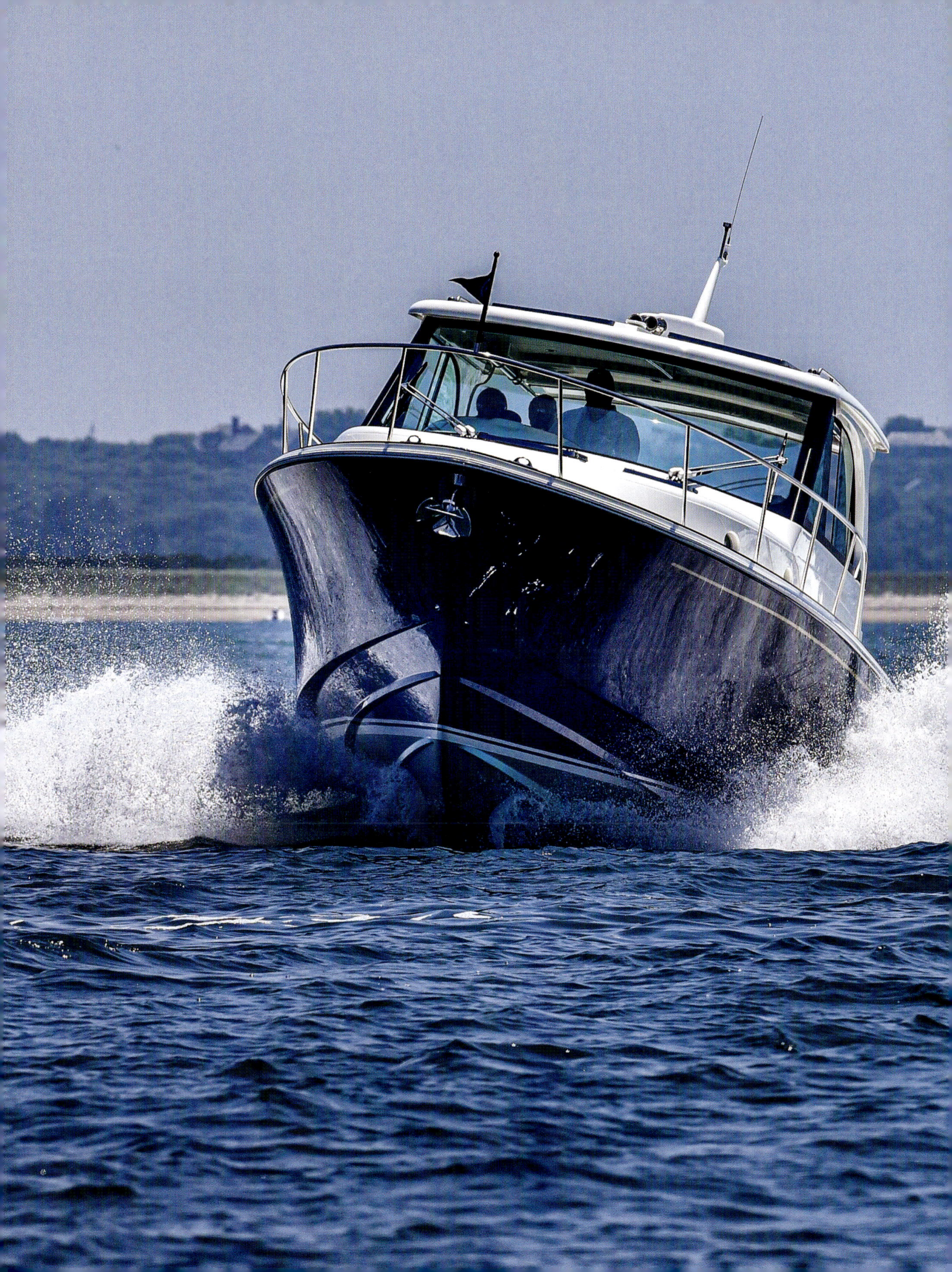

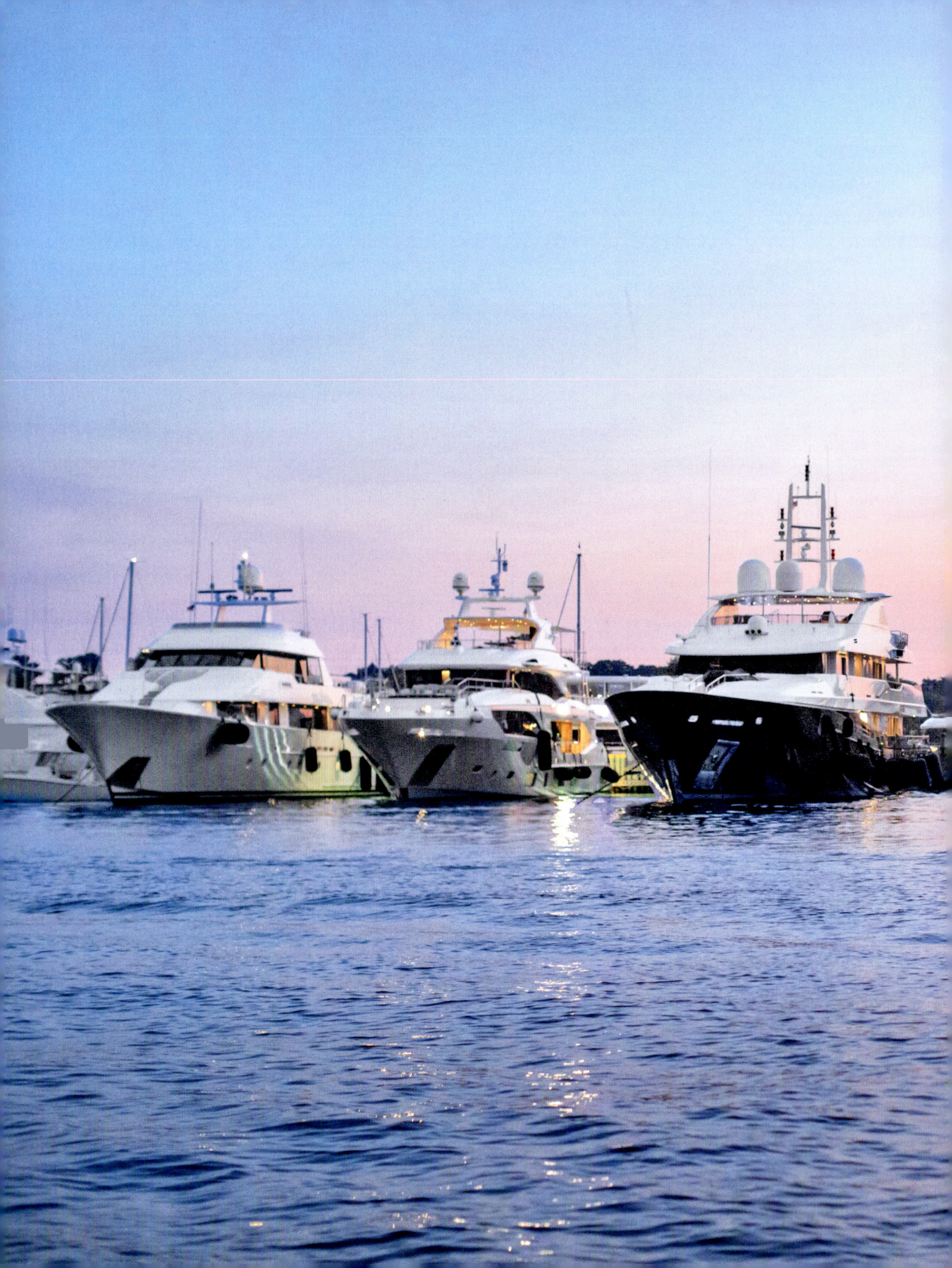

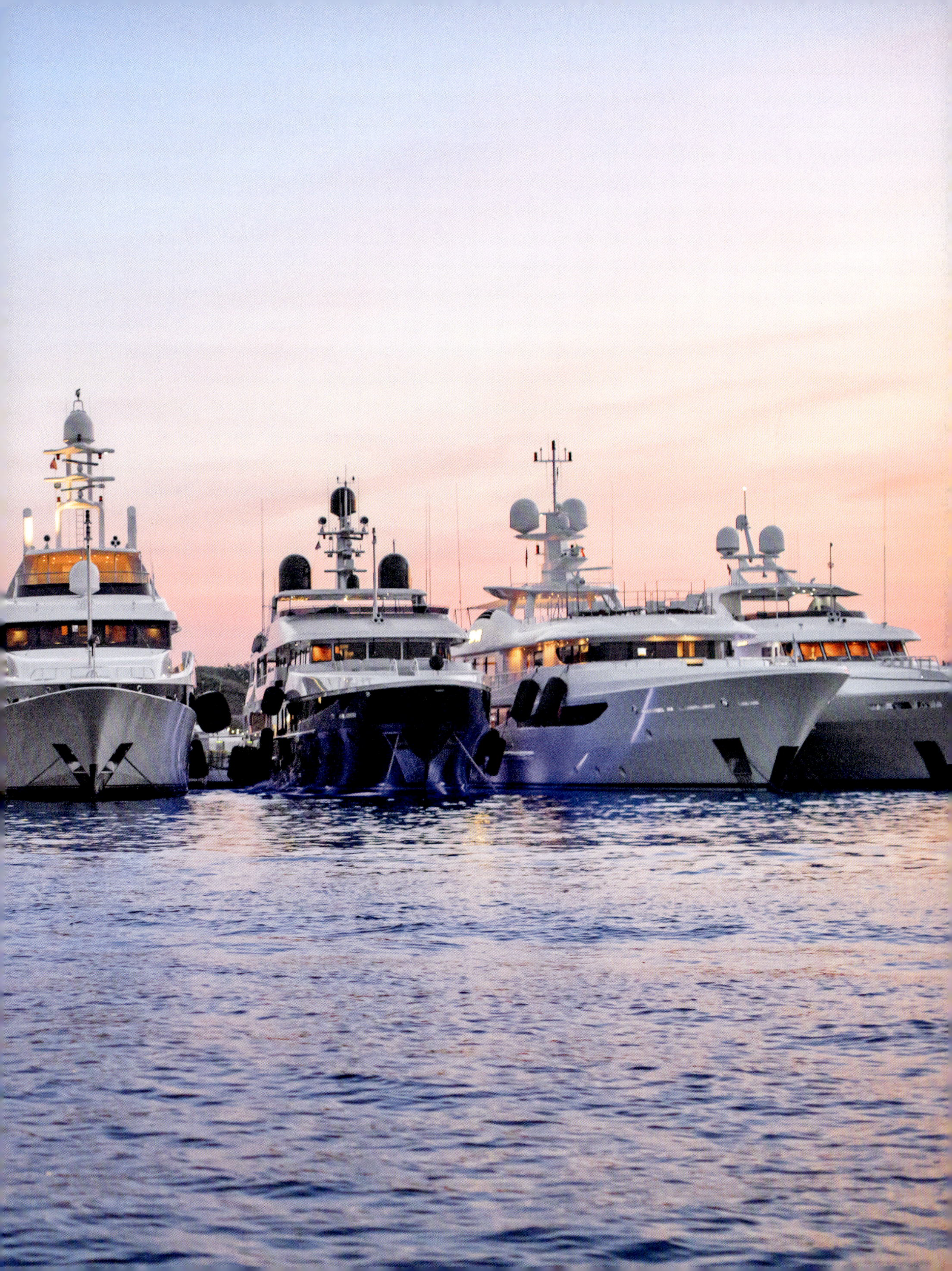

“For me, the most special time to be here is during a hurricane, to hear the wind whipping and the shutters flapping, it's like, yes, Mother Nature is in charge. We think we can manage her but we really can't. To me the most important thing about this island is how fragile it is. Its history is fragile. Environmentally it's fragile. It's an island sitting in the Atlantic Ocean. It moves!”

—**Lissy Bryan, lifelong summer resident**

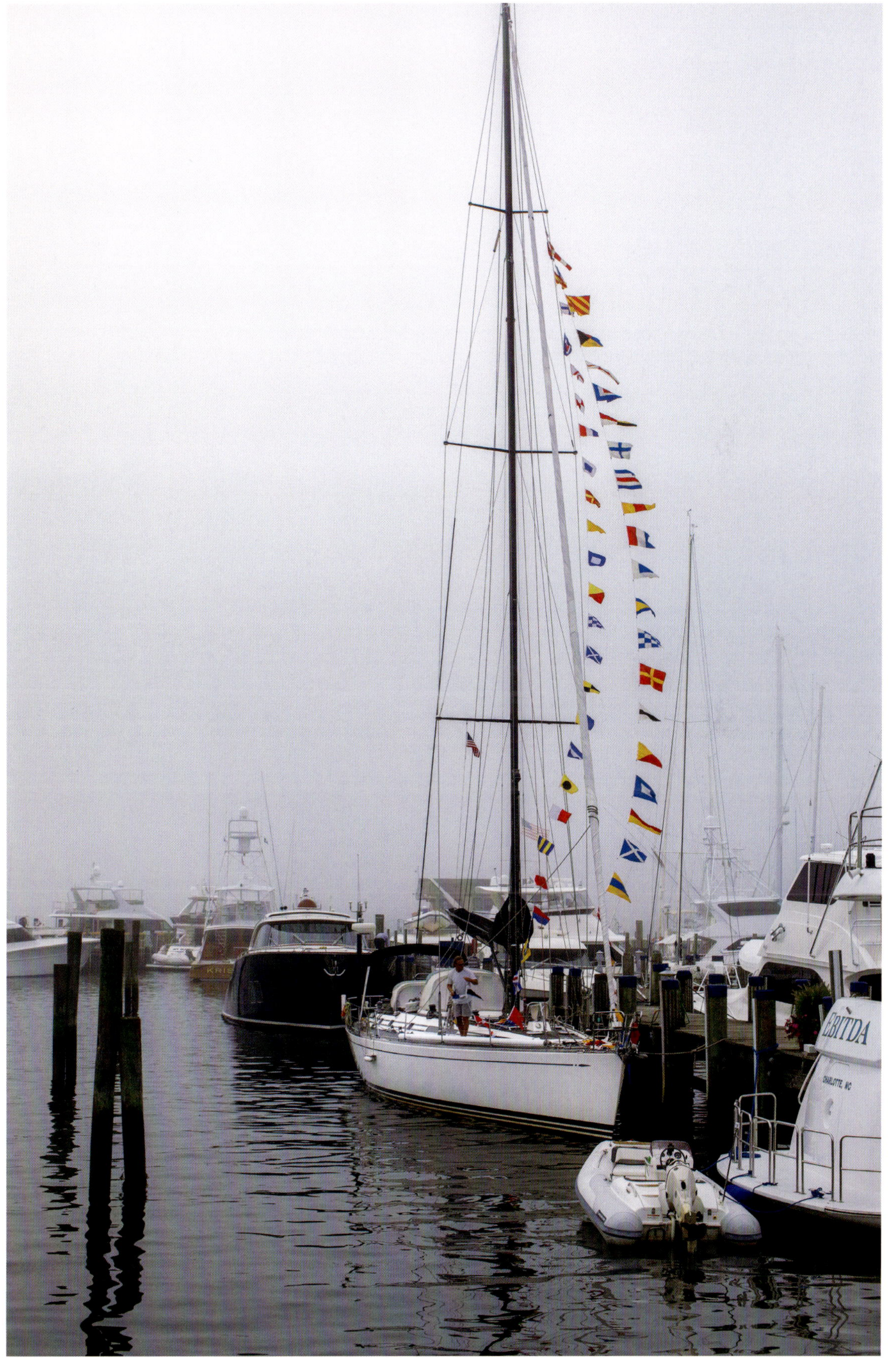
EBITDA
CHARLOTTE, NC

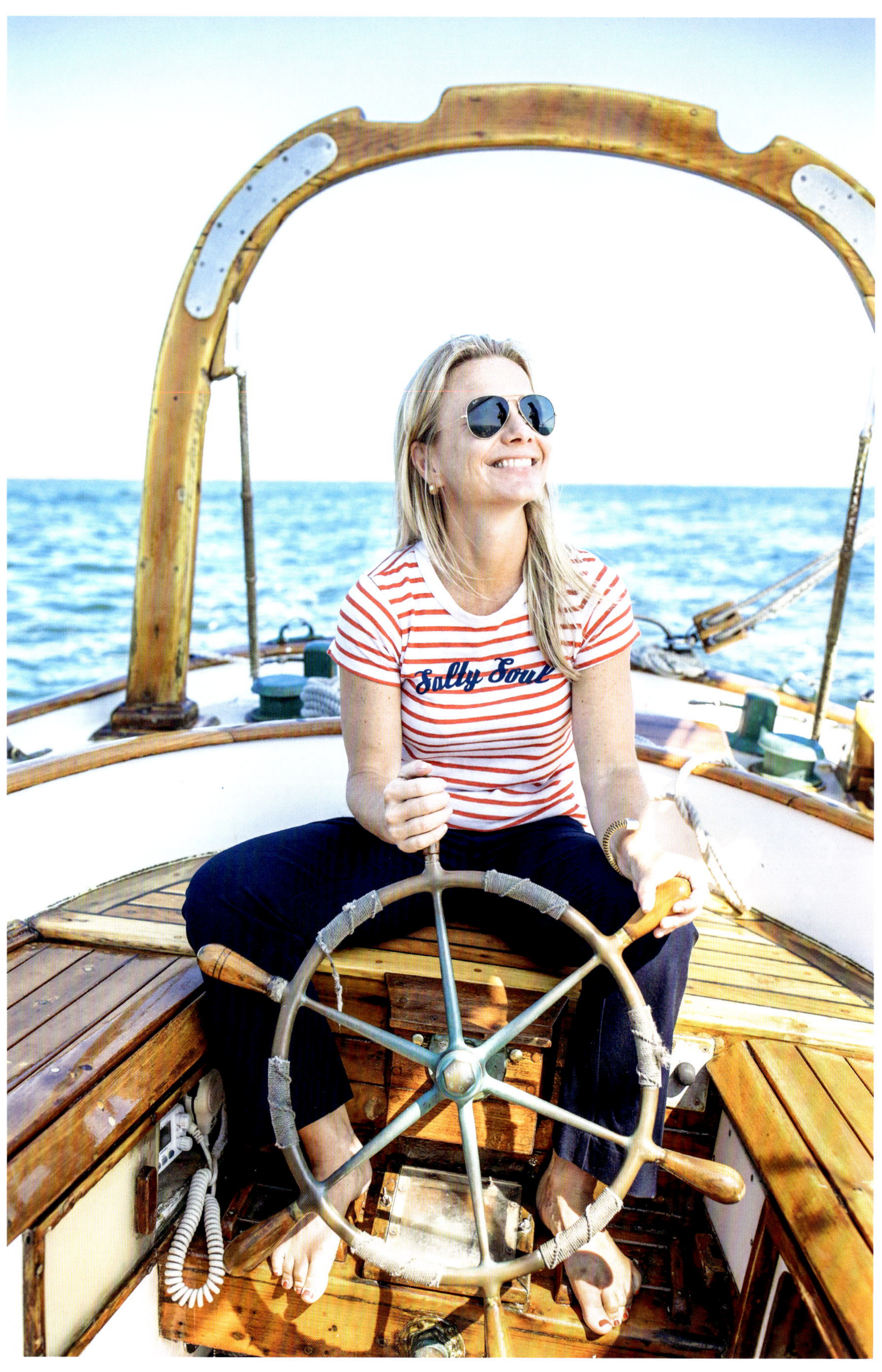
Salty Soul

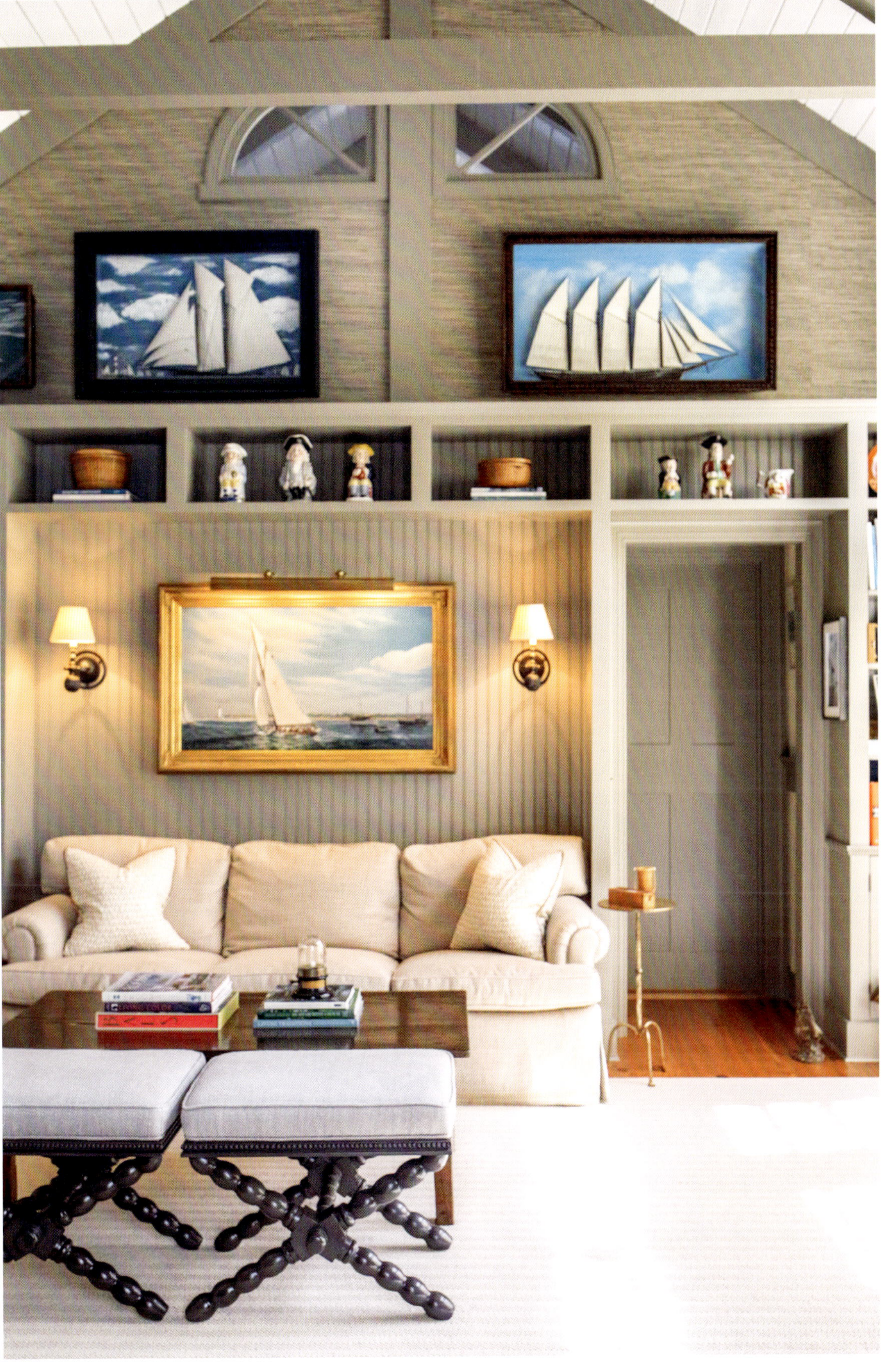

PHILANTHROPY

"It turns out Nantucket is a very big family," says actor-director John Shea. "If you are in trouble or you need something, the community supports you in miraculous ways."

A key tenant to Nantucket life, philanthropy is an island value ingrained in both summer and year-round residents. More than 100 nonprofits make an impact on the community, with causes ranging from preserving history and the natural environment, to building up resources for islanders and bolstering its arts and cultural offerings.

One major island resource Nantucketers have rallied around is the new Nantucket Cottage Hospital complex—which includes housing for staff—built at a cost of more than $200 million. That's a healthy campaign for an island population of just 50,000 at the height of summer. The ninety-year-old Hospital Thrift Shop donated half a million dollars from sales and support in just one year.

Much of the summer season is devoted to large and small charitable events, and even for those not directly involved in nonprofit giving, the events offer fun and glamour for an otherwise low-key island. The island's busiest weekend happens mid-August, when the Boston Philharmonic plays in support of the Hospital Foundation to around 40,000 people on beach chairs and blankets along Jetties Beach.

For many island residents, giving back is often a family legacy as well. Entrepreneur and filmmaker John S. Johnson is devoted to the Nantucket community, as were his parents, Seward and Cecilia Johnson. His belief in looking at where one's passion meets another's need led him to found the Nantucket Film Festival and to get involved in the Dreamland Theater when it was in danger of being lost. Johnson and others ensured that the summer movie house, with a 180-year cultural history on the island, was saved and now serves as a resource for arts and education year-round in a state-of-the-art, environmentally sensitive facility.

"We're talking about people with phenomenal gifts and they share them because they have an understanding that Nantucket can't just be beaches and restaurants to be a home," says Shea. "To be a spiritually nourishing home it has to be multi-dimensional and the cultural life of a place like Nantucket is vital to everybody's wellbeing, whether it's theater, art, literature, or poetry. And it takes benefactors, patrons of the arts—the modern Medicis—to help support that. And that happens on Nantucket, which makes it a very special place."

Naturally, charity events are plentiful, filling the summer social calendar for many. With camera-in-hand, longtime islander Gene Mahon reports on them in his weekly newsletter, **Mahon About Town**, snapping pictures of benefactors in pastel-colored party attire.

The philanthropic mindset is by no means reserved to summer residents. Islanders are deeply civic minded. There is a recognition of the interdependence between year-rounders who often rely on each other for mental and physical survival. Shea tells one remarkable story of a beloved island carpenter, "the last of the hippie carpenters," who was felled by ALS. When he was nearing his death, the community organized a fundraiser that generated enough money to buy a home for his wife and children, which is no small feat on an island where affordable housing is a scarcity.

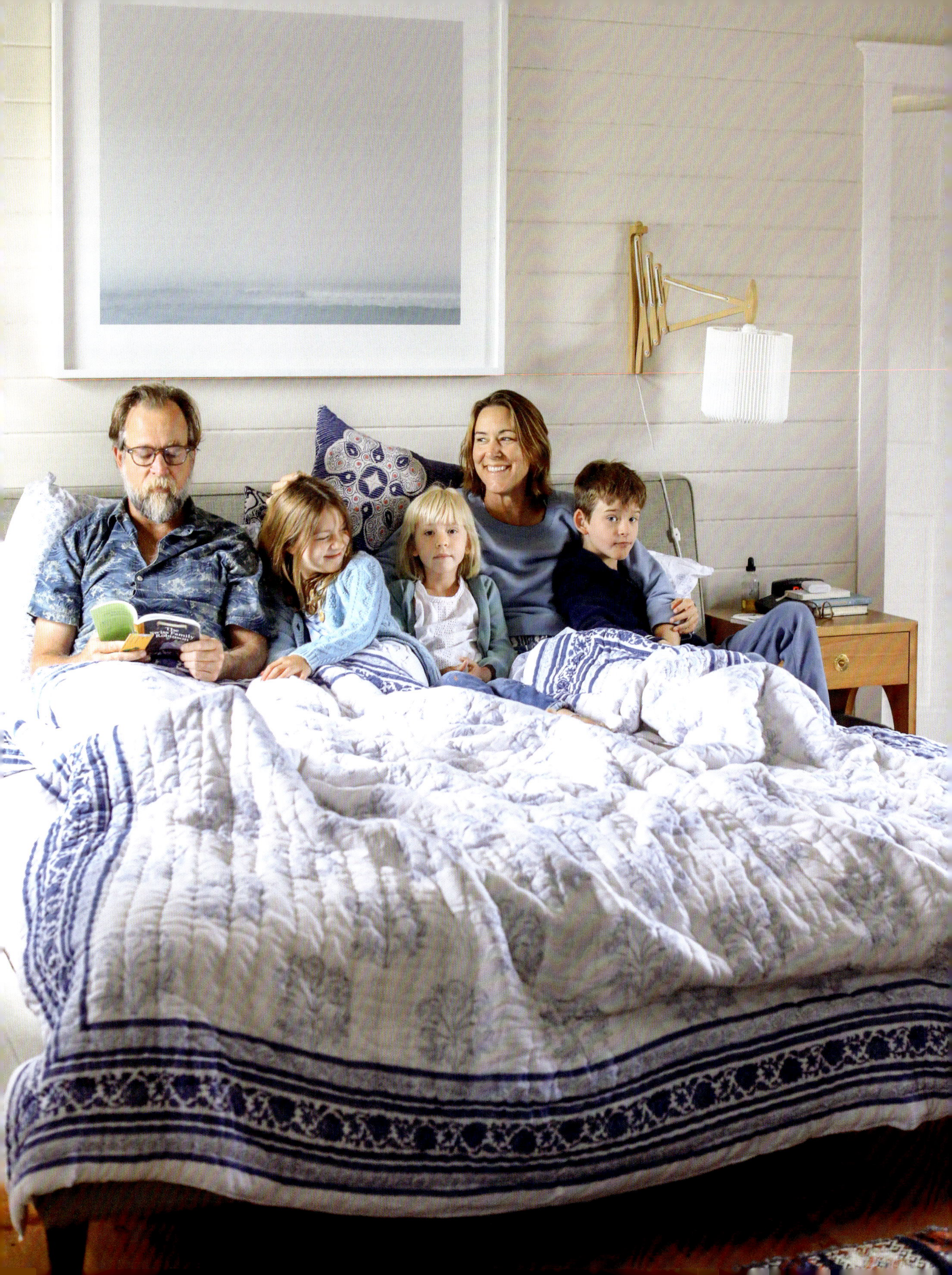

John S. Johnson III, co-founder of BuzzFeed; founder and chairman of Harmony Labs; founder of Almanac Arts Colony on Nantucket; The Harmony Hotel in Nosara, Costa Rica

YEARS ON NANTUCKET: *Fifty-three years on the island; mostly summers and a few gorgeous autumns.*

ISLAND HOME: *Tupancy Links/Cliff Road area*

HOW LONG HAVE YOU BEEN GOING TO NANTUCKET? *My parents met on a plane to Nantucket that got fogged out. I was there before I was born, always as a summer kid with some exceptions where we stayed into the fall.*

FAVORITE BEACH: *Totally depends what you're out to do. For swimming you want the north shore, unless you're out to play in waves then you want to be on the south shore. As a surfer I'll tend to be somewhere south of Cisco Beach.*

NANTUCKET UNIFORM: *Fjällräven quick-dry shorts, Birkenstocks, and a t-shirt. I'm quarter Bermudian so I wore shorts, long socks, and a jacket to a couple of events this summer and thought, "this is brilliant".*

MOST DAYS ON NANTUCKET I … *am finding a way to get outside. Mountain biking these single-track trails out to Madaket and foraging for blueberries and blackberries in summer, and for wild grapes in the fall.*

ASPECT OF LIFE ON NANTUCKET THAT'S THE SAME AS ITS ALWAYS BEEN: *Relating to nature in a really immediate way that not all folks on the mainland are used to doing.*

FAVORITE THING/SPOT ON NANTUCKET? *Our vegetable garden at home.*

COMMON MISCONCEPTION ABOUT NANTUCKET? *That all the artists have left.*

NANTUCKET HISTORICAL FIGURE THAT SPEAKS TO YOU? *Absalom Boston, such a cool dude, he was a whaling captain, maybe the first African American whaling captain. One of the things I really loved about that dude was that he sued the state of Massachusetts so his daughter, who was brilliant, could go to school past a certain grade. He effectively de-segregated schooling on Nantucket.*

NECESSITY ON NANTUCKET: *Bike*

IDEAL DAY: *Getting out on the water in some way with my family; surfing together or out on our little Hobie [catamaran]. Followed by lunch back home and me getting some time hitting a croquet ball. That's my time to think or meditate in the sense that I'm totally immersed in hitting that ball.*

MOST TREASURED EXPERIENCE/THING ON-ISLAND: *Time with my wife and kids. The second would be my memories growing up there with my parents. Also first crushes and summer nights when I was first independent as a kid and could go out with friends.*

HOW DO YOU DEFINE NANTUCKET STYLE? *I think that's pretty hard to define because there have been so many different constituencies there. There was this incredible, cosmopolitan history and then, later on, this reductive country club preppy thing, and now with the great wealth that's settled in on the island it's gone more global but in a less accessible way.*

HAS THE ISLAND INSPIRED YOUR OWN CREATIVITY? *Oh definitely, more indirectly these days. I'm less interested in setting stories on Nantucket and more interested in the mental space and solitude that all the places you can get away to do for me.*

WHY DO YOU BRING ARTISTS TO NANTUCKET? *Typically we get artists from cities staying at this 200-year-old farmhouse on the island, and beyond the freshness of the novelty, there's the interchange. The island is still chock-full of interesting people.*

"There is definitely a rivalry between Nantucket and Martha's Vineyard. The Thanksgiving football game between the high schools is the only time some people ever go to the other island. For summer residents, you feel like you're on a little slice of heaven so why would you take a day from here to go there? Also, with Nantucket being further out to sea—it's 22 miles further from the Cape—it has a kind of magical feeling for people in the summer. You just can't believe a place looks like this and it's not in a theme park."

—Gwen Snider, owner of The Nantucket Hotel and The Winnetu resort on Martha's Vineyard

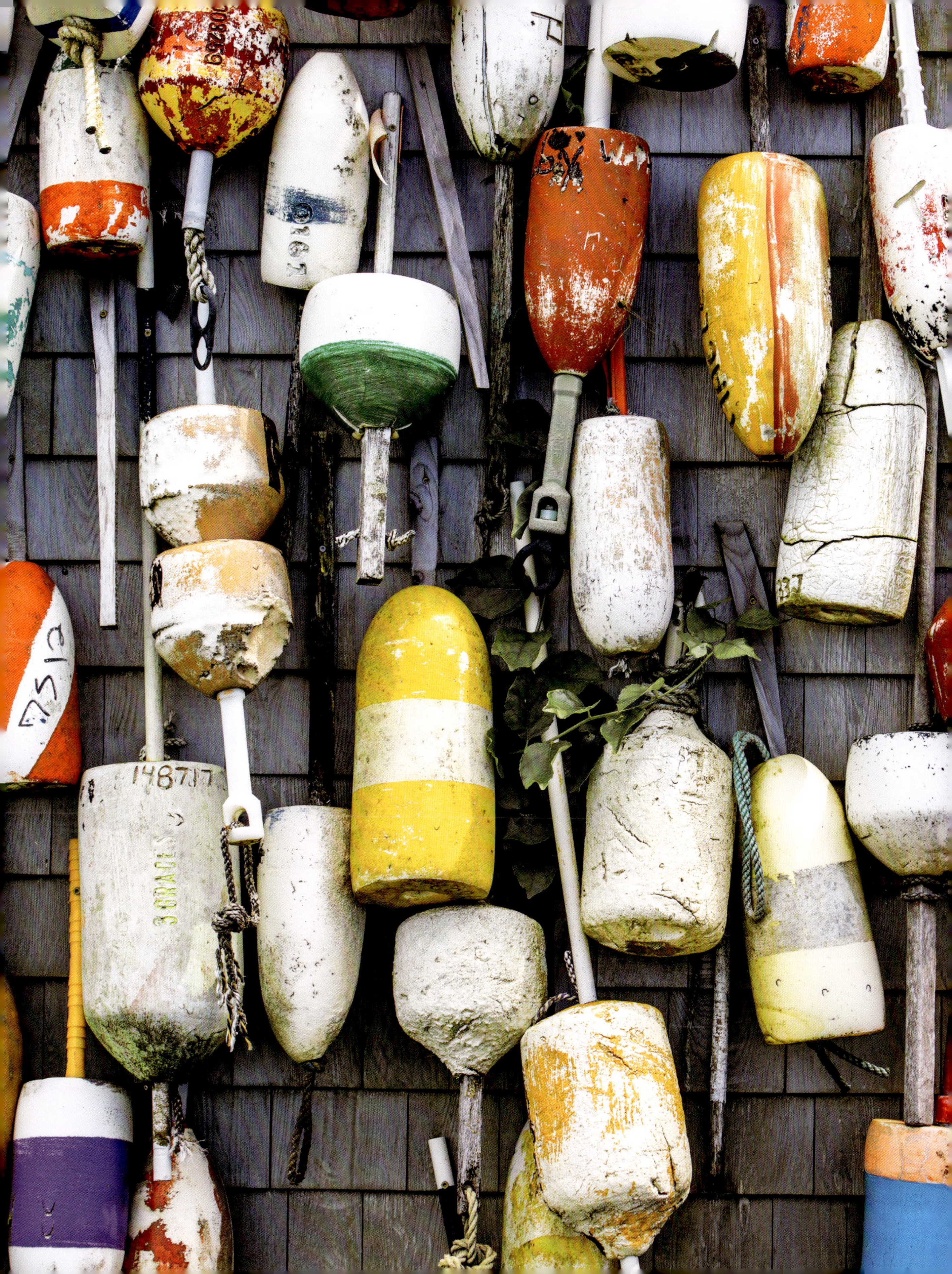

CONSERVATION AND HISTORIC PRESERVATION

For design buffs, history enthusiasts, anyone with an eye for aesthetics, stepping off the ferry on to Nantucket's Straight Wharf can seem like a dream. Legions of visitors are wowed by two striking characteristics of the island. First, the impeccably maintained historic architecture of Nantucket Town and beyond, and second, the large swaths of wild nature on the island. Not just the beaches (which are all free and open to the public) but the acres of fields, moors, cranberry bogs, as well as many biking, hiking, nature paths and trails snaking the land. The historic built environment and natural beauty work to transport visitors to another time, and headspace, on the island. One feels permission, even obliged, to adopt traditions of a simpler time when a milkshake at The Pharmacy or stroll through the Moors at Altar Rock is all the action you need in a day. The eternally lengthy line winding out of the Juice Bar ice-cream shop may be proof of that.

Walking through town, particularly at night when few cars are driving, can transport you to another time. Wavy glass windows,

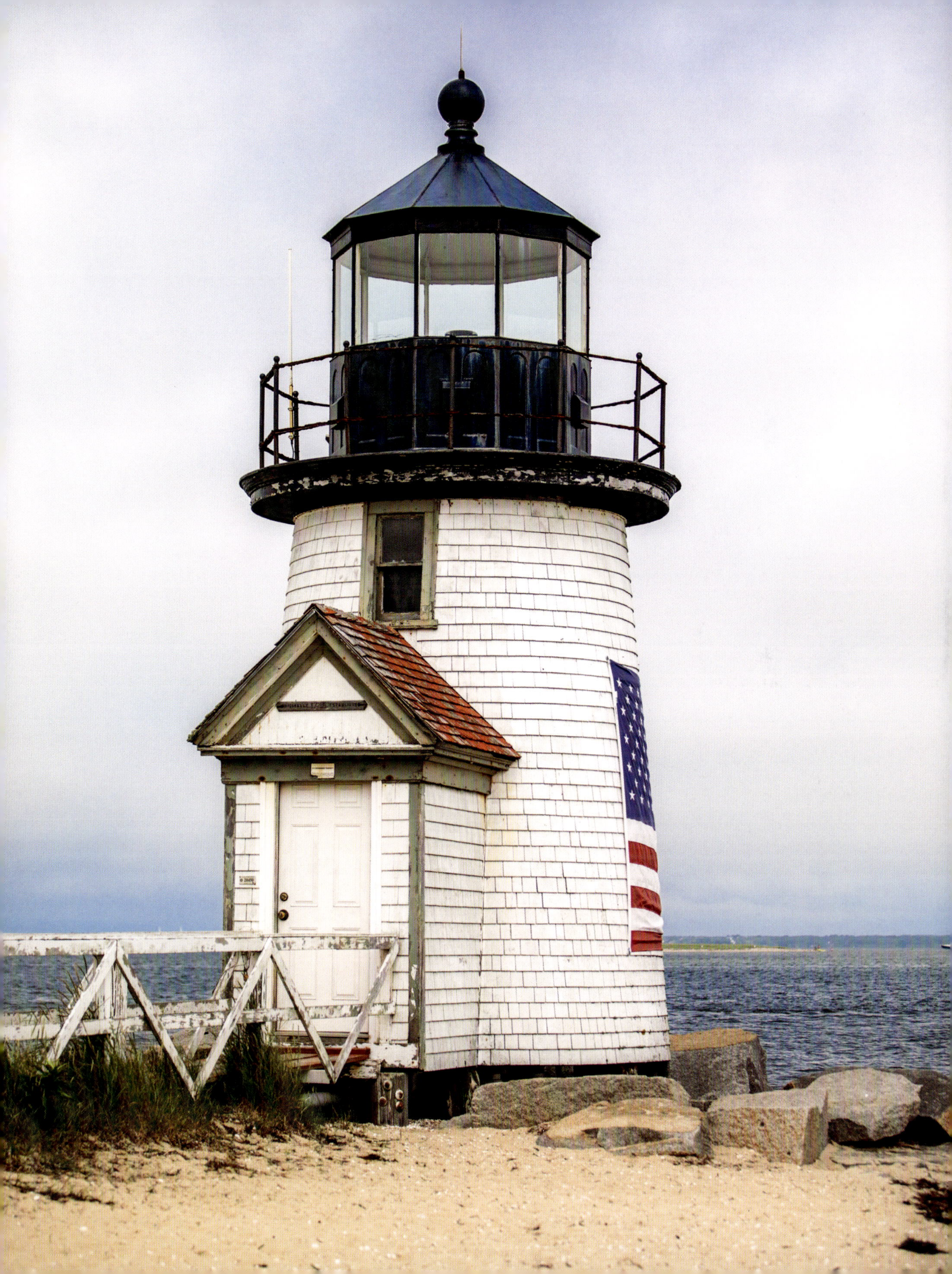

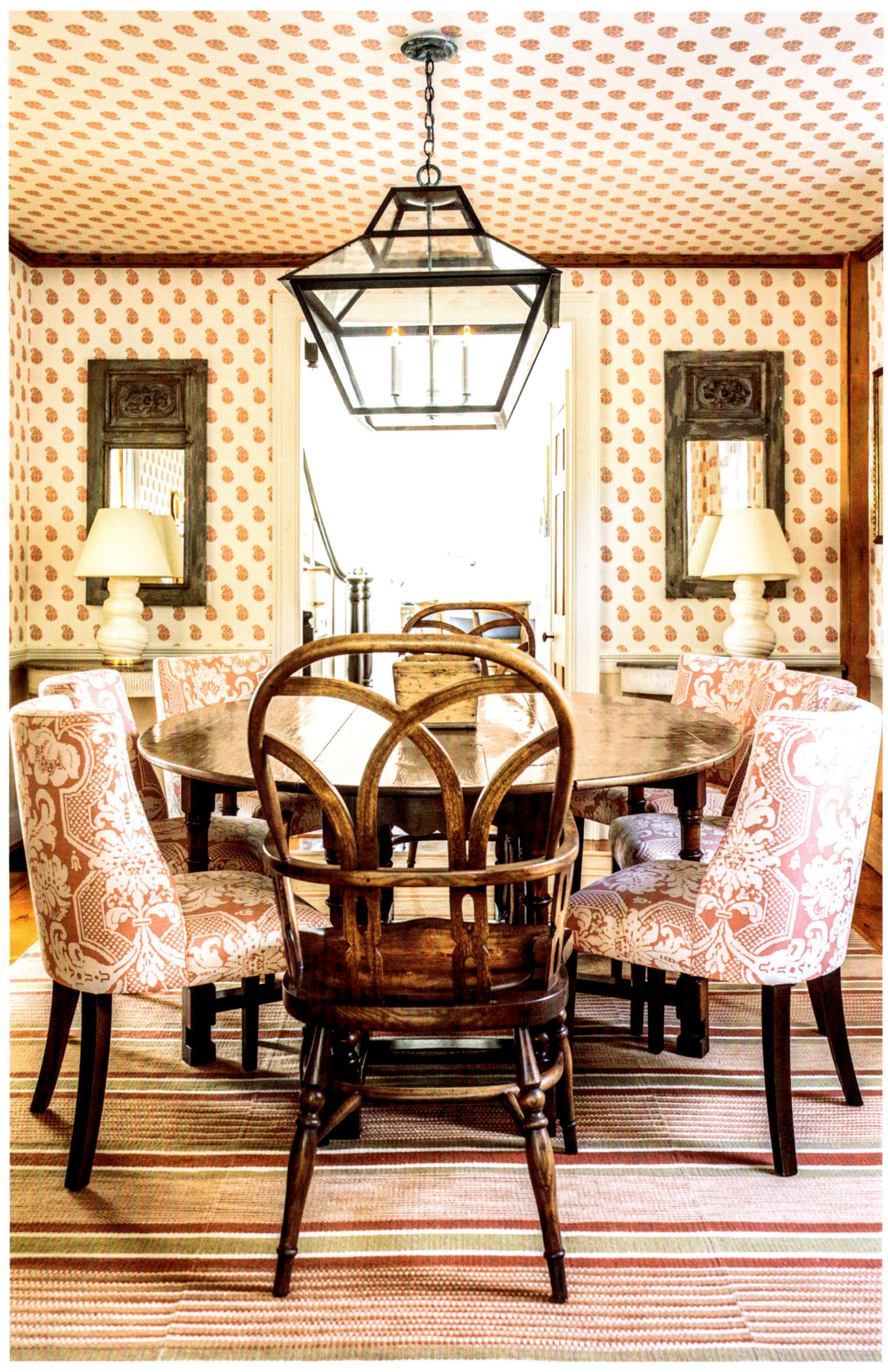

cobblestones and gas lamps all contribute to the aura. It's not hard to imagine the ghosts of the past. According to the Nantucket Historic District Commission, the town's more than 800 buildings built before the Civil War—still lived in and used today—represent "one of the best intact collections of late-seventeenth to mid-nineteenth century buildings in the United States." When whaling came to an abrupt stop in 1850, so did the development of Nantucket (until recently). For that reason, the island has few structures from the ornate Victorian era. The prevailing aesthetic is colonial and simple: Quaker-style shingle homes with impeccable craftsmanship, likely because they were said to be built by shipbuilders.

A conscious effort by many preservationists and philanthropists over the years has protected this character. In a 1995 document, "Building With Nantucket in Mind" (by Christopher Lang and Kate Stout), outline guidelines for building and landscaping on the island, the Commission points out that unlike places like Colonial Williamsburg in Virginia and Old Sturbridge Village in Massachusetts, Nantucket is not a "recovered" glimpse at early American life, it's a living and breathing community. "Here, it is possible to live it, not just gaze in over velvet ropes. This privilege, however, bears with it the weight of great responsibility, hence why everything from design to trim color is subject to approval, why preservation on Nantucket is, simply, a way of life."

The Commission's preservation policy goes beyond "minimal intervention" to include "avoiding architectural irresponsibility." Good taste is demanded by town leaders. Ostentation is not welcome, and never was. Although, that austere simplicity is changing today within interiors of homes, and there is quite some discord between old and new. Fewer than thirty homes exist that haven't been remodeled, and the new look of modern, white interiors is a point of contention for many Nantucketers. If bumper stickers tell the truth, then this ubiquitous one: "Gut fish, not houses" on the back of many island cars, is most revealing.

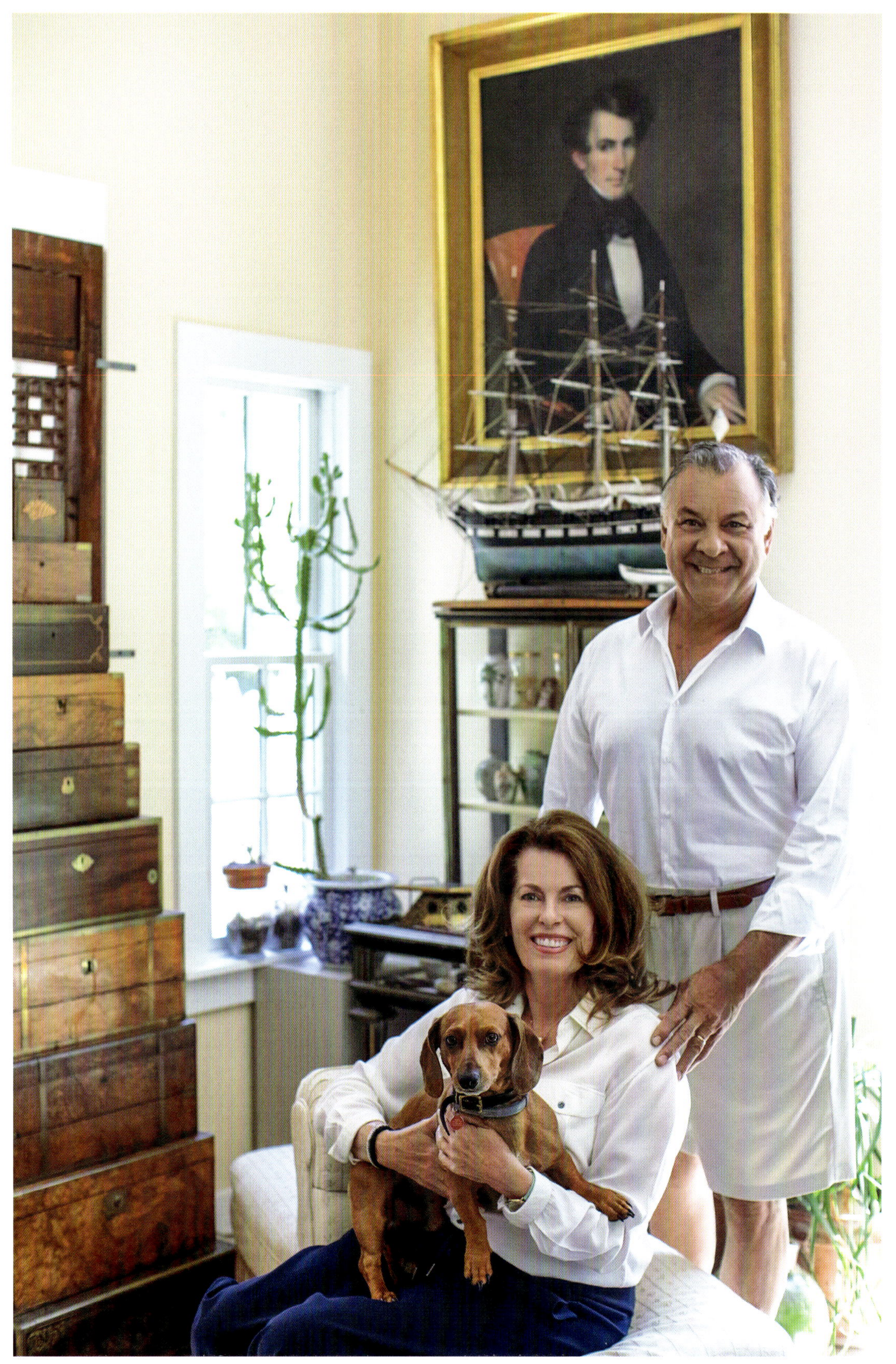

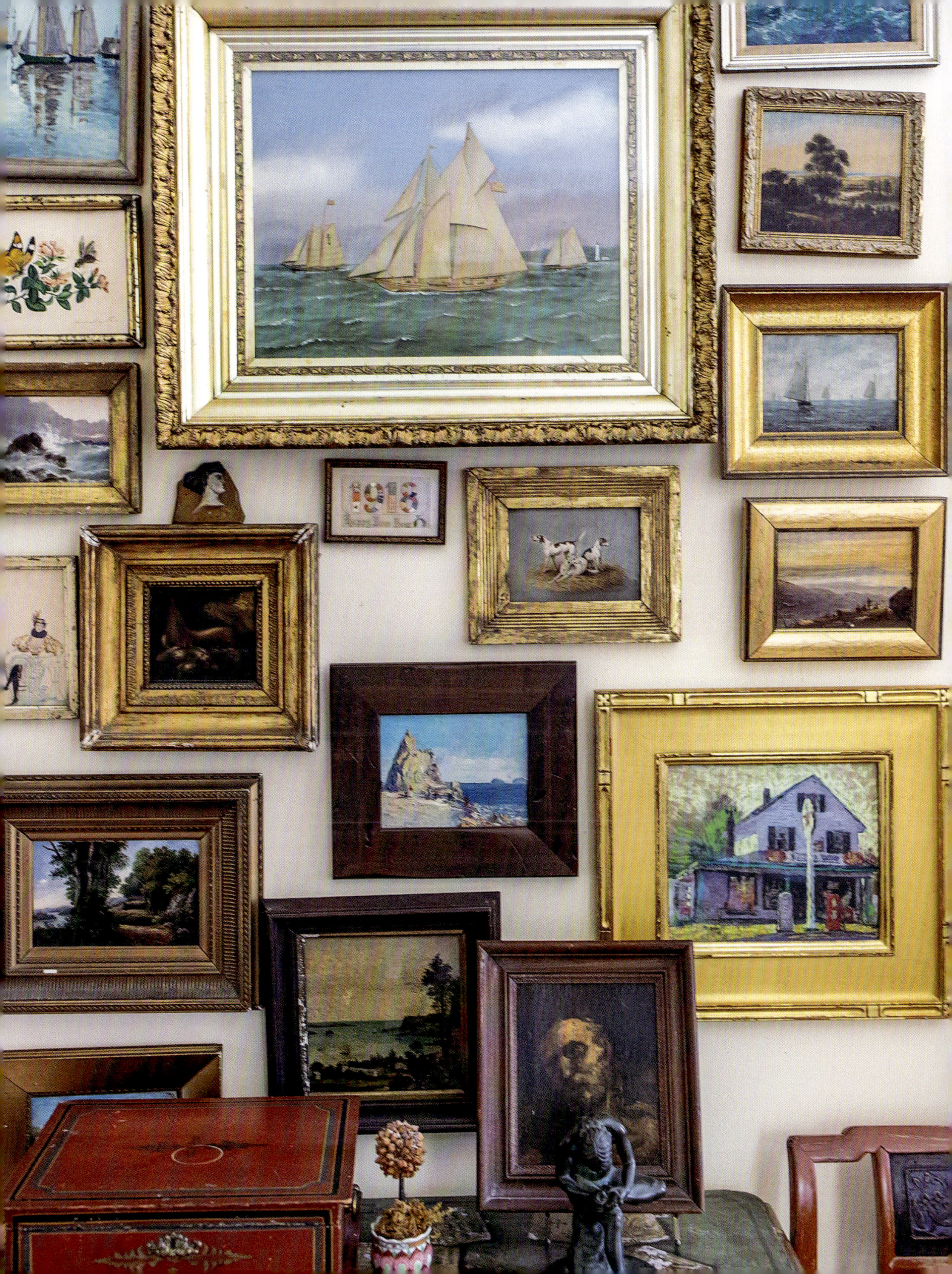
1918

Nantucket remained in a sleepy phase from 1850 until the 1950s when a man named Walter Beinecke, Jr. had a major impact on the island. Controversial at the time, prompting islanders to don pins declaring "No man is an island," Beinecke set the stage for Nantucket's tourism boom which hit its stride in the 1980s and continues today: the island's population of 11,000 year-round residents multiplying five-fold with July and August tourists. From the early 1960s Beinecke invested heavily in transforming the industrial wharf into what it is today, with shops and restaurants and slips for mega-yachts steps from town. He turned the scallop shanties along Old South Wharf into charming retail shops. He beautified by burying Main Street's power lines, planting trees, and bringing landscaping down to the waterfront.

In the early '60s another important moment came for the island. Beinecke, along with other wealthy island families, established the nonprofit Nantucket Conservation Foundation to forever protect the island's open areas from development. Today, the nonprofit is the largest landowner on Nantucket; its holdings, either donated or purchased, make up 30 percent of the island, comprising beaches, hardwood forests, dunes, bogs, marshes, meadows, ponds, and more. The town added to the effort in 1983 by voting to establish the Land Bank, the first of its kind in the nation, which receives a percentage from island real estate sales, to acquire, preserve, and protect land on Nantucket. Today Land Bank trails run through town and beyond. Those key efforts by forward-thinking island citizens, along with a 100-acre state forest in the center of the island, and several Mass Audubon holdings including an 875-acre wildlife sanctuary at the eastern end, ensure that not only will half of Nantucket be forever saved from development, but it will be proactively preserved for recreation and ecological purposes.

Erosion plays a large theme in island culture today, and in the past decade several homes have literally fallen into the sea. There is considerable effort and thought put toward this as the climate change necessitates future planning. 'Sconset and Madaket are most at risk, and residents there are hyper-involved in creative thinking about how to not only preserve their own homes, but in how to preserve the island at large, which will be mostly underwater in centuries to come. Like Venice, Nantucket has an encroaching sea, and an environmental summit occurs now each June to address the issue.

Since 2012, billionaire Wendy Schmidt has become a major player preserving Nantucket and launching sustainability efforts. Schmidt is known for swooping in when local institutions, such as beloved Main Street bookstore Mitchell's Book Corner or the Dreamland movie theater, were in danger of being lost. Her philanthropy is marked by a concern for raising the quality of life for its year-round residents, instituting such things as a windmill on top of the high school, and an environmentally sound bus service across the island called The Wave.

Those who fall for Nantucket fall hard. And as a result, the island has a long history of visionary, civic-minded patrons and citizens willing to go to extraordinary lengths to preserve what makes it so special.

"There's a pride and a sense of respect that we're just passing through here and to take care of it."

—D.W. Coffin, thirteenth-generation descendant of founding Nantucket settler

D.W. Coffin, Nantucket native; thirteenth-generation descendant of one of Nantucket's earliest English settlers

YEARS ON NANTUCKET: *Thirty-six, mostly summers after I moved off for boarding school at fifteen years of age.*

ISLAND HOME: *Polpis*

MODE OF TRANSPORT: *Jeep Wrangler or Land Rover LR4*

FAVORITE BEACH: *Squam*

SUMMER UNIFORM: *Board shorts and a linen shirt.*

_ IS BETTER ON NANTUCKET: *Everything*

NANTUCKET STYLE IS ... *laid-back but formal, with flip-flops.*

MOST DAYS ON NANTUCKET I ... *work, but no one believes me.*

CLASSIC NANTUCKET IS... *fishing at Smith Point or Great Point, depending on the tide, then grilling out through sunset with bonfires on the beach.*

FAVORITE SPOT ON NANTUCKET? *Not giving that one up.*

COMMON MISCONCEPTION ABOUT NANTUCKET? *That it's the Hamptons.*

NANTUCKET HISTORICAL FIGURE/EVENT THAT SPEAKS TO YOU: *I'd be remiss if I didn't say my own ancestor Tristram Coffin, who was head of one of the seven families that founded the island.*

NECESSITY ON NANTUCKET: *Four-wheel drive.*

MOST TREASURED EXPERIENCE ON-ISLAND: *Getting a chance to grow up here.*

THING YOU ONLY WEAR ON NANTUCKET: *Lilly Pulitzer pants and Artemis shoes, usually have a t-shirt on with Pulitzer pants. Can't take yourself too seriously.*

WHAT INSPIRES YOU ABOUT NANTUCKET: *There's a pride, comradery, and toughness that every single person has who's from here. There's an honor to it. And a sense of respect that we're just passing through here and to take care of the island.*

SLANG ISLAND SAYING: *Keep ya secret.*

ON NANTUCKET I NEVER ... *go through a red light.*

WHAT'S SPECIAL ABOUT NANTUCKET: *The beauty of it. Nantucket has its own presence, its own soul. It's basically a real life "Chadtucket."*

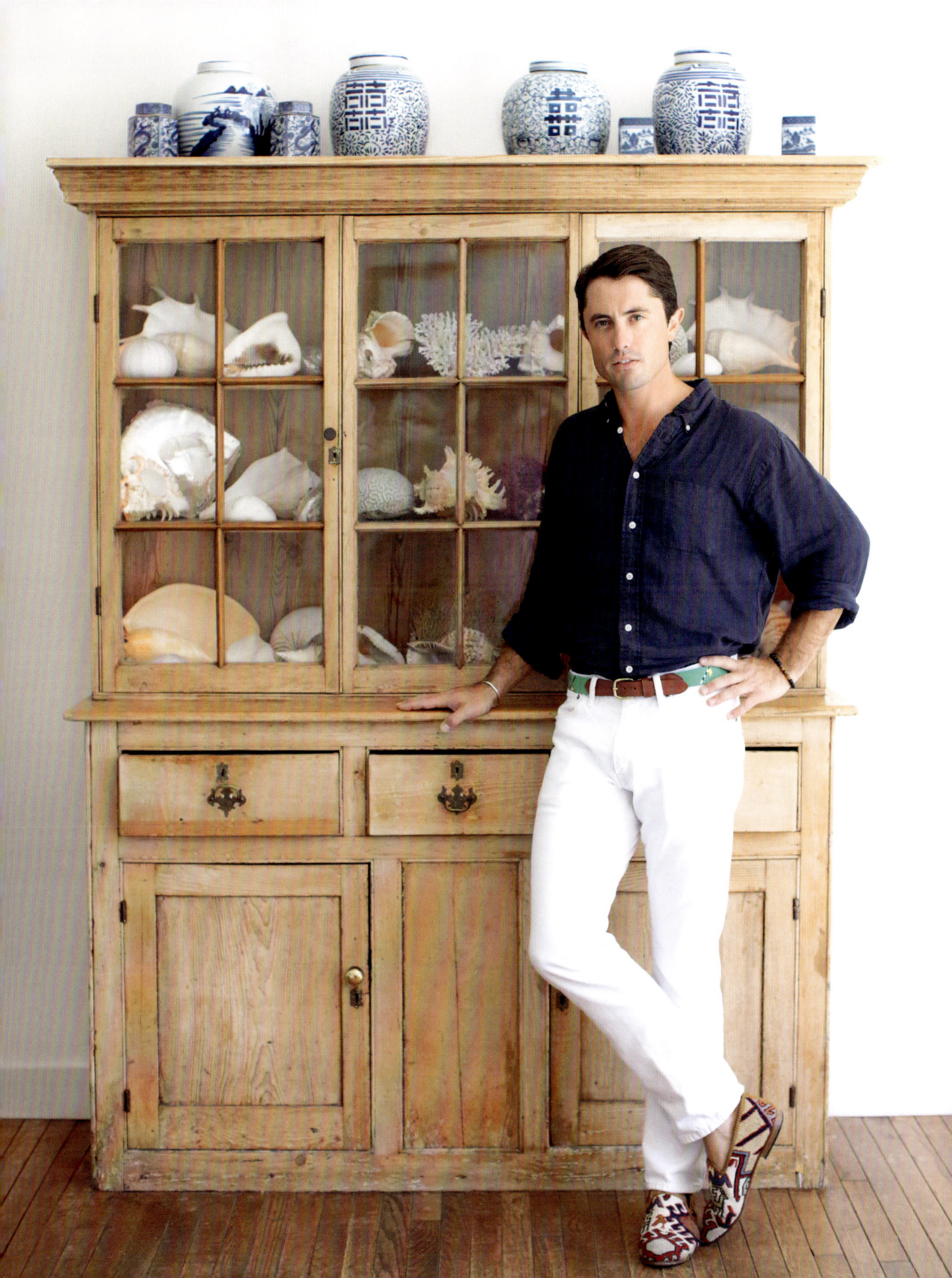

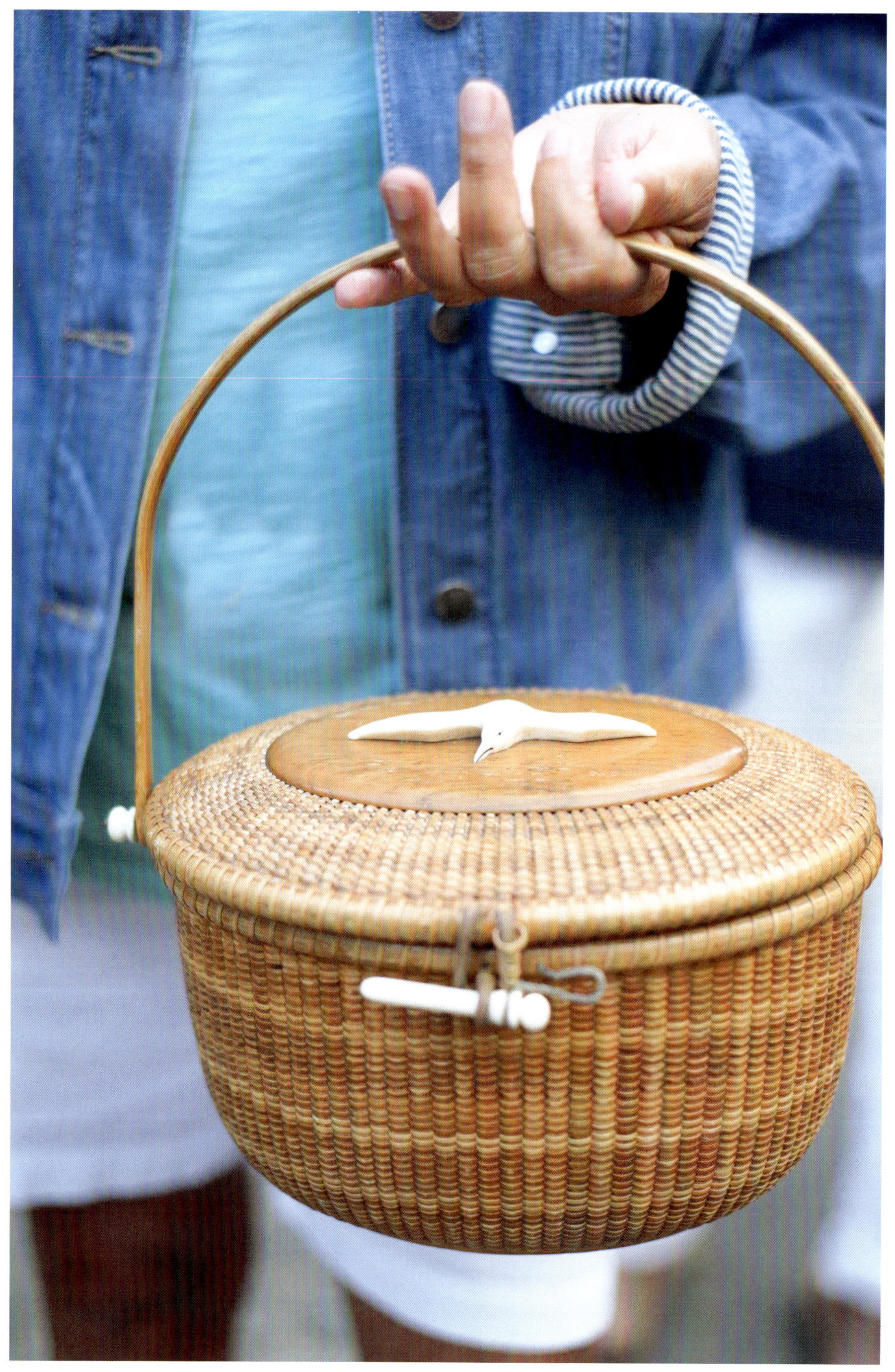

ISLAND TRADITIONS

Nantucket Dictionary

ACK Nantucket's airport code

AMERICA The landmass and attitude that's 30 miles to the west

BLUEFISH PÂTÉ A local island fish and cocktail party staple

CHADTUCKET Describes a stereotypical visitor who populates Nantucket during spring and summer

COATUE Hard to get to, but this remote eastern part of the island has good swimming and warm sand in the summer. Best to take a boat.

DRESS FOR DINNER Blazer and slacks for men, dresses for ladies

GHOSTS Nantucket is a haunted spot for sure! Take a ghost tour to learn about the island's eerie residents from the past.

GREY LADY A Nantucket island nickname because of the thousands of grey shingles adorning buildings across Nantucket and the often-foggy weather

ISLANDER Someone born and bred on Nantucket. Often tracing back multiple generations.

LIGHTSHIP BASKET A woven rattan and solid wood base basket design originating from Nantucket in the early eighteenth century

NANTUCKET REDS Inspired by the sailors' pink cotton pants of Brittany, Murray's Toggery Shop designed these fashion staples for island living. Reds have become synonymous with the summer Nantucket lifestyle. Once featured in "The Official Preppy Handbook."

SHAKE-A-DAY Find this game at local bars for a roll of the dice and winnings

SUMMER PEOPLE Island residents who come only for the summer months

TAKE IT OR LEAVE IT (AKA MADAKET MALL) Used goods for free at the island's garbage dump

THE "SEASON" Refers to summer from Memorial Day to Labor Day

WASHASHORE A newcomer/non-native resident

WEEKENDER Visitor who arrives by ferry or plane only for a short visit

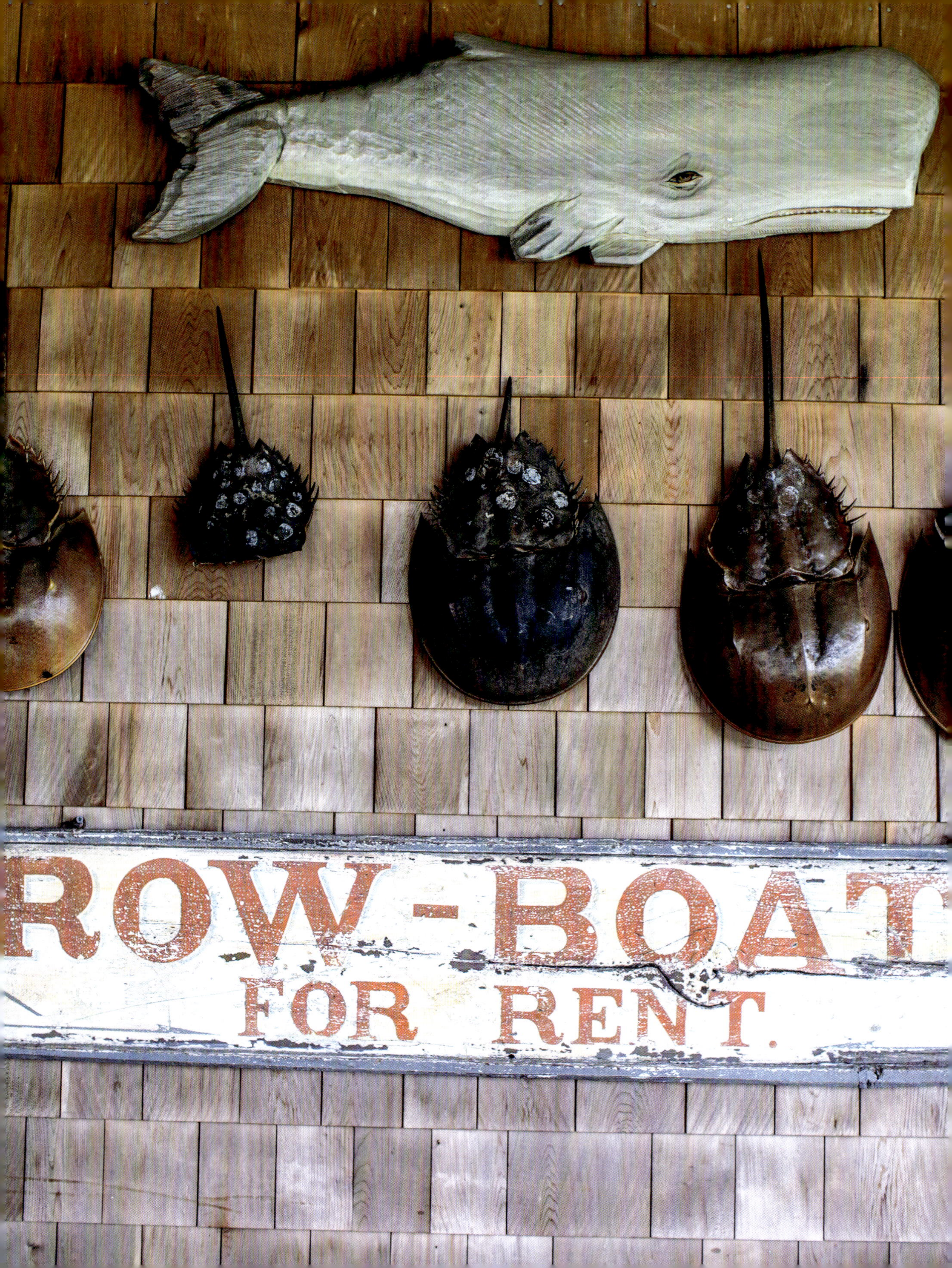
ROW-BOAT
FOR RENT.

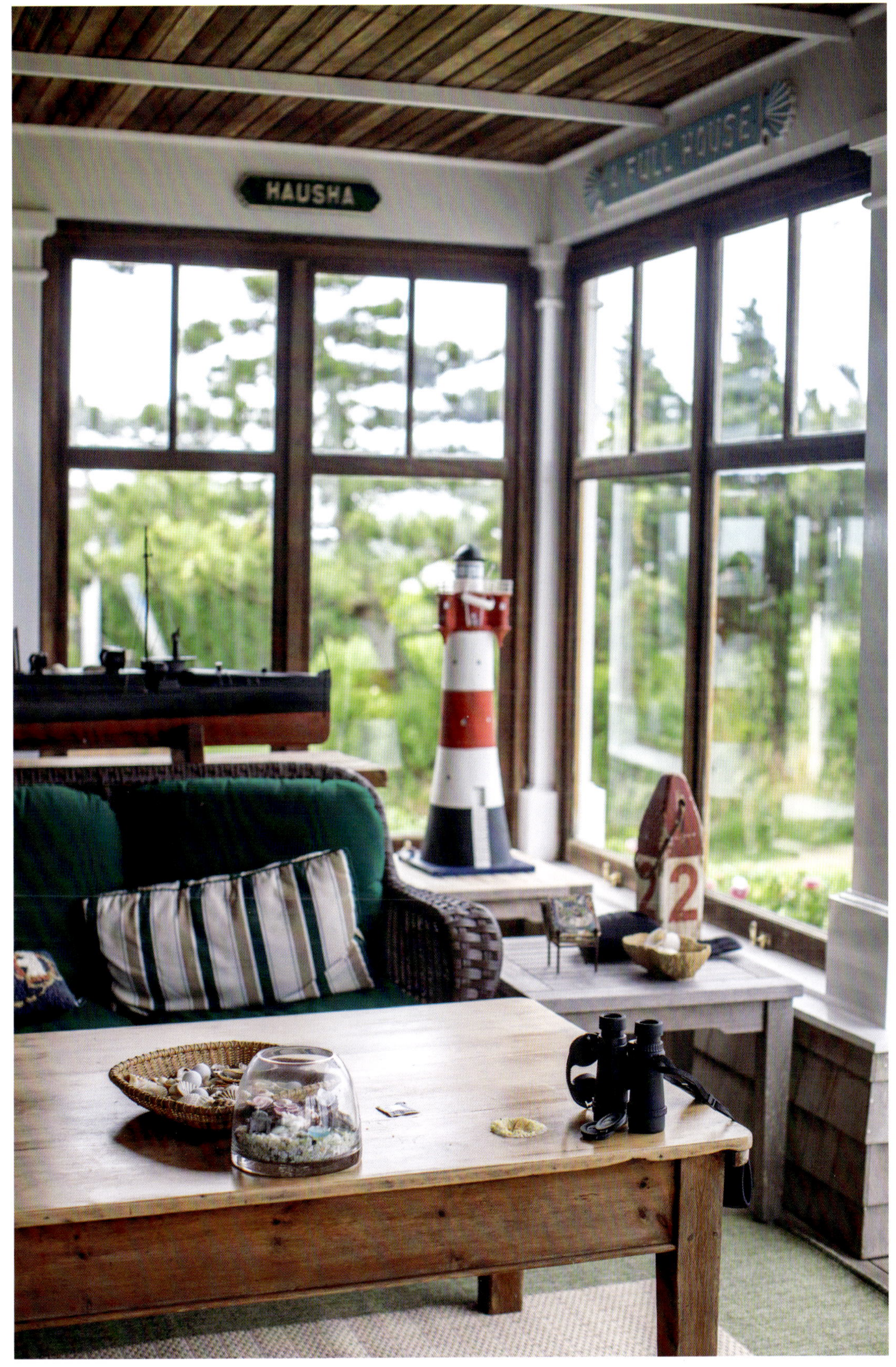
HAUSHA
FULL HOUSE
22

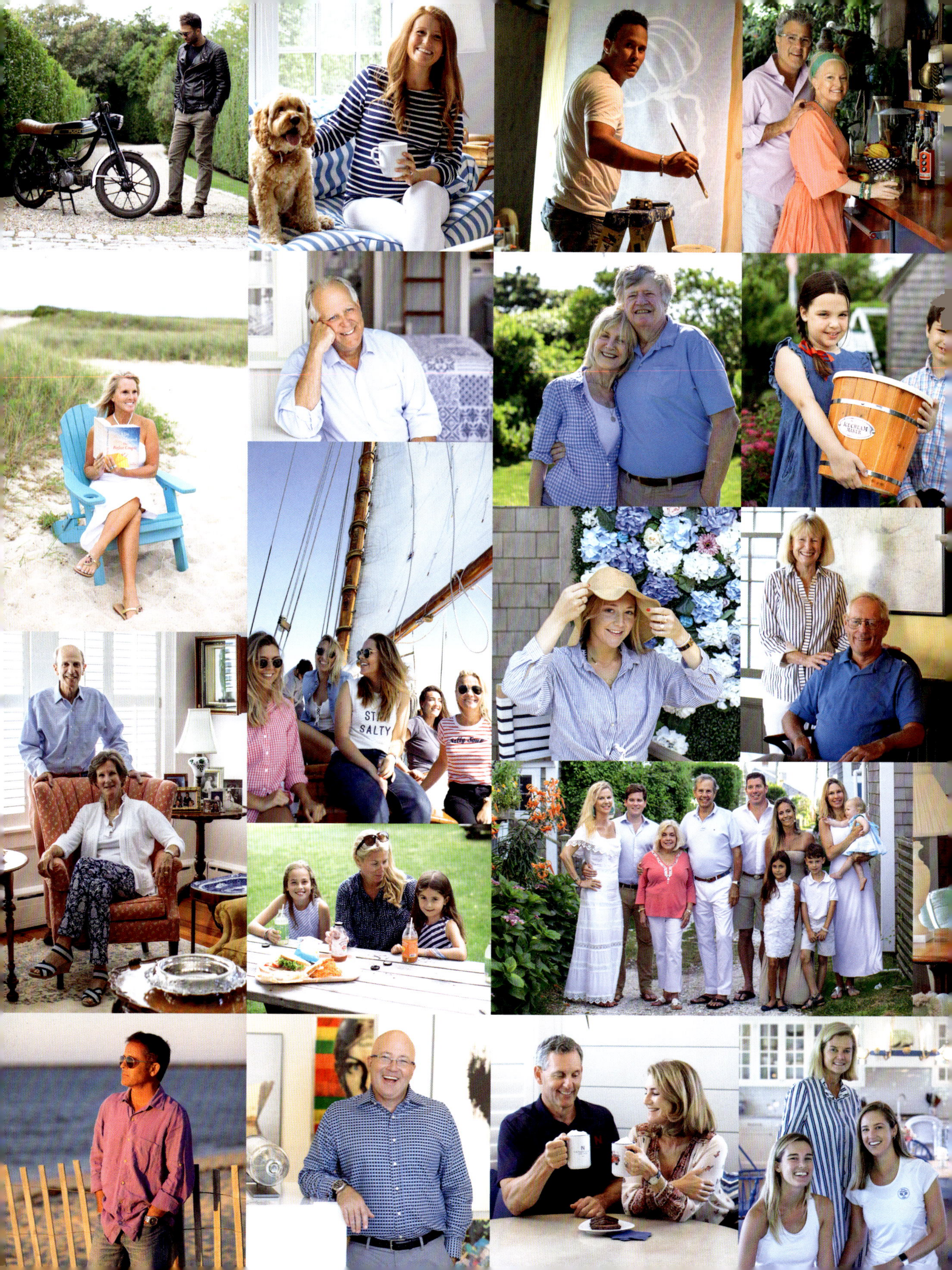
SALTY

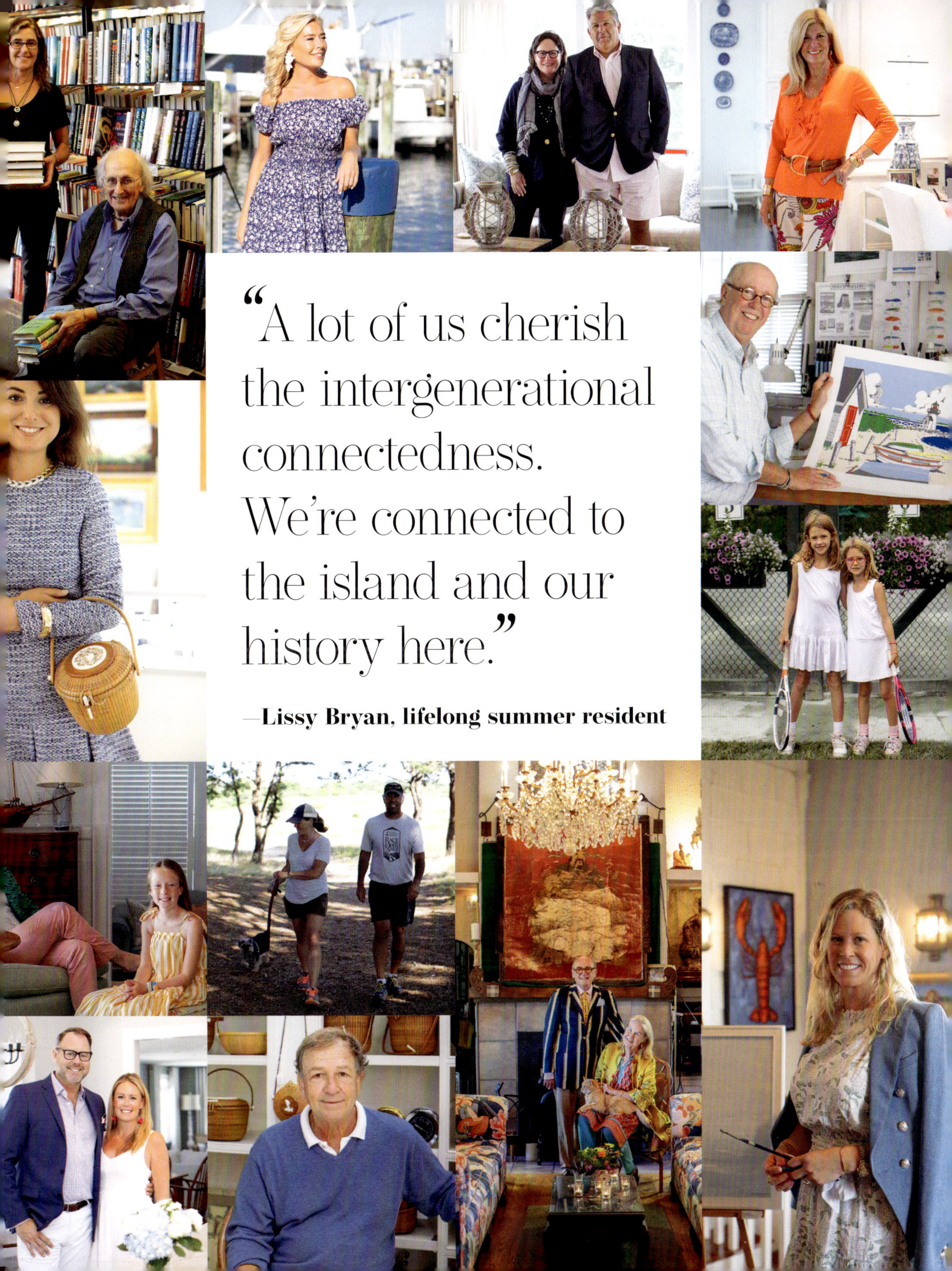

"A lot of us cherish the intergenerational connectedness. We're connected to the island and our history here."

—**Lissy Bryan, lifelong summer resident**

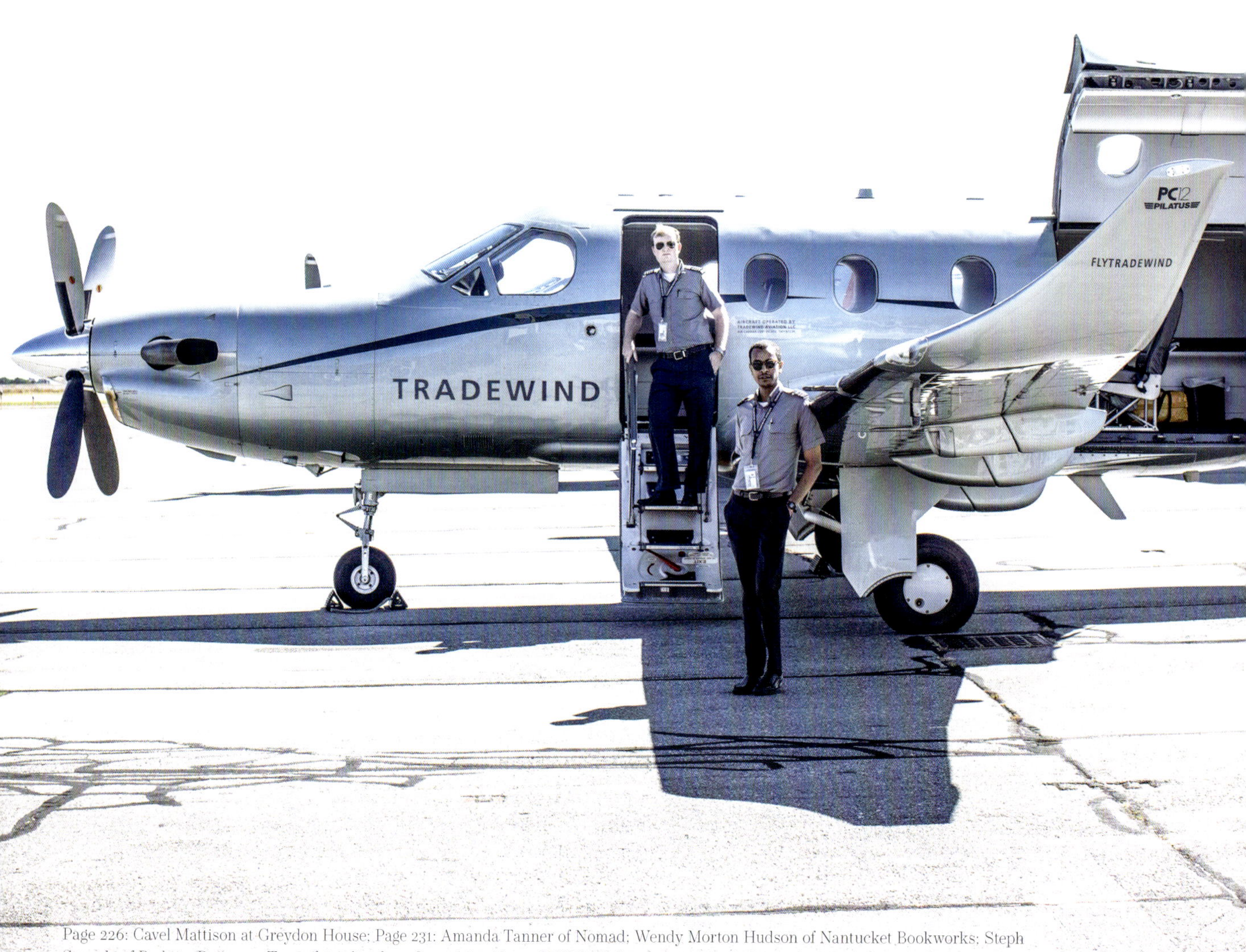

Page 226: Cavel Mattison at Greydon House; Page 231: Amanda Tanner of Nomad; Wendy Morton Hudson of Nantucket Bookworks; Steph Sproule of Bodega; Page 232: Tray of goodies from Something Natural; Nick Nashington and staff; donuts from Downyflake Donuts; Sam and Tyler Herrick; Page 234: Jennifer Lake; Becky Peraner, Bess Clark, Stephanie Hall of Nantucket Looms; Carrie Nieman Culpepper (center); Page 235: Colleen Darby Wurts of Atlantic; Townsend and Spyder Wright of Spyder Wright Surf Shop; Elizabeth English of Current Vintage

NANTUCKET TRAVEL GUIDE

The island itself is quite small, with Nantucket town surrounded by small areas comprising Coatue, Madaket, Muskeget, Pocomo, Quidnet, Siasconset, Tom Nevers, Tuckernuck, and Wawinet.

How to Get to/from Nantucket

The fast ferry from Hyannis takes approximately an hour. Duration of flights from key mainland cities: Boston (30 minutes); New York City (1.5 hours); and Washington, D.C. (3 hours).

CAPE AIR (www.capeair.com)
HY-LINE CRUISES (https://hylinecruises.com)
JETBLUE (www.jetblue.com)
STEAMSHIP AUTHORITY (www.steamshipauthority.com)
TRADEWIND AVIATION (https://www.flytradewind.com)

How to Get Around Nantucket

The island is enjoyable for those who wish to explore on foot, but there are several car hire facilities dotted about the island, and bike or scooter rental options. Visitors can also take the shuttle bus service, The Wave (https://nrtawave.com).

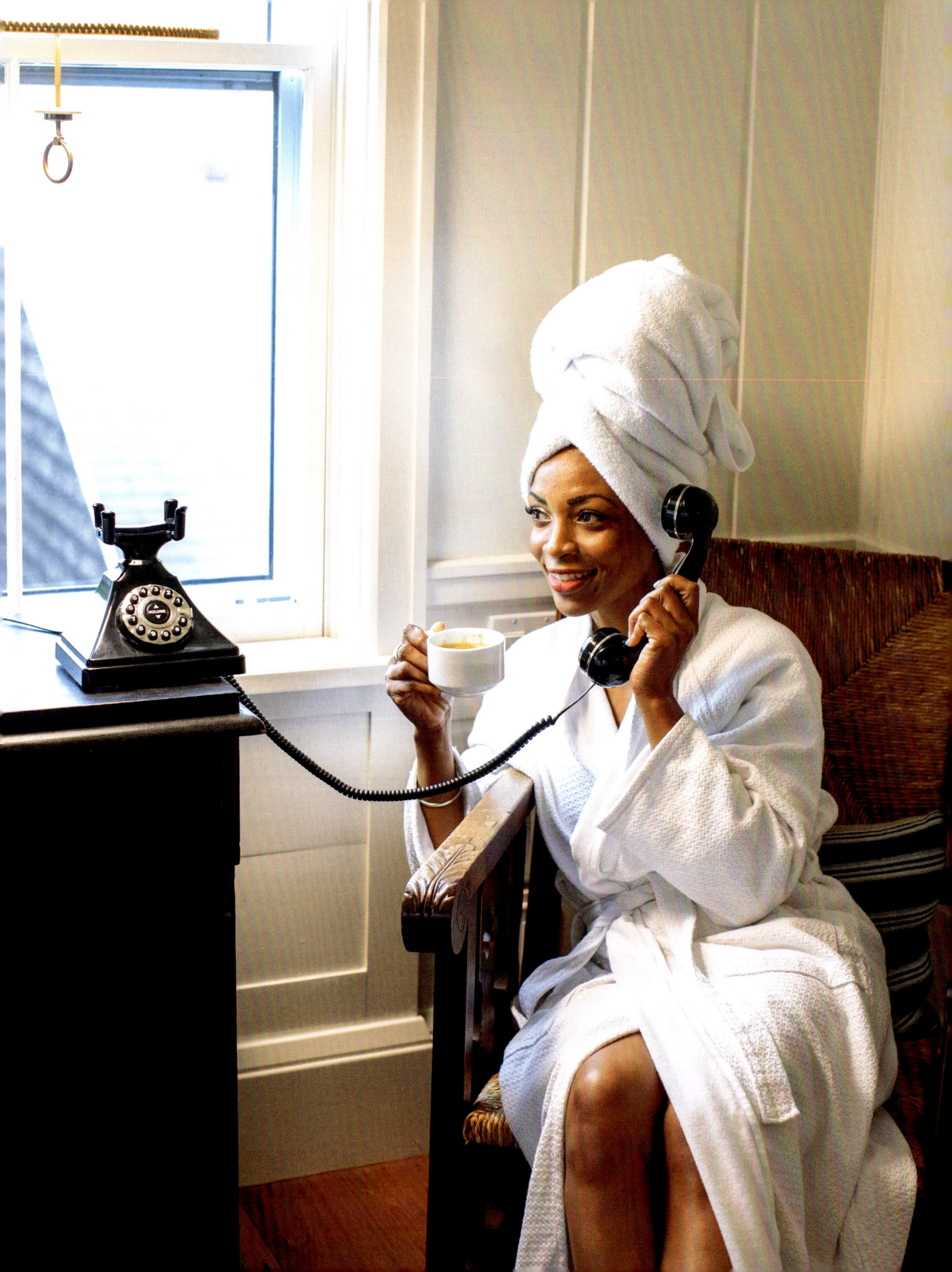
VOLUME

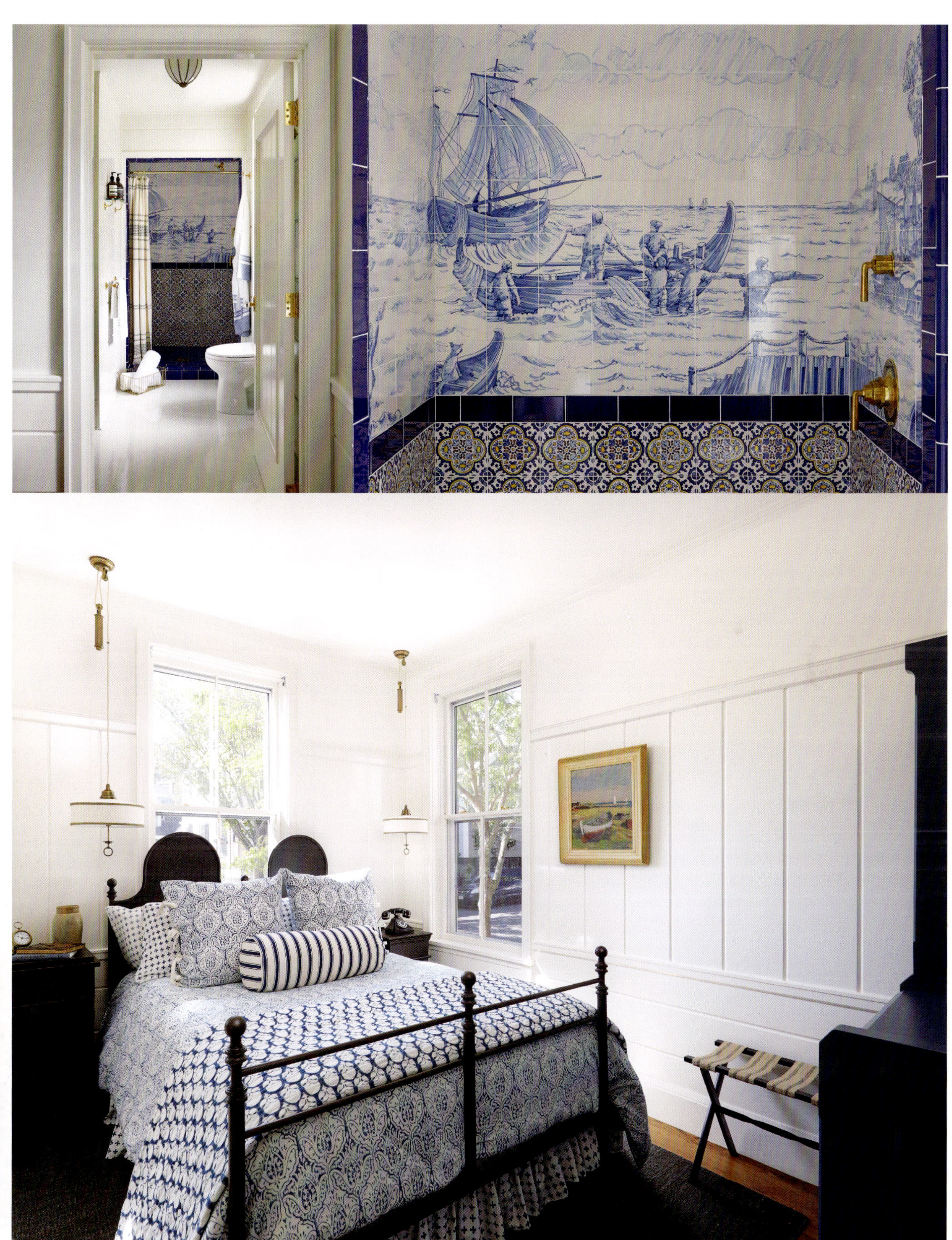

Where to Stay on Nantucket

ANCHOR INN (anchorinnack.com) Four-poster beds with crisp white linens fill the thirteen rooms at this bed-and-breakfast on downtown's Center Street.

CLIFFSIDE BEACH CLUB (cliffsidebeach.com) White-washed beach club and resort facing a North Shore beach that's been run by the same family for sixty years.

THE COTTAGES AT NANTUCKET BOAT BASIN (www.thecottagesnantucket.com) Tiny grey-shingled cottages with kitchens.

GREYDON HOUSE (greydonhouse.com) Boutique inn in a sea captain's house steps from Steamboat Wharf with impeccable interiors blending whaling-era chic with a modern sensibility by super-star designers Roman and Williams. [pictured previous spread]

HARBORVIEW NANTUCKET (www.harborviewnantucket.com) A series of lovely multiroom cottages, ideal for small groups, gathered around a sweet garden and private waterfront on the harbor with loaner kayaks, sunfish, and paddleboards.

HAWTHORNE HOUSE (hawthornehouse.com) Nine-room inn with minimal décor in a nineteenth-century home in town.

HOTEL PIPPA (https://hotelpippa.com) Modern boutique hotel in a historic clapboard house set right in town with loaner coolers and beach chairs.

MARTIN HOUSE INN (www.martinhouseinn.net) Nineteenth-century home turned inn with canopy beds, mahogany furnishings, and comfortable covered side porch.

THE NANTUCKET HOTEL (www.thenantuckethotel.com) Family-friendly historic hotel lovingly brought back to life with fun details like a moving sculpture in the lobby, antique fire truck rides, and s'mores on the patio.

PERIWINKLE INN (periwinklenantucket.com) Traditional bed-and-breakfast in a Greek Revival House on North Water Street's "Guest House Row" steps from the ferry.

SUMMER HOUSE (thesummerhouse.com) A dream of an inn dating back to the 1880s, comprising charming shabby chic cottages on a bluff across from the pool, café, and beachfront. Also a romantic restaurant with a legendary pianist who takes requests into the night. The owners also run three inns in town whose guests have access to the Summer House pool and beachfront via a shuttle service.

UNION STREET INN (www.unioninn.com) Classic Nantucket inn exactly as you'd want it with Frette linens, brick patio, and impeccable service.

THE WAUWINET (wauwinet.com) A 150-year-old inn perched on the northeastern end of the island, with a special and remote setting in the Coskata-Coatue Wildlife Refuge with Nantucket harbor or Atlantic beaches to choose from and an award-winning restaurant, Topper's.

WHITE ELEPHANT (whiteelephantnantucket.com) Popular with families and couples, this large complex of grey-shingled buildings clustered near Brant Point Lighthouse has a variety of hotel rooms and home rentals on the harbor, as well as lofts in town nearby.

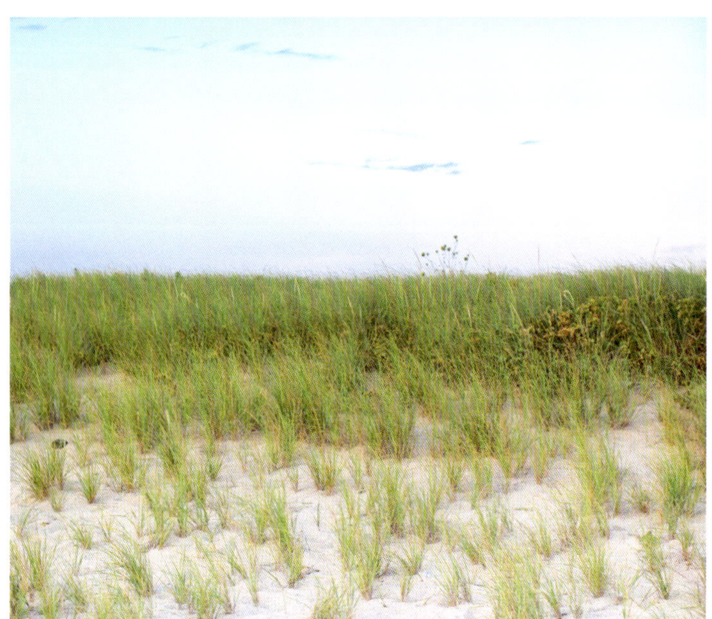

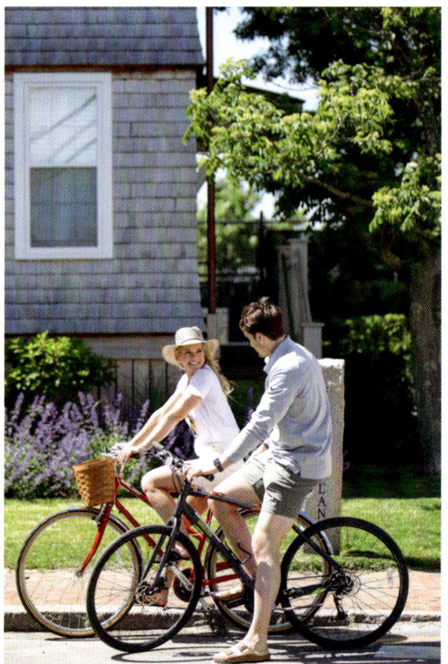

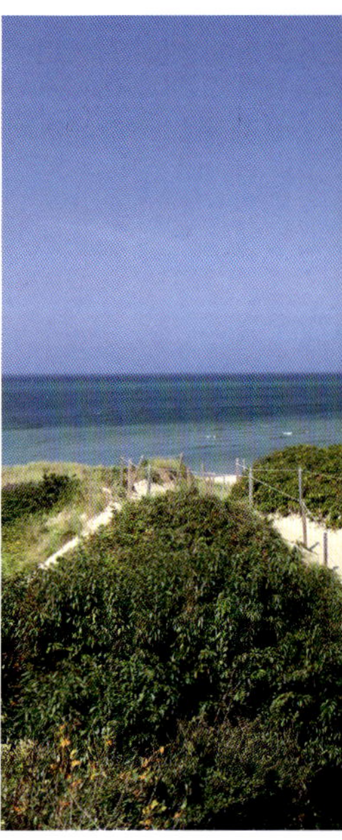

What to Do on Nantucket

Enjoy a boat trip (shearwaterexcursions.com)
Sail the "Endeavor" (www.endeavorsailing.com)
Experience the "Lynx" tall ship (https://tallshiplynx.com)
Get involved with community sailing (nantucketcommunitysailing.org)
Join community tennis (jettiestennis.com)
Be thrilled with ghost tours (ravens-walk.com)
Seek out National Historical Association tours (https://nha.org)
Visit the Whaling Museum (https://nha.org/visit/museums-and-tours/whaling-museum)
Learn to Surf (nantucketsurfing.com)
Take basket-making classes (nantucketbaskets.com)
Tour Cisco Brewers (www.ciscobrewersnantucket.com)
Hike or bike in the wild (nantucketconservation.org)
Walk the 'Sconset Bluff Walk (nantucket-ma.gov)
Visit Brant Point, Sankaty Head, or Great Point Lighthouses
Go stargazing at Loines Observatory (mariamitchell.org)

NORTH SHORE BEACHES Gentler surf and warmer water, these beaches are more suitable for easy swimming and for children. Most are walkable from town and all have views of Nantucket Sound or the harbor. North Shore beaches include 40th Pole, Brant Point, Children's, Dionis, Jetties, Steps, and Washing Pond.

SOUTH SHORE BEACHES The Atlantic side of the island. Most South Shore beaches on Nantucket are known for surfing, seals, and even a few shark sightings. Often the beaches have strong currents and shifting sands. South Shore beaches include the Cisco, Fisherman's, Low, Madaket, Madequecham, Miacomet, Miacomet Pond, Nobadeer, Smith's Point, Surfside, and Tom Nevers.

EAST SHORE BEACHES The curved, eastern end of the island also features waves and sea life such as sea lions and seals. East shore beaches include Codfish Park, Siaconset, and Quidnet.

INNER HARBOR BEACHES The outer beaches of Coatue and Great Point require a boat or a four-wheel drive with beach permits to drive to them. Some car rental companies can provide you with a permitted vehicle.

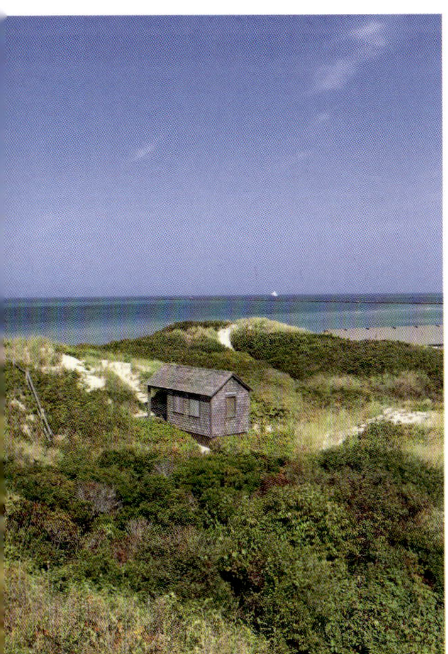

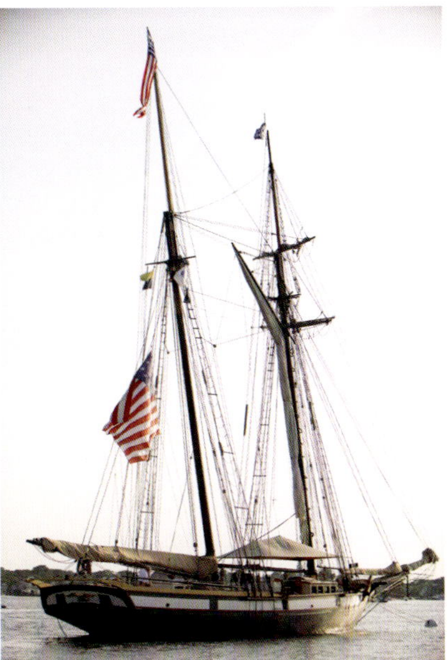

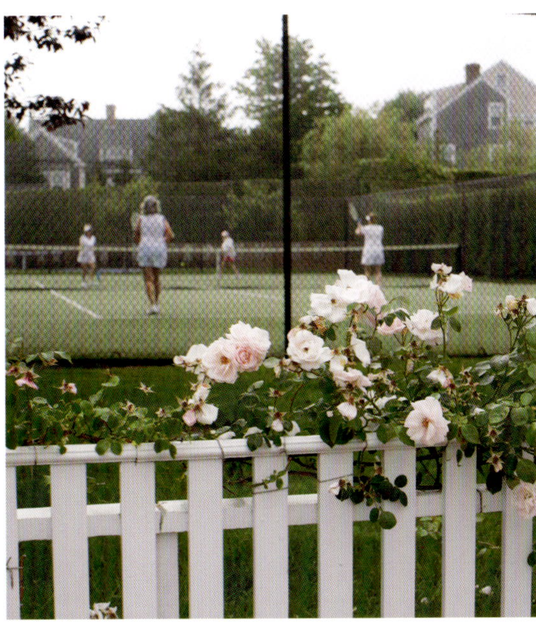

Where to Shop on Nantucket

28 CENTRE POINTE (28centrepointe.com) Modern beach-house furniture and home shop with elegant jewelry and art.

ACK 4170 (ack4170.com) Cute shop for unique Nantucket-themed gifts and accessories.

ATLANTIC (16 Federal St. Nantucket) Clothing, jewelry, and housewares sourced from small designers around the world.

BODEGA (https://bodeganantucket.com) Rare and refined but eclectic collectables and homewares, stationery, bedding, and accessories.

CJ LAING (https://cjlaingshop.com) Boho-chic sundresses, jewelry, and cashmere sweaters at this colorful shop with locations in town and 'Sconset.

ERICA WILSON (ericawilson.com) Founded by America's mother of needlepoint, now run by her daughter who introduced elevated boho chic clothing and accessories to the mix.

EYE OF THE NEEDLE (facebook.com/eyeoftheneedleack) Longtime shop for womenswear with a touch of glitz.

HOSPITAL THRIFT SHOP (https://hospitalthriftshop.org) Ninety-year-old second-hand shop with housewares, books, furniture, tools and more in a converted home on India Street in town.

THE HUB (thehubofnantucket.com) Coffee and gift shop with cards, books, and tasteful souvenirs.

ISLAND CASHMERE (cashmerebeach.shop) Sweaters, ponchos, and other womenswear for windy Nantucket days and nights.

ITS FOR NOW (itsfornow.com) New island shop promoting and selling small regional brands with a story.

LADYBIRD LINGERIE (ladybirdlingerie.com) Large selection of fine lingerie from independent labels.

THE LOVELY (thelovelynantucket.com) Beachy bohemian clothing and accessories.

MILLIE & GRACE (millyandgrace.com) Hip clothing, jewelry, and home accessories plus wedding planning in one ivy-covered shop.

MITCHELL'S BOOK CORNER (mitchellsbookcorner.com) Beloved Main Street book shop with large section of books about the island.

MONELLE (monelle.com) Trendy boutique with everything from an evening gown to beach cover-up.

MURRAY'S TOGGERY SHOP (www.nantucketreds.com) Iconic department store filled with classic preppy labels for the whole family. Murray's even has a makeup counter downstairs, and a shoe department too. Famous for inventing

NANTUCKET BOOKWORKS (nantucketbookworks.com), a welcoming bookshop with gifts and a kids' corner with events.

NANTUCKET LOOMS (www.nantucketlooms.com) The most classic Nantucket shop, the Looms is famous around the world for its fine home goods and hand-woven blankets. A working loom.

NOMAD (www.nomadnantucket.com) Beautifully curated, rustic-modern home store selling throw pillows, tableware, and even dresses.

PARCHMENT (http://parchmentnantucket.com) A careful curation of fine papers and stationery.

PATINA (patinanantucket.com) Stylish jewelry, independent label European designer clothing, and home objects.

PETER BEATON HAT STUDIO (peterbeaton.com) Island hatmaker Darcy Creech's collection of traditional straw hats and a selection of grosgrain ribbons in this quaint shop down an alley off Federal Street.

THE PHARMACY (center of Main Street) A true old-fashioned pharmacy with gift items and a soda counter.

REMY (https://remycreations.com) Many of her own designs, Remy is known for capes, tunics, and jewelry.

RES IPSA (resipsausa.com) Levi's, letter jackets, and kilim loafers mingle in this men's and womenswear shop with an upcycled vintage outlook.

THE SKINNY DIP (https://shopthedip.com) A collection of small-label clothing, jewelry, bags, and shoes rooted in the preppy aesthetic.

SPACE (https://www.facebook.com/SPACEnantucket) On the wharf, an eclectic collection of beautiful pieces, including paintings, jewelry, bags, and clothing.

THE SUNKEN SHIP (www.sunkenship.com) An island favorite, this catchall has everything you need (and might have forgotten to pack); grab a raincoat, hat, or even a toy.

TOUJOURS MIDI (tourjoursmidinantucket.com) Fine accessories for the tabletop and home.

VIS-A-VIS (visavisnantucket.com) Clothing, accessories and home goods, many Nantucket-themed gift items.

Antiques, Art Galleries, and Artisan Shops

CECILIA JOYCE AND SEWARD JOHNSON GALLERY (nantucketarts.com) Official gallery of the Artists Association of Nantucket showing work by artist members year-round.

COE + CO PHOTOGRAPHY GALLERY (www.coeandcogallery.com) Nantucket photographer Nathan Coe's gallery showcasing his landscapes and work by other well-known photographers, including celebrity portraits by Terry O'Neill and Harry Benson.

ERIC HOLCH GALLERY (ericholch.com) Home gallery by Nantucket printmaker whose work is inspired by island sites and his sailing hobby.

FOUR WINDS CRAFT GUILD (fourwindscraftguild.com) Seventy-year-old shop selling art and crafts from local artisans. Large selection of carvings, scrimshaw, and Nantucket baskets.

HOSTETLER GALLERY (www.hostetlergallery.com) Sculptor David Hostetler's Main Street gallery shows work by him and a handful of contemporary artists working in various media.

JEANNE VAN ETTEN (jeannevanetten.com) Nantucket artist's whimsical shop is filled with her mermaid inspired crafts and drawings.

NANTUCKET ESTATE JEWELRY AND FINE ART (nantucketjewelryandart.com) A great shop to score a piece of fine estate jewelry or paintings. Tucked into a side street off Main Street.

PETE'S FRESH FISH PRINTS (petesfreshfishprints.net) Small shop selling artist Peter Van Dingstee's "flat taxidermy" prints of fish on rice paper in the nineteenth-century Japanese Gyotaku style on Old South Wharf.

ROBERT FOSTER FINE ART (robertfosterfineart.com) Downtown gallery selling established Nantucket artists.

QUIDLEY & COMPANY (www.quidleyandco.com) Main Street gallery featuring the work of contemporary American artists. Other locations in Naples, Florida, and Westport, Connecticut.

RAFAEL OSONA AUCTIONS (rafaelosonaauction.com) Forty-year-old auction house specializing in Nantucket and nautical art and antiques from the eighteenth and twentieth centuries sold at weekly auctions during the season.

SAMUEL OWEN GALLERY (www.samuelowen.com) With Greenwich, Connecticut, and Nantucket locations, Samuel Owen shows colorful contemporary art with pop art and pop culture references.

SILVIA ANTIQUES (sylviaantiques.com) Main Street antiques store and nearby showroom selling new and antique nautical folk art, furniture, jewelry, and a large collection of Nantucket baskets.

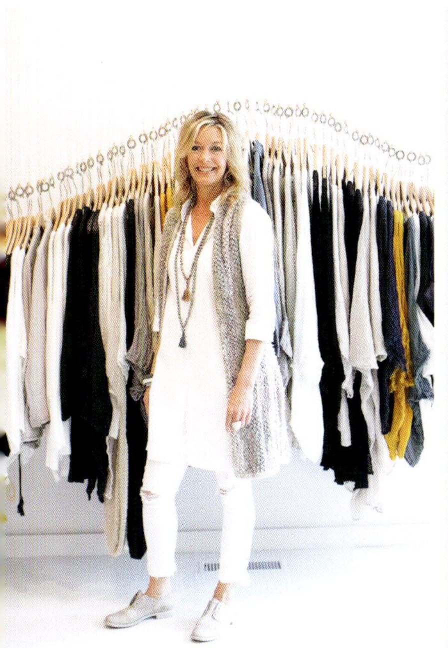

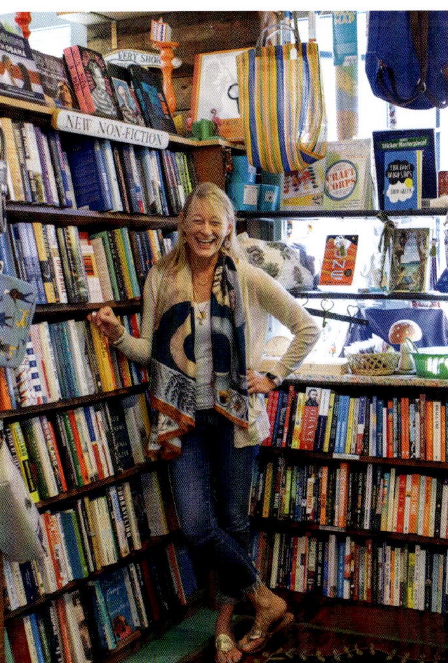

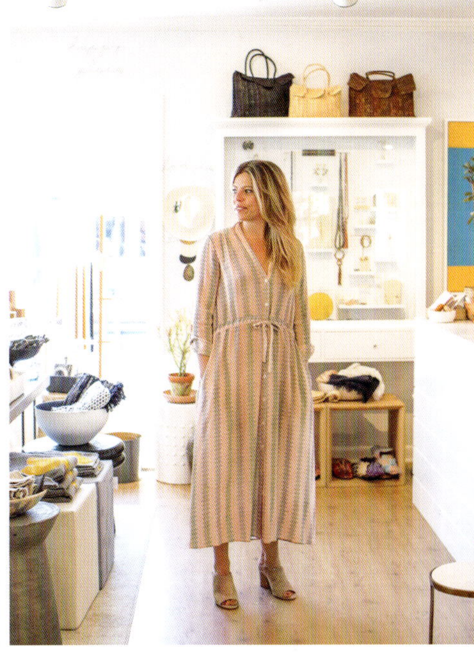

Where to Eat on Nantucket

167 RAW (http://167raw.com/nantucket) Forty-year-old seasonal fish market with picnic tables in the garden for events, also operating a raw bar truck out of nearby Cisco Brewers.

AMERICAN SEASONS (www.americanseasons.com) A Gordon Ramsay protege with one Michelin star opened this quaint spot in 2015 with atmospheric indoor dining and covered patio under twinkle lights, on a quiet street just out of town, and serving elegant preparations of duck breast, Nantucket bay scallops, and more.

BARTLETT'S FARM (https://bartlettsfarm.com) Gourmet market with prepared foods and fresh fruit, veggies, and flowers from the 120-acre farm, an island institution run by the Bartletts for seven generations.

BLACK-EYED SUSAN'S (https://black-eyedsusans.com) Wildly popular brunch and BYOB dinner in a cozy tavern setting on a side street in town. A local favorite. Cash only.

BOARDING HOUSE (http://boardinghousenantucket.com) Thirty-year institution in the center of town with an enviable patio; the menu is inspired by both local ingredients and the owners' international travels. Award-winning wine list.

BROTHERHOOD OF THIEVES (brotherhoodofthieves.com) Exposed beams and fireplace make this multiroom English-basement restaurant a great hideaway spot for elevated pub grub and a pint of craft beer.

CHANTICLEER (https://chanticleernantucket.com) A restaurant serving seasonal menu offerings in a charming 'Sconset setting.

CLAUDETTE'S (10 Main St, Siasconset) Cash-only breakfast, lunch, and BYOB dinner spot in 'Sconset.

CLUB CAR (https://theclubcar.com) Upscale food on one side, and a sing-along piano bar in a converted train car on the other.

COMPANY OF THE CAULDRON (https://companyofthecauldron.com) Candle-lit atmospheric spot by Michelin-star chef Joseph Keller (Thomas's brother) serving farm-to-table French cooking from a nightly prix-fixe menu.

CORNER TABLE CAFÉ (www.cornertablenantucket.com) Healthy, house-made grab-and-go food and great coffee.

CRU (www.crunantucket.com) Premier raw bar and seafood fare with jaw-dropping views of some of the world's most expensive super-yachts. What's not to love?

DUNE (https://dunenantucket.com) Popular dinner date spot helmed by a Culinary Institute of America graduate who serves elegant, seasonal seafood and poultry dishes in a minimal modern setting with atmospheric lighting indoors and out on the covered patio.

GALLEY BEACH Pricey outdoor dining on the beach. Eternally snaking line at this popular spot for homemade ice cream.

LE LANGUEDOC BISTRO (https://languedocbistro.com) Forty-year-old island inn and French-American bistro set in an eighteenth-century home in town with blue-and-white checkered tablecloths and two decades of Wine Spectator recognition.

LEMON PRESS (https://lemonpressnantucket.com) Healthy breakfast and lunch. A popular spot for sushi and cocktails.

LOLA BURGER (www.lolaburger.com) Family-friendly spot outside of town for gourmet burgers.

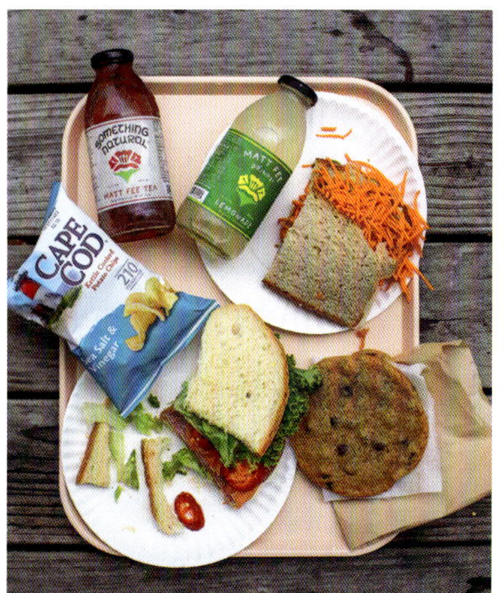

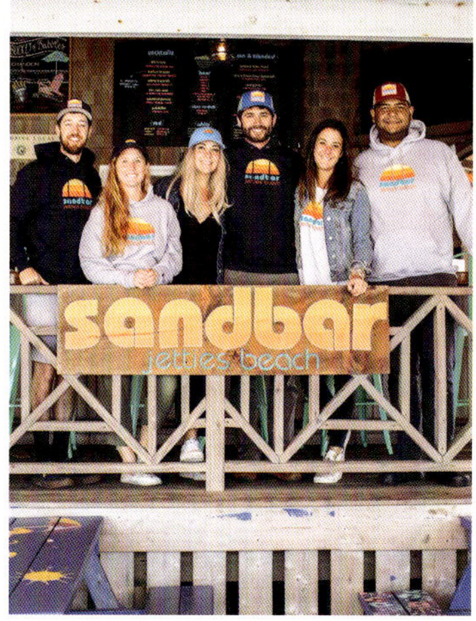

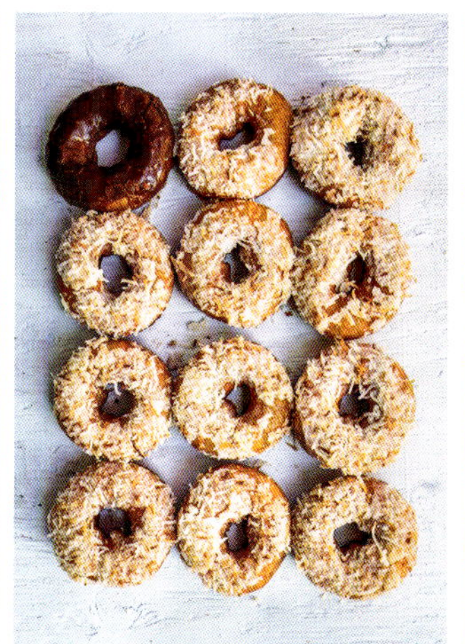
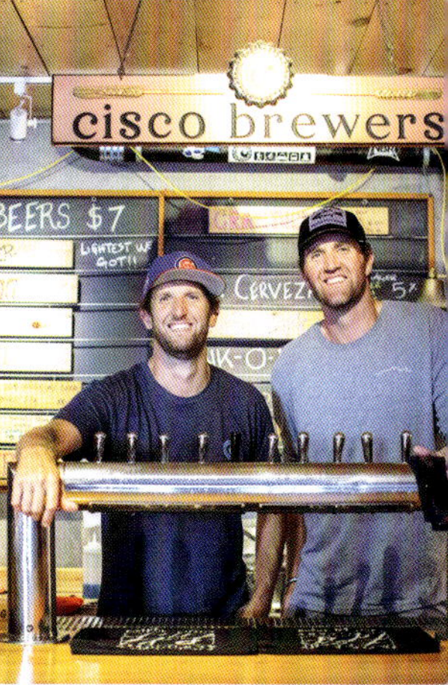

MILLIE'S (https://milliesnantucket.com) Mexican fare out in Madaket. Family-friendly and a classic spot for island fun and sunsets.

THE NANTUCKET LOBSTER TRAP (https://nantucketlobstertrap.com) Strap on your lobster bib at this casual, family-friendly lobster and raw bar restaurant staple since the 1970s. Try the rum punch and sit on the covered patio. Buzzy spot featuring Southeast Asian–inspired small plates and creative craft cocktails. Upscale seasonal American cuisine served on the second story of a historic house.

THE PEARL (http://thepearlnantucket.com) Seasonal shellfish and seafood with some Asian inspiration in a modern setting in town.

THE PHARMACY (center of Main Street) Throwback pharmacy with a lunch counter serving hot dogs and other simple sandwiches.

THE PROPRIETORS BAR & TABLE (proprietorsnantucket.com) Light wood and Edison lights set a hip-tavern mood for a menu of internationally influenced comfort food inspired by whalers' travels.

PROVISIONS (provisionsnantucket.com) Gourmet sandwiches and Nantucket Nectar juices to go, right off the wharf. Try the Turkey Terrific. Cash only.

QUEEQUEG'S (http://queequegsnantucket.com) Warm, cozy, indoor/outdoor seasonal American restaurant named after the harpooner from "Moby-Dick" and adjacent to The Tree Bar.

SANDBAR AT JETTIES (jettiessandbar.com) Kid-friendly and fun, one of the few casual restaurants on the with tables on the deck and in the sand. Live music every afternoon.

SCONSET MARKET (https://sconsetmarket.com) Convenience store with some prepared foods and ice cream. Get there in the morning for a just-baked scone.

SHIPS INN (www.shipsinnnantucket.com) Brasserie-style dining with a Wine Spectator award in an 1831 ship captain's mansion-turned-inn.

SLIP 14 (www.slip14.com) Cozy seafood restaurant with large covered patio dining on quaint Old South Wharf.

SOMETHING NATURAL (www.somethingnatural.com) Sandwich shop known for its homemade Portuguese-style bread, juices and picnic tables in a parklike setting. Kids love playing in the boat perched on the lawn. Forty-plus year seafood institution in a lovely rustic setting on the wharf.

SUMMER HOUSE RESTAURANT (thesummerhouse.com) Charming restaurant in 'Sconset's classic inn with candlelit dining on the front porch and inside the 1880s inn. Known for its piano bar that inspires nightly sing-a-longs into the night.

TOPPER'S (www.wauwinet.com) New England seafood restaurant with large town patio bar that breaks into a nightly dance party.

VIA MARE (www.viamarerestaurant.com) Venetian-inspired small plates and pastas at Greydon House.

Where to Drink on Nantucket

AFTERHOUSE SEAFOOD BISTRO & WINE BAR (www.afterhouse.net) Modern, subterranean wine bar with extensive menu of tinned seafood from Spain and Portugal.

THE CHICKEN BOX (www.thechickenbox.com) Mid-island spot and a major island social hub. Beer, wine, and spirits made on-site, live music, food trucks, and picnic tables adjacent to a farm offer a welcoming spot to spend an afternoon. All ages (and dogs) welcome!

CLUB CAR (https://theclubcar.com) This drinking and sing-a-long spot with the piano in a converted train car turned bar is a Nantucket classic.

THE GASLIGHT (https://gaslightnantucket.com) Bar and live music venue with windows that open to the street on Straight Wharf in summer. Mudslides are the tradition here.

GREYDON HOUSE (greydonhouse.com) One of the island's most atmospheric spots for a cocktail. The bar at this gorgeously renovated sea captain's house turned inn is outfitted by notable designers Roman and Williams with antiques to transport you to the whaling days. Don't miss the mural behind the bar.

PETRICHOR WINE BAR (https://petrichorwinebar.com) Enjoy a glass in a leather armchair at this wine bar with a large selection of share plates; located mid-island.

THE TREE BAR (Instagram: @treebarnantucket) Outdoor patio bar where locals and tourists belly up to a wooden bar built around a central tree. Serving food from adjacent, sister restaurants Town and Queequeg's.

Annual Events

DAFFODIL FESTIVAL Late April | www.daffodilfestival.com
A weekend of events to celebrate springtime awakening on Nantucket. The first occasion (a very simple affair in the 1970s) included an antique car parade in which islanders showed off their classic cars, followed by a community tailgate picnic in 'Sconset.

NANTUCKET WINE FESTIVAL Mid May | www.nantucketwinefestival.com)
One of the nation's most celebrated wine and food events.

FIGAWI MEMORIAL WEEKEND Late May |www.figawi.com
This event is a competitive sailing regatta in Nantucket Sound that gives back to local Cape Cod and Nantucket Charities. With fifty years of sailing excellence, decades of local philanthropy, and benefiting over 100 local charities, Figawi attracts many from all walks of life.

NANTUCKET FILM FESTIVAL June | www.nantucketfilmfestival.org
Running for more than two decades and one of the premier destination film festivals in the world. Visitors flock from all over to experience preview screenings, signature programs, and standout hospitality.

NANTUCKET BOOK FESTIVAL Mid-June | https://nantucketbookfestival.org
Author readings, panel discussions, and social events in an informal atmosphere that encourages conversations between writers and readers. Most of the festival events are free and held within walking distance of the ferries.

NANTUCKET COMEDY FESTIVAL July | www.nantucketcomedyfestival.org
Founded in 2007, this is an annual summer experience that brings top comedic talent to Nantucket as the major fundraiser for Stand Up & Learn™, an island-based, year-round comedy education program serving Nantucket's children. The Nantucket Comedy Festival fosters a sense of community connection through laughter.

NANTUCKET GARDEN FESTIVAL Mid-July | www.ackgardenfestival.org
This event celebrates gardening through creative workshops, exquisite garden tours, children's workshops, and an opening night soirée.

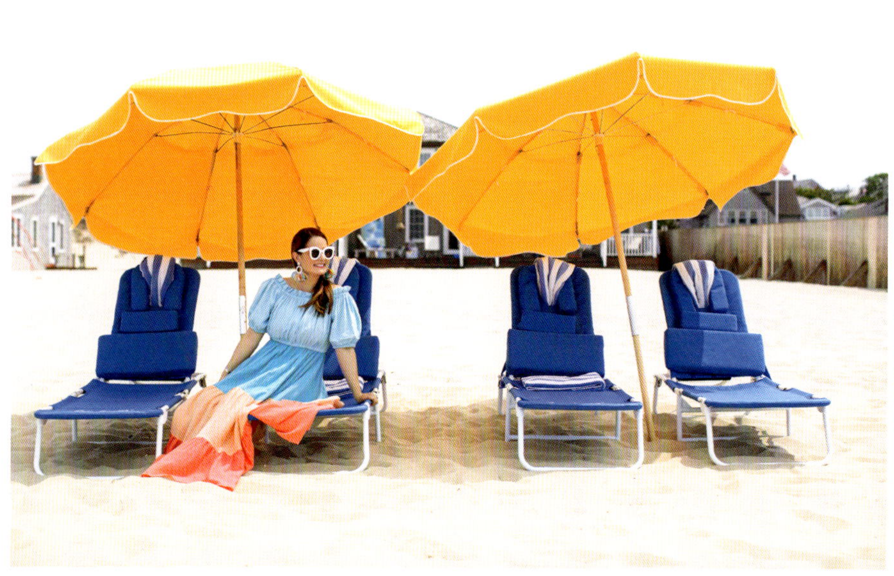

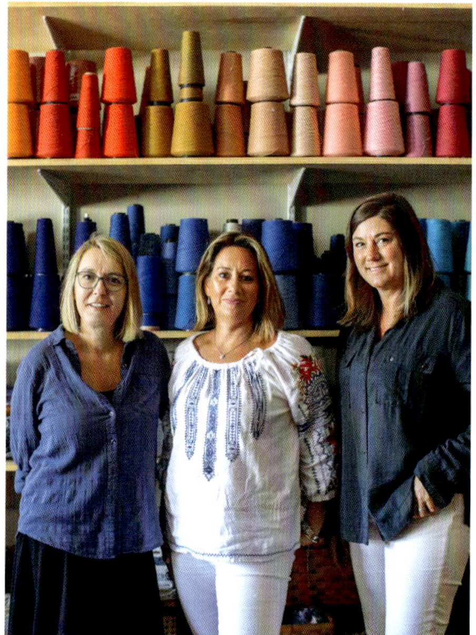

BOSTON POPS Mid-August | www.givenantuckethospital.partners.org/popsga
The Boston Pops Esplanade Orchestra performs live on Nantucket at Jetties Beach in one of the island's stellar summer events.

NANTUCKET RACE WEEK Mid-August | www.nantucketraceweek.org/page/nrw
Nine days of regattas, awards ceremonies, and parties hosted by Nantucket Yacht Club and Great Harbor Yacht Club to benefit the nonprofit Nantucket Community Sailing organization.

SHORTS FESTIVAL Early fall | www.nantucketshorts.com
Founded in 2013 by five local Nantucket artists interested in creating a community of support and a forum for filmmakers (both amateur and professional) to present their work.

THE NANTUCKET PROJECT Late September | www.nantucketproject.com
Features marquee presenters, change makers, artists, live music, and more in an ideas symposium focused on concepts that spark conversation. Founded by Tom Scott, one of the Nantucket Nectars juice company founders, and island local Kate Brosnan, TNP is intimate and has approximately 600 attendees.

NANTUCKET ARTS FESTIVAL
September–October | www.nantucketartscouncil.org/news/nantucket-arts-festival
Many of the island's arts and cultural groups schedule special programs during the festival.

CRANBERRY FESTIVAL
October | www.nantucketconservation.org/event/16th-annual-cranberry-festival
The Nantucket Conservation Foundation's Milestone Cranberry Bog is transformed into the most unique and beautiful of festival grounds for this special event. Visitors can expect to learn about the history of cranberry farming on Nantucket through educational displays and harvesting demonstrations, participate in family activities, sample delectable cranberry treats and other New England classics, or simply enjoy the music and the spectacular autumn scenery.

CHRISTMAS STROLL First weekend in December | www.christmasstroll.com
Nantucket's Christmas Stroll is a much anticipated annual tradition that began as a way to encourage visitors to do their holiday shopping on-island. Today it's a popular weekend for summer residents to return to kick off the holiday season on-island. This event is part of the Chamber of Commerce's "Nantucket Noel," and preparations begin just before Thanksgiving.

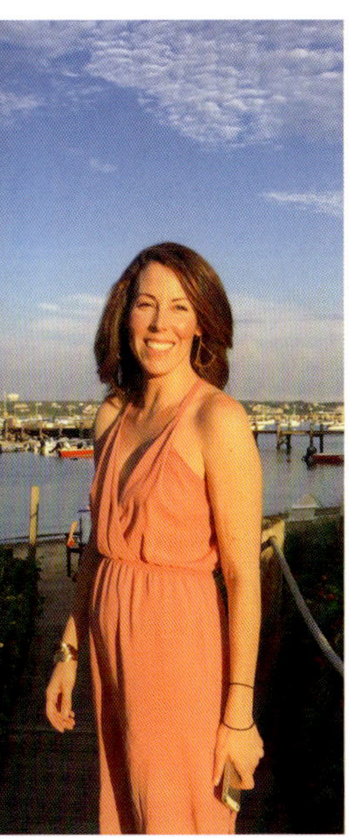
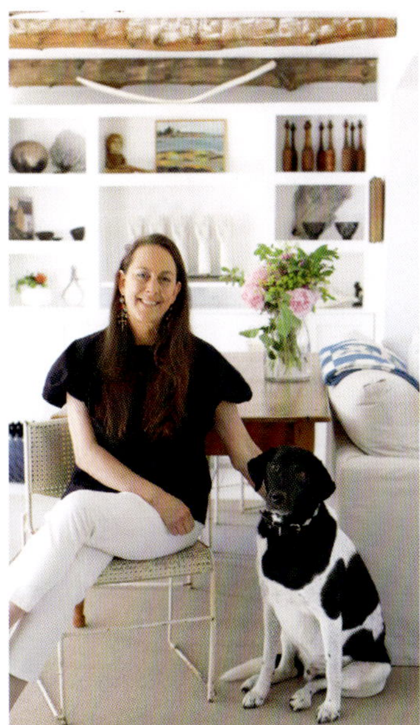
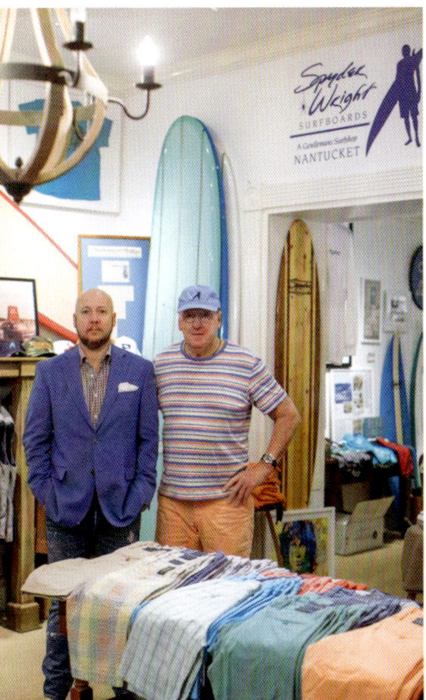

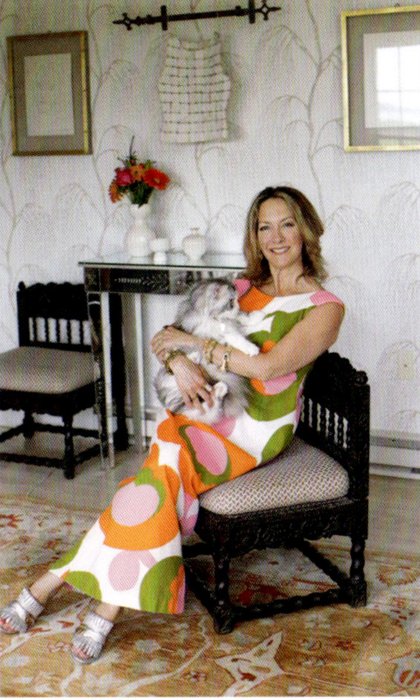

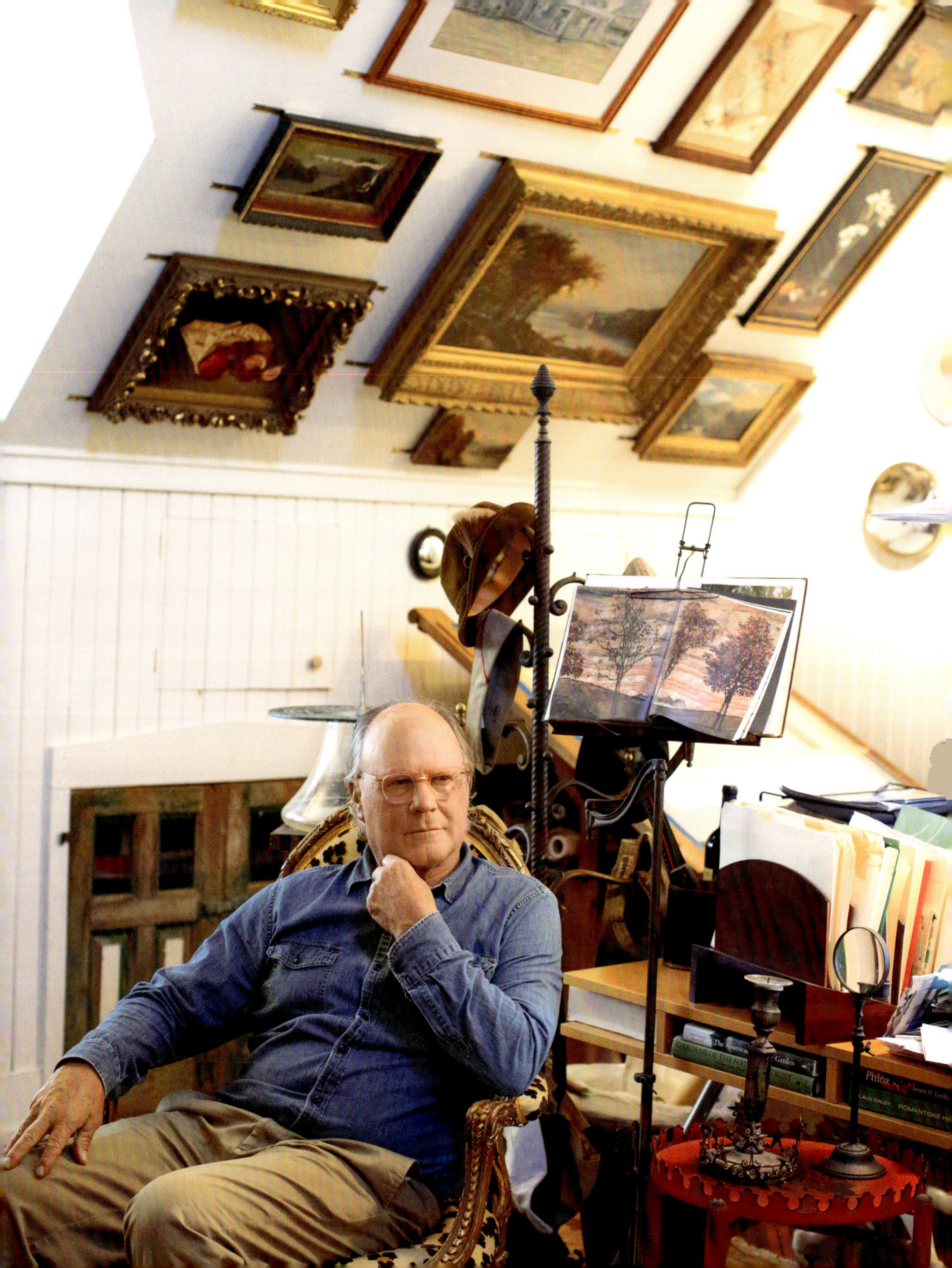
Garden
Phlox

THANKS

We are grateful to so many people on Nantucket. Mostly to Marty (at left) and Holly McGowan for bringing us together. Scott Culpepper for making it happen. Aiden Bourke, our fearless intern and local insider; Thomas L. Macy for friendship; Thomas and Patricia Anathan; Liz Anathan; Xani Feldman; Bambi Constantine; Angela Raynor; Maddy Grayson and Jocelyn Gailliot; Lisa Soeder and Immanuel Chac; Bess Clark and the women of Nantucket Looms; Alex Gil; Maria Waicowski; Stephanie Hubbard; Sara Rossi; Taylor Ivey; Page Bond; Edward Sanford; Gwenn and Mark Snider of The Nantucket Hotel; Elliot Gould, Alexander Leventhal and the Greydon House team; Kayla Hedman at Fishers Island Lemonade; Jennifer Stocker of Sail to Sable; Alex Saletin at Hinckley Yachts; David Zipkin of Tradewind Aviation; Ashley Frisbie; John S. Johnson; Lee and Cindy Millazo; John Shea and Melissa MacLeod; Sue and Jim Genthner; Kevin Withrow; Eric Holch; Lissy Bryan; D.W. Coffin; Meredith Hanson; Lloyd Hussey; Jennifer Lake; Beth Aschenbach and Danielle Norcross; Nancy Gershman; and at Images Publishing: Joe Boschetti, Georgia (Gina) Tsarouhas, and Nicole Boehringer.

ABOUT THE AUTHORS

Liza Gershman | A Nantucket summer resident, best-selling author and Winner of the Gourmand Cookbook Award (2018), Liza has fifteen published books, including **Cuban Flavor**, which was touted on CBS, **National Geographic**, **Travel & Leisure**, NPR, and more. Liza was honored to speak for "Talks At Google", and on the prestigious campuses of Twitter, Oracle, and Disney. Clients: Williams-Sonoma, Goldman Sachs, Hyatt Hotels, Restoration Hardware, Getty Images, AirBnB, Visa. In 2010, Liza was Governor Jerry Brown's campaign photographer, and in 2014 was a photographer for America's Cup. She's photographed in more than fifty-four countries and forty-seven states! She specializes in creative direction, art direction, styling, writing, photography. (Find her on page 84, row three, center.)

Carrie Nieman Culpepper | An award-winning journalist and brand strategist who covers culture, design and lifestyle around the world, Carrie's passion is reporting on the people, art and ideas shaping culture. She is a Contributing Editor for **Architectural Digest** and has worked for many major media outlets over the last two decades, including **The New York Times**, **The Washington Post**, **Travel + Leisure** and **House Beautiful**. She first came to Nantucket on assignment and hasn't stopped writing about the island since. Carrie also works in marketing and brand strategy and has been recognized by the Public Relations Society of America for excellence and innovation. Recent clients include American Express, The Corcoran Group, and The Carnegie Corporation. (Find her on page 234, center.)

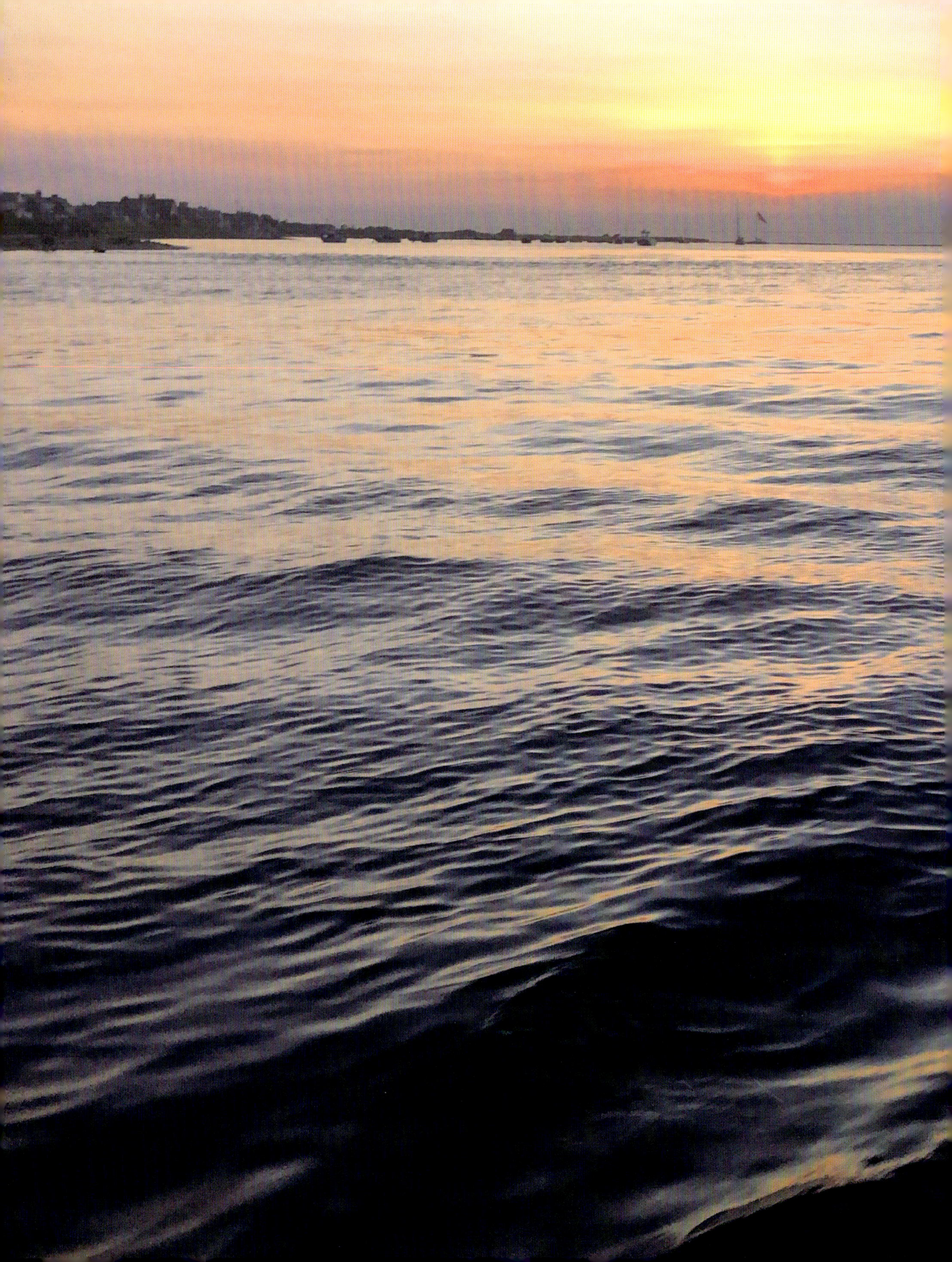

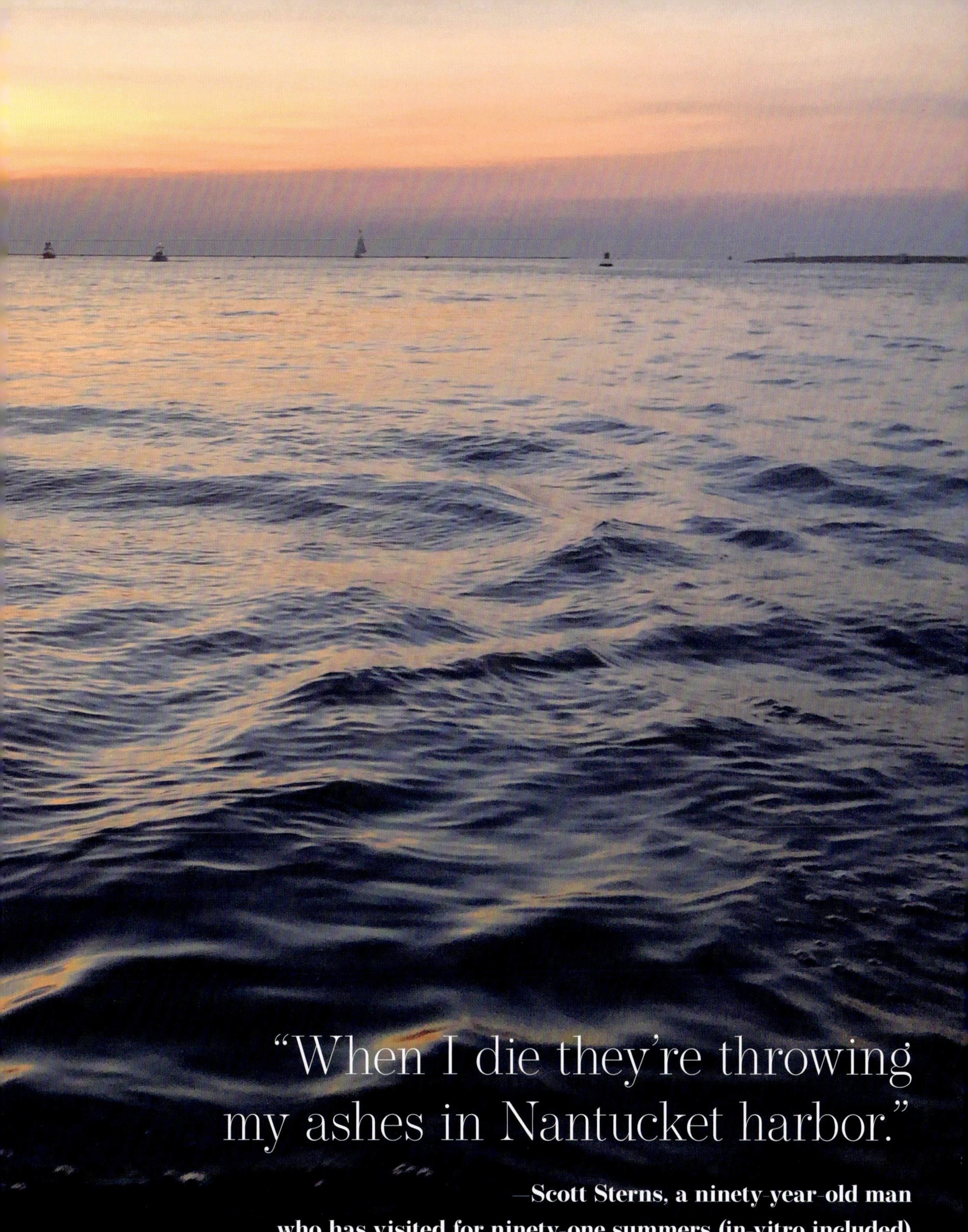

"When I die they're throwing my ashes in Nantucket harbor."

—**Scott Sterns, a ninety-year-old man who has visited for ninety-one summers (in-vitro included)**

First reprinted 2025
The Images Publishing Group Reference Number: 1630

First published in Australia in 2020 by
The Images Publishing Group Pty Ltd
ABN 89 059 734 431

Offices

Melbourne
Waterman Business Centre
Suite 64, Level 2 UL40
1341 Dandenong Road, Chadstone,
Victoria 3148
Australia
Tel: +61 3 8564 8122

New York
6 West 18th Street 4B
New York, NY 10011
United States
Tel: +1 212 645 1111

Shanghai
6F, Building C, 838 Guangji Road
Hongkou District, Shanghai 200434 China
Tel: +86 021 31260822

books@imagespublishing.com
www.imagespublishing.com

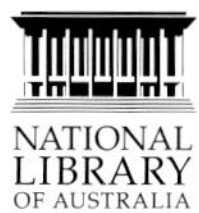

A catalogue record for this book is available from the National Library of Australia

Title: Nantucket: Classic American style 30 miles out to sea
ISBN: 9781864708707

This title was commissioned in IMAGES' Melbourne office and produced as follows: **Editorial** Georgia (Gina) Tsarouhas, **Art direction/production** Nicole Boehringer

Printed on 157gsm Chinese OJI matt art paper (FSC®) in China by Artron Art Group

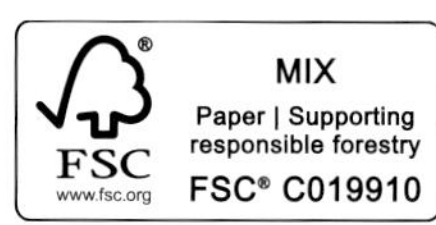